CAMERA POLITICA

CAMERA
POLITICA

The Politics and Ideology of
Contemporary Hollywood Film
By
Michael Ryan and Douglas Kellner

Indiana University Press
Bloomington and Indianapolis

First Midland Book Edition 1990

© 1988 by Michael Ryan and Douglas Kellner

Manufactured in the United States of America

Library of Congress Cataloging-in-Publication Data
Ryan, Michael, 1951-
Camera politica.
Bibliography: p.
Includes index.
1. Motion-pictures—Political aspects—United States.
I. Kellner, Douglas, 1943-   . II. Title
PN1993.5.U6R93   1987   302.2'343   86-45477
ISBN 0-253-31334-1
ISBN 0-253-20604-9 (pbk.)

3 4 5 6 94 93 92 91

PN
1993.5
U6
R93
1988

For my parents.
—D.K.

For Jim Fleming and Julie Rivkin,
winter friends.
—M.R.

Drama, more than any other literary
genre, needs a resonance in history.

—WALTER BENJAMIN

Cinema . . . is a contest of phantoms.

—JACQUES DERRIDA

Until we can understand the assumptions in
which we are drenched we cannot know ourselves.
. . . A radical critique . . ., feminist in its impulse,
would have to work first of all as a clue to
how we live, how we have been living, how we have
been led to imagine ourselves. . . .

—ADRIENNE RICH

It may be time to move from the prisonhouse of
language to the slaughterhouse of history.

—CORNEL WEST

CONTENTS

Preface

Our study focuses on the relationship between Hollywood film and American society from 1967 to the mid-eighties, a period characterized by a major swing in dominant social movements from Left to Right. We began writing this book in 1980 because we were disturbed by the changes in dominant cultural representations which that large political tidal shift seemed to bring with it. We noticed particularly that Hollywood film, which seemed to us to be gaining in importance as a mobilizer of public energies, was actively promoting the new conservative movements on several fronts, from the family to the military to economic policy. Our initial impulse, therefore, was critical and negative, a leftist response to a rightward turn that worried us. While we retain a great deal of concern over the conservative, frequently neofascist ideals and images that came to populate the American cultural scene, we have also, as we pursued our research into the relation between film culture and society, come to sense that the system of domination and inequality which those cultural representations help to hold in place is not as stable or well grounded as some of its self-idealizations make it appear. Indeed, as we pursued our project we came to realize that the very ferocity of those conservative representations, the very thing that inspired our initial concern, was itself a testament to other forces, other movements and changes which were quite progressive in character or which bore the potential of becoming progressive. We became convinced that it is in the very nature of conservative reaction to be indicative of the power of forces which threaten conservative values and institutions.

Moreover, we have come to understand that the flow of forces in social history is such that social movements, like the hegemonic conservatism of the eighties, are usually responses to threats posed by other social movements. In examining the conservatism of the eighties, we were forced to return to the radicalism of the sixties, which made tremendous inroads into the old world of traditional family, patriotic, economic, and religious values that conservatives seek to defend. Feminism, the civil rights movement, economic democracy, the sexual revolution, antimilitarism, and environmentalism blossomed in the sixties and seventies, and although they met with fierce resistance from the Right in the eighties, they have also permanently transformed American social consciousness, so much so that conservatives found themselves in an irreducible quandary in the late eighties: although they possessed political power, they were incapable of instituting the conservative social agenda. Americans were not willing to follow the Right into war in places like Central America, to buy into born-again calls to abolish abortion, or to accept the destruction of the government's role as provider of social security. During the sixties and seventies, American social consciousness was liberalized to a remarkable degree, and although conservative counterattacks against the forces

xi

of liberalization have been quite successful at seizing power and using it, we suggest that this change in consciousness bodes well for progressives interested in changing American society in a radical direction. Our book, then, is as much about cultural history and social change as it is about film. Our purpose has been to use film to gain an understanding of American political life which we hope would ultimately be of use to those interested in changing it.

Many people aided the composition of this book. Our students and colleagues over the years contributed insights and observations which were far too numerous to cite in each case. The following friends and colleagues aided our research, suggested ideas or changes, or provided criticism of various drafts of the text: Carolyn Appleton, Peter Biskind, Louis Black, Stephen Bronner, Jackie Byars, Harry Cleaver, Jim Fleming, Gerry Forshey, Bill Gibson, Bob Goldman, Lisa Gornick, Margaret Homans, Fredric Jameson, Lewanne Jones, Chuck Kleinhans, John Lawrence, Flo Leibowitz, Richard Lichtman, Bill Nichols, Elayne Rapping, Tony Safford, Tom Schatz, Kay Sloan, Paul Smith, Clay Steinman, and John Stockwell. And we are especially grateful to Judith Burton and Julie Rivkin for their thorough, thoughtful, and painstaking critical readings of the book. Many changes and improvements were a result of their suggestions and insights.

We also wish to thank Emily Seager, Barbara Humphreys, and all those others at the Library of Congress Film Division who helped us get access to films now out of circulation. The audio-visual services at the University of Virginia, Miami University, Northeastern University, and the University of Texas (Austin) also helped enormously with time, labor, and equipment. Ellen McWhirter, the director of the English Department film series at the University of Virginia, was especially helpful, as were Eric Eubank, Juvenal Mendez, Kevin West, and John Mechaley of the language lab at Texas. We thank the English Department of Miami University, and especially the Executive Secretary, Susan Deckhart, for all of its assistance during the writing of this book, and the English Department of Northeastern University, especially Eileen Smith, for assistance during the final preparation of the manuscript. Both Jerry Schrader of Northeastern and Alicia Montoya of Texas provided invaluable help with the illustrations. In addition, we are grateful to Alan Trachtenberg for arranging a Visiting Fellow appointment for Michael Ryan in the American Studies Program at Yale University which gave us access to otherwise unavailable research materials at the Sterling Library, and to the University of Texas Faculty Research Institute for providing a grant which enabled Douglas Kellner to work on the book.

Our research into audience responses to Hollywood movies was greatly helped by the advice of Pat Golden of the Sociology Department at Northeastern. Tommie Lott of African American Studies, Herman Gray of Sociology, and Carol Owen of Anthropology at Northeastern also provided invaluable counseling and help. Marisa Belmonte helped type in the data, and Wu Yue provided needed assistance with the research program.

Finally, we thank all of those friends who accompanied us to movie theaters over the years, putting up with what must have appeared to be rather bizarre preferences in film.

The composition of the book entailed a long process of consultation, draft writing, and mutual criticism. We initially divided the chapters between us. Doug Kellner did the first drafts of the chapters on horror, disaster, and conspiracy films. Michael Ryan did the drafts on war, working class, and women's films. Other chapters were put together from both our work. The drafts were exchanged, criticized, and rewritten a number of times. We also discussed the book often over the phone, developing ideas and debating differences, and we had occasion to meet on a regular basis over the years at conferences as well as at each other's institutions to work together. Several different versions of the manuscript were written in this way. The final version for the press was written by Michael Ryan. We think of this book as a genuinely collaborative project. Neither of us alone could have written it. We encourage readers to participate in that process of collaboration by writing to us with comments or criticisms.

CAMERA POLITICA

INTRODUCTION

Some radical critics argue that Hollywood film operates to legitimate dominant institutions and traditional values and that its representational conventions help instill ideology. Those institutions and values include individualism (with its emphasis on self-reliance and its distrust of government), capitalism (with its values of competition, upward mobility, and the survival of the fittest), patriarchy (with its privileging of men and its positioning of women in a secondary social role), racism (with its unequal partitioning of social power), etc. The representational conventions include form as well as subject matter. The formal conventions—narrative closure, image continuity, nonreflexive camera, character identification, voyeuristic objectification, sequential editing, causal logic, dramatic motivation, shot centering, frame balance, realist intelligibility, etc.—help to instill ideology by creating an illusion that what happens on the screen is a neutral recording of objective events, rather than a construct operating from a certain point of view. Films make rhetorical arguments through the selection and combination of representational elements that project rather than reflect a world. In so doing, they impose on the audience a certain position or point of view, and the formal conventions occlude this positioning by erasing the signs of cinematic artificiality. The thematic conventions—heroic male adventure, romantic quest, female melodrama, redemptive violence, racial and criminal stereotyping, etc.—promote ideology by linking the effect of reality to social values and institutions in such a way that they come to seem natural or self-evident attributes of an unchanging world. The conventions habituate the audience to accept the basic premises of the social order, and to ignore their irrationality and injustice. The mapping of personal life stories over structural social issues like war and crime makes the existing order seem moral and good. And personal identification with representations of public order creates the psychological disposition for inducement into voluntary participation in a system of exploitation and domination.

Much of what happens in Hollywood cinema is indeed ideological in the sense outlined above, but not all Hollywood narrative realist products are inherently ideological. This conception of cinematic ideology flattens out necessary distinctions between different films at different moments of history, and it overlooks the distinctive and multiple rhetorical and representational strategies and effects of films in varying social situations. The recourse to

1

static, formal, abstract categories like "the subject" in structuralist film theory obliterates situational differences as well as the possibility that films generate multiple, highly differentiated effects. If the category of history helps break down and differentiate the somewhat monolithic model of Hollywood film which the structuralist theory of ideology takes for granted, the pragmatic determination of a film's meaning or its ideology in terms of the rhetorical operation it addresses to audiences (rather than in terms of a preordained category of ideological closure that operates the same way everywhere without differentiation) also opens the analysis of film out onto a plural social and political terrain. Films cease to appear to be inherently ideological simply by being Hollywood narratives. Their political meaning is more a matter of specific arguments made, concrete representational strategies adopted, possible effects generated. Films function differently in different contexts, as the film survey we conducted for this study confirms (see Appendix), and we would suggest that the determination of their political meaning may be more complex, contested, and differentiated a matter than some structuralist film critics assume.

For instance, Hollywood film since 1967 is quite distinct from what it was in the preceding era, and we will argue that its political role in American culture during the period from 1967 to 1987 is varied and multivalent. Within certain predictable limits, popular films of this period debate significant social issues, and many, operating from a left-liberal perspective, attempt to use the traditional representational formats and conventions for socially critical ends. The limits are fairly recalcitrant, the breadth of political scope not very wide. But a study of the contemporary era suggests that Hollywood is not monolithically ideological. Its forms may have served predominantly conservative ends, but the current cinema proves that those forms can be reframed, given new political inflections. And even ideological films, we have found, permit an analysis of potentially progressive undercurrents in American society by delineating, frequently inadvertently, the salient fears, desires, and needs that make up the everyday fabric of American culture during a time of enormous change and that are the bearers of radical possibilities.

During the first Cold War period, from the late 1940s through the mid-1960s, the Hollywood cinema was dominated by cinemascope spectaculars like *Ben-Hur* and *Cleopatra*, romantic musicals like *Oklahoma* and *The Sound of Music*, family melodramas like *Picnic* and *Giant*, anticommunist films like *Red Menace* and *I Was a Communist for the FBI*, Cold War spy thrillers like *The Manchurian Candidate*, beach blanket films like *Gidget*, Jerry Lewis comedies, Rock Hudson and Doris Day romantic comedies like *Pillow Talk*, paranoid monster films like *Them* and *The Thing*, conservative or at best liberal pluralist genre westerns like *The Searchers* and *Broken Arrow*, Hitchcock's woman-punishing thrillers like *The Birds* and *Psycho*, and moralistic social problem films like *The Man with the Golden Arm* and *Rebel without a Cause*. While the overall ideological atmosphere of the cinema of the period is usually considered to be predominantly conservative or at best complacent, there were a number of socially conscious or critical films like *High Noon, Attack,*

The Wild One, *The Defiant Ones*, *Paths of Glory*, *The Day the Earth Stood Still*, *The Lawless*, *All That Heaven Allows*, and *On the Beach*. In *Seeing Is Believing: How Hollywood Films Taught Us to Stop Worrying and Love the Fifties*, Peter Biskind demonstrates that many films of the period, even apparently "conservative" ones, question dominant myths and values.[1] Still, it was not until the mid-sixties that Hollywood films began to adopt the critical and experimental thematic and stylistic modes that had characterized European and Third World filmmaking for some time. Biskind concludes his study by describing a "coming apart" of the social consensus of the fifties in films of the sixties.

In fact, if one considers a list of the major films of the early to midsixties, one notices indications of what Biskind calls "creeping leftism" throughout the period: 1960—*Spartacus* depicted a slave revolt, *The Apartment* satirized business sexism, and *Inherit the Wind* attacked fundamentalist religion; 1961—*Raisin in the Sun*, *The Outsider*, and *West Side Story* criticized racial intolerance, *Splendor in the Grass* explicitly attacked the suppression of youth sexuality, and *Judgment at Nuremberg* advocated a liberal indictment of intolerance; 1962—*The Birdman of Alcatraz* took a benevolent approach to criminal rehabilitation, while *Sweet Bird of Youth* criticized evangelical hypocrisy; 1963—*Lilies of the Field* depicted racial cooperation, *To Kill a Mockingbird* sympathetically portrayed racial interaction in the South and condemned racism, and *Days of Wine and Roses* dealt frankly with the problems of alcoholism; 1964—*Failsafe* criticized nuclear ideology, *Seven Days in May* carried out a liberal attack on the radical Right, *Dr. Strangelove* satirized nuclear war madness and right-wing paranoia, and *Nothing but a Man* depicted southern black life from a black point of view; 1965—*The Bedford Incident* depicted the real possibility of accidental nuclear war, *Patch of Blue* indicted racial intolerance, and *The Pawnbroker* dramatized the effects of bigotry; and 1966—*A Man for All Seasons* argued for the right to dissent, *The Russians Are Coming* satirized Cold War thinking, and *Who's Afraid of Virginia Woolf?* exposed a despairing side to suburban life.[2]

Film historians point to 1967 as a "revolutionary" year, the moment when a significant opening occurred in Hollywood film: that year *Cool Hand Luke* criticized authority, heroized rebellion, and denounced southern conservatism; *Guess Who's Coming to Dinner* diagnosed the subleties of racism among liberal whites; *Bonnie and Clyde* romanticized social banditry; *The Graduate* addressed the new antibourgeois rebelliousness and growing alienation then taking hold of a large segment of the younger generation; *In the Heat of the Night* portrayed racism in the South; *Hurry Sundown* depicted a corrupt southern aristocracy; *The Group* presented a liberal take on women in American culture; *The Flim-Flam Man* celebrated rambunctious bohemianism; *Marat/Sade* dealt with the French Revolution and, indirectly, the problem of exploitation in contemporary society; *In Cold Blood* provided a journalistic examination of the psychology of murder and punishment; *The Trip* brought a new liberalism regarding drugs to the screen; *Point Blank* advanced critical perceptions of business values in an experimental style; *Dutchman* put on

1967. A turning point year in Hollywood film. The period between 1966 and 1968 is a watershed of the sixties, a time when the economy was expanding, liberals in government were seeking to reform society, blacks were in revolt against oppression, drug use and sexual experimentation were changing traditional social values, and protest movements against the Vietnam War were gaining national attention for the New Left.

1967. But already signs of the future were present—military defeat, a collapsing economy, a right-wing populist leader-figure on the rise, and the beginnings of what would become the New Right of the late seventies and early eighties.

screen an Amiri Baraka (Leroi Jones) play about racism; *Reflections in a Golden Eye* dissected the pathologies of the military personality; *Beach Red* argued for pacificism and an understanding of the humanity of one's national enemies; and *Up the Down Staircase* showed the new liberalism at work in schools. Social criticism would become even more striking during the following years with the appearance of *Midnight Cowboy, Easy Rider, The Mad Woman of Chaillot, Medium Cool,* and numerous other films.

Economic and institutional changes in the film industry contributed to the transformations underway in Hollywood. During the sixties, what remained of the old studio system was bought up by corporations; other studios transformed themselves into conglomerates. Increasingly, films were put together as "deals" by independent producers or agents, who then secured funding for production from the major studios, who also handled distribution. The demise of the studio system gave filmmakers more control over their product than had been the case during the previous era, and this development helped facilitate the production of more socially critical and innovative films. The elimination of the Production Code and the initiation of a new rating system in 1966 made it possible to deal with previously forbidden subject matter. At the same time, film schools were producing directors literate in film history and interested in making more films that were personal statements. A growing number of "art film" theaters imported European film movements which influenced the style and thematics of Hollywood film. As a result, some Hollywood films of this period began to resemble the sorts of complex cinematic texts that were being made by British social realist filmmakers, French New Wave directors, and such influential filmmakers of the time as Fellini and Bergman. These changes were related to new industry perceptions of the audience and the marketplace. An emerging baby boom youth population was quickly becoming the center of American culture, and audience surveys indicated that a young, more liberal and cineliterate audience was responding to newer, more socially conscious and innovative films.

Perhaps the crucial reason for the increase in socially conscious and stylistically innovative films in the late sixties was the liberal and radical social movements of the period—civil rights, antiwar, feminism, consumerism, gay liberation, the hippie counterculture—and the general loosening of previous strictures against sex and drugs. Radical social and political issues of the sort banished during the Cold War were once again possible topics of popular films.

Any history of the post-1967 era would note that during this period the United States ceased to be the sole world power; the American empire was curtailed on several fronts; and the postwar era of "Pax Americana" came to an end. The country's economy experienced several major crises. The nation's leadership from Nixon to Carter was shown to be corrupt or ineffectual. The liberal pluralist consensus that had held the country together for decades was broken by the social movements of the sixties and seventies. The split in that consensus widened throughout the seventies, and previously stable social institutions like the family and cultural representations like "the nation" and "freedom" became objects of contestation. Grassroots movements arose around issues of the environment, consumer rights, sexual politics, rent control, corporate power, and militarism. They inspired a fierce counterattack by conservatives in the late seventies and eighties.

These conflicts and changes produced significant shifts in national mood and national self-image which register in popular films of the period. The psychosocial effects of economic instability, the loss of the Vietnam War and of national prestige, social divisiveness, threats to the traditional patriarchal family and to conservative sexual mores, revelations of corruption in government and business, fears of environmental poisoning and of nuclear war are on ample display in film. In many ways, to study films of this era is to study a culture in decline, trying to come to terms with severe economic, political, and social crises and to adjust to a world in which the United States had much less power, both economically and politically. Films portray the extremes of anxiety, tension, hope, and fear undergone in this process of transformation and themselves participate in and further the process of social change. The shift from the depiction of alienation from the "American Dream" in *The Graduate* (1967) to the affirmation of white middle class male opportunism in *Risky Business* (1983) tells us something about the changes in U.S. society in the period between the two films. An understanding of the ideology of contemporary Hollywood film is therefore inseparable from the social history of the era.

Three narrative strands demarcate some of the major changes of the period: the fruition and further vicissitudes of the social movements of the sixties, the failure of liberalism in the seventies, and the triumph of conservatism in the eighties. The sixties were characterized by a radicalization of major sectors of the American population. Blacks rose up against poverty, discrimination, and disenfranchisement. Women reignited the feminist movement for reproductive rights and civic equality. Young whites rejected the American Dream of bourgeois success, turned to drugs and music as symbols of alternative values, and refused to collaborate in American imperialist adventurism in Southeast Asia. Capitalism ceased to be a taken-for-granted institution in American life, and a radical intellectual culture developed in the universities particularly. In addition, grassroots movements struggling for equality for Native Americans, Chicanos, and other minorities came into being, as did powerful ecological and environmentalist currents which spurred opposition to nuclear power and the toxic pollution of the environment. This groundswell of radical energy transformed American society, forcing significant changes in U.S. institutions, from the patriarchal family to laws regarding civil rights, the environment, and war.

Popular agitation obliged liberals in government to legislate for major changes in the way poor people, blacks, and women were treated in American society. Liberals used such government programs as welfare, public housing, busing, and affirmative action hiring requirements to alleviate the most obvious surface symptoms of structural inequality. The federal government and the courts intervened actively to remedy racial discrimination, pollution, un-

fair treatment of criminals, the denial of control over their bodies and sexuality to women, and so on. From a liberal perspective, it was a period of
great reform, when liberals dreamed of creating a Good Society through
federal spending, legislation, and regulation.

The sixties are also significant as the beginning of the end of the complicity of the American population in the imperialist aspirations of their
business-government leaders. The Vietnam War was the cause that catalyzed
opposition to the use of U.S. governmental and military power by the business
class to wage war against nonwhite, generally anticapitalist liberation struggles
in the Third World. Young men refused to fight, and by the early seventies,
most adults opposed the intervention. The United States was obliged to withdraw. More important, perhaps, the war meant that business leaders in government could not count on the support of the American population when
business-government decided to use force against its enemies abroad. The
sixties thus mark the end of a long period during which the business class
could act with impunity and great violence against popular liberation movements overseas.

Yet to speak of the sixties as an event in this way is somewhat misleading.
They are in fact the culmination of a long movement under way since the
mid-fifties, when the McCarthy era ended, the Beat Generation began, blacks
turned on their white oppressors, and radical thinkers like Herbert Marcuse
and C. Wright Mills began to voice the sorts of new ideas that have come to
be associated with the New Left. Moreover, the sixties spilled over into the
seventies, and the shadow of the sixties movements hangs over the liberalism
of the mid-seventies, down at least until 1977.

Cinema and television were integral to the dissemination of the new
radical ideas and values. Films like *The Graduate, Bonnie and Clyde,* and *Easy
Rider* redefined the prevailing representations of the world for many young
people, offering touchstones and providing points of reference for constructing alternatives to the conformist ethos of the preceding era. In the
late sixties particularly, radicals in the "New Hollywood" had more access
to filmmaking than ever before. Blacks especially were noteworthy for producing strong political statements in film, and women like Barbara Loden
were beginning to experiment with the use of film to represent previously
unrepresented dimensions of women's experience in a patriarchal society.
Films exercised the same transgressive tendencies that were breaking down
old principles of order in the world of the radical movements and the counterculture. They questioned the sanctity of the white male hero, the ico-
nography of capitalist individualism, the ideal of conservative family life (so
powerfully promulgated in fifties television), the prevailing ethos of sexual
repression, and so on. Films broke down the generic boundaries and principles of propriety that segregated life into discrete sectors for men and
women, rich and poor, black and white.

But the New Hollywood of racial themes and liberal values was dependent
on a secure economic climate, as indeed were the movements themselves.
And the seventies were to be a time of severe economic crisis and material

suffering for many as a result of inflation, unemployment, and a conservative backlash against labor militancy. Payment for the simultaneous hawkish guns and liberal butter of the Johnson years began to fall due in the early seventies in the form of the first economic recession of the period (to be followed by more severe ones in the mid-seventies and early eighties). At the same time, the crisis of confidence in government and economic institutions that characterizes this period was initiated by revelations of government and corporate wrongdoing (the Pentagon Papers, the Watergate scandal, the ITT and Lockheed disclosures, media exposure of unsafe automobiles, and so on). In addition, the liberalism and radicalism of the sixties had two unintended effects. Radicalism drove many moderate liberals into the conservative camp, and liberalism ignited a reaction in the form of a virulent opposition to welfare, abortion, busing, and government regulation, and a firm advocacy of the traditional family, patriotism, and fundamentalist religious faith. The "new" conservatives were already active opponents of liberalism and radicalism in the early seventies in such journals as *The Public Interest*. The second, less intellectual and more populist reactionary movement did not emerge as a powerful social force until the late seventies, when it would come to be called the "New Right."

The conservative reaction against the liberal programs of the Great Society and the radical agenda of the New Left appeared in cinematic representations that challenged the predominantly critical outlook of many late sixties films. It promoted values that were more counterrevolutionary than countercultural. Whereas blacks and the poor were victims with whom one empathized in the sixties, they became disturbers of order in early seventies films like *Dirty Harry*. Women, whose struggle for independence had received some sympathetic attention, now suffered a fierce and violent male backlash in the form of horror films like *The Exorcist*.[3] And the forces of law and order that were depicted as unjust and repressive in sixties movies were championed as social heroes. Conservative themes, characters, and styles began to dominate Hollywood film once again. The success of films like *Love Story, Airport, The Godfather, The Exorcist*, and *Jaws* (the first or second top grossing films for 1970, 1971, 1972, 1974, and 1975) motivated Hollywood producers to seek blockbuster hits in more conventional and predictable genre formulas. Whereas the late sixties are characterized by generic discontinuity and innovation, genres return in the early seventies as a major film form in the demonic horror and disaster films. Moreover, the ironic and critical social realist styles of the late sixties give way to a mixture of grandiose, bombastic, and mannerist styles in the early to mid-seventies. The conservative chiaroscuro of *The Godfather* and the misogynistic horror of *The Exorcist* supersede the critical reflexivity of *Midnight Cowboy* and the experimental style of the early Altman (*M*A*S*H, Brewster McCloud, McCabe and Mrs. Miller*). The resolution-oriented narrative of the classic Hollywood cinema returns in full force, and the crest of reflexivity and experimentation in narration, image, and character that one finds in the more radical films of the late sixties recedes.

Nevertheless, in the early to mid-seventies conservatism was still on the defensive, and a questioning of American institutions and values is carried out throughout these years in Hollywood film. It makes itself felt in conspiracy films, in the new black, women's, and working-class films, in the revived social problem film, and in the transformations of such traditional genres as the western, the detective, and the musical. What these films suggest is that the radical social movements of the sixties did not disappear after 1971, but instead produced effects that spread like waves through U.S. society and put some of its most powerful social and cultural institutions in question. Even conservative films that point to the radical movements by reacting against them evidence the effects of those movements.

By the mid-seventies, some of the most significant effects of the movements of the sixties were strikingly visible. In 1975, the war in Vietnam finally ended with the liberation of Saigon. The Clark Amendment forbade foreign intervention in Angola. Abortion had been legalized, and the Equal Rights Amendment was moving toward passage. The civil rights movement extended to Chicanos and Native Americans. Strong environmental protection laws were in effect. Blacks made significant political gains in electoral politics, and black cultural production in film was at its height. Liberals in Congress were hauling major corporations as well as the intelligence apparatus over the coals for wrongdoing. The popularity of antiauthoritarian films like *One Flew Over the Cuckoo's Nest* and *All the President's Men* (the two top grossing films in 1976) suggests that representations of a sense of distrust toward those in power were resonating with audiences. At the same time, films articulating perceptions of conspiracy among corporations and ruling elites were prevalent and popular—from *Network* and *Coma* to *The China Syndrome*.

But victories also take their toll by generating countermovements, and the high point of one movement can be the starting point of another in reaction to it. A new, much deeper economic recession in the mid-seventies helped foster white middle class resentment against affirmative action, in part because of the pinch of unemployment. Conservative opposition to peaceful coexistence and arms reduction talks with the USSR grew and became hysterical when the Soviets invaded Afghanistan in 1979. The attainment of relative parity in nuclear weapons also provoked right-wing fears regarding the "Present Danger." The liberation of Angola and Nicaragua gave rise to cries of "creeping communism." Conservative men and women launched what would be a successful campaign to turn back the ERA. Blacks suffered most through the recessions, and as the economic crisis was exacerbated, there were increasing white conservative outcries against federal welfare spending. An antitax movement sprang up around the country. Moreover, greater international economic competition made corporate profit difficult to maintain in America's relatively high-wage climate; in consequence, corporations began to divest and deindustrialize, to move overseas in search of lower wages, and to launch a campaign against unions and labor in general.

By 1978, the New Right was becoming a powerful force in American culture and politics. The "revolt against the state," that is, against the liberal use of the federal government to curb the negative effects of capitalism on people and the environment and to promote social welfare, was well under way. The movement was given a unified philosophy through the combination of a rehabilitated classical free market economic theory (Friedman and Laffer) with the new fundamentalist evangelism of the likes of the Moral Majority's Jerry Falwell. These were linked with the highly combustible militarist patriotism that emerged in the late seventies in response to Soviet expansionism, the "loss" of Vietnam, and the Iran hostage crisis. What gave the movement coherence was a "politics of return," the combined call to return to pre–New Deal, pre–social welfare economics (with its faith in the free market), to the traditional, male- supremacist family (in which children were disciplined and women subservient to men), to fundamentalist religious values (especially as allied with the "right-to-life" movement and with an eschatology that equated the Second Coming with the destruction of the Soviet antichrist), and to a time when the United States was the most powerful military nation on earth. By 1980, the New Right had been united into a religious crusade to restore the free market and the social discipline it required through the destruction of its two greatest opponents, the New Deal federal government and the Soviet Union.[4]

The new conservative spirit in American culture informs many popular films of the seventies and early eighties. In the *Star Wars* series, a very Soviet-looking Empire is successfully blown away by "republican" champions of "freedom." Feminism is put in its place in *Kramer vs. Kramer*, a film that demonstrates that father does indeed know best (even about mothering). If *Death Wish* had not taught blacks that they had better watch out for whitey, their return to Bojangles roles in films like *Trading Places* at least taught them how to get along with their newly gentrified oppressors. A slew of post-Vietnam, promilitarist films, including *The Deer Hunter* and *Rambo*, made it clear that the hawks were determined not to let "it" happen again. After a mid-seventies crest of popular disillusion and projected anxiety in disaster and conspiracy films, American culture seemed to turn predictably in the late seventies to fantasies of power (*Star Wars* and *Superman* were the top films of 1977 and 1979) and fantasies of romantic, nostalgic, or religious transcendence of the world of inflation, unemployment, and loss of national prestige (*Grease, Close Encounters*, and *Animal House* were the top films of 1978).

In the early eighties, under the leadership of Ronald Reagan, the revived conservative social movements managed to turn back many of the liberal social gains of the preceding fifty years. Films that promote right-wing positions regarding feminism (*Terms of Endearment*), war (*Rambo*), economics (*Risky Business*), and social structure (*Return of the Jedi*) were prevalent during this time. The most popular films of the early to mid-eighties—*Raiders of the Lost Ark, E.T., The Empire Strikes Back, Return of the Jedi, Beverly Hills Cop, Rambo*—suggest that conservative values, escapist fantasies, and cinematic regressions to traditional social forms were resonating with audiences by now exhausted by economic crisis and the resulting insecurity and ready to identify with images of a reinvigorated patriarchal family (*On Golden Pond*), a revived male-centered romantic couple (*An Officer and a Gentleman*), a renewed military (the *Star Wars* series), new stronger male heroes (*Indiana Jones*), and triumphant Americanism (the return-to-Vietnam films).

But, as we have argued, the social movements of the sixties carried over into the seventies and eighties, and significant cinematic statements against social injustice, nuclear weapons, and U.S. foreign policy continued to be made (*War Games, Missing, Silkwood, Under Fire, Salvador*). This phenomenon indicates a discrepancy between cultural production and political power. But the simultaneous popularity of both liberal films like *E.T.* and militarist fantasies like *The Empire Strikes Back* also suggests that there were cultural forces at work in contradiction to the hegemonic conservative power bloc. While describing the history of the relation between film and society during the period between the passing of the New Left and the rise of the New Right, then, we will be concerned with delineating those forces and analyzing their consequences.

We conceive of the relationship between film and social history as a process of discursive transcoding. We do so in order to emphasize the connections between the representations operative in film and the representations which give structure and shape to social life. Social life consists of discourses that determine the substance and form of the everyday world. For example, the discourse of technocratic capitalism, with its ideals of progress and modernization, embodies certain material interests, but it also consists of representations that shape and transform the social world. Indeed, one could say that the very substance of capitalist modernity depends on such representations; it could not exist without them. The ideal of "progress" is a metaphor, a figure which allows specific economic interests to be transported across class lines and universalized, while also underwriting the reshaping of material life. The same can be said of people's social roles and psychological dispositions in a capitalist culture. Businessmen live by one set of representations, housewives by another. The prevailing cultural representations that shape a businessman's life prescribe certain patterns of behavior, thought, and feeling, and set boundaries over which he cannot cross. Similarly, the housewife internalizes representations which prescribe a quite different set of attitudes and habits, different boundaries on thought and action. The acceptance of such boundaries or limitations constitutes one's life as a synecdoche, a part which stands in for a whole, in that one allows one's life possibilities to be curtailed, reduced to a part, in order to fulfill a function in the larger whole of technocratic capitalist social life. One's being is thus shaped by the representations of oneself and of the world that one holds, and one's life can be described in terms of the figures or shapes which social life assumes as a result of the representations that prevail in a culture.

Films transcode the discourses (the forms, figures, and representations) of social life into cinematic narratives. Rather than reflect a reality external to the film medium, films execute a transfer from one discursive field to another. As a result, films themselves become part of that broader cultural system of representations that construct social reality. That construction occurs in part through the internalization of representations.

Recent "object relations" psychoanalytic theory emphasizes the role of representation in determining the direction and development of psychological life. Psychological maturation and health are foremost a matter of developing a capacity for mental representation. And certain forms of mental dysfunction, like schizophrenia, have come to be seen as consisting in part of a failure to develop such a capacity. Representation is important because it allows the person to mark out boundaries between the self and the world as well as between objects in the world. At the earliest stages of development, representation enables the child to tolerate separation from initial caretakers; by representing them to herself in their absence (by "internalizing" them), the child can learn to accept the sense of loss separation entails. If that initial separation is executed successfully with the aid of mental representations, then the child is likely to continue to develop a capacity to represent the world in a way which is not neurotic and that is distinct, complex, articulated, and differentiated. Neurotic representation is either too indistinct or too distinct; it erects excessive representational boundaries between objects or between self and world which are designed to protect a vulnerable self, or it has trouble constructing representational boundaries, with the result that the self is excessively oriented toward fusion with others.[5] Such "boundary disturbances" appear as mental representations that replace representations of the actual object world with private representations that are either exaggeratedly developed, distinct, and articulated, but which have no bearing on reality, or characterized by a failure to distinguish the imaginary from the real or to make clear distinctions between objects.

Representations are also taken from the culture and internalized, adopted as part of the self. When internalized, they mold the self in such a way that it becomes accommodated to the values inherent in those cultural representations. Consequently, the sort of representations which prevail in a culture is a crucial political issue. Cultural representations not only give shape to psychological dispositions, they also play an important role in determining how social reality will be constructed, that is, what figures and boundaries will prevail in the shaping of social life and social institutions. They determine whether capitalism will be conceived (felt, experienced, lived) as a predatory jungle or as a utopia of freedom. Control over the production of cultural representation is therefore crucial to the maintenance of social power, but it is also essential to progressive movements for social change.

Film is a particularly important arena of cultural representation for carrying out such political struggles in the contemporary era. Film is the site of a contest of representations over what social reality will be perceived as being and indeed will be. Films have been used to reassert traditional representations of women in order to counteract feminism, but they have also permitted the prevailing representations of capitalism and of capitalist government to be questioned. Significant changes in American attitudes toward such institutions as government and the family have occurred in the past two decades, and cultural representations like film have been part of that process. In addition, the sorts of economic and political crises that have occurred during this time provoked psychological crises which were also crises of representation. Traditional ways of representing the world broke down; there was a tremendous loss of confidence in institutions. The cultural representations of leaders and of public virtue were eroded, and people whose psychological integrity depended on the internalization of those representations felt what psychologists call a loss of "object constancy." That is, their private representations no longer stabilized a secure world, and that loss of stability provoked anxiety. In such a situation, either new representations can be forged which take change into account or old ones can be revived which reinstate stability. To study American film of this period is to observe this dual process in action.

The political stakes of film are thus very high because film is part of a broader system of cultural representation which operates to create psychological dispositions that result in a particular construction of social reality, a commonly held sense of what the world is and ought to be that sustains social institutions. This conception of the role of film necessitates expanding the traditional Marxist notion of ideology, defined as the system of ideas and images which operates to enlist the oppressed in their own subjugation—control without the exercise of force. In our view, ideology needs to be seen as an attempt to placate social tensions and to respond to social forces in such a way that they cease to be dangerous to the social system of inequality. Ideology carries out this task through cultural representations which, like mental representations in relation to the psyche, orient thought and behavior in a manner that maintains order and establishes boundaries on proper action.

Rather than conceive of ideology as a simple exercise in domination, we suggest that it be conceived of as a response to forces which, if they were not pacified, would tear the social system asunder from inside. Indeed, one could say that the very necessity of ideology testifies to something amiss within society, since a society that was not threatened would not need ideological defenses. By attempting to pacify, channel, and neutralize the forces that would invert the social system of inequality were they not controlled, ideology testifies to the power of those forces, of the very thing it seeks to deny. Even conservative films, therefore, can yield socially critical insights, for what they designate in a sort of inverse negative is the presence of forces that make conservative reactions necessary. By reacting against the structural tensions and potentially disruptive forces of an inegalitarian society in a way that attempts to render them invisible, film ideology must also simultaneously put them on display—just as excessively washed hands testify to offstage guilt, or as an abundance of white blood cells points to disease. It is for this reason that we see ideology itself as being a testament to the presence of forces in American society which have the potential for becoming sources of progressive change.

We would contend as well that ideology needs to be redefined more concretely as certain specific rhetorical and representational techniques which, when internalized, give rise to particular ways of constructing (perceiving and acting in) the social world in keeping with the prevailing institutional setup. Ideology, we have found, is primarily a metaphoric way of representing the world that is linked to a particular way of constructing social reality. A metaphor replaces an image with an ideal or higher meaning. The ideal meaning "freedom" is substituted for by a concrete image (for example, the eagle). The metaphoric replacement of the actual object with a higher meaning parallels the way in which, in ideology, certain ideal meanings come to stand in for an accurate perception of actuality. Someone who adopts such ideological representations of the world as "freedom" will think, feel, and act as if the ideal of class mobility were real, and will not see the structural reality of class inequality. Nevertheless, actuality cannot be erased entirely, if for no other reason than that the necessary vehicles of all ideological metaphors are actual, concrete, literal, and material, and this discursive reality cannot be transcended. The idealism and ideology which a metaphoric rhetoric permits (by creating sense of meaning that is above materiality) are trapped by their own material literality. Some connection, some material tie or contiguous link between the ideal metaphoric meaning and the reality it supposedly transcends and determines, will always obtrude. We will use the term *metonymy* to refer to these links. Metonymy is the trope of connection between objects which are in contiguous relation to each other or which relate by part to whole. Eagle is by metonymy not a sign for an ideal like "freedom" but rather is significant of, because literally connected to, some part of material reality like the threat hunters and land developers (whose material activities are sanctioned by an ideological ideal like freedom) pose to the wilderness and the environment. You can see why we might want to privilege the metonymic mode of representation. Rather than promote an idealized understanding of the world which overlooks material connections, metonymy is the mode of representation that foregrounds the contiguous, material, contextual interconnections between different dimensions of the actual social system. It is an anti-ideological representational form in that it acts to deconstruct the pretensions of ideological meanings like "freedom" by anchoring them in their material contexts.[6]

We also see the metonymic undermining of ideological metaphors as indicating real forces at work within the society of domination that threaten its stability and identity. If metaphor is an ideological representational form which sanctifies the status quo because it posits a hierarchy of ideal meaning over material image, code over context, and determination over the dissemination of reference, metonymy, in contrast, is a leveling and equalizing form which defuses metaphoric hierarchies and with them the social hierarchies they stabilize. The metonymic connections that undermine the idealizing pretensions of social metaphors instantiate real forces and possibilities in society that tend toward an equalization of all the inequalities ideological metaphors sanctify, a breakdown of social boundaries, and an erosion of such spurious ideals as property, propriety, and individual self-identity. By pacifying the tensions endemic to an inegalitarian society, ideology points toward those forces, and it cannot help but register the effects of those other possibilities in its very representational form. What we will be concerned with primarily in this book, then, will be what we call a diagnostic critique of those ideological strategies whose dual purpose is to analyze the sources, the morphology, and the limitations of conservative and liberal ideological cultural forms and to ferret out the forces and possibilities that ideology seeks to deny, forces that point beyond the society of domination toward a more equal social form. Using deconstructive analysis, we attempt to go beyond the usual charting of successful domination in the critique of ideology by studying how films undermine their own ideological premises and by asking what about ideology points toward the reconstruction of society along progressive lines, not on the basis of a utopian aspiration for another world, but on the basis of immanent possibilities within this world.[7]

1. FROM COUNTERCULTURE TO COUNTERREVOLUTION, 1967–1971

In the late 1960s many Hollywood films, responding to social movements mobilized around the issues of civil rights, poverty, feminism, and militarism that were cresting at that time, articulated critiques of American values and institutions. They transcoded a growing sense of alienation from the dominant myths and ideals of U.S. society. Film served as both an instrument of social criticism and a vehicle for presenting favorable representations of alternative values and institutions. "New Hollywood" films like *The Graduate, Bonnie and Clyde, Midnight Cowboy,* and *Easy Rider* were important not only for their social content. Some subverted the traditional narrative and cinematic representational codes of Hollywood filmmaking. Many employed a disjunctive editing that undermined passive viewing (*The Graduate, Point Blank*), used experimental camera techniques as thematic correlates (*Midnight Cowboy*), mixed genres like slapstick and tragedy (*Bonnie and Clyde*), employed color as an ironic or critical rather than expressive correlate of meaning (*They Shoot Horses, Don't They?*), broke down the classical narrative patterns that had dominated the 1950s and early 1960s (*Little Big Man*), introduced camera and editing techniques derived from television that significantly altered the pace and format of film (*M*A*S*H*), and undermined the mixture of blithe cynicism, complacent naiveté, and strained optimism that characterized the Cold War period (in some respects, a "Restoration Period" in Hollywood).

These films provided audiences with a new set of representations for constructing the world, new figures of action, thought, and feeling for positing alternative phenomenal and social realities, sometimes apart from, sometimes within the interstices of the dominant social reality construction. These alternative representations and figures were as important as the new institutions and laws brought into being by the direct actions of blacks, students, and women in the streets and legislatures during the period. Even though the social movements themselves could be repressed or contravened, those new figures of social understanding and behavior would become a permanent

part of American culture. Perhaps the most important of these representations was that of the self or subject in rebellion against conservative authority
and social conformity. It was the figure that marked the end of the fifties
ideal of functional selflessness. Related representations included that of the
"Establishment" as a set of outdated conservative values, of the police as an
enemy rather than a friend, of the patriarchal family as an institution for the
oppression of women, of the liberal ideal of consensus as a cloak for white
racial domination, of the government as the slave of economic interests,
especially war industry interests, of foreign policy as a form of neoimperi-
alism, of Third World liberation struggles as heroic, of the value of subjective
experiences related to mysticism and drugs, of the importance of the preservation of nature, of sexuality as a rich terrain of possibility rather than as
an evil to be repressed, and of capitalism as a form of enslavement instead
of a realm of freedom. This transformation of the dominant representations
which determined how the commonly held sense of social reality was constructed would have lasting, indeed permanent effects. It would be impossible
to return unquestioningly to the imposed discipline of the fifties or to restore
the conservative order of sexual and moral propriety that prevailed prior to
the sixties. A radical alternative culture came into being, one immune to the
sort of McCarthyite repression that had silenced the radical culture of the
twenties and thirties, because the new radicalism was as critical of the Soviet
Union as it was of the United States. And that meant that the impunity with
which the business-government class had acted, especially overseas, could no
longer be assumed without opposition. Resistance had become a staple of
American culture.

1. Alienation and Rebellion

The major movements of the sixties were the black struggle for civil
rights, the struggle against the Vietnam War, the feminist movement, and
the New Left student movement. The sixties were also characterized by a
high level of disaffection on the part of white middle class youth from the
values and ideals of fifties America, the world of suburban houses, corporate
jobs, "straight" dress and behavior, sexual repression, and social conformity.
These alienated and rebellious youth took to the roads, dropped out of school,
started communes, grew long hair, listened to rock music, took drugs, and
engaged in the creation of alternative lifestyles to those associated with the
bourgeois "Establishment." We will begin our consideration of the sixties by
looking at the phenomenon of alienation from and rejection of the "American
Dream."

The American ideology which came to be rejected by so many during
this period consisted of a set of codes for understanding the world and living
in it that derived from American institutions and helped reproduce and legitimate them. Those codes provided an essentially metaphoric version of
U.S. history and society. A metaphoric representation is one which replaces
a real version of events or an accurate account of social reality with an elevated

ideal. An understanding of the phenomenon of alienation from and rebellion against such ideals is therefore inseparable from an understanding of the representational strategies used to undermine such ideological idealizations.

Crucial among these representations is the individualist male hero, the ideal of the just American war, a righteous vision of U.S. history, and the frontier myth of expanding possibilities for achievement and wealth that are available to all. Many revisionist films criticize the myth of the traditional American hero through reconstructive representations that clash with the hitherto prevalent Hollywood conventions. For example, in *Little Big Man*, one of the most popular films of 1970, General Custer is portrayed as a megalomaniacal butcher who deserved his fate. The critical representational strategy of the film consists of adopting the position of the Native Americans and of depicting the U.S. soldiers from outside as the enemy. At a time when domestic opposition to the Vietnam War was on the rise, a number of satiric and tragic films like *M*A*S*H* and *Johnny Got His Gun* departed from the tradition of the just American war by representing war as something stupid and inhumane. The mythic representation of the frontier is undermined in films like *Soldier Blue* and *McCabe and Mrs. Miller*, which depict it as brutal. And the traditional representation of the ladder of individual success open to all talents is revised in critical films like *Midnight Cowboy* and *They Shoot Horses, Don't They?*—a film based, like *Johnny*, on a Depression-era novel. The revival of thirties leftism is also signaled by three critical films by directors from the heyday of the social problem film—Dassin's *Uptight*, Biberman's *Slaves*, and Polonsky's *Tell Them Willie Boy Is Here*—all of whom had been blacklisted.

The development of new narrative strategies in a number of these films is inseparable from their critiques of the major tenets of the American imaginary. The theme of individual success, like that of the great American patriotic tradition, is based in a narrative form. It is a *story* that entails a character, a plot, and a conclusion. Similarly, American history is a narrative with good and bad characters projected over actual events that moves from a happy beginning (the Founding Fathers) to an even happier conclusion (the present, or if that doesn't work, the future). The frequent use of discontinuous, reflexive, and interrupted narratives in these films is thus not only a playful formal device. It gets at the heart of the American imaginary, inasmuch as that is based in narratives (of individual success, of American history, and so on).

The fact that the American imaginary is inseparable from cultural representations implies that its critique is inseparable from formal and generic revisions. Consequently, that critique is frequently carried out at the level of image construction, camera technique, editing, generic mixing, and so on. Neoexpressionist camera techniques are used in many films (*The Graduate*, for example) to transcode a sense of disillusion with bourgeois life, to connote the then-prevalent existentialist philosophy of the fleetingness of existence, and to render cinematically the new Romantic ethos of experience ("living for the moment"). These films represent in a positive way an alternative world of pleasure usually excluded from the bourgeois narrative of what a good life should be, what it should "look" or "read" like. Other films go to the other end of the stylistic spectrum, using exaggerated realism or naturalism to portray poverty and suffering, things omitted from the classical narrative of American life which were brought to public attention by Michael Harrington's *The Other America* in 1962. The hovel scenes in *Midnight Cowboy* are shot in a flat documentary style that contrasts with the expressive rendering of the young anti-hero's disillusionment. In addition, the traditional generic conventions that were consubstantial with the period of uncritical dominance of the tenets of the American imaginary began to be undermined. Alienated youth rebelled against the separation of work from meaning and value or the hiding of suffering behind happy, conformist façades. These topics are rendered cinematically as the mixing or undermining of genres that had in the previous era helped stabilize the world by dividing it into segregated, discrete realms (melodrama for women, westerns for men, comedy in a realm apart from tragedy, and so on). Now, the walls between the genres come down, permitting a crossing of representational boundaries that disrespects the principles of social order. One could sum up all of these revisions by saying that they represent a shift away from a metaphoric construction of social reality toward a more metonymic construction. Rather than present elevated ideals which transcend the material reality they supposedly represent or endow with meaning, these films tend to wrench those ideals out of the transcendental air and anchor them firmly in the rather messy materiality of history.

The Graduate (1967), one of the first alienation films, is the story of a college graduate who rejects his parents' upper-class career track, has an affair with a much older woman, and finally flees with her daughter. Images of immersion in water suggest the claustrophobia of the bourgeois world, the cloying sense of its hypocrisy and emptiness, which many young people of the time were experiencing. And the career advice Ben (Dustin Hoffman) receives—"Plastics"—sums up what many young people of the era thought of the fifties world of their parents and of the career imperatives of the American Dream—that they were crass and artificial. Directed by Mike Nichols, *The Graduate* was a key alienation film of the period and was also the biggest box-office success of the late sixties. It was innovative in style, relying on imported French New Wave techniques—jump cuts, long takes with hand-held cameras, tight close-ups—to render the experience of alienation from the American ideal of material success. Though weighted down by Christian imagery (Ben uses a cross to fight for his beloved Elayne) and a traditionalist romantic conclusion, the film nonetheless expanded the lexicon of the American cinema through editing and music primarily. In the credit sequence, Ben's air of passivity as he is carried along an airport conveyor belt while a loudspeaker issues recorded instructions is reinforced by Simon and Garfunkel's song "The Sounds of Silence." The music and the imagery suggest he is a cipher in a world of mass conformity and social control, the mode of being alienated young people claimed a technological and technocratic society was imposing on them. The film's critique is also executed through editing. Nonrealist transitions permit Ben to walk out of one space (his parents' outdoor pool) and into another quite different one (the hotel room where he carries on his affair), thus establishing contiguous links that suggest the interchangeability of upper-class luxury and cynical adultery. The metonymic leveling of the metaphoric idealization of bourgeois success is realized fully at the end when the escaping young couple ride a common bus to freedom and leave behind their parents' wealth.

In the other great rebellion film of 1967, *Bonnie and Clyde*, the story of two young Depression-era outlaws who are ultimately murdered by the police, images of imprisonment and confinement (the bars of a bed which represent the constraints a young woman feels in her working-class world) are juxtaposed to images of the open fields of nature to establish a simple trajectory of escape. Contrasts in visual texture and tempo code the escape as one from confinement and fragmentation to openness and continuity. Throughout the film, images of open fields, single tone colors, an expansive camera frame for exterior shots, and jaunty banjo music suggest liberation from the tight focus shots in small-town settings. While the young rebels are associated with brown earth, blue sky, freedom of movement, and dynamic music, the figures of Establishment authority are represented negatively in association with bleak, whitewashed prison settings and images of urban confinement. The film thus evokes the romanticism that was prevalent in the late sixties, which counterposed nature as a realm of freedom and equality to the authoritarianism of the Establishment. The style of the film is itself romantic. Close-ups are used expressively; the model of classically linear narrative is scuttled in favor of a more episodic mode of storytelling; color is used symbolically; and the frame functions to create significant still images of the interrelations between the protagonists and nature (the outlaw car set in a field at night). If metaphoric representational forms rely on codes to supply the meaning for the images, *Bonnie and Clyde* is metonymic to the extent that it enacts a process of decoding, of breaking down traditional meaning structures, by displaying the literal or material underpinning of the encoded metaphoric ideals. The traditional ideal of the good Texas Ranger is undermined when he is shown to be a cruel and cynical man who torments injured prisoners and cold-bloodedly kills the outlaws. Moreover, the film transgresses the boundaries that maintain generic propriety and unity by mixing several different modes, from comedy to slapstick to tragedy. The generic code is broken, as is the traditional code of the idealized hero. Neither Bonnie nor Clyde is isolated as a superior individual; indeed, it is the somewhat tragic interrelationship of the two that is probably the most metonymic feature of the film. They exist in contiguous association, common victims of a very brutal material reality.

Yet both *The Graduate* and *Bonnie and Clyde* evidence the limitations of the sixties version of alienated white middle class rebellion. The alternatives posed to bourgeois conformity frequently took the form of a search for more personal, self-fulfilling experiences. The self ("doing one's own thing") became a criterion of authenticity, and in many ways this representation cohered

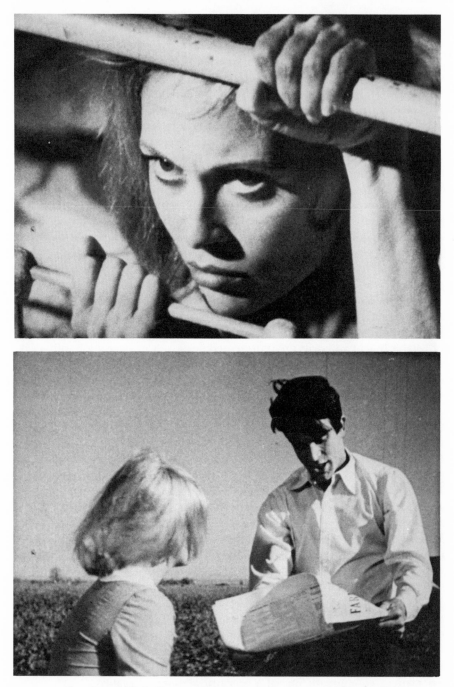

Bonnie and Clyde. From entrapment to the romance of nature.

perfectly with traditional American individualism. The subjective and expressive style of *The Graduate* (frequent point of view shots, meaning-laden similes—parents = fish in a bowl) thus correlates with the personalist alternative the film proposes. While the film positively affirms a refusal of work which was available at least to some at the time, it also portends the seventies social idiom of white professional class self-complacency (quiche, chablis, and hot tubbing). The radical gesture of *Bonnie and Clyde* is plagued by a similar limitation. It offers a permanent code-breaking as an alternative to passive suffering; yet, just as it is in the nature of this picaresque narrative style never to be able to terminate in any image of success (thus to become a domestic melodrama), so also it is in the nature of the social alternative of picaresque decoding never to be capable of offering the suffering "Okies" or displaced farmers of the Depression anything but a transient image of folk heroism (more Marx brothers than Marx). It is indicative of the prematurity of this social vision that it confines itself to thumbing its nose at the "Establishment" and complaining of the institutional violence of the law. In some respects, this also was a shortcoming of the rebellious and alienated white middle class side of the sixties.

Alienation from the "American Dream" assumed its most striking form during the period in the hippie counterculture. Founded on the values of a return to nature, of the virtue of preindustrial social forms like the commune, of the need to liberate oneself from "straight" behavior, especially regarding sexuality, of the ideal of a simple and more authentic life experience, usually gained with the aid of drugs, the counterculture seemed for a time to be in the process of constituting a genuine and permanent alternative to bourgeois life. But the effort was itself dependent on a well-fueled capitalist economy, which began to fizzle out in 1970, and dropping out soon gave way to caving in. Law school followed a quick shave and haircut for many former hippies.

Easy Rider (1968) was produced by Bert Schneider and Bob Rafelson's BBS company, which also was responsible for other alienation classics of the time like *Five Easy Pieces* (1970) and *The Last Picture Show* (1971). The story of two motorcycle-riding hippies who travel from Los Angeles to New Orleans to sell drugs and who are murdered by rural rednecks in the end, the film turned a small budget into a large profit and helped launch the "New Hollywood" of more "personal" and artistic independent films. It is in this film that the ambivalent ideology of sixties individualism is most evident. Such individualism is usually male and highly narcissistic. Consequently, the ride into nature which the bikers undertake is both a metaphor for the escape from urban oppression into the freedom of self-discovery and a synecdoche for male narcissistic regression to a warm, comforting maternal environment in the face of the constraints of modern mass life (signaled by the metal structures that seem to be devouring the bikers in a scene just before their death). Women are noticeably marginalized in the film; they appear as compliant sexual partners, prostitutes, or devoted wives. Moreover, although the hippie quest permits a critique of small-town southern provincialism, it is also essentially aimed toward an ideal of freedom that is highly traditional.

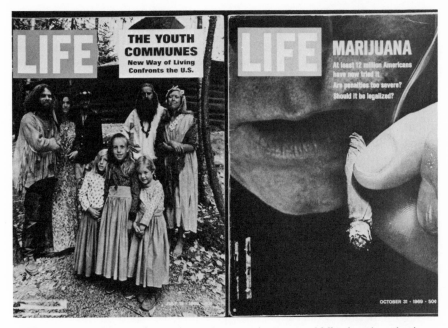

The counterculture seeks an alternative to mainstream middle class America in mysticism, drugs, ecological naturalism, communes, and karma.

Indeed, it recalls the Jeffersonian yeoman ideal of small rural capitalism. For example, at one point the bikers are compared to cowboys shoeing a horse in a medium shot which includes both within the frame. In a certain sense, the bikers' ride is as much into the past as it is into the heartland.

While it is an exemplary sixties film, *Easy Rider* is also a good indicator of why much of what seemed radical in the hippie counterculture blended so easily with mainstream capitalist culture in the seventies. The most telling example of this tendency is Ken Kesey's *One Flew Over the Cuckoo's Nest*, a best-selling novel of the time which became a major film in 1976. A romantic celebration of inspired male individualism and rebellion, it projects onto women responsibility for curtailing the great male's quest, and the solution offered to this misogynist vision of castration is flight to nature. In *Easy Rider*, similarly, nature is portrayed as a utopian space of narcissistic self-fulfillment. This narcissistic vision is coupled with paranoia or distrust regarding everything that curtails male desire, and indeed, the bikers are divided psychologically between the paranoid Billy (Dennis Hopper) and the narcissistic Wyatt (Peter Fonda). As in *Bonnie and Clyde*, the only solution to the quandary of having to live in a world of constraint while seeking a regressed "freedom" of maternal bonding is tragedy. Metaphorically, nature can be a mother (especially when suffused with rock music), but literally, all open roads lead eventually to modern cities, and the motorcycle that makes one natural and free is itself a modern technological device, not a horse. It is because this insistent literality cannot be transcended that the transcendent quest must

Easy Rider. The bikers' cycle is compared to the western cowboy's horse.

end with death and a whine of self-pity. Politically, the film suffers from a similar conundrum. It is critical of a certain America, but it can also be read as merely enacting the fundamental principle of capitalist America—the freedom of the market, which is in some respects metaphorized as the freedom of the open road. The primary complaint against America in the film is that it is not American enough.

Late sixties "alienation and rebellion" films like *Easy Rider* are thus dominated by tropes of pathos and deviation. The camera is frequently in close-up, or else the lone individual is isolated in the frame against over-coded shots of natural settings. Narratively, the hero's life progresses along a path away from normality rather than toward its discovery or restoration. By positioning the primary characters within order initially and developing them away from it, the films suggest a deficit, a poverty within normal life. They also suggest the constructedness of such normality, its basis in variable conventions. It is perhaps a drawback of the available lexicon for constructing alternative modes of social perception, alternative norms and social ideals, that few films exploit the theme of conventionality by positing alternative social constructs. Instead, most point to nature, an other which is outside civil society as the site of a new world. The films are dominated by metaphors which establish equivalences between nature and behavior counter to patriarchal, mainstream conformist, or legal norms.

The nature metaphors are part of a larger romantic rhetoric that characterizes the era. In film, this romanticism takes the form of eliciting empathy and identification with characters rather than situations, with pathic rather than ethical dilemmas. The assumption of the point of view of the primary characters places the audience outside the law of normal institutions in each case. But this potentially radical or critical gesture is undermined in certain instances by a pathic or emotive subjective focus which prevents a contextual understanding of the situation of the characters. Nature is that which is supposedly without history, at least in ideology, and the myth-quest of *Easy Rider* particularly is resolutely ahistorical. *Bonnie and Clyde* most successfully incorporates an ethical perspective, especially in such scenes as the encounter between the wounded outlaws and the impoverished Okies. The camera assumes an overhead position and neutralizes the pathos of the scene by incorporating the Okies into the frame. The suffering of the outlaws is implicitly compared with another sort of suffering—the everyday experience of the poor farmers. To a certain extent, then, the film undercuts its own premise, which is to depict the outlaws in such a way as to generate an uncustomary identification with those who break rather than maintain civil order. By suggesting a broader span of suffering, the film undermines the pathic empathy which directs audience identification toward Bonnie and Clyde.

Something similar occurs in the famous death scene, which shifts from empathetic identification (the outlaws sharing an apple in their car) to a distanced ethical consideration of the event of their murder by faceless law officers who hide behind a bush. The juxtaposition of empathy and distance (slow-motion shots of the bodies being pulverized by bullets) heightens the sense of mechanical brutality. It is an ethical rather than a pathic rhetorical strategy, a matter of the creation of meaning through contrast, situation, and context rather than character identification. The rhetoric of death in *Easy Rider*, on the other hand, evokes identification with the primary character through his rather significant absence from the final frames. One only sees his motorcycle flying through the air and exploding. The camera pulls up and away into the heavens, reinforcing the meaning that he has been transmuted by death into something higher, mystical, and natural. He and the camera quite literally transcend, and the audience is invited to participate empathetically in this aggrandizement of the suffering and beset male. In this case, pathos displaces ethics. Yet at their best, the alienation films of the late sixties combine both in effective social critique. For example, *They Shoot Horses, Don't They?* evokes identification with an exploited young woman who tries to win a dance contest in the thirties. Having lost everything, she asks a fellow participant to shoot her. The pathic identification is linked to a critique of the capitalist system of competition which is allegorized in the dance contest. Similarly, in *Midnight Cowboy* the concluding pathic evocation of empathy with the death of a poor bum on a bus to Florida is indissociable from a broad context which includes critical depictions of upper-class decadence and rural oppression.

While hippie romanticism can be conservative, it also helped spawn the ecology movement, legislation to protect the environment, and the rediscovery of natural agriculture and foods. In its benign progressive forms, the counterculture became a culture of alternative values based in nature that led eventually to such important later social movements as the antinuclear campaigns of the late seventies and Greenpeace. In light of the value of "nature," some of the more negative aspects of conservative capitalist life came into focus—toxic waste, pollution, etc.—and became objects of social opposition. Thus, hippie romanticism was not univocal. Even though its inflection in *Easy Rider* is male individualist and narcissistic, it also gave rise to a mental health movement which questioned the prevailing definitions of psychological normality, emphasized the psychological costs of living in a capitalist society, and promoted ideals of self-expression as a way of gaining mental health. The very important subjective psychology movement of the seventies (the so-called "culture of narcissism") derives from the counterculture's emphasis on expressivity. Although it was often limited to white professionals, that movement pointed toward the necessity of a focus on issues of mental health in any progressive vision of social reconstruction.

We have concentrated on films celebrating the values of alienation and rebellion, but many films of the era cast both the counterculture and the new hip rebelliousness in a somewhat more critical light. Richard Lester's *Petulia* (1968) and Paul Mazursky's *Bob and Carol and Ted and Alice* (1970), for example, criticized the alternative lifestyles of the new sexual revolution. And films like *Panic in Needle Park* (1971) and Arthur Penn's *Alice's Restaurant* (1969) depicted the countercultural use of drugs negatively. Penn's film also suggested the fragility of the communal experience. By 1971, the dark side of the counterculture would be revealed for many in *Gimme Shelter*, the film of the Rolling Stones concert at Altamont which culminated in violent death. Film itself contributed to the standardization of the counterculture. The "capturing" of the experience of Woodstock, the major commercial "happening" of the late sixties, in a film of 1970 was also a freezing of the supposed spontaneity of the occasion. What could be filmed and commercialized was to a certain extent already inimical to the countercultural rejection of bourgeois values in favor of more noncommercial and natural ideals. To be "counter" cultural was to place oneself at odds with the mainstream of American culture, and while taking advantage of so commercial a form as the rock concert or the rock movie could help spread the countercultural message, it also necessarily contradicted the essential values of the counterculture.

2. Feminism, Black Radicalism, Student Rebellion   (ourse

More than the counterculture, the feminist, black, and student movements would have a lasting impact on U.S. society. The feminist and black movements in particular gained ends (affirmative action, for example) which would become objects of great debate and struggle in the seventies and eighties, as white male conservatives counterattacked against the inroads made on their traditional prerogatives and power. The student movement would give rise to a radical Left culture that would make protest, opposition, and contestation legitimate parts of modern American life. At the same time, the gay and lesbian movement and the movement for sexual liberation would transform accepted structures of sexual relations in the culture and create alternatives to heterosexual patriarchy. Except in independent films made by participants in the various struggles, these movements are not represented with tremendous accuracy in Hollywood films of the time.

Indeed, the feminist movement was greeted by more opposition than support in Hollywood. Films like *Such Good Friends* (1971), *The Happy Ending* (1969), and *The Rain People* (1969) portray women attempting independence and failing, while *Up the Sandbox* (1972) is an overt attack on feminism. One possible reason for this phenomenon is that while most men (and men controlled the film industry) could be liberal regarding civil rights or war, it was more difficult for them to embrace a movement which saw them as oppressors and which questioned their most ingrained psychological dispositions regarding sexual identity. One major exception within Hollywood was *Diary of a Mad Housewife* (1970), the story of a housewife who has an affair in rebellion against her brutish husband, an opportunistic social climber. Tina (Carrie Snodgrass) is not presented as a figure of female strength, and her husband is so exaggeratedly reprehensible that her departure seems less motivated by feminist principle than by simple repulsion. The film thus risks making patriarchal domination seem the work of a few bad eggs. In addition, like later women's films, the exit from patriarchy has to pass by way of a sexual affair which if anything merely repositions Tina as the passive victim of men. The equation of liberation with the attainment of orgasm would remain in effect down through later films like *Coming Home* (1978). Tina's dilemma is in some ways symptomatic of the incipient character of feminism at the time. A strong women's community had not yet developed, and support groups were not yet available to help women like Tina out of brutal marriages. It is an additional comment on that early stage of development that the film was directed by a man (Frank Perry). Women filmmakers were not yet being trained in large enough numbers and had not yet made their way into Hollywood with sufficient power to make an impact on the dominant representations of women.

Yet women were working in the independent sector, and one of the most critical independent films about women was Barbara Loden's *Wanda* (1971). Loden plays a working-class housewife who leaves her family and becomes involved with a petty criminal after being refused work in a sweatshop. He is killed in a robbery. Alone, she is sexually assaulted by a man and then incorporated into a drunken group of revelers. The film ends bleakly with a shot of her sad face as she sits mourning in the midst of celebration. The film marks a radical departure from the idealizing style of Hollywood film production. It focuses on an ordinary and inarticulate underclass woman who is in no way heroized. The style of the film is remarkably unedifying and nonillusionist. No attempt is made to stage events; characters speak as they would in real life on that social level; and the metonymic narrative ends nonclimactically, merely drifting off, like the main character's life.

To say that Hollywood did not noticeably further the feminist movement at this time would be an understatement. The movement was perhaps still

The radical uprisings of the sixties include a wide range of discourses, from feminism and black power to student radicalism and Third World revolutionism.

The mid to late sixties is a time of major social upheaval among women, workers, blacks, and students. The labor movement is at the height of its postwar power, and the womens' movement, aided by the founding of the National Organization for Women in 1966, becomes a powerful new force reshaping U.S. society and culture.

too new, its slogans and ideas still too limited to educated groups and not yet sufficiently popular with a broad public. Most audiences still seemed to accept the traditional idea of woman's secondary social role, and those who were struggling against that idea were obliged to shout louder in order to be heard at all. "Feminists" were easily recognizable as women who deliberately flouted traditional behavior and dress, refusing to wear makeup or to shave legs. The ideas of feminism thus were positioned in what appeared to be a minoritarian space, inapplicable to the rest of the female population, let alone to the male population. In addition, unlike the black movement, which could base itself in longstanding organizations like the NAACP or the more recent Student Non-Violent Coordinating Committee, the feminist movement favored small groups. Indeed, for many feminists, who saw feminism as a critique not only of the content of patriarchal society but also of its organizational forms, such coordination was antithetical to feminist ideals of equality, democracy, and participation. Moreover, while the black movement benefited from the support of northern liberals and from the training of its leaders—those like Martin Luther King who were churchmen especially—in public speaking, the feminist movement had to develop its own forms and agendas in a universally hostile male environment, and its leaders did not have the sort of institutional training and support that an organization like the church provided blacks. By the end of the sixties, however, it was

Riots by urban blacks help give substance to the analysis of black oppression by members of the Black Power movement.

clear that feminism was becoming a permanent part, indeed a very revolutionary part, of the American cultural scene, and Hollywood, if it did not like the idea, at least indicated its importance by reacting to it with a mixture of hesitation and outright hostility.

The mainstream black movement of the sixties was liberal and reformist. Leaders like King sought change within the existing system, using nonviolent tactics. By the late sixties, a younger, more revolutionary black movement had also come into being, associated with leaders like Stokely Carmichael and Huey Newton and with organizations like the Black Panthers, whose armed revolutionary public image contrasted with the much less violent reality of their community work in schools and food centers for children. The revolutionary blacks refused to work with whites for reform; they saw black oppression as being too deep to be ameliorated by voting rights or welfare checks. Many argued that it was inseparable from capitalism, while others, who argued for "black nationalism," sought to revive the black African cultural heritage and to make an alternative black nation. The differences between the liberals and the radicals is dramatized in *Uptight* (1968), a remake of Ford's *The Informer*, in which blacks debate whether or not to work with white liberals. One radical tells a white: "If you want to help us, send us some guns." Another voices the nationalist and separatist black position regarding whites: "No people are more nonviolent than blacks. Whitey is the mother of violence." Surprisingly, perhaps, it is this more radical outlook that makes its way into film at the time.

From the forties to the sixties, in films like *Pinky*, *The Defiant Ones*, and *Raisin in the Sun*, Hollywood had demonstrated liberal attitudes toward the cause of black liberation. Occasionally, black filmmakers like Ivan Dixon, whose *Nothing but a Man* in 1962 was one of the first (post-World War II) films to examine black life from a black perspective, could gain access to the mode of cinematic production, but for the most part, it was Hollywood liberals like William Wyler (*The Liberation of L. B. Jones*) and Stanley Kramer (*Guess Who's Coming to Dinner*) who portrayed black life sympathetically. The late sixties saw the appearance of a new generation of young white and black radical filmmakers like Robert Downey, whose *Putney Swope* is a send-up of advertising from a black perspective, and Melvin Van Peebles, whose *Watermelon Man* satirizes white racism by depicting a white man who wakes up one day to find he is black and who eventually becomes a black nationalist. Black films by blacks are distinguished by their cinematic and thematic radicalism. Peebles's *Sweet Sweetback's Baadasss Song* (1971), for example, sets the tone of the time by being dedicated to the "Brothers and Sisters Who Have Had Enough of the Man." It uses the metaphor of the black male sexual performer in a club frequented by whites to make its case that blacks need to cease being subservient to whites. Sweetback begins as an unassuming man, but by the end he is a revolutionary. His complicity in black oppression is signaled by the fact that he is at one point handcuffed to a policeman who beats up a young black radical after a demonstration. Sweetback's moment of conversion comes when he decides to attack the policeman and defend the radical. Songs throughout the film act as an ironic chorus exhorting him to action: "We're talking revolution, Sweetback. I want to get off these knees." The film thus draws on the emerging discourse of black revolutionary thinking at the time, and it translates it into a cinematic practice that is itself quite radical, resorting to discontinuous narration, unconventional editing and camera angles, overexposed color techniques, overlap images, and split screens to convey a sense of Sweetback's departure from the conservative realism of black passivity into a more disruptive and revolutionary attitude. The represented reality is literally transformed in conjunction with the character.

Ivan Dixon was responsible for one of the most radical film statements of the era—*The Spook Who Sat by the Door* (based on the novel by Sam Greenlee). It is probably an indicator of changing political times that when it appeared in 1973 it was received with widespread criticism for depicting black youths who take up arms against the National Guard. Later critiques have focused on its sexist portrayals of women. The story concerns a black man who is trained by the CIA, but who quits when he learns his job will be to "sit by the door" as a receptionist. He returns to Chicago, where he uses his new skills to train youth gangs to be revolutionaries, and they engage in armed warfare against whites. It is a sobering and angry film, one that was not likely to please either white or black liberal audiences (though it was also taken to task in the Panther newspaper). It is significant for arguing that white liberalism has its limits at a time when that had not yet become evident. Affirmative action is shown to be a token gesture. Perhaps its most radical—

and troubling—rhetorical move is to equate the black cause with that of Third World revolutionary movements and to suggest that blacks need to use the weapons of the enemy against the enemy—fight force with force. *Spook* thus places itself far beyond the scope of liberalism, the belief that oppression can be lifted through a negotiated harmony of interests. By dramatizing (indeed merely documenting) the violent nature of white oppression, the film argues for the necessity of much more radical forms of structural change.

A plot summary makes *Spook* sound simplistic, but it is an astute rhetorical exercise. Its political analysis is presented dramatically, rather than being argued discursively. Moreover, complexities of plot prevent its politics from being reduced to an unproblematic formula. The hero loses his family and friends as a result of his radicalism. His actions are portrayed as in contradiction with his ideals, and the contradictions create tensions that are absent from other radical films. Nor is the film unidimensional or unironic. The black guerrillas soon learn that black brothers are working as National Guard troops, and they, along with the whites, must be killed if the war is to go on. This adds a tragic dimension to the uprising that defuses the possibility of simplistic self-righteousness and communicates a palpable sense of social and historical contradiction.

Attitudes and actions of the sort portrayed in *Sweetback* and *Spook* provoked the ruling white males of the United States to make certain concessions. Often those concessions took the form of infusions of liberal money into ghetto communities. This did little to change the general structure of inequality, which for blacks remained both racial and economic. Blacks were not only socially excluded but also more economically oppressed on the whole. Moreover, the new black leaders who were accepted into the white establishment belonged to the black bourgeoisie and believed in the fundamental values of capitalism. Their induction did not pose a serious threat to the system that kept less entitled fellow blacks under the heel of well-to-do whites. The cooptation of the mainstream black movement coincided with the violent repression of radical blacks by the police, who hounded the Panthers and occasionally murdered their leaders (Fred Hampton and Mark Clark in Chicago, for example). Hollywood was in step with these developments. Black radicalism would be argued against in numerous "black" films of the early seventies, from *Shaft* to *Claudine*, and mainstream liberal attitudes toward blacks would be privileged in sentimental films like *Sounder*. Yet all of this should not be read as simple cooptation. The process of mobilization and conciliation takes movements to higher levels than before; blacks "made gains," as liberals put it, even though the structures of oppression remained intact. What this means is that the demands would necessarily be higher the next time around, when the inegalitarian structure becomes either too obviously evident once again or else too painful to bear.

The movement for which the sixties is perhaps most notorious historically was the "student movement" against the war in Vietnam. With the black and feminist movements, this one contributed to a ripping apart of the consensus which had characterized American life since the fifties. Students refused to

Medium Cool. Police riot in Chicago.

serve, and their opposition to governmental authority spread to include university administrators, the police, and such other figures of the "Establishment" as businessmen. Arguably, this movement forced a president out of office and obliged the government to end the war. Its tactics were generally nonviolent, although after the police riot against demonstrators in Chicago in 1968, the methods came to include violent direct action. The movement had always included a strong anticapitalist component, especially in the critique of the "military industrial complex" which was seen as responsible for the war. With the shift to violent methods came as well a sharpening of the anticapitalist position into a revolutionary one which drew on such foreign examples as Mao in China and Che Guevara in Latin America. The "New Left" reintroduced a radical outlook into American culture and for a time at least made the business of making four-fifths of the people work and fight wars so that one-fifth could enjoy themselves and live in peace more difficult.

Hollywood made an effort to exploit the phenomenon, but the results were not terribly successful. *The Strawberry Statement* (1970) and *Wild in the Streets* (1968) were lame attempts to capture an aura, but the first, the story of a student who becomes radicalized, came out little better than a dull high school play, and the second, the story of a revolution by youth against adults, was extreme enough to seem farcical. It took those who were directly engaged in the movements to make cinematic statements that accurately reflected their motivations and ideals. Haskell Wexler's *Medium Cool* (1969) was a major

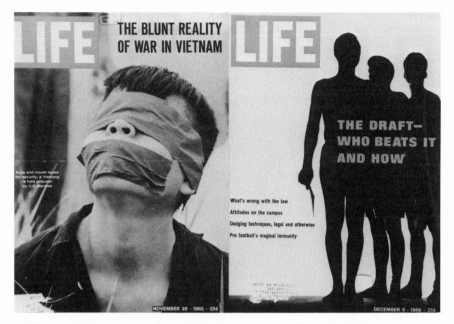

The war in Vietnam provokes resistance against the military draft of young men.

statement of the radical position. It depicts the coming to political consciousness of an apolitical news cameraman. This trajectory is rendered as a move from fiction to documentary in the narrative, as if the character's conversion consisted of a departure from a fictional universe and entry into a more real world. By the end, the movie consists almost entirely of documentary footage which was shot during the Democratic Convention in Chicago in 1968. Relying on methods established by French filmmaker Jean-Luc Godard and the neorealists, Wexler attempts to demystify the Hollywood conventions of dramatic action and character. Such metaphoric narrative conventions as romance and adventure are muted, and the characters behave like ordinary people who happen to have wandered in front of a camera. The purpose of these devices is to force the audience to identify less with the adventure or the hero and to think more about the documentary events. Yet the price paid for this strategy is an emotionally flat drama. The main character may move from behind the cool medium of his camera and become more involved, but the cool intellectual rendering of the story allows the audience to watch without becoming emotionally engaged. Nevertheless, the film stands as the summation of an era, for it records the process of political enlightenment that was the sixties. And it brings together the three major movements that demarcate the decade—black radicalism, in the story of the main character's journey into the black ghetto, feminism, in the story of a poor Appalachian woman he befriends, and the student antiwar movement, in the documentary depiction of the protests of 1968.

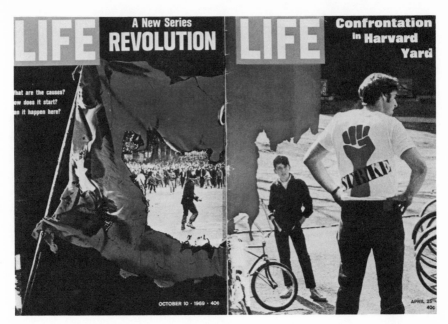

The student movement becomes more radical as the sixties progress, turning from resistance to calls for revolution.

Perhaps the headiest issue of the day among white student radicals was revolution. The Weather Underground actually set about the task and blew itself up in the process. The promotion of revolution in film was only slightly more successful. *The Revolutionary* (1970) views like a good sermon on all the available revolutionary positions of the era, from Leninism to anarchism. The more popular *Billy Jack* (1971) elicits audience sympathy for righteous violence against oppressors, but its dramatic setting—a small rural town— precludes deriving any broader political lessons. Michelangelo Antonioni's *Zabriskie Point* (1970) brings to the issue a modernist style of the sort that characterizes much late sixties radical filmmaking, and in so doing it suggests that changes in perception and representation are integral to the new political consciousness. The narrative of the meeting between a young male revolutionary who has shot a policeman and a hippie woman who is on her way to work for a wealthy businessman is intercut with nonnarrative segments that enact fantasies and transform reality (thousands of hippies copulating in the desert, for example). The two protagonists argue the merits of countercultural pacifism and political radicalism, and each is modified by the other. The young man decides to return to face justice, while she, having argued the pacifist position, fantasizes the destruction of her boss's home (and with it of American consumer culture) upon hearing of his shooting by the police.

Like *Spook*, *Zabriskie Point* suggests that the peace of civil society is a false one; it conceals an institutional violence. An inegalitarian civil society declares violence to be criminal and thereby legitimates its own covert and implicit violence. What Antonioni suggests is that revolutionary violence merely holds a mirror up to the society against which it is directed. But the film also draws attention to a major drawback in the radical political gesture Antonioni seems to advocate. At the time, no popular movement was available to serve as a mass base for revolutionary action. Consequently, fantasies of individual or small group political action found credit with the New Left. A political model that privileges violent interventions over the building of mass movements finds its corollary in the modernist cinematic strategy of the film. That strategy touches on surface perceptions without attempting to get at the unconscious processes which are the root of ideology. Similarly, the political strategy it enacts (the destruction of consumer culture) is itself directed at the surface of capitalist life—consumerism—and not at the root system of production and workplace exploitation which underlies it like a repressed unconscious. Modernism in politics as in film suffers from being too attentive to surface forms at the expense of invisible structures, perceptual patterns at the expense of unconscious processes, be they psychological or social.

No single lesson can be drawn from this. The weakness of the political movements of the sixties, their quick disappearance as publicly organized movements after 1970 and their failure to translate radicalism into an idiom acceptable to a broad mass of people, probably owes something to an excessive reliance on the sort of youthful, explosive, pyrotechnic antinomianism whose shortcomings are evident in *Zabriskie*. While many radicals sought to establish contacts with American workers in the early seventies, for the most part the New Left situated mainstream America as an other with whom there could be no compromise. Rather than attempt to forge new modes of life for the mass of people, radicals separated themselves from that world to engage in revolutionary violence whose rationale could not be made evident to people without relying on such contaminated instruments of capitalist culture as the media. Moralistic self-righteousness was indeed self-defeating. Nevertheless, the New Left reintroduced a long-repressed radical spirit into U.S. culture and made possible many grassroots movements which militated for change throughout the seventies and eighties, around such issues as the environment, the workplace, nuclear energy, and war. It was also, with the counterculture, feminism, and black radicalism, responsible for one other major event of the seventies. With its economic security threatened by recession in the early seventies, the white middle class began to turn sour and intolerant. And there began what is one of the most remarkable outcomes of the sixties—the reaction against it.

3. The Hollywood Counterrevolution

The struggles and movements of the sixties began to provoke a conservative backlash by the early seventies. Polls indicated a change during this period toward more "conservatism" and toward more concern with material self-satisfaction. Whereas only 1% of the people listed national unity as a major concern in 1959, the figure had risen to 15% by 1971. Adults also

The Silent Majority backlash of the late sixties and early seventies crystallizes in calls for "law and order."

registered a reduced sense of integration into the social structure, more anxiety accompanied by an increased search for intimacy, an increased concern about an uncertain future, and a move to less social, more personal and individuated integration and well-being.[1] There seems to be a relation between the new conservatism and the onset of the first major economic recession of the period at the same time. But the social struggles of the sixties also took their toll, giving rise to a countertendency desirous of unity, order, and peace. The demolition in the sixties of the cultural representations essential to the traditional order seemed to lead to a search for alternative forms of representational security and ego-integrity. But the sixties' assault on traditional values also provoked a reassertion of exaggerated versions of conservative ideals. The fearful retreat from the public world of disharmony and conflict was accompanied by a resuscitation of security-providing patriarchal representations. One finds evidence of the turn to personalism in the great popularity of *Love Story* (the top grossing picture of 1970) and of the desire for patriarchal unity in the success of right-wing police dramas like *The French Connection*, the Oscar winner in 1971, and *Dirty Harry* (1971), one of the most notorious films of the period.

    Conservative films had been made during the late sixties. But on the whole, conservatives were then on the defensive, and the terrain of social struggle was determined by the insurgent liberal and radical social forces. The killing of student radicals at Kent State and Jackson State by National

Straw Dogs. The homosocial impulse behind misogyny is displayed in the closing image of an all-male utopia supposedly purged entirely of female traits.

Guardsmen and police in 1971 marked a turning point in the limits of conservative tolerance for social revolt. By 1972, the Nixon counterrevolution was in full force, and the Nixon administration successfully mobilized conservative sentiments against young radicals, minorities, and feminists in the 1972 election by painting liberal Democrat George McGovern as the candidate of the three A's—abortion, acid, and amnesty for draft resisters. A meaner, more cynical discourse began to emerge as the dominant mode of Hollywood film. In 1971 alone, *The French Connection*, *Dirty Harry*, and *Straw Dogs* articulate an antiliberal value system that portrays human life as predatory and animalistic, a jungle without altruism.

At stake in Peckinpah's *Straw Dogs* is the law of the patriarchal family. In the late sixties, women were striking out for independence from male law in the home, and sexuality, long a secure domain of male power, became problematic. *Straw Dogs* sets the tone for the antifeminist counterrevolution of the seventies. The woman in the film is depicted as a treacherous sex kitten who betrays her "wimpy" husband, David, and entices men who finally rape her, an act she is portrayed as enjoying. In the final segment of the film, the same men attack their house, and she attempts to join them but is prevented from doing so by her husband, who is eventually transformed into a warrior who ultimately kills the attackers. His ascent to true manhood is associated with learning that liberal civility and law are useless against brute force, and that women need to be disciplined if they are not to go astray. At one point he calls out to his attackers that what they are doing is against the law, but of course his plea is ineffective. The local constable, whose ineffectuality is signaled by his lame arm, ultimately hands power over to David, telling him he is "the law here now." The benediction seems also to apply to the domestic sphere. David immediately tells his wife, "Do as you're told," and smiles beatifically. In the end, he separates out from her altogether and rides off into the night with another man, a sign of the homosocial origins of misogyny.

Peckinpah's style earnestly expresses the ideal of male redemption through violence. The color tones suggest a dark nature of instinct and passion, and the violence has all the frenzy of a sexual encounter; indeed this is a telling feature for understanding its origins. *Straw Dogs* opens with a shot of children playing against gravestones, a scene reminiscent of the juxtaposition of innocence and violence that opens *The Wild Bunch*—children tormenting a scorpion with ants, then setting it on fire. Even the innocent harbor bestial desires and violent instincts, the film suggests. *Straw Dogs*, therefore, concerns regression, the falling back upon a supposedly more basic or natural reality of violence when social order breaks down. Yet the film can also be said to undermine or deconstruct its own premises.

David is educated in the process of the film. He learns to be violent, to regress from civility to bestiality, and to be a "man." The film presents this metaphorically as a recognition of primordial realities (through the metaphors of primitive hunting devices), but it depicts the regression as a process of training or socialization, a random, contingent, and metonymic process, in other words. The constable's benediction is the most telling evidence of the initiatory or artificially induced character of David's learning experience. Moreover, his relation to his wife is characterized by a mixture of fear and dependence that situates his aggressive domination of her and his ultimate flight into the night with another man as further evidence of the social origins of this particular male "nature." In the penultimate scene, David is about to be overwhelmed by one of the aggressors. He lies on his back, with the other man on top, an explicitly "feminine" pose. He is passive and helpless, and his wife has to save him with a shotgun blast. She stands at the top of the stairs, he at the bottom, a curious literal denial of all the film figuratively asserts. The passive male's rage against woman is in fact an anger against dependence, against the possibility of being "on the bottom," that is linked to fears of passivity in regard to other men in a competitive male world. Violence permits an escape from those feelings, as well as an overthrowing of female power and potential independence. What is really regressed to is an earlier stage of psychic development when women have power over men as their primary caretakers. That power must be purged in order for the man to acquire a patriarchally defined male identity. But male anxiety is not limited to an abreaction of earlier experiences of female power, a metaphor of a narcissistic, atemporal simultaneity or fusion. It also concerns female sexuality. When David's wife almost leaves to join the other men, she displays the origin of male sexual anxiety in a female sexuality which is not ultimately beholden to male power, which, like the literal metonymic associations that trouble self-idealizing metaphors, can "go astray." Violence also cures this threat to impropriety.

Straw Dogs evokes these tensions between female independence and male dependence, impropriety and domination, and it seems to resolve them. But the metaphoric resolution which establishes a pure identity by transcending all metonymic ties and feminine links displays its own failure. It depends upon the exclusion of woman altogether, yet "woman" can never be purged from male identity. The restored family at the end seems an all-male one. The woman is absent, ejected from this metaphoric utopia of male self-identity in which sexual difference and the possibility of dependence and sexual indeterminacy represented by the metonymic connection to the woman are excised. Yet a tension persists between the metaphoric ideal, with its singular, proper, absolute meaning or identity, and a metonymic literality that characterizes that ideal identity as differential, material, and relational, dependent still on the position of the woman. The woman has been replaced by another man, who occupies the "wife's" position in the passenger seat of the car and who, because he is slightly retarded, weak, and "effeminate" (he has long hair), is a more ideal partner, one more likely to allay male anxieties. This metaphoric substitution excludes woman literally while retaining her figural place, and the self-identity of male power shows itself to be dependent on a metonymic connection, an other which provides a boundary for the self. The film thus displays how male identity can only be metaphoric, which is to say artificial and contingent, the effect of a rhetorical construction whose purpose is to permit a nonrecognition of the very real, material constituents of that identity.

The process of regression to a more brutal or primitive nature in these films is related to the different processes of representation. Such regression implies that the world of civility consists of signifiers without any meaning in themselves; they are contingent and variable, and their real truth resides in the realm of nature which lies hidden behind them, just as meaning lies behind the empirical signifiers in metaphor (eagle = "freedom"). To privilege the regression to a truer nature is in some respects to fulfill the structure of metaphor, to move back to a truer meaning behind ultimately meaningless images. The difference between a liberal or radical outlook and this conservative one is that the former sees what passes as "nature" as itself a product or effect of that seemingly meaningless level of representation. What conservatives posit as nature is merely an illusion created by a metaphoric representational structure which creates the sense of a hidden meaning, a true identity, a fundamental stratum behind historical contingency. The liberal and radical attitudes accept the realm of metonymic contingency, the possibility that meaning is not determinate, identity not fixed, as the only one that exists and consequently see the social world posited by such rhetoric as malleable and indeterminate.

The other major conservative films of 1971—*Dirty Harry* and *The French Connection*—were crime dramas. These "law and order" thrillers transcoded the discourse of the campaign against crime and drugs waged by Nixon and

Agnew in the early seventies. They are also vehicles for conservative counterattacks against the liberalism that many conservatives blamed for the crisis in domestic order brought about by the sixties. Both films contest the liberal theories of criminal justice, exemplified in the Miranda decision, that gave more rights to criminal suspects and curtailed the powers of the police. In this vision, liberal criminal justice is unjust because it prevents good cops from doing their job, and it lets criminals go free to commit more crimes. Cops are portrayed as heroes whose zeal to protect the innocent and society is misinterpreted as brutality by liberals. Like *Straw Dogs* and *Clockwork Orange*, these films portray conservatism as a regression to primary process thinking, to a privileging of force and instinct over civil procedure. Unsublimated drives such as competition and domination are presented as more fundamental than such liberal civil modes as negotiation, mediation, and cooperation—all connective or metonymic ways of proceeding which encroach upon the firmly boundaried identities that conservative metaphors establish.

In *The French Connection*, a tough cop named Popeye Doyle (Gene Hackman) manages to crack a heroin smuggling operation, but all the criminals are let go in the end for lack of evidence. The suggestion is that liberals are responsible for the failure of the system, while the individualist cop is a better solution. The film is metaphoric to the extent that it presumes certain axioms that are not open to negotiation; the narrative obliges the audience to agree with the premises of the film because there are no spaces where reflection is possible. The cop reacts instinctively to the "problem" of crime (which, significantly, has not yet been committed), and the audience is given little time to do anything but react with equal rapidity to his actions, thus assuming guilt without judicial process. This is made clear in the famous chase scene. The subjective camera lodged in Popeye's car identifies the audience with his point of view in a way that works against reflection on the motivations and consequences of his actions. The audience's desires are manipulated into supporting a restoration of order or the achievement of the goal of catching the criminal, no matter what the cost in life or liberty (and Popeye almost does harm a number of people during the chase). When he finally does kill the hit man (unnecessarily; he could just as easily have wounded the disarmed man), the audience is prepared to desire the release of tension that ensues. Police brutality is thus legitimated stylistically.[2]

A more overt and articulated statement against the sixties in general and against liberal criminal justice in particular is made in Don Siegel's *Dirty Harry*. Liberalism in crime prevention is outrightly condemned, and the evil figure in the film is a fanatical and "effeminate" killer named Scorpio who is associated with peace symbols, long hair, and other countercultural paraphernalia. The rhetorical procedure of this film is to position the audience as being knowledgeable of the criminal's guilt, then to show liberals letting him go after Harry has risked his life to capture him. When Scorpio kills again, the audience knows that Harry's only choice is to sidestep the liberal criminal system and use force. The style of the film is designed to produce

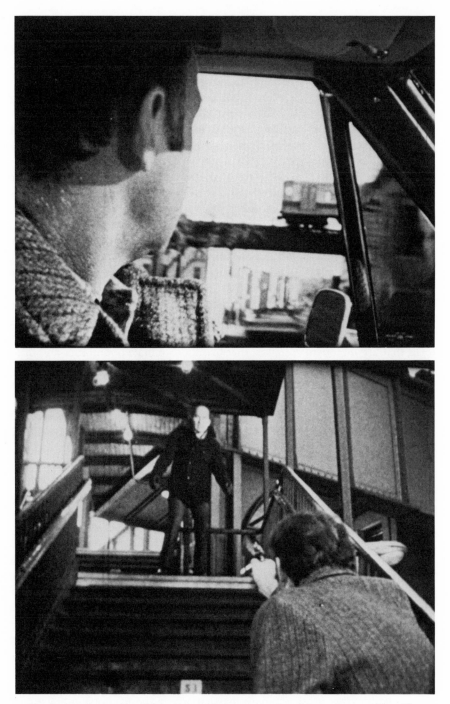

The French Connection. The subjective camera in the chase sequence identifies the audience with Popeye and justifies slaying the disarmed French hit man.

both repulsion and idealization (two conjoined attitudes that reappear in a number of conservative films). It mixes naturalistic representations of violence and brutality (a raped adolescent girl being removed from a hole in the ground where she has been allowed to suffocate) with monumentalizing celebrations of white male individualist power (Harry standing alone against the sky overlooking the city like a Hobbesian sovereign). The representational mix is significant because such metaphoric idealization (which establishes Harry's higher meaning as a savior while separating him from the mass) is often a means of turning away from or denying something threatening or repulsive. In this case, the idealization is of extremely "male" traits such as aggressivity, toughness, lack of affect, and individualism. What is repulsive is "feminine" or, worse, indeterminate. Scorpio is associated with gays ("My, that's a big one," he remarks of Harry's gun, after Harry has mistaken a gay for Scorpio), and he is depicted as whining, weak, and very un-"manly." What this suggests is that male-defined ideals of conservative law and order are bound up with the representational dynamics that construct male sexual identity. Metaphoric male idealization comes down to an insecurity in males over the determinacy of sexual identity, over being a "man" and not being confused with a "woman," an insecurity associated with representational patterns that are metonymic, that is, that break down male boundaries and male identity by establishing empathetic connections with people or differential relations between supposedly hermetic realms. Because Scorpio represents such a breakdown, he must be eliminated.

But the breakdown is operative as well within the identity that is secured by Scorpio's annulment, and this is the deconstructive significance of the film. Both Harry and Popeye are metaphoric idealizations, but they are also marked by lower middle class characteristics and ties, metonymic connections which detract from their ideal meaning or identity by anchoring them in a material universe. The metaphoric idealization works by isolating Harry from his environment, creating distances between subject and object which define the contours or boundaries of the subject's identity, reducing the metonymic interference of empathy and "effeminacy," and creating a sense of freedom through the metaphoric transcendence of social ties. Women and liberals represent external ties which constrain freedom, curtail natural impulses, and contravene the subjective will of the hero. Freedom necessarily assumes the form of idealization, a narcissistic exaggeration of one's own rights, a privileging of one's own will over that of others, and a separation from social ties. It has to deny the metonymic or contextual reality of social relations and communal responsibilities. The most obvious emblem of this magnification is Harry's handgun, "the most powerful handgun in the world."

Yet all such idealizations deconstruct, and the deconstruction of these lower middle class idealizations is particularly pathetic. Popeye envies the expensive dinner of the mafioso he is tailing, giving voice to petit bourgeois resentment against ostentatious wealth. Harry worries that a doctor will cut his pants, because they cost so much. It is in these marginal moments that the material values of the films inhere. The idealization denies context, but it requires a context of fallen materiality, something it transcends, if it is to have meaning. Harry seems to transcend material everyday life, and his metaphoric meaning for audiences particularly resides in his ability to overcome everyday constraints. But he is also the victim of those very (metonymic) constraints. This undecidability is irreducible, and it is what gives films like *Dirty Harry* their tremendous ideological resonance. Contextual or metonymic connections anchor the metaphoric figure of the hero/detective in a social reality that situates him as a common person, a link in a series or chain of equality. The ideologizing isolation of him is a way of attempting to overcome that metonymic seriality. Neither one of these terms can exist without the other; nor can they be separated into a decidable opposition which declares the meaning of the film to be one of the terms alone. Harry takes on meaning for audiences through his transcendence of his middle-class context, but he has no meaning except as part of that context. This problem is a common representational dilemma of conservative films during this period. The ideological strategy of conservatism is to isolate a hero from social contexts and to idealize him. This is why nature will be such an important metaphor for conservatives; it is the symbol of all that is not constrained by liberal civility. (Both Harry and Popeye experience their redemptive apotheoses outside the city, in a version of nature.) But in order to be plausible representations, conservative idealizations or metaphors must invoke the reality they address, the economic constraints on self-worth for which they serve as therapeutic antidotes. Ideology is always double and undecidable in this way. Harry's pants are as important as his handgun.

Dirty Harry was not a significantly popular film, at least in regard to box-office receipts. Its sequels would fare much better. Our audience survey also suggests that it wasn't successful in winning large segments of the population over to its viewpoint: 77% of our sample felt Harry's methods were the wrong way to deal with crime, and 73% felt that the D.A. represented necessary constitutional protections as opposed to unnecessary red tape. While 40% perceived Harry as a rebel against American society, a significant 68% characterized him as a reactionary. It may be important as well that nearly 30% of our sample had not seen the film, though some of these no-views may be due to the age of the film. While our survey suggests that many viewers rejected the film's vision of the world, we should also note that in our oral interviews we encountered a number of people who fully held the position of the film, and in a number of cases where people disagreed with the solution to crime, they nonetheless confessed to buying in temporarily to the action format and the plot premises of the film. This splitting of the ego between a reserved judgment and participation in the spectacle characterizes a number of audience response patterns to different films. It suggests that the popularity of right-wing films is not necessarily a testament to the prevalence of right-wing opinions in the film audiences. But it also points to the possibility of false consciousness and of unconscious influences. It is noteworthy, for example, that 79% of those polled also support stronger punishment for criminals.

French Connection and *Dirty Harry* are reactionary films, yet they also contain immanent critiques of American society. To be able to proclaim their right-wing solutions, they must inadvertently describe a disintegrating society which is incapable of finding real solutions to its fundamental problems of economic, political, and social inequality. The films depict the failure of liberal solutions to the problems of crime and poverty generated by capitalism. More accurately than liberal films, they portray the real exercise of force that underlies seemingly apolitical problems like crime. Right-wing films in certain ways portray the harsh truth of a society which must rely on authoritarian and repressive police force, generally directed overwhelmingly at minorities, in order to avoid coming undone as a result of its structural imbalances.

Dirty Harry and *French Connection* show right-wing conservatism to be isomorphic or specular. That is, it projects its own animus into the world, seeing there only what it itself is. Against Scorpio's seemingly warrantless violence, Harry musters an equally unrestrained and irresponsible violence. The first is deemed the cause of the second within the film's ideological scenario, but in fact the film can be read in such a way that it intimates that the first is merely a projection of the second. The primary process of conservative violence is projected in an inverted form into the world and perceived as an external threat, but in fact that violence emerges from right-wing conservative social principles themselves. It is not surprising then that in both films, two men are pitted against each other, and that each pair entails an inversion of traits—Popeye's streetwise populism vs. the heroin smuggler's aristocratic mannerisms, Harry's toughness vs. Scorpio's effeminacy. For these films are essentially about rightists gazing into mirrors. Mirrors can only give back what is projected, and what right-wing conservatives project is the motivating energy of their own social ideal—force, violence, and a disregard for law. Both Harry and Popeye are characterized by a rather resentful attitude toward legal restraint which makes them mirror images of their opponents. Thus, these detectives foreshadow the images of rightist putschism that distinguish later films of the era, which will argue against rational, liberal, legal processes in favor of the exercise of personalized force.

In 1971, American culture was still very much a contested terrain. It would be a mistake to assume that the appearance of films reacting against the sixties constituted a full-fledged capitulation on the part of Hollywood to an emerging conservative movement. Just as 1968 witnessed the popularity of such right-wing fare as *The Green Berets*, so also in 1971, radical films continued to make a strong showing. For example, though few films of the era can be said to deal p itically with issues of class, Stanley Kubrick's *A Clockwork Orange* might be read as an exception. It concerns a working-class adolescent whose criminal predilections are cured by state controllers using behavior modification. But Alex, deprived of his criminal instincts, is soon victimized by all those he himself victimized, and he attempts suicide. The failed attempt destroys his new, reformed conditioning, and he reverts to his previous criminal nature. The film is complicated ideologically, and it pivots on an irony that can be read either as debunking statist attempts at reform in favor of a recalcitrant working-class reality or as delineating a rather nasty and brutish human nature behind all of society's pretensions to civility. The latter possibility—the fatedness of evil and the unredeemability of a violent human character, a theme evident in Kubrick's *2001: A Space Odyssey* that was also a favorite of popular literature during the period—is suggested by the seeming inevitability or clockwork character of Alex's encounters with his former victims. Even good, "normal" people who live in a house called "Home" are portrayed as capable of a violence equal to Alex's "abnormal" behavior. The style appropriate to this debunking of the illusions of liberal civil society is satiric and ironic. Alex's bestiality is emphasized through the speeded-up shooting of an orgy, while his violent acts are choreographed in a slow motion that renders them aesthetic. At one cut, the camera lingers on an ornate design while classical music plays; it then descends to a derelict theater, where a gang is performing a gang rape. The ironic juxtaposition of high culture and low entertainment demolishes the myth of bourgeois civilization signified by the music and the setting. But all of these elements of the film are available for an alternate reading that would argue that the film depicts a working-class anger against wealth and privilege that cannot be quelled. When Alex stares at the camera at the end, fantasizing about "ultra-violence" as a state reformer attempts to use him to gain publicity, the sense conveyed is that this is one working-class lad who will not be "saved" quite so easily.

These two thematic strains—the fatedness of evil, the recalcitrance of working-class anger and violence—demarcate the semantic tension at the core of the film, a tension that can be described rhetorically. The idea of endemic violence is presented through a predominantly metaphoric rhetoric that suggests an implicit order in the world that transcends the contingencies of history. Such order is spatial rather than temporal; it denies social and historical differences in favor of analogies that establish metahistorical or ideal semantic identities. Thus, Alex's violent fantasies cut across historical boundaries and posit a basic violent identity of human nature. Metaphor enables the theme of a natural basis to society because a metaphor consists of an evident vehicle or image and a hidden tenor or meaning, and this structure implies a truth (nature) lying behind a meaningless appearance (society). The highly metaphoric form of the film easily accommodates the idea of a violent nature underlying civility. Most notably, the narrative is structured as a repetition of events; the camera situates action within extremely ordered spatial compositions; and the temporal pacing is choreographed as a slow unfolding of conclusions determined in advance. The overall impression is of a world of order, regularity, and proportion which possesses the rigidity of an unchanging nature. Against this backdrop, the criminal acts of the working-class youths take on the aura of disruptions of an inherent meaning, a random metonymic displacement by improper associations (Beethoven juxtaposed to musical numbers like "Singin' in the Rain" in Alex's repertoire of favorite hits). Metonymy, the representational form which emphasizes the artificiality, contingency, indeterminacy, and displaceability of putatively eternal or natural meanings, takes on a radical connotation in this context. Alex represents a metonymic possibility by stealing the signs of bourgeois propriety (classical music) as much as the signs of bourgeois property. His cultural juxtapositions and genre mixings represent a transgression of a cultural order in which everything has its place and its boundary. He thus displays the ungrounded character of bourgeois culture, and this is as threatening to a system based on cultural hierarchies as any theft of property.

Thus, the film cuts two ways—toward a theme of violence in human nature that cuts across class lines, and toward a theme of the rhetorical contingency of signs of cultural class differences. But it is the latter which ultimately seems the more powerful. The theme of violent nature is sustained by a narrative repetition that creates a sense of unchanging sameness, yet that narrative is inescapably temporal, and this anchors the idea of nature in social and historical contingency. The ironic ending seems to establish Alex as a sign of a violence that cannot be redeemed, making him a metaphor of human nature, but it also no less portrays him as a metonymic sign of that radical contingency within society which is the recalcitrant anger of those society exploits.

Despite the appearance of a critical, even radical, film like *Clockwork Orange*, 1971 nevertheless signaled a new development in Hollywood culture. Films like *Dirty Harry*, *French Connection*, and *Straw Dogs* were only the beginning. Very soon, films promoting conservative positions on the family, sexuality, unions, human nature, crime, war, politics, and society as a whole would crowd the Hollywood screen. At the same time, in courts and in Congress, conservative forces would mount a decade-long counterattack against New Deal liberalism and New Left radicalism that would culminate in the election of Ronald Reagan to the presidency in 1980. In the next chapter, we will examine some of the major early seventies films that articulate the values and ideals of this growing conservative countermovement.

2. CRISIS FILMS

The seventies has been characterized as a period when the United States underwent a "legitimacy crisis." Major institutions that previously had been fairly immune to significant popular criticism lost the confidence of the American people. In *The Confidence Gap: Business, Labor, and Government in the Public Mind*, S. M. Lipset and W. Schneider point out that distrust of government rose from 24% in 1958 to 73% in 1980, and that between 1967 and 1971 confidence in leaders fell from 42% to 28%.[1] Confidence in the executive branch fell from an average of 39 points in the mid-sixties to 15 in 1980. Confidence in all institutional leadership fell from 55% in 1966 to 23% in 1982. Antibusiness feeling grew enormously between 1965 and 1975. Belief in the social benefits of profits fell from 67% in 1965 to 41% in 1975. The favorability rating of business fell from 70% in the early sixties to 48% in 1975. Declines for specific industries were sharper, falling from 75% to 40% in some cases. An average of 65% of the population came to view business negatively (hold it in disdain, as the authors put it). The sense that business is fair fell from 70% in 1968 to 19% in 1981. The authors conclude that real events—political, economic, and social crises—account for this "legitimacy crisis," this "deep and serious discontent" beneath the surface of American society. Those real events included revelations of corporate wrongdoing (price-fixing, bribery, the manufacture of unsafe products, deliberately harmful pollution), economic recessions accompanied by inflation that led to a dramatic rise in the price of goods and to major unemployment, revelations of unethical practices by government officials, highlighted by the disclosure in the Pentagon Papers of Lyndon Johnson's lies during the Gulf of Tonkin incident and by Republican Vice-President Spiro Agnew's downfall, a collapse of the legitimacy of the presidency as a result of the Watergate scandal, which forced Richard Nixon out of office, and the disclosure of illegal practices by the nation's intelligence agencies.

This sort of crisis has, we noted in the introduction, two kinds of effects. It can promote a regressive reaction, whereby more familiar and secure traditional social models and cultural representations are revived, or it can lead to a progressive attempt to construct new representational codes and social attitudes. We will look at this latter possibility in the next chapter. Here we will consider those films that evidence a more conservative turn in the popular imaginary. What we call "crisis films" articulate the sense of discontent in

49

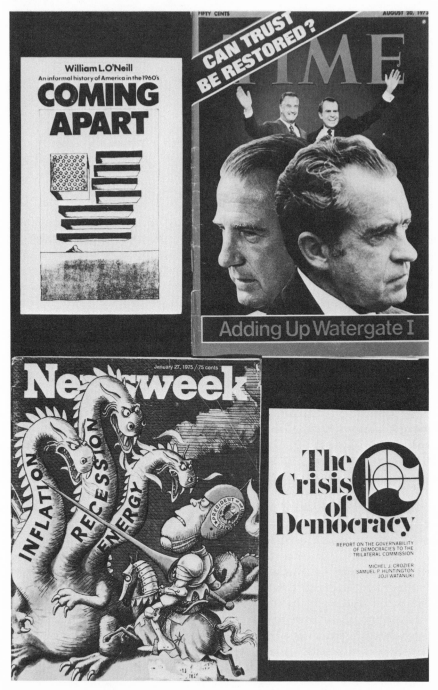

With the revelations around the Pentagon Papers, Watergate, and corporate malfeasance, public trust in the major institutions of the society begins to erode.

American culture during this time, while also offering compensatory models of redemptive leadership that are in some respects representational proto- types of the new conservative leaders of the eighties.

Crisis films (*Jaws, Exorcist, The Godfather, Airport*) generally operate on a high metaphoric level. The metaphor of catastrophe in such films permits anxieties to be avoided in their real form, but metaphor is itself a kind of aesthetic/psychological defense against threats to social ideals, a therapeutic turning away. It is through a deciphering of the metaphors by asking what they turn away from, therefore, that those symptomatically absent sources of anxiety can be deduced. Generally, they concern changes brought about by the movements of the sixties, feminism particularly. They also concern the threat to social authority and male paternalist power which the rebel- liousness of sixties youth represented. Natural disaster in early seventies films is often a metaphor for the "immorality" and "disorders" of the late sixties, or for the "democratic distemper" which conservatives saw at work during the period. In crisis films, a stern paternalist male order is reimposed on such troubles. Thus, the conservative metaphors of many of these films can be read as harboring actual metonymic or contiguous connections with the social discourses of the period as well as with some of the crucial flows of desire and need that were subliminally shaping the social universe.

Furthermore, as the seventies progressed, crisis films acquired an ad- ditional meaning. With the decline of the economy, the increased threat of joblessness, and the reduction of income through inflation, the sense of a lack of confidence spread. If in the early seventies crisis films seem preoc- cupied with responding to and pacifying the feistiness of the sixties, by the mid-seventies they are more concerned with economic issues and with the negative psychological effects of back-to-back recessions. The mood of mid- seventies films is markedly less optimistic.

Crisis films are also symptomatic of the relationship between industrial changes and film ideology. They were among the first blockbuster hits of the early seventies, and they inspired the quest for the blockbuster as the dom- inant marketing trend of the era. The phenomenal success of *The Godfather, The Exorcist, Jaws,* and, later, *Star Wars*—all of which successively became the top box-office hits of all time—led Hollywood to concentrate on lucrative genre spectacles. In addition, between 1969 and 1972 the studios lost 500 million dollars, and the failure of films like Hopper's *The Last Movie* and Fonda's *The Hired Hand* signaled the eclipse of the "New Hollywood" brand of experimentation. Studios therefore focused on making fewer, more prof- itable movies rather than a large spread of films. To guarantee large box- office returns, we suggest, these films had to address broadly felt popular fantasies and fears. This probably explains in part the prevalence of family themes, as well as the concern with healing the "crisis of confidence" in government and business. The intersection of industrial strategy and social psychological change also influenced the style of the crisis films. Their form had to appeal to a large constituency; hence, they are characterized by classical realist narratives and representational codes (romance, male heroism, tension-release plots, simple unproblematic resolutions, etc.), which are made attractive to the burgeoning youth audience of the period by the use of high levels of physical shock effects and extreme narrative tension.

1. Disaster Films

Disaster films were one of the most popular genre cycles of the early to mid seventies;[2] they exhibit a return to more traditional generic conventions and depict a society in crisis attempting to solve its social and cultural problems through the ritualized legitimation of strong male leadership, the renewal of traditional moral values, and the regeneration of institutions like the patriarchal family. Yet disaster films are not unidimensionally conservative; they warn about the dangers of unrestrained corporate capitalism and show how the unchecked pursuit of profit leads to catastrophe. The critiques of the excesses of business, however, are usually moralistic, and the films advocate corporatist solutions whereby an elite of leaders, usually professionals or technocrats, enable groups of people to survive through coordinated, even obedient action.

The contemporary disaster cycle began in 1970. By 1976 four of the top twenty money earners of all time were disaster films—*Airport*, *Towering Inferno*, *Poseidon Adventure*, and *Earthquake*.[3] Disaster films have a fairly simple narrative structure which moves from stability to disorder to a series of tests which select out a leader/savior and finally to transcendence of the disaster. They bring together a diverse group of characters whose personalities and foibles are sketched in quick, broad strokes, relying on familiar stereotypes. The ensemble usually represents a microcosm of American society and is often enclosed in a building or in some form of modern transportation that is threatened by catastrophe. The marks of their environment are usually luxury and modernity; advanced technology and communications systems are almost always on display. The films thus posit a predisaster norm of a patriarchal, capitalist, technological order in which everyone has a preordained place and function; the disaster coincides with the breakdown of this order.

The first film of the cycle, *Airport* (1970), concerns a bomb threat on an airplane. The airport is a conservative's nightmare: nothing is working quite right, and the "democratic distemper" (i.e., demonstrators protesting noise levels) is interfering with the smooth and efficient management of the airport by professionals. In fact, one complainer meddles on the plane and allows the bomb, planted by a disgruntled unemployed worker, to go off. The worker's problems are represented as his own fault, and the rescue is carried out by an individualist troubleshooting maintenance man who uses native knowhow and determination to clear a runway so that the damaged plane can land. At the end, one of the triumphant crew, looking admiringly at the aircraft, says: "Remind me to send a thank-you note to Mr. Boeing."

Airport celebrates both traditional individualism and the new corporatism. The welding together of the two is summed up in the reference to "Mr. Boeing," a rhetorical gesture that personalizes the impersonal, bringing male individualism and the corporate system represented by the airport together. The purpose of this is to enlist allegiance for the subordination of personality to impersonal, functional corporate roles. The mentally troubled worker is depicted as being incapable of such an attitude; he insists on rebelling, though he is told by his wife, "Stop dreaming. Just hold onto the job." The meddler-complainer is an analogously anticorporate anomaly who is responsible for the airport's almost being shut down as the damaged plane is about to land. The audience is thus positioned to think negatively of such democratic-ecologistic meddling in the smooth running of things by corporate professionals.

The alternatives to wimpish whining and democratic meddling are the values of obedience and respect for male authority which guide the solution to the crisis. Petroni, the maintenance man, is the only one who is skilled enough to lead the runway rescue operation, which he runs in an authoritarian manner, defying effeminate experts and proper procedures alike. The rhetoric of class and sexuality in the film is striking. The airport manager's handicap is a rich wife who attempts to run his life. An anomaly in comparison to his decidedly more cooperative female sidekick, she is predictably dumped by the end of the film. The airport's salvation parallels a liberation from her thrall, as it does a decision by a stewardess not to get an abortion. Male sexual and social power, as much as an airplane, are at stake in the film, and middle-class family values prevail over the new sexual liberalism and over upper-class "decadence."

The potential for social authoritarianism in this vision of order is indicative of the middle-class ethos of the film. The middle-class traditionally occupies a position of extreme vulnerability in a society characterized by a structural anxiety, the possibility that anyone might fall to the bottom. The constant threat of descent provokes this stratum to cling tenaciously to its material possessions, making it susceptible to arguments against taxation and affirmative action hiring, as we shall see happening later in the decade. It is also appealed to by authoritarian political models which guarantee its safety by enforcing discipline on workers and order on the economic market. The tremendous growth of this class sector in the boom period after the Second World War meant that by the seventies, a large number of Americans were part of this group—people who make between $15,000 and $40,000. This may account for the rhetoric of a film like *Airport*. It constructs a world of people at home with cocktail lounge Muzak, repressed sexuality, nice little old ladies, fireplace warmth, soap-opera decor, and moral oppositions instantiated in the difference between bright, unshadowed lighting in middle-class settings and underground darkness in working-class settings, where music from fifties horror films codes the world as one to be feared.

Airport closes with images of rejuvenation. It is sunny in the Midwest, and planes are landing safely. The troublesome protesters are gone, as is the troublesome worker. It is a golden moment for mid-American ideology. Corporations still look virtuous. The doubt, distrust, and skepticism that will characterize the seventies have yet to set in. Few later disaster films match the arrogance of this vision of American hope.

As the crisis in confidence intensified during the seventies, more was needed than a tough maintenance man to clear the runways. At this time, many people began turning to evangelical religion and born-again Christianity for relief from a world of disappointment, insecurity, and frustration that inflation and unemployment helped usher in. *The Poseidon Adventure* (1972) depicts a religious solution to corporate irresponsibility and failed secular leadership. A ship is overturned by a tidal wave because the corporate owners wanted to save money. A tough individualist priest, Reverend Scott (Gene Hackman), convinces a small group to follow him in a quest to find the top of the ship and salvation. They undergo numerous tests, and the weak (two women, most notably) fall by the wayside. In the end, Scott sacrifices himself to save the survivors.

One can determine what the projected fear and the real social threat underlying the film disaster are by turning inside out the solution proposed. That the narrative progress toward salvation valorizes the family, intergenerational harmony, respect for authority, faith, a return to traditional values, individualism, sacrifice, etc., would seem to suggest that the tidal wave is a metaphor for threats to those values and institutions—secularism, generational conflict, dissent, feminism, etc. None of these actual problems or threats is present on the screen, but their absence is made more significant by the presence of such strong antidotes.

The strongest antidotes are faith in one's own personal salvation, proven through individual rather than collective effort, and obedience to strong leaders. Each of the group's trials emphasizes individual rather than communal efforts. And it is the strong individualist leader who saves the pilgrims, not the standpat bureaucrat who advises waiting against striving. The film demonstrates the curious congruity between individualism, the Protestant religion, and the leadership principle in American capitalist culture. A sense of singularity fuels the entrepreneurial capitalist drive, and this is backed by a religion of personal salvation, part of which entails pleasing a patriarchal figure. The film thus mediates individualism with corporatist cohesion. Faith in oneself comes down to faith in one's place in a sacred hierarchy. Subjective conviction links up with faith in objective structures of public authority. The film is thus a good example of how individualism can have extremely conservative forms, forms that seem patently anti-individualist in that group loyalty takes precedence to rebellion or deviation. *Poseidon* is a lesson in how to choose to belong.

The film is noteworthy as well for the particular narrational rhetoric it employs and for the populist critique of capitalism it proposes. It is the first disaster film to sympathetically incorporate young people, and it clearly aims for a family effect. The family structure and the class background of the survivors suggest that the film is addressed to a traditionalist middle-class American audience, one that would be distrustful of the power of big business and susceptible to right-wing, religiously based authoritarian solutions. This audience is likely to be appealed to by more simple plot narratives. The narrative of stasis, crisis, and resolution is, moreover, a striking projection of a psychology of fear, disconfidence, and yearning for help. That the solution to this crisis is a strong male leader who inspires trust and self-reliance is an indicator of the extent to which the film transcodes actual psychological vectors which are prefigurative of future political realities.

The conventions of the disaster film crystalized into a readily recognizable and much discussed genre form with the appearance of *Earthquake* and *The Towering Inferno* in 1975. Both joined the list of most popular films of all time. *Inferno*, like *Airport '79*, concerns corruption in corporate capitalism at a time when the economy was inflicting hardship on people and corporations were revealed to be callous and unscrupulous. A fire erupts during a party at the opening of the world's largest building. On a metaphoric level, it is as if the elements were punishing capitalist hubris, greed, and luxury. And indeed, responsibility for the fire lies with the building contractor who cut costs. As a solution, *Inferno*, like *Airport*, proposes an alliance between a lower middle class hero, a fireman (Steve McQueen), and an architect (Paul Newman) who is a member of the professional managerial class, that group of corporate executives whose power became increasingly solidified during this era. Throughout the rescue attempt, they exchange meaningful glances which establish their bond. In the end, they promise to discuss ways to prevent future disasters. The film thus suggests that the worst evils of the system can be cleaned up by heroic male authority figures. And, like other disaster films, it reinforces the sense that professional managers, the new corporate executive class, not traditional economic elites, are the rightful leaders of society.

That *The Towering Inferno* succeeds in distinguishing a good brand of capitalism from a bad variety is suggested by the results of our audience survey. While 71% thought that the depiction of business in the film was realistic, 78% felt that the corrupt construction people represented one bad sector of capitalism rather than the way most big business operates, although there are significant distinctions within these figures. A greater percentage of those who make over $30,000 thought the depiction unreal, felt it referred only to one bad sector, and indicated the film had no effect on their positive opinion of business. Similarly, while 44% of those from working-class backgrounds thought the film's villains represented the way all big business operates, only 12% of those from upper middle class backgrounds felt so. The figures were inverted for the one bad sector option; 89% of the upper middle class people chose that as opposed to 56% of the working-class participants. In addition, 29% of those surveyed said that the film reinforced a sense that business puts profit before human life, and 23% answered that the film *initiated* their suspicion of business.

The vision of hope offered by the disaster films is a response to troubled times, and the need for those conservative solutions is made to seem all the more pressing by the increasingly hopeless literality of the disaster metaphors. If *Airport* ends with an intact airplane, *Poseidon* leaves a boat overturned and a priest dead, while *Inferno* concludes with a burned-out skyscraper, and *Earthquake* leaves nothing standing. The metaphors of transcendent rebirth required a vision of a fearful and deadly material reality. But there is a

psychological significance to this as well. It is as if, as the economic and
political crises of the seventies deepened, an increasingly frustrated white
middle class was wishing death on more people, imagining hotter conflagra-
tions to consume class and moral enemies. There were more bodies around
at the ends of the films, a literal sign, perhaps, of negative urges operating
through the metaphors.

By 1975, plurivalent disaster films like *Towering Inferno* would articulate
both the populist distrust of business which characterized the era and the
conservative yearning for an alternative which such distrust necessarily generated. The confusion of liberal and conservative strains of thinking in the
film is itself indicative of the crisis of confidence and the sense that no clear
solution was at hand. The disaster metaphor is thus undecidable, both rhetorically and historically. Rhetorically, it welds a vision of transcendent or
metaphoric redemption to a recalcitrantly literal metonym of social destruction, neither of which can be affirmed without the other. Historically, it
articulates both a populist distrust of conservative institutions and yearnings
that could only be satisfied by conservative solutions (at least in the existing
social context). This undecidability of meaning is therefore indicative of a
very real problem in American culture. The crises of a conservative economic
and political structure generate distrust and desires for a better community.
But the available lexicon of political, economic, and social possibilities limits
what can be envisioned as an alternative. What stands in is what is most
familiar, and a literalization of the metaphoric solutions—priest, fireman,
etc.—indicates how important neighborly familiarity and traditional middle-
class representational and institutional figures were becoming in the time of
greatest crisis in the mid-seventies. And what is most familiar is, of course,
the family.

The disaster films therefore provide therapeutic narratives, which enact
crisis, then assuage it. At the same time, they point to desires for care and
community which will, in American culture, be increasingly addressed by
conservative and traditionalist ideals. For this reason, it is very important
that the ethos of the disaster genre is markedly middle-aged, middle-level
managerial, and mid-American. It seems directed to that middle class, which
fears both big business and liberal urban modernity, and which clings to
traditional values of home, self-reliance, and faith. The disaster film is in
some respects the anxious imaginary of these people particularly, the world
of Amway distributors, Rotarians, Masons, and the local Chamber of Commerce, the very white middle class Ronald Reagan would appeal to with his
vision of an America of restored small-town life, folksy communities where
friendly white businessmen and their wives could thrive without being bothered by big government or the urban poor and non-whites. This older, middle-
class, middle-American world was particularly sensitive to the threats disaster
films metaphorize—social critics, disgruntled workers, decadent rich people
flouting traditional morality, corrupt capitalists, liberated sexuality, economic
recession. The same fears and desires articulated in these films would be
answered, beginning around 1978, in films like *Close Encounters of the Third*

Kind, *Raiders of the Lost Ark*, *Star Wars*, and *The Deer Hunter*, which offered antidotes to disaster. What is projected negatively as anxiety in the disaster films of the early to mid seventies will appear positively beginning in 1978 as an affirmation of the traditional ideals of the American Way (Amway, for short).

Yet the films also enact a problem which cannot be resolved by conservative ideals. They accurately depict the negative consequences of the conservative economic policies which are inseparable from the traditionalist social structures which seem most to respond to the needs the films articulate. The films therefore point to an irresolvable dilemma or antinomy of conservative ideology in American culture. Conservative ideology most readily responds to the need for care and community because it celebrates family and patriarchal authority, yet it also regenerates the very problems which inspired that need in the first place. Thus, the films are both reactionary and radical, both a closing off of significant desires and a blueprint for the inevitable reopening of them.

2. Metaphors of Fear

Two of the major "crisis" films of the early seventies—*The Exorcist* and *Jaws*—can be read as metaphoric representations of anxieties generated by contemporary social movements like feminism and by the crisis in confidence in business and civic leadership. In *The Exorcist*, demonic possession is a metaphor for fears about independent women and female sexuality; the resolution offered reassures a threatened patriarchy that male paternalism will restore discipline and authority to an unruly post-sixties society. *Jaws* projects metaphoric fears of the dissolution of community and family as a result of the venality of business and the weakness of traditional authority figures, and depicts the passage to power of a patriarchal savior of the community who dispatches the threat and restores order.

The Exorcist (1973), directed by William Friedkin, was one of the most discussed media events of the decade.[4] Its success accelerated the blockbuster phenomenon, and it helped spawn a genre cycle of occult horror films featuring demonic possession. The story concerns the possession of Regan MacNeil (Linda Blair), and the attempts of her mother, Chris (Ellen Burstyn), to rid Regan of the demon. After consulting medical and psychiatric authorities, Chris calls in a priest, and an exorcism is performed. A parallel plot centers on one of the priests who performs the exorcism, Damien Karras (Jason Miller). His impoverished mother dies, and, overcome with guilt and religious doubts, he carries out the exorcism by sacrificing himself for the girl.

In *The Exorcist*, Chris's husband has left her, and several scenes underscore the father's absence. The demon's arrival occurs as Chris lies alone in bed, working. She becomes increasingly incapable of coping with the crisis and eventually collapses. One of the film's implicit messages, then, is the need for a father to protect and discipline women and children. Summing up the film's sexist stereotypes, Ruth McCormick writes: "All the women—the whole-some, average young woman who turns into a hermaphrodite monster; the pseudosophisticated but basically vulnerable and hysterical mother; the in-nocuous, prep-school-girlish secretary; and Karras' frail, dominate-through-guilt mother—are passive, helpless, and lost in a cruel world without male help and guidance."[5]

The Exorcist can also be interpreted as an attack on independent feminine sexuality. Author William Blatty based his plot on the story of a fourteen-year-old boy, but transformed the protagonist into a young girl in his novel. During the final scenes of the film, she is strapped to the bed, and the images around her project phallic shadows of bedposts and other objects. Many feminists argued that these scenes promoted bondage and rape fantasies. Each of the scenes depicting Regan's possession contain derogatory images of female sexuality. Cumulatively, they represent women's sexuality as wild, uncontrollable, and dangerous, a depiction reminiscent of the ideology of witchcraft, which promoted the punishment of women for being too sexually active. This depiction, of course, is a male projection, a symptom of male sexual anxiety. The demonic possession can therefore be decoded as sexual aggression against men, and the exorcism can be interpreted as an attempt to repress a threatening female sexual power. Literally, of course, the prob-lem is a woman with a man inside of her—a woman who behaves like a man. If she is a figure of a deviant power, she is also a figure of a confusion of sexual identity, an additional threat to a gender power system based on the absolute segregation of sexual traits.

The bondage-pedophilia images also play on male sexual fantasies of the helpless girl-child, and Regan's tantrums evoke images of the naughty child who needs punishment. Throughout the film, the girl behaves like an exor-bitant brat. At the conclusion of the exorcism, she sits on the bed in the pose of a temptress, and Karras beats her until she submits to his power by crying out and becoming a good little girl again. The final scene in particular high-lights this point. Regan is again a sweet and submissive girl, returned to a state of innocence. She smiles at a priest, looks at his clerical collar, impul-sively kisses him and runs off, a perfect example of devoted submission to patriarchal authority. Chris, too, once so independent and sassy, is restrained, chastened, and ready to become a doting mother once again. Both are re-turned to their "normal" roles; the spirit of feminism and of independent female sexuality has been exorcised.

Camera rhetoric and scene composition work to the benefit of the pa-triarchal and irrationalist ideology of the film. The exorcist is positioned opposite an icon of the demon in an early scene, and his large shadow is projected against the house the demon occupies in another, connoting his power. The mother, on the other hand, is shot from a high camera angle when she enters the house, suggesting her lack of power in relation to the demon upstairs. And when she is attacked by the girl-demon in the bedroom and flung on the floor, the camera assumes her low position as an armoire hurls itself across the room toward her, connoting her powerlessness. The incapacity of science is signaled by the juxtaposition of off-putting images of surgery with scenes of Karras saying mass in a peaceful, pious environment. The contrast suggests that "evil" is impervious to rational solutions.

The Exorcist mystifies the social origins of suffering, and it puts liberal reformism and rational science in doubt by depicting "evil" as something immune to existing institutional remedies. The demon survives, despite its exorcism. In a conservative vein, the film thus seems to posit the irreducibility of "evil." The metaphysical pessimism of this and later satanic conspiracy films reproduces the worldview of reactionary social forces like evangelical-fundamentalist Christianity which were at this time beginning to become powerful. As in this film, in evangelicism Satan is often projected onto real social groups like feminists, communists, homosexuals, or whoever else threatens the holy order of monogamous reproduction.

The Exorcist is also interesting historically for depicting the susceptibility of patriarchy to the threat posed by feminism and sexual liberation. From this perspective, the ideology of the film can be turned inside out, like a glove. Once that is done, once the internal stitches of the seams that hold the glove together are delineated, the polarities that define the film's value system (possession/faith, female hysteria/male power, science/dutiful obedience, etc.) become equally reversible. Seen as a symptom of male anxiety and fear of the sort provoked in the early seventies by feminism's challenge to male domination, the film itself comes to seem like a kind of hysteria, a shrieking, rageful, "possessed" act of male representational violence against women. As in paranoia in which the characteristics of the external enemy are merely projections of internal psychological features of the paranoid subject, in the film the negative characteristics of the two female characters—violent rage, uncontrollable sexual desire, helplessness, weakness—can be read as externalized projections of male psychology as it confronts and reacts to feminism. A diagnostic reading of the film would suggest that at this moment in history it is clearly men who are feeling at once rageful and weak, violent because rendered helpless by the feminist attack on male privilege. That privilege was traditionally accompanied by a positioning of women as caretaking mothers, which implied a male reliance on female care and a certain male vulnerability. The abandonment of that role by women would thus produce tremendous pain, a sense of weakness, and rage against the perpetrator. We suggest that this equation probably has something to do with the representational violence the film mobilizes against women.

Thus, the central metaphor of the film constructs a representational world that assuages the feminist threat to male psychological integrity, an integrity founded on the positioning of women in passive social roles. Like all ideological artifacts, however, the film displays the literal basis of its metaphor, its roots in material and social concerns. The women literally become passive in the end, and this passivity retroactively recodes the metaphoric possession as the opposite of passivity, as indeed a threatening excess of female activity. The narrative resolution provides the key for understanding the motivation of the narrative metaphor. Moreover, the narration is dual, and the relations between the two strands become clear in the light of this reading. The second narrative concerns Karras's feelings of doubt and guilt regarding the death of his mother. A violence against the mother, implied by guilt, thus lies under the more metaphoric violence against women in general in the narrative. The symbolic murder of the mother parallels the subordination of the independent woman. In both instances, power over the man is reversed.

Like *The Exorcist*, *Jaws* (1975), directed by Steven Spielberg, depicts a society weakened internally by a loosening of traditional institutions and values and a failure of traditional authorities; those critical weaknesses that undermine society and threaten its integrity are projected onto an evil that only appears to come from outside. Like disaster films, *Jaws* deals with economic corruption, the failure of traditional leadership, and the way the integrity of a community is at first threatened, and then restored. After a number of people are killed by a shark, the town's sheriff, Brody, sets out with a seaman and a scientist and eventually kills it.[6] Although the overt villains of the film are the small town's economic elite, who put profit before safety, the crisis around which the film's thematics revolve has to do with sexuality, manhood, and leadership. Critics noted the sexual dimension of the phallic shark (and the movie poster played to this perception). But the shark is less the sign of male sexuality than the sign of what goes wrong when the male sex is not fulfilling its duty of patriarchal leadership. Brody is the crucial figure in this scenario. He is at first inept, bureaucratic, and weak. He submits to the cover-up fostered by the town's business elite. His weakness as a leader is reinforced by his ties to his wife and to female sexuality. At one point, an attempted seduction by his wife which distracts him from his duties is linked with a threat to his own child. At another point, her attentions immediately precede a shark attack that results in a child's death. If economic venality corrupts leadership, then an excessively independent female sexuality undermines male public action and responsibility. Indeed, the shark's first attack is on a girl who has just seduced a boy into going skinny-dipping with her. As she runs toward the ocean, shedding clothes, she leaves behind the palings that connote the strictures and boundaries of civil society. Her transgressively independent sexuality is suitably rewarded.

When Brody's family is first presented, the palings metaphor reappears, this time as a latticework fence protecting his wife and child. Thus, it signals male protection as well as sexual control within the family form. It is associated with the law of the father (quite literally, since Brody is a policeman), that which protects the family from threats that lie beyond the pale, so to speak. Independent feminine sexuality seems to bring about a threat to the community that is aggravated by a failure of leadership. The solution is to restore male leadership and to refuse female sexuality by privileging male socialization and initiation rites. To accomplish his task, Brody must sever himself from the cloying intimacy and domesticity associated with his wife. Indeed, as the three men prepare to set out on the hunt, Brody and his wife are shot in a foreground close-up, connoting intimacy, while in the back-

Jaws. Seduction distracts the patriarch from his duties, and a child is eaten.

ground the two other men bustle about boisterously. The demarcation between the male public world of the hunt and the female domestic sphere is clear. Later, the men will compare shark scars, and Brody will peer down into his pants, looking for his own and not finding one. The initiation ritual is complete when at a moment of weakness Brody seeks to call home to his wife and the old fisherman Quint severs the umbilical radio cord. Only then does the reborn patriarch emerge.

The alternative to the dangerous female world of threateningly independent sexuality is the all-male group. Male bonding is carried out stylistically as well as through plot and theme. When one significant male walks off silently alone (Brody after being slapped by an angry mother; Quint in rejection from the town meeting), another significant male watches his back

Jaws. The opening sequence. A young woman runs to the water, removing her clothes, and leaves behind palings of patriarchal law.

Jaws. Hail to the Chief. The palings reappear in their proper place. The point of focus is the word "police" on the side of the patriarch's truck.

for several extended moments. The camera assumes the position of his gaze, and in each case the audience is placed in the position of sympathetically identifying with the rejected male. This device establishes both the importance of the lone male, through the duration of the shot and the centering value it accords him in the frame, and a community of male bonding through the admiration from the other male that the lingering camera signifies. The audience is alerted to the importance of the bond between the three heroic men, as well as the singular significance of each.

Thus, while the film offers a corporate liberal critique of small-business venality and promotes the interests of a technocratic class of professional managers against that of the old Chamber of Commerce sector, it is also important historically as a major response to the crisis feminism and independent feminine sexuality were posing for traditional patriarchal values and institutions. The power of the Father/Leader needs to be reasserted, the film seems to say, and indeed it soon would be in U.S. society.

The film also demonstrates how the public and the private institutions of society reciprocally legitimate each other through the analogical comparison of one to the other. Leadership of communities by males is legitimated by establishing a parallel between the community and the patriarchal family, just as the patriarchal family derives its model from the royalist tradition of public order. Indeed, the cross-fertilization of the two social models is particularly strong in *Jaws*, since the shark poses a dual threat to community and family. What is noteworthy from a deconstructive perspective in this analogical or metaphoric exchange of traits between family and polis is its reversibility. The use of one category as a metaphor for another institution— family patriarchy for community leadership—is designed to accomplish an idealization, a sense of the meaningfulness and therefore necessity and uni-

versal importance of that institution. Yet the very vehicle of that metaphor
implies literal metonymic connections which cannot be closed off and which
interfere with the ideal the metaphor promotes. All meaning rests on associations, the creation of relations between terms. But this implies as well that
all meaning is unstable, because nothing prevents further associations from
being possible, other meanings from being created. This is especially true of
meanings which rest on the exclusion or subordination of one term by another. For instance, patriarchal power in *Jaws* clearly is meaningful only
inasmuch as it excludes and subordinates woman. She means something which
must be external to patriarchy, if it is to mean what it pretends to mean. The
idealizing patriarchal meaning deconstructs at those moments when literal
material connections back to woman emerge. This is especially clear during
the metaphoric quest for the shark, a quintessentially male, public adventure,
severed entirely from female-dominated family life. Yet that quest cannot do
without certain literal motifs of sexual power and potency. Brody's literal
glance into his pants in search of the missing phallus establishes a metonymic
connection which both enables and disables the sexual metaphor of the quest.
For the quest doesn't make sense except as a confirmation of manhood, that
is, as the ability to perform with women. Woman is always there, in other
words, as threatening perhaps as the shark. The literal associations deprive
the patriarchal metaphor of its idealizing pretensions, but more important,
they suggest that the literal and the metaphoric might be reversible. The
metaphoric ideal of patriarchal public order might be nothing more than an
illegitimate transfer of material interests into cultural idealizations which have
become self-evident assumptions, constantly replicated in the field of representation and psychology with the aid of artifacts like *Jaws*. All in the family
indeed.

Like the disaster films of the same era, these crisis films are hinges
between periods of major cultural activity. They mark the running down of
the sixties, the transmutation of radical energies into fearful reactions, as
economic and political events removed the secure ground that permitted the
radical critiques to thrive. Even as these films articulate a withdrawal to
imaginary models of redemptive violence and leadership, they also point
forward to the next historical period when those models would be realized
in concrete form. Their rhetorical strategy of evoking crisis only to heal it is
something more, therefore, than an invitation to audiences to indulge in
fantasies of destruction. It is also indicative of an actual change in the cultural
representations, the figures which construct the world in a certain way, providing psychological security, a feeling of integrity with the world around
one. The films indicate the loss of a certain object constancy, a stability of
mental representations which regulate the internal world and which are bor-
rowed or internalized from the culture and from the institutions of society.
They point therefore to the close relationship between psychological integrity
and the stability of social institutions, and inversely, by carrying out a restoration of social institutional order on the level of psychological representation, they also point to the power of cultural representation in preparing

and enabling institutional change. The films both depict the imaginary return of redemptive representations of order and pave the way for an actual restoration by directing the representations which code the communal construction of a common sense of social reality in a conservative direction. Not that the viewing of crisis films accounts for the conservative political triumphs of the late seventies. Rather, the films enact the collapse of representational security which was itself a factor in that turn of events, and they representationally construct institutional solutions. Audiences made representations of crisis popular because disasters on the level of communally held representations had occurred which disturbed the security that derives from such representations. The films transcode the crisis of representation, the undermining of confidence and security, but they also provide the new representations which will have a socially therapeutic effect a few years later. The narrative of crisis in these films, therefore, is itself an enactment of what would occur historically. The leader was on his way—if only in people's minds.

Yet in one way, these apparently successful exercises in ideology were themselves counterideological. Conservative cultural or cinematic texts invariably contain a fissure line that troubles the apparently victorious ideology of the text. Ideological antidotes always point out disease even as they try to remedy it or, as in the case of some film representations, try to pretend it doesn't exist. The success of the ideological operation is always a testament to failure, since ideological representations would not be necessary if indeed there were no trouble in the system, if indeed all's right, as ideology claims, in the world. *Jaws* and the other crisis films are interesting because they depict patriarchy as on the defensive. Father could no longer claim to know best if he had to argue his position.

3. Francis Coppola and the Crisis of Patriarchy

One lesson of the crisis of order and patriarchy is that political authority and male sexual and social power are interconnected and interdependent in a patriarchal society. Therefore, the failure of legitimate leadership articulated in disaster films frequently appears as a crisis of male power over women and in the family. This dual crisis seems to be felt most acutely in recent American history by the economic sector most vulnerable to the kinds of economic recessions that have plagued the country during this period—the competitive as opposed to the corporate sector. The ideal self-image of this petit bourgeois sector is the small father-run family business, which survives on a mixture of irrational blood loyalty and brutally rational marketplace calculation.

The values, ideals, and figures of the small-business ideology are most saliently on display at this time in the films of Francis Coppola. Coppola initially confronted the social crises directly in realist styles, but as time passed he turned to more romantic and expressionist forms, compensating for the sense of loss engendered by the crises of the family, of the economy, and of public leadership through increasingly aestheticist fantasies and regressive genre forms. We shall argue that the ideology mobilized in his films as a response to crisis is authoritarian, petit bourgeois (small-business based), and neopatriarchal, and that with time, that ideology has assumed more overtly rightist forms.

From *You're a Big Boy Now* (1967) and *The Rain People* (1969) to *Rumble Fish* (1983) and *Cotton Club* (1984), Coppola's films display an inability to come to terms with the crisis of patriarchy initiated by feminism. *You're a Big Boy Now* poses an ideal girl against a "bad" girl and argues that its hero is better off choosing the good one. The traditionalist attitudes of the film do not bode well for a happy marriage with feminism, and indeed, Coppola's next "auteur" film, *The Rain People*, carries out a covert attack on feminism. A pregnant wife suddenly leaves home and drives across country, fleeing from the responsibility of motherhood and marriage, and intent, it seems, on getting an abortion. Her bad experiences at trying to be a "liberated" sexual vamp lead her in the end to decide to rejoin her husband, a bossy Italian patriarch named Vinnie (a nice autobiographical touch). The theme of failed "liberation" is enunciated through the style and structure of the movie. The narrative forms a closure that suggests inescapability; the spaces in which the significant actions occur are oppressively closed; and the tone of the images, as of the story, is one of a sad, nostalgic sentimentality that makes the past seem a dream to be cherished and home life an ideal to be preserved. In other words, the style and structure of the movie also advocate its conservative politics.

The antifeminism of *Rain People* carries over into the very popular *Godfather* films (first in gross in 1972, fifth in 1975). The "saga" chronicles the history of a mafia family as it develops from a moment of security, harmony, and power at the beginning of the first film to a point of dissolution at the end of the second. The first film depicts the rise to power of a young mafia don, Michael Corleone (Al Pacino), who earns his right to rule through displays of vicious violence. The second film concerns the falling apart of his family and his empire. The films are strikingly multivalent. They can be read as transcoding the mid-seventies populist distrust of big, corporate institutions, and, in a sense, they are highly critical of capitalism and of its negative impact on traditional communities and on family life.

If the *Godfather* films lend themselves to a radical reading, they also provide insights into the conservative reaction to cultural modernization and to the increasing corporate dominance of American economic life.[7] The economic theme closely parallels the antifeminist theme. Economic harmony in the first film seems indissociable from the positioning of women in a subsidiary position of care in relation to men, who are the primary economic agents. The two worlds are in fact carefully demarcated. Business takes place in dark interior rooms from which women are excluded. The camera work in these scenes is organic; it suggests unity and harmony, and the lighting is generally shadowy yet warm. As one of our students remarked, the dark rooms resemble a womb. Not accidentally, then, when the family business leaves its roots in *Godfather II*, becoming increasingly impersonal and corporatized ultimately

to collapse, the women also display nontraditional, nonmaternal characteristics. The separation of male business from the female home in fact presupposes a strong connection between the two. The idealized, father-run,
small business of the films is dependent on the empathy and care provided
by women socialized to remain at home, out of the business jungle. If the
market world is an arena of danger for men who are socialized to survive by
ridding themselves of all "feminine" traits, such as empathy, the home world
is their only haven. Confined to the domestic or family sphere, empathy easily
becomes exaggerated and cloying, a sentimentality of blood loyalty which
makes up for the lack of empathy in the external world. Thus, economics
and sexual politics are closely intertwined. The conservative elegizing of the
small-business world is inseparable from a nostalgia for the patriarchal family
because the brutal, aggressive, and calculating emotional configurations of
that world require a compensatory locus of care, one provided in traditional
conservative socialization by women in the family.

Godfather I begins with an account of violence done to a young woman,
and it concludes with an ejection of a woman from the inner male sphere of
business and her positioning in a proper role as a caretaker of men. The two
moments are profoundly related, for it is the threat of male violence in the
public world that obliges women to submit to domestication. The price of
protection is subservience. And the assumption of the feminine role of caretaker legitimates and helps reproduce the dichotomizing of gender roles,
which results in the male assumption of the right to exercise violence in the
public world—against each other and against women. A circle of cultural
reproduction is formed by linking the beginning and ending of the film. But
that circle doesn't quite close. To understand why, it will be necessary to
stress the importance of framing and scene composition to the elaboration
of the film's themes.

Cinematography, visual texture, and narrative structure operate thematically in the film. The conservative themes—that brutality and the struggle
for survival lie just beneath the surface of civilization and that strong leaders
and firm order are therefore needed to prevent the chaos of nature from
erupting—are highlighted formally in several ways. The film's style is classical;
that is, each segment is structured as a unity of establishing shots and stable
shot transitions that suggests social order. Similarly, the frame compositions
display a high level of organization and symmetry of disposition among elements which bolsters the political theme. For example, in one segment, the
men of the family are in the foreground at a table, awaiting news of Michael's
assassination of their enemies. The telephone rings, and Sonny, the new Don,
walks to the background to answer. He is positioned at the focal center of
the frame; the others are arranged around him symmetrically. He is literally
positioned as the new center of order in the social world. Likewise, when a
horse's head is put in the bed of a troublesome movie producer, the segment
begins with a classical establishing shot of his house. The camera moves in
like an intruder to the scene of ruthlessness and horror. The segment concludes with the same external establishing shot of the house, stylistically rein-

forcing the cruelty of the trick. Order frames the violence, making it seem part of nature and intimating that such horror and brutality are part of the fated order of things.

Many segments like these suggest that firm order is needed because the world is cruel. This, we would contend, is the significance of the famous final segment in which church scenes are ironically intercut with scenes of murder. Civilization merely covers over the brutality of nature, and the film works to elicit from the audience both exultation in the violence and admiration for Michael's leaderly genius. In the ensuing scene, Michael confronts his brother's betrayer, and because the man's guilt is not prepared for in the narrative, this narrative surprise endows Michael with an air of intuitive genius similar to that lent the Godfather when, out of nowhere, he predicts exactly how enemies will attempt to kill Michael, as if recounting a law of nature.

Finally, color texture is used as a thematic correlative. The film is structured around an inside/outside opposition (family vs. world, especially) that is signaled initially by the difference between the intimate darkness of the family rooms, in which close-ups and orderly camera changes prevail, and the lit world outside, where medium and long shots predominate, suggesting less intimacy and less control over the environment. Michael first sits on the rim between the family house and the backyard wedding party, half in light, half in darkness. Eventually he moves into darkness and assumes command. The clarity, simplicity, and "orderliness" of his commands are coded chromatically in the Nevada scene when he tells his brother never to speak against the family in public. Michael is filmed against a blue carpet that fills the screen with a simple color that is as unambiguous as his words.

There is a male anxiety operating both thematically and stylistically in the film, and it originates in an inability to tolerate disorder, complexity, and ambiguity. Coppola flings so many symbols (candles, bierlike canopies, etc.) at the world that it is as though he fears it might not have any meaning or order. And, of course, the yearning for a great leader like the Don or Michael is evidence of a similar anxiety. All such metaphoric meaning schemes can be deconstructed, simply because it is in the nature of such anxiety, as we have argued, both to turn away from the source of anxiety and, in turning, inadvertently to point to the source. For example, at the end Michael's wife, Kay, stands in the foreground, a rather large figure filling half of the frame. In the background, in the center of the frame, is a door leading to Michael's room, where he stands, after having been honored as Godfather by his men. Framed by the door, Michael is idealized in a metaphoric portrait. The door is then closed, and the woman/wife/mother is shut out. The gesture of separation establishes the prevailing opposition of the film between the inside of the men's world and the outside of the women's world. But what is presented as an effect of male superiority and self-identity (the necessity of keeping women out) is in fact its cause, and the cinematography signals this inadvertently. The literal cause of the film's metaphoric aggrandizement of the man is fear of woman, of being mistaken for a woman (passive, nonviolent, dependent, etc.). That fear is also a fear of a representational form like

The Godfather. The frame of the door constitutes a literalization of the psycho-logical boundary the male creates around himself by aggressively ejecting the woman from the male sphere.

metonymy that would reveal the metaphoric male ideal to be constituted through real material connections with and dependencies on a powerful woman. The final image executes an anxious, violent exclusion of the woman because, as the mother all men first identify with and upon whom men are dependent as children, she is in fact potentially threatening and powerful. In the concluding image, the cause (fear of woman's power) is inverted into an effect of the very male pathology that fear in fact generated (exclusion of woman from the male world because of her weakness). The woman's exclusion is made to appear a result of male self-empowerment and inde-pendence.

But what is interesting from a deconstructive perspective is that the woman remains so large within the frame. We are shown the literal source of the film's anxiety, the metonymic or material basis of its metaphoric ideal-ization. The woman/mother's power is literally displayed, even as it is fig-uratively denied. This tension between the figurative and the literal dimen-sions of meaning signals an aporia at the heart of male sexual identity. That identity is constituted as independence from woman, but it is dependent on woman to guarantee that independence. In the final image, the enlarged woman gazes down at the man in an illogical spatial arrangement. His em-powerment is dependent on that gaze, that confirmation of his power. Ex-cluded from the man's world, the woman nevertheless has power quite literally over it. Without her confirming gaze, it would have no identity as that which is male, that which excludes woman, and that which elicits female adulation. But the gaze is more than adulatory; it is also maternal. For the metaphoric hero is literally a small man-child within the composition of the frame. Woman is needed as a larger-than-life ideal mother even as she is denied existence as a literal person. The independent male betrays his dependency and his relational connectedness, just as the metaphor which secures the ideal of independence and power betrays its anchoring in a metonymic literality that cannot be transcended. This reverses the hierarchy and polarity the film seeks to establish. And the possibilities opened up by this are highly indeterminate, for if such strong male identity and independence are in fact dependent on what they give out to be weak and effeminate, if the ideal meaning of the metaphor is produced by the sign or vehicle (the literal image of the woman) which was supposed to be a merely secondary transportation device for its true meaning, then no secure identity is possible which is not also interme-diated and derived in a similar way. The literal and the figurative, the met-onymic and the metaphoric, can no longer be distinguished in a hierarchy that gives the latter in each case precedence over the former. And this is precisely why the film resorts to metaphoric representational forms, for, given all this, it is only through semantically overdetermined representations that this indeterminacy and undecidability can be overcome—at least apparently.

Coppola's films always contain such confusions of tropological levels, and we contend that this relates to a desire, which is very much the one instantiated in this final image, to return to a fused state of non-separation from the mother, a narcissistic paradise of spatial static harmony into which no difference, no temporality, no indeterminacy intrudes. In such a state, the literal and the figural would be indistinguishable, for the difference from the object world that initiates the need to represent things in their absence would not yet have occurred. This is the significance of the fact that the final image resembles a portrait, a fixing of identity in a metaphoric fusion of image and meaning that seems exempt from all the contingencies of mo-dernity.

This reading permits us now to reconsider the political and economic themes of the *Godfather* films, their evident tendency to hark back to a golden age of family unity and small-business integrity. Male narcissism informs both of these instances, as it does the implicitly authoritarian political values. Pri-vate male narcissism is exercised publicly as authoritarianism, a political form which resembles the metaphoric rhetorical form in that a spatial order (hier-archic, coded, determinate) displaces all metonymic dissonance, indetermi-nacy, and equality. All the differences that characterize modern, urban de-mocracies dissolve into the will of the ruler. The seamless unity desired in narcissism means that these themes are found in every dimension of the films, from the sentimental blood ties which overcome the distance between people resulting from modernity and big business, resolving alienation into a fused corporate family, to the chiaroscuro that blurs distinctions and creates the aura of an old photograph throughout the films. Fittingly, the films them-selves were fused into a narrative sequence for television, and it is structured as a nostalgic evocation through flashback of a golden age prior to the erosion of male leadership, the breakdown of family unity, and the introduction of indeterminacy into the fixed meaning that ended the first film. Like the flashbacks in *film noir*, which always occur in conjunction with the presence of powerful women, this narrative structure signals a flight from a threat, just as indeed the predominantly metaphoric rhetoric of the films points to an anxious turning away from something which must be kept absent.

Coppola's other films, especially those of the late seventies and early eighties, provide further evidence of a psychology at odds with corporate modernity, troubled by feminism, and attracted to authoritarian patriarchal ideals. Harry Caul of *The Conversation* (1974) is a small businessman who seems powerless in the face of the large powerful corporation with which he contends. He ends up being partially responsible for the murder of the paternal corporate head by his deceitful wife. *Apocalypse Now* (1979) is an allegory of Vietnam that redeems the loss of war with a myth of rejuvenated male leadership. *One from the Heart* (1982) concerns a petit bourgeois couple who experiment in the new sexuality, then decide to reestablish a safe hearth. An attempt to revive the traditional studio musical, the film is shot in a pastel style that separates it entirely from historical actuality, while establishing a metaphoric medium purged of metonymic contamination. *The Outsiders* and *Rumble Fish* (both 1983) are about young boys yearning for strong leaders, and both use expressionist techniques that replace reality with symbols and exaggerated representational surfaces. Finally, *The Cotton Club* (1985) is an oedipal fantasy in which a young man kills off papa for mama that is distinguished by representational forms which suggest a withdrawal from a potentially threatening world into a narcissistic and paranoid realm of private fantasy. As in Coppola's other films, this is associated with the incursion of big capital into small business.

In these films, representation, politics, and psychology form a nexus. The psychoanalytic theory of object relations argues that the constitution of the self as an autonomous and differentiated entity occurs through representation. The child learns to represent the object world, and in so doing, it achieves a sense of separation from it. Clear and distinct representations of objects place them apart from the self and establish the boundaries that separate the self from the world. That world initially is defined by primary caretakers (especially mothers in a patriarchal society), and the child must learn to transcend its sense of undifferentiated fusion with such caretakers. By developing a capacity to represent them, the child poses them as objects and establishes a boundary between them and the self. These mental representations also provide a surrogate security or satisfaction that permits the child to live apart from caretakers, to function in their absence.

What matters for our analysis of Coppola is that representational distinction is crucial for male sexual identity. A power of mental representation, by establishing boundaries around the self and separating it from the object world, also secures an identity for the male child which distinguishes the child from the mother. (Remember the boundary marked literally by the door frame in the concluding image of *Godfather I*.) But if the male child fails to develop mental representations that permit separation and that establish boundaries, his sense of sexual identity will become confused. The ties of care and empathy with the mother (the first "object") will come to appear as threats to his hermetic boundaries and to his identity. This failure appears most importantly at an early stage of psychic development in the failure to represent the mother in her absence. Incapable of providing himself with the security and care he takes from her presence through his own mental representations, the child experiences her absence and his inability to compensate for it as abandonment and loss. The resulting narcissistic wound leads to feelings of insecurity and to desires either to fuse with the maternal object or to withdraw entirely from an object world that is felt to be threatening and inconstant. Such withdrawal from the representation of objects leads to the development of compensatory private representations that are highly resolved and hypertropic. These hypertropic or exaggerated private representations overcome the confusion of boundaries that the early failure entailed by rejecting the object world altogether and thereby establishing extremely firm boundaries around the self which radically separate the self from that world and from the threat of empathetic ties to it. The stronger the needed boundaries the more powerful and developed are these private mental representations in distinction, differentiation, quality, etc. The extreme instance of such fantasies is schizophrenia. These representations tend therefore to replace public reality, which is metonymic, contingent, and indeterminate, with private meaning systems that are metaphoric, overdetermined, and fixed. The resulting security of boundaries helps reestablish a determinate sexual identity, since the object world associated with maternal inconstancy is left out of the picture. The final ingredient in this psychopathology is violence. The need to establish exaggerated boundaries through hypertropic representations is carried out aggressively, and that aggression is directed against the mother, who is experienced as being responsible for the initial abandonment, loss of object constancy, and failure of mental representation. If care is linked to metonymic ties that confuse the boundaries of identity, then its inverse—uncaring aggression—will be valorized as the means of salvaging sexual identity. In Coppola's films and in patriarchal culture in general, the fixing of male sexual identity through idealizing metaphoric representations that establish firm boundaries will be linked to violence against women.

It is noteworthy that *Godfather, Apocalypse Now, The Conversation,* and *Rumble Fish* all end with images of lone males cut off from a world that cannot be trusted or that has proved threatening. In all four films, men either live separately from women in all-male groups or else violently reject women. In *Rumble Fish,* the explicit cause of the demise of the gangs whose virtues the film celebrates is women, and the boys live in a family which has been abandoned by the mother. The films are all characterized by an absence of clear representational boundaries, either between objects or between private fantasies and realist depictions. According to the psychoanalytic theory we are using, this would indicate an anxiety over sexual identity, a loss of object constancy which defines self boundaries that is played out aesthetically or representationally. Compensation for the loss of object constancy occurs both through a turn to authoritarian political forms which promise to secure objectival determinacy and through a turn to representational forms that are extremely developed and that fuse images and meanings in overdetermined symbols. In *Rumble Fish*, the Motorcycle Boy "reigns" (as graffiti constantly remind the viewer), and the gangs are looked back to nostalgically as a time when everyone was "loyal" and "organized." Kurtz in *Apocalypse Now* is an authoritarian leader. Both films are stylized allegories in which expressionist images, heightened nonrealist effects, and symbols abound.

Each of the heros is also an individualist, since it is the purpose of the political model and of the representational form of each film to establish a boundary around the self, a sense of representational distinction between the self and the threatening, because inconstant, maternal object world. The individualist resists being "boxed in" (as the theme song of *Rumble Fish* puts it), and in all of the films figures representing limitations on the hero are overthrown or rejected. The leader is someone who brooks no limitation on a triumph of his will; he represents a conservative male desire to regress to a narcissistic state in which all desires are immediately satisfied, especially by the mother. The perfect fusion of command and execution in the leadership principle is a correlate of the perfect fusion of self and world, self and mother which the narcissistically wounded male child desires yet can never attain. The mother's ineluctable difference, experienced as a loss of object constancy, thus motivates the rightist political thematics.

Restitution also occurs through the very formal properties of the films, which fuse signs and meanings into symbolic spatial unities that deny temporal difference. Authoritarianism appears as the desire to control the cinematic medium fully, to bend it to one's private fantasy and will, to replace a threatening indeterminate depiction of historical or material objects with a highly privatized vision of meaning, to subsume metonymy to metaphor. Through representation, through surrogate control over the world of inconstant objects (especially female or maternal objects, the object relation that usually underlies all later ones), a sense of male sexual identity and power is achieved, and the sense of loss is overcome.

In *Rumble Fish*, for example, the highly metaphoric style of the film is a correlate of the kinds of mental representations which would compensate for instability in the male narcissist's object world. It both distances the threatening maternal world of inconstant objects and restores its presence through a substitute medium, for the extremely developed representational surfaces of the film fulfill the same function as accurate representations of that lost object without being prey to any of its threatening contingency. The film's representational dynamics stabilize a defective self-identity, and this representational strategy constitutes an ideal of fusion whose political analog is the hero-worshiping corporate gang. The representational fusion of world and will, image and meaning, is realized in the symbol of the fish, for example, the only color objects in this otherwise black and white film. Like the colored fish (which only the visionary, natural leader, The Motorcycle Boy, has the

power to see), ordinary things are endowed with transcendental, highly metaphoric significance through the use of nonrealist camera angles, speeded-
up film, and fantasy sequences, strategies that evoke an attitude of veneration
parallel to that inspired by leaders, a sense of the mysterious, transcendental
power or meaning in things. If the all-male group is a defense against women,
so also is the representational form of the film, which, like the confusion of
reality and stage performance at the end of *Cotton Club*, overcomes difference,
and replaces an indeterminate public reality with a fused private fantasy of
semantic overcoding in which no difference, no loss, no indeterminacy is
possible.

All Coppola's later films are highly metaphoric for this reason. They
seem to neutralize the potential dissemination of meanings through random
interpretive connections and material networks that are a consequence of
the metonymic forms Coppola so carefully avoids. The streets of Harlem in
Cotton Club, for example, will for this reason be rendered as a stage set whose
artificiality is scarcely concealed, for such signs of artifice suggest this world
is one of one's own making, something, unlike the historical reality of Harlem,
in one's control. Private fantasy replaces public reality, but also the sub-
sumption of the material historical world to one's own magisterial meaning
replaces a threatening possibility that this world might have a disturbingly
separate objectivity or materiality, one marked by multiple indeterminate
meanings of a sort that threaten the firm boundaries of identity. If this
difference is the difference between authoritarianism and democracy, it is
also the one between a conservative male sexual identity and a more liberal
or radical concept of the innocuousness of sexual indeterminacy, as well as
the difference between metaphoric and metonymic representational forms.

In Coppola's films, then, one notices a combined desire for fusion and
separation that has political, representational, and sexual components. Representational fusion (of image and meaning) permits a separation of metaphoric form from the constraints of reality, just as political fusion (in the
fascist organization or all-male gang) separates the exalted male from worldly
threats to his power. And a fusion of sexual identity waylays threats of indeterminacy by establishing a boundary that separates the "male" from the
"female."

Coppola's films indicate the extent to which culture (that is, certain forms
of representation) is essential to the kinds of conservative political and economic mobilizations that would occur in the seventies and eighties. They
display the pathological representational forms that result when a world of
stable and constant objects begins to collapse, as it did in the seventies for
numerous vulnerable people. A desire for fusion with a security-providing
object and a desire for withdrawal from a threateningly unpredictable object
world (economic, political, social) result from such instability. Coppola's films
are crucially prefigurative because they record a breakdown of stable object
relations inasmuch as such a breakdown is a failure of representation. They
point toward the replacement of such lost stable relations with fantasies of
semantic fusion and with retreats into compensatory, overcoded private rep-

resentations. And indeed, this is what will occur in American culture as people withdraw from an unstable social world in search of increasingly hypertropic private fantasies of power over that world which provide a sense of fused unity with lost objects. Film and the other media (including that medium of representation which is most obviously effective—politics) will be important for supplying the representations that enable and enact these psychosocial processes.

3. GENRE TRANSFORMATIONS AND THE FAILURE OF LIBERALISM

The "crisis in confidence" we described in the previous chapter coincided in the seventies with the appearance in film of desires for powerful leaders and secure institutions, desires that would be realized in the 1980s with the coming to power of a right-wing president. If culture precedes and prepares the way for politics, then in this case politics followed culture with a mimetic vengeance, filling in all the psychological gaps that are so evident in films of the period. But the crisis of confidence also led to a set of critical demolitions and reconstructions on the level of cultural representation. Previously respected institutions like government and business were cast in a negative light, and the crisis of confidence gave rise to a confidence of criticism. Indeed, it was what conservatives later would call the spirit of "self-flagellation," the liberal and radical critique of American society which culminated in the mid-seventies, that provoked many to turn to a more affirmative and positive vision offered by conservatives in the eighties.

Here we will examine from a historical perspective the impact of that critical spirit on the generic patterns of Hollywood film. Genre films have been some of the most powerful instruments of ideology, as we saw in the last chapter. They secure a sense of object constancy by providing a sense of repetition and familiarity. But the close tie between genre films and social ideology means as well that genre films are among the most fragile forms, the most vulnerable to the effects of social change. A crisis of confidence in public institutions is necessarily a crisis of the cultural representational forms that construct the social world in a way that helps hold those institutions together, endowing them with the psychological glue of credibility and legitimacy. Distrust of leaders leads predictably at this time to a debunking of the cultural icons associated with the ideology of business and government leadership. The basing of self-identity on cultural representations of public authority implies that disappointment on the public level is felt as a personal disappointment, wound, or loss. For this reason, perhaps, Jimmy Carter, widely perceived as a somewhat ineffectual leader, was the final straw in conservative tolerance of liberal criticism. The middle of his reign coincides with a turn from criticism to affirmation in American culture (1977–78) that marks the beginning of the triumph of conservatism in the contemporary era. Thus, a study of generic transformations at this time also entails a study of the failure of liberalism in the seventies.

The cultural radicalism of the sixties initiated the debunking of public institutions and generic stereotypes through camp parody. The darker, more pessimistic mood of the mid-seventies emerges in the generic *noir* revival, as well as in the development of a new generic cycle of conspiracy films. These changes describe a trajectory from criticism to pessimism that culminates around 1977. This is the highpoint of liberal reappraisal, but it is also the point when the failure of liberalism during the contemporary period is most clear. The Carter presidency signaled that the Democrats were no longer capable of handling the sort of economic crisis that two major recessions had brought about. While Carter was blaming Americans morally for the country's economic dilemmas, the people were demonstrating, through the appeal of certain films around 1978, that they wanted a more positive sense of the future, a more affirmative political vision. After the peak of pessimism around 1977, more affirmative and optimistic generic transformations occur—the rediscovery of fantasy adventure films (*Star Wars*, *Raiders of the Lost Ark*), sports success films (*Rocky*), neomilitarist war films (*The Deer Hunter*), mindless musicals (*Grease*), urban neowesterns (*Every Which Way but Loose*), and conservative family melodramas (*The Turning Point*). If these latter events prefigure the resurgence of conservatism in American political life, the mid-seventies films can be read as cinematic articulations of the failure of liberalism that would pave the way for that resurgence.

1. Western, Detective, Musical

Genres hold the world in place, establishing and enforcing a sense of propriety, of proper boundaries which demarcate appropriate thought, feeling, and behavior and which provide frames, codes, and signs for constructing a shared social reality. We are speaking now of genres in a broad sense which includes the different areas of social behavior—public as well as private. Each area is a locus of conventionally determined behavior, and we have argued that the prevailing generic division in American social life segregates a hypertropically empathetic or sentimental "home" and family life from a capitalist work world whose conventions prescribe either cutthroat competition or obedience, separation or fusion. Film genres participate in this process by sorting out the different values and ideals a social order requires to be internalized if it is to survive. The traditional western, for example, aided the construction of a social reality in which it was believed that males appropriately dominated the public sphere, while the traditional melodrama constructed a social reality, a commonly held set of precepts, attitudes, and beliefs, which promoted the domestic sphere as the one appropriate to women. Transformations in these social arenas necessarily provoke changes on the level of the cultural representations that hold them in place. This is what seems to have happened as a result of the movements of the sixties and the social crises of the seventies. Fundamental social attitudes like patriotism, optimism, trust in government and business, sense of social security, and so on were either deliberately overturned by such things as the counterculture or undermined by events like Watergate. As a result, the generic divisions which maintained boundaries around proper public dress and behavior or between public morality and immorality were crossed. Idealized cultural representations of public authority in the western and detective genres, for example, could no longer hold in a society in which young people scorned public figures and repudiated authority. Similarly, the cultural ideals seemed less valid the more the people they figuratively idealized (presidents, for example) proved corrupt and inept.

Some of the most critical revisions of traditional genres during this period were carried out on the western, the detective, and the musical. Each was associated in the American cultural tradition with ideological values and institutions—the frontier myth, individualism, the ladder of success, magical romance. During this period, all three genres underwent transformation, and these transformations coincided with changes in the values and institutions that the generic representations helped construct.

Genres depend on receptive audiences who are willing to grant credibility to the conventions of the genre to the extent that those conventions become invisible. Once that is accomplished the generic illusion can assume the character of verisimilitude. It no longer seems to be constituted through the manipulation of coded formulae. A certain occlusion of rhetoric and convention, therefore, is crucial to the successful transmission of ideological beliefs to the audience. What this means, however, is that once the generic conventions are foregrounded, the genre can no longer operate successfully as a purveyor of ideology. The conventions become unstable and variable; history increasingly intervenes in the realm of myth; and the generic signifiers themselves increasingly become signifieds, the referents of films rather than the active agents of cinematic practice, a matter of content rather than a vital form.

This process can also be described rhetorically. Genres are metaphors. Generic idealization (of the western hero, for example) enlists those who might be moved to dispute the reigning social divisions, as a result of material oppression, into the maintenance of their unequal position. The western hero made capitalism legitimate even for those on the out because, as a metaphor, he universalized specific concrete interests, making them abstract and transportable across class lines. Detached from their specific capitalist class anchor, they could be moved and adopted by other class groups.

What undermines generic idealization is the reduction of the metaphor to its literal components, the framing of the metaphor so that it ceases to be universal and becomes citable as an example of a specific rhetorical strategy. The ideal thus becomes historicized and materialized. All of these can be described as metonymic rhetorical moves. Each renders the generic ideal material in a way which displays the concrete connections which link it to the specific social realities that metaphor seemed to transcend.

All genres create a tradition that can become an object to be cited, an occasion for reflexivity. In the western, this tendency is exacerbated by the fact that the western is linked to a specific historical moment that has passed. The classical Hollywood western resolved contradictions between economic reality and cultural ethos in a way that permitted the changing configurations of American capitalism to be made legitimate for the public. It was an essentially conservative genre. Perhaps for this reason alone it was damaged by the cultural revolutions of the sixties, which were characterized by a liberal ethic that rejected many of its major values. By the mid-seventies, the western had all but disappeared from the screen.

Classic westerns like *Red River* and *Shane* promoted values of competitive individualism at a time when the U.S. economy was still relatively market-oriented, while later westerns like *The Professionals* and *The Wild Bunch* legitimate the technocratic-elitist ideology of corporate capitalism.[1] As U.S. capitalism becomes more corporatist, technocratic, and "postindustrial," it is no longer appropriate or effective for western myths to portray a world of rugged individualist competition in a frontier setting that is an allegorical version of the capitalist marketplace. Nor is a myth of a corporate elite on horseback sufficient. The social alliances that capitalism must forge to survive require myths that contain a range of character types which can represent government, labor, and business, as well as different professions and ethnic groups. These diverse groups must then be able to band together against a shared external enemy in order to legitimate the new class alliances. The western could no longer supply these needs by the mid-1970s. No external enemy from the western repertoire could be placed on the horizon, and the western's range of characters, designed for heroizing entrepreneurial capitalism within the context of a threatening frontier-market, could not supply the ideological needs of a transnational capital faced increasingly with a threat less from domestic government (which could easily be reined in) than from the Soviet Union and from national liberation movements that increasingly turned to socialism rather than capitalism. High-tech transnational westerns like *Star Wars* seem to be the solution. They have the needed character range, the external enemy who represents various forms of the current nemesis of capital, and a technological environment that is itself an advertisement for a robotized, automated, and computerized economic system. Capitalism in crisis would seek more mythic and fantastic fare to purvey its ideology of superior entrepreneurial individuals to whose elite executive power all of society should submit while forming a seamless corporatist order—Jedi Knights, for example.[2]

Instead of legitimating entrepreneurial individualism or corporate professionalism, by the early seventies the western tends either to demystify the myth of the West or to depict the closing of the frontier and the end of the mythic space of the traditional western (*Will Penny*, *Monte Walsh*, etc.). During this period, the western undergoes a process whereby its conventions are made visible; it increasingly assumes the form of a tradition that is reflected on and referred to in film. That process takes several forms—elegy, historical realism, and genre subversion and satire. Perhaps the most elegaic filmmaker of the era is Sam Peckinpah. In films like *Ride the High Country*, *The Wild Bunch*, *The Ballad of Cable Hogue*, and *Junior Bonner*, the western conventions are signaled as being lost. The usual generic motifs of individual heroism and male bonding are represented as under siege from mass urban society and from corporate interests that put values of money and efficiency before the blood and friendship bonds that define the ethos of Peckinpah's West. His "post-westerns" nostalgically mourn the passing of the West and the increasing obsolescence of the western hero in the modern world. The conventions are cited as belonging to an earlier era.

His films are particularly interesting ideologically because the theme of the passing of the West is invariably linked to a nostalgia for a small-business world of heroic entrepreneurship prior to the ascendance of corporate capitalism. For example, in *The Ballad of Cable Hogue* (1970) and *Junior Bonner* (1972) the main characters are latter-day cowboys or individualist small businessmen who are out of place in a modernizing and corporatized world. For each, the end of the frontier where individual courage can be proven is associated with big money (either banks or businessmen) and machines. The disappearance of the frontier is signaled by the car, a symbol of modernity, that kills Cable and the bulldozer that destroys Junior's father's house. Whereas Junior's brother commercializes the West by turning it into a tourist attraction, Junior upholds the cowboy values of individualism and silent courage. On the other hand, Cable Hogue stands for small-business values against a stagecoach company; in his case, the theme of the end of the frontier is joined to a statement about the end of a small-business economy.

In Peckinpah's films, the idealized myth is still operative, but now there is some separation of the myth from its signifiers. Without any real content, the signifiers themselves are exaggerated and shifted to the foreground. The cinematography of the death scenes of *High Country* and *Wild Bunch* is self-consciously mythologizing; departing from the usual reality effect of the traditional western, it makes the dying men larger than life and highlights the conventionality of the hero. (An even more self-consciously cinematic version of the separation of myth from reality is evident in Siegel's *The Shootist* (1976); as much an elegy to John Wayne as actor as to the western character he plays, it begins with a series of clips from Wayne's western movies.)

A cycle of more historically "realistic" westerns, initiated in the 1960s, depicted the West as dirty, hostile, and violent. These representations undermined the mythology of the western hero and the generic idealization which legitimated the violence of the "good" hero against "bad" Native Americans, Mexicans, or villains. The historical realism of films like *Cheyenne Autumn*, *Soldier Blue*, *McCabe and Mrs. Miller*, *The Great Northfield Minnesota Raid*, *The Life and Times of Judge Roy Bean*, and *The Missouri Breaks* presented both outlaws and established authorities as vicious killers whose use of violence was equally arbitrary and destructive; in addition, the films frequently presented Native Americans sympathetically.[3] These films also often display the conventionality of the western by ignoring the conventions altogether, or by explicitly recoding them. Far from being a conventional western hero, McCabe is a brothel owner who shoots men in the back, while Brando's "regulator" in *The Missouri Breaks* is a paid executioner who dresses in drag and shoots men while they're at toilet and the central character is a rustler who grows cabbages as a cover.

Finally, in satiric films like Robert Downey's *Greasers' Palace* (1972) and Mel Brooks's *Blazing Saddles* (1974) the conventions are made fully visible. Brooks's film ends by breaking the fictional frame entirely—the actors leave the western set, get into a fight on the set of a musical, and go watch themselves in a theater. And Robert Altman's *Buffalo Bill and the Indians* (1977) self-consciously exposes the pretentiousness of western myths and ideals.

The eclipse of the western was thus fostered both by the subversion of its generic conventions and by its exhaustion as a mode of ideological legitimation. The change confirms the triumph of liberalism over traditional conservative interest groups, which is the political hallmark of institutional politics during the sixties. And it signals the transformation of the United States from a small-business economy into a full-blown transnational corporate economy. Yet first indicators of the ultimate faltering of liberalism in the late seventies are signaled by the absence of any affirmative alternatives to the western, of anything asserting a post-western, post-conservative set of liberal values and ideals. The Hollywood liberals could debunk the conservative myths of the traditional genre, but by not filling the gap with an alternative vision, they portrayed themselves as a negative force and left the discovery of a positive alternative to the conservatives. One major problem, of course, was that liberals had no alternative vision to offer, and as the mid-seventies ushered in the closest thing to a depression the United States had seen in half a century (the social discomfort index was the highest since the thirties), that lack became striking. Thus, the political triumph of Democratic liberals in the mid-seventies (the post-Watergate war on government corruption and CIA wrongdoing, as well as the overthrow in 1976 of an incumbent Republican president) coincided unfortunately with economic recession, and the negative critical spirit of seventies liberalism could not respond to the psychological needs for reassurance generated by this crisis. An increasing sense of frustration is especially apparent in the transformation in the detective genre during this time.

Mid-seventies private and police detective films like *Serpico* and *Chinatown* articulate the mid-seventies liberal ethos by depicting a society that is controlled by corrupt economic and political elites. *Chinatown* (1974), directed by Roman Polanski and written by Robert Towne, inserts into the private detective genre the figures of skepticism and pessimism that were prevalent in the post-Vietnam, post-Watergate era. The story depicts the effects of water and land monopolies in 1930s Southern California and portrays a society dominated by a corrupt economic elite. Detective J. J. Gittes (Jack Nicholson) investigates a public water scandal and learns that water is being diverted for

Chinatown. The formulaic *film noir* long shot situates the characters in an uncontrollable and menacing environment.

private ends by a ruthless mogul, Noah Cross (John Huston). Gittes falls in love with Cross's daughter, Evelyn (Faye Dunaway), who agrees to help Gittes because her husband was murdered by Cross, the father of her illegitimate child by incest. Cross is an unscrupulous capitalist patriarch, and "Chinatown" (a generic reference to the concluding setting of Welles's *noir* classic *A Lady from Shanghai*) is a metaphor for an environment controlled by ruthless men and for a world where the good intentions of decent individuals only result in the death of innocents.

Chinatown, in an anti-heroic gesture consistent with the sixties sensibility that lies behind it, recodes the figure of the detective hero by portraying Gittes as a flawed man who cannot control events. Throughout much of the film he wears a bandage on his nose, signifying his weakness and vulnerability. The tough guy detective of Hammett, Chandler, and others, by contrast, is a paragon of individualism who is courageous, resourceful, and usually successful. He stands outside of the corrupt universe that he inhabits, subscribes to his own code of honor, and usually succeeds in exposing and defeating evil. Such a figure, *Chinatown* suggests, is an anachronism. In the film's pessimistic conclusion, Evelyn is killed by the police, and Gittes's involuntary complicity in her death is suggested by the fact that he is handcuffed to the policeman who shoots her. Gittes tries to explain what has really been going on, but is rebuffed; one of his associates tells him at the end, "Forget it Jake. It's Chinatown." A formulaic *film noir* crane longshot of the street, as the camera elevates (a reference to the opening sequence of another Welles *noir* film, *Touch of Evil*), shows the dark environment enveloping and overpowering the small human figures, powerless against the dominant social powers.

Chinatown is a striking articulation of mid-seventies cultural pessimism, and it suggests the direction the liberal critique of traditional conservative economic interests was taking. Indeed, the entire *film noir* revival of the mid-seventies can be said to instantiate the emerging reality of political liberalism—that it was powerless against the entrenched economic power blocs of the country. It could do nothing against steep price rises and the bleeding of the country by oil companies. It is in the tragic figure of the *noir* detective, determined to do right yet incapable of changing the basic realities, that the liberal ideal, with all of its well-deserved self-pity, finds its strongest expression at this point in time.

Traditionally the *film noir* of the late forties and early fifties depicts a dark world of contending, sometimes ambiguous, moral forces, in which deception, treachery, and murder are commonplace. Dialog is frequently abrasive, and the style is usually characterized by night shooting, dark shadows, sharp lighting contrasts, askew camera angles, symbolic environments, and convoluted narratives (the classic example of which is *The Big Sleep*). These films frequently feature detectives who operate on the edge of the law as hard-bitten loners only marginally able to relate to women (who are frequently the source of evil). The films usually expose corrupt wealth and power; crime and business often seem interchangeable.

Indeed, the *noir* world is characterized by crossed boundaries. In films like *Out of the Past*, moral transgression is connoted by backlit figures whose boundaries merge. The breakdown of representational clarity is associated frequently with a collapse of conservative moral imperatives. More often than not, these transgressions are recuperated, and many *noir* films end moralistically, affirming traditional morality, often in natural settings. Nevertheless there is something troubling to a conservative social ideal of proper distinctions in this breakdown of representation. That the lines can be crossed at all suggests that they are conventional, rather than natural. These films thus underscore the link between styles of representation and the institutions of social order.

The revival of the *noir* form after 1967 (*Point Blank* and *Bonnie and Clyde*—considered as a reprise of *They Live by Night*—arguably the initiators) could be said to coincide with the breakdown of conservative moral and social boundaries that characterized the sixties. As in earlier *noir* films, in contemporary films like *Night Moves* (1975) it is difficult to sort out good from evil in a clearly boundaried way. Normal institutions like motherhood are corrupt; and the trust usually associated with family relations is betrayed. The supposedly innocent delve into incest, but their death is not in any way justified as moral retribution. The moral dilemma is often due to the incursion of the past, the return of the repressed. *Noir* flashbacks often highlight the power of past guilt in determining the present, and this abreactive form undermines the "eternal present" of Hollywood film, the appearance that everything occurs in a nonhistorical space. The narrative turns in these films are part of a general moral rhetoric which confuses simplistic conservative moral judgment by overturning the logic of moral responsibility. If individuals are evil, it is usually because they are examples of a class structure.

The contemporary *noir* revivals can be said to pertain, then, to that strain of populist distrust or loss of confidence which animates so much of the critical activity of the era. The rich and powerful are usually portrayed as corrupt, and this representation was not very distant from the actual characterization of them in the media at the time. Yet the films also say something about the transformations in liberalism during the era. The demise of public confidence and the erosion of public institutions took a toll on public psychology that could not ultimately be remedied by liberal kindness and self-reflection. In 1967, the *noir* hero of *Point Blank* could walk away from wealth after having struggled to recover what was rightfully his. It is a sixties gesture, a righteous rejection of a corrupt world in favor of personal salvation. By 1975, after the rejected world had proven just how corrupt it really was, it was no longer possible to pose a realm of personal righteousness against the structures of power.

The mid-seventies *noir* revivals are distinguished by a sense of pessimism devoid of even the individual triumphs that the traditional *noir* detective enjoyed. Marlowe (Robert Mitchum) in the remake of *Farewell, My Lovely* (1975) remarks, "I've run out of trust in this joint" and "Everything I touch turns to shit." Distrust constitutes wisdom in this world, and power is defined exclusively in monetary terms. The detective is even more flawed in Penn's *Night Moves*. "I didn't solve anything," Harry Moseby says. "I just fell in on top of things." Moseby is a virtuous man, but even the ethical gestures that seemed to redeem things a bit in *Farewell* count for little in *Night Moves*. Everyone double-crosses; all are out for profit; and the innocent are slaughtered in the process. The plight of the detective is that, like Gittes, he himself becomes an inadvertent perpetrator of evil. He ends up in a boat which goes around in circles.

Thus, the mid-seventies peak of liberalism in American culture is characterized by a sense of hopelessness about structural, especially economic, corruption. As the decade progressed, the shortcomings of the liberal agenda became more emphatically marked, and the people eventually fled from an ineffectual Democrat to an affirmative Republican. Not surprisingly, perhaps, the detective genre swung back into line. And despite the portrayal of a humane and successful *noir* detective in Burt Reynolds's *Sharkey's Machine* (1982), by the early eighties Clint Eastwood was back as a tough detective in *Sudden Impact* (1983) and *Tightrope* (1984), and he and others like Lawrence Kasdan even attempted to revive the western (*Pale Rider, Silverado*). The period of contestation leaves its mark, however. After criticism, ideology cannot simply continue as it was. It must recompose itself in the terms of its adversary. It is significant, therefore, that a seventies Dirty Harry film like *Magnum Force* (scripted by John Milius and Michael Cimino) must respond to criticism of vigilantism aimed at *Dirty Harry* by showing Harry fighting police vigilantes, or that *The Gauntlet* (1978) seems to respond to charges of sexism by showing a strong woman. The genre even comes to incorporate its own satire in *City Heat*, in which Reynolds and Eastwood play detectives who at one point comically compare the size of each other's guns. The continued popularity of macho detective films like *Sudden Impact*, however, confirms the power and success of conservative representations in the early eighties.

Transformations in another traditionally ideological genre—the musical—substantiate our claim that there is a strong relation between changes in sociocultural configurations and changes in generic representational forms. Early to mid-seventies musicals evidence the critical spirit we have noticed in certain western and detective films. Later musicals, however, indicate the turn American culture was taking in the late seventies toward more conservative visions.

Barbra Streisand's characterization of singer Fanny Brice in *Funny Girl* (1968) and *Funny Lady* (1975), two of the most popular musicals of the era, depicted Brice's failures to find love and happiness within her musical career. Both were strikingly pessimistic in comparison to earlier musicals. Bob Fosse's *Cabaret* (1972) projected an even darker vision of life in Nazi Germany on the eve of Hitler's ascension to power; it uses the musical review format to engage in social critique through songs that satirize bourgeois values. The story of the sexually freewheeling Sally Bowles and her gay friend—Christopher Isherwood—in Berlin is recounted in a quasi-Brechtian narrative that ironically intercuts scenes of Nazi violence with images of cabaret performances. The juxtaposition of historical realist scenes with melodramatic segments creates a sense both of menace and of blithe ignorance. The rhetorical strategy is evocative, a warning of sorts against naiveté. The love story, once again, is of failed rather than successful romance.

If *Cabaret* breaks down the boundaries between conventional stage performances and historical events, it also crosses sexual and moral boundaries of the sort a conservative mentality would prefer held fast. It instantiates the personal or cultural radicalism of the era, which sought to reconstruct structures of social relations around such issues as homosexuality and women's sexual liberation. Its style is metonymic or disseminatory, rather than metaphoric. The rhetorical strategy of juxtaposition suggests contiguous relations between stage art and real events, and it thereby demystifies the aura of art which usually operates to elevate certain values into metaphoric absolutes. In this film, values are contingent, matters open to decision and construction, and representation pertains as much to the social as to the artistic world. Such a viewpoint, however, imposes responsibility, and it is a significant indictment of the characters' naiveté regarding the rise of fascism that their irresponsible lives are narrated in juxtaposition to that event. Yet the film is not moralistic on this point. It celebrates their very nonfascist liberality, while also questioning it. If the rhetoric of the film is metonymic, it is also to a certain extent undecidable—a refusal to draw absolute moral boundaries or to exercise judgment. Even the Nazis are presented for what they are—blond-haired singers of charming songs who are capable of murder.

Martin Scorsese's *New York, New York* (1977) is equally pessimistic, another articulation of the critical spirit pervading American culture down through the mid-seventies. A "realist" musical, it situates the narrative of failed love between a singer and a musician in the era of the great musicals. The film is critical to the extent that it depicts a man's inability to accept the independence and success of his female partner. The segregation of music onto the stage in critical musicals of this sort suggests that the transformation of everyday life in traditional musical numbers was becoming an impossibility for modern audiences and calls attention in itself to the artificiality of musical conventions.

It is significant that *New York* was made in 1977, roughly the high point of the critical, satiric, pessimistic vision of the seventies. It is the year of *Annie Hall, Missouri Breaks, Twilight's Last Gleaming*, and other countergeneric, critical, or pessimistic films. With that year, the critical *noir* revival also comes to an end. If the major box-office films of 1976 are *One Flow over the Cuckoo's Nest* and *All the President's Men*, the hits of 1977 are *Star Wars* and *Rocky*. They signal the beginning of an affirmative tendency that would continue into the eighties. Criticism gives way increasingly to ideology. It is of course also the first year after the end of the "Watergate era," the first year of the tenure of a new president who promised national renewal (only to fail).

The changeover is marked in the musical genre by *Grease*, the most popular film of 1978, which returned to the conventional musical format and revived as well patterns of ritualized romance, traditional gender modeling, and masculinist posturing. It also participated in the nostalgic return to simpler times that would mark the youth film of the period and brought back defanged fifties popular music, women in bobby socks, and "greaser" ducktail haircuts. All the social crises and tensions that made the seventies so insecure, and escapist fantasies like *Star Wars* or *Grease* so popular, evaporate into worries over dates.

A history of significant generic transformations during this period thus can be mapped onto sociopolitical changes. And those transformations indicate important movements in the metamorphosis of American culture from liberalism to conservatism. The demolition of the western myth under a satiric and critical liberal gaze from the late sixties through the mid-seventies helps create a vacuum of ideology, the lack of a reassuring set of beliefs, ideals, and values in a culture whose traditional institutions had been undermined. That vacuum gives rise to a sense of loss, pessimism, and despair that appears cinematically in the mid-seventies *noir* revival films as a hopeless vision of the social universe. But out of the night, affirmations emerged. The vacuum began to be filled in the late seventies, with revivalist visions of the sort on display in some musicals of the era. The only problem is that those visions sometimes took the form of men who carried whips, which they occasionally used on women and non-whites, or rode space battleships that fired torpedoes at Soviet-like enemies. The night coincided with the failure of liberalism during this epoch, and the emergence into light in consequence coincided with affirmations of conservative values and ideals.

2. Social Problem Films

The social problem film genre has traditionally been a battleground between conservatives and liberals regarding such social issues as crime, political corruption, drugs, and youth gangs. In the late forties especially, the social problem genre was characterized by liberal and leftist points of view. The susceptibility of the genre to political change was demonstrated in the fifties, when, during a period of conservative ascendancy, the percentage of social problem films fell off markedly.[4] The leftist revival of the sixties brought with it a renewal of interest in the genre. Indeed, one of the major generic transformations of the era is a revival of the social problem film in the seventies and eighties. These films testify to the power of the new anticonservative voices that were unharnessed by the social radicalism of the sixties. Yet they also are a major indicator of some of the crucial shortcomings of liberalism which would lead to its defeat in the late seventies.

In the seventies and eighties, crime and problems of criminal justice were a major focus of social problem films. While liberals continued to militate for more humane ways of dealing with crime, conservatives countered with arguments for harsher punishment. Eventually they would win out, and one sign of their success is the eventual return of the death penalty accompanied by strong public support.

While liberal social problem films of the early to mid-seventies like *Serpico* (1973) concentrated on corruption in the institutions of criminal justice, conservative films tended to portray crime as a problem best solved by violence. Crime in these films is the result of an evil human nature, not of social conditions. The popular "Dirty Harry" films (*Dirty Harry*, number 5 in box-office gross in 1972; *Magnum Force*, number 4 in 1974; *The Enforcer*, number 8 in 1977) are the most notorious examples. In these films, Harry generally has as difficult a time battling liberals as he does criminals or terrorists.

A less strident antiliberal statement is made in Paul Schrader and Martin Scorsese's *Taxi Driver* (1976). Scriptwriter Schrader's usual heavy-handedness is salvaged somewhat by Scorsese's lighter, more ironic touch. An inarticulate bumpkin, Travis Bickle (Robert De Niro), is stranded between a cosmopolitan liberal social world that has no place for the likes of him and the underworld of drugs, sex, and youth gangs that he detests. He drives a taxi, a ploy that permits him to observe the seedier side of city life. After being rebuked by a blonde campaign worker for a liberal politician, Travis meets a young prostitute, buys guns, and eventually cracks up. His attempt to assassinate the liberal politician fails, so instead he decides to liberate the prostitute by killing her pimp. He becomes a media hero. Travis's choice of targets is not altogether fortuitous, for it is the liberals, according to conservatives, who are responsible for the "moral" corruption Travis turns to instead of the poli-

Crime is a major focus of conservative mobilization in the seventies.

tician. The narrative displacement suggests that liberal permissiveness and hypocrisy allow crime and vice to flourish.

The film displays the shortcomings of the moral response to social inequality. The categories of moral thought are personal and individualistic. The notion of systemic "evil" is alien to it. Moral programs thus seem inevitably to demand the punishment of individuals, rather than the transformation of systems. The moral conscience is fetishistic because it breaks down complex ethical problems into discrete elements—individuals and individual acts—and because it privileges single acts of violence as vehicles of individual redemption.

Visual texture correlates with Travis's moralistic paranoia and instantiates the ethical fetishism of the film. The recurrent images of smoke, expressionistically represented colored lights, and the pervasive use of red visually code the city as an inferno. Like his moralism, the style is fetishistic. The opening shots of the taxi emerging from the fog to the sound of neo-fifties Bernard Herrmann music suggests both terror and reverence, two components of paranoid fetishism. Like a fetish, the taxi seems to transcend its surroundings and to elicit a riveting attention. Moreover, throughout the film, Travis's experience of the city is represented through images that underscore the fragmented nature of that experience. As he drives, images of small parts of the taxi—the outside mirror, the windshield, the rearview mirror—make up the composite of his phenomenal world. The style concentrates on fragmented and isolated parts instead of wholes, and the camera is enclosed, like Travis himself; it looks out on a world that can only appear threatening from so circumscribed a point of view. The representational rhetoric of the film, therefore, is as fragmentary and fetishistic as Travis's moral vision. It touches on surfaces and immediate street-level experiences, but it does not indicate the interconnections of the system that gives rise to the things that repulse Travis and motivate his actions. A more radical filmmaker might have used the vehicle of the taxi driver to depict the tremendous inequalities of wealth that are on display in large cities like New York. And such a depiction would have probably required a different representational style altogether, one that would be less fetishistic, one more concerned with the metonymic relations between the different parts of the social system, more tolerant in consequence of difference in point of view, and therefore more multiple in its perspective. The alternative to conservative representations of fusion or isolated withdrawal into hyperbole is therefore not "realism" in its banal empirical sense, but rather a complex, systemic, and differentiated representation of the object world in its interconnectedness. And such a representation entails a conceptual and abstract understanding of the operative principles and underlying or nonempirical rules of the social system.

The social problem film that made the most explicit statement for the conservative position on crime was the vigilante film *Death Wish* (1974), in which a liberal who is initially tolerant of urban crime converts to a radically conservative position when his wife is murdered by a gang of young thieves. It is noteworthy that the vehicle of his conversion is a Sunbelt rightist, the

Taxi Driver. The fetishistic moral vision. The taxi driver noses in on urban corruption.

social type that would indeed take over from the liberals in the eighties as the dominant social policy voice in the country. His social views are bolstered by an ideology of nature—that new housing developments, which are meant to be white enclaves, should conform to the shape of the land—which will, as the decade advances, come increasingly to be the justification for a number of right-wing themes—the market, the family, patriarchal authority, etc.

A comparison of the film with a liberal film of the period—Sidney Lumet's *Dog Day Afternoon* (1975)—dramatizes the differences between the conservative and liberal postures on crime while displaying the ways different representational or rhetorical strategies construct distinct realities.

The rhetorical format of *Death Wish* combines ironic cynicism with romantic sentimentalism. The film signals the sentimentalist basis of its predatory conservative social ideology at the outset. Paul Kersey and his wife are in nature (a white middle-class tourist nature—Hawaii), basking in romantic sunsets. She is his fetish object, a treasure captured in photographs. Throughout the film, women are associated with whiteness, purity, and religion. It is significant that it is an attack on this sepulchral femininity that motivates Paul's conversion to conservatism. The dual structure of private sentimentalism and public violence is, we have suggested, characteristic of conservative social thinking. The necessity of male public violence is associated with the hyperbolic elevation of the female private sphere as a locus of empathy. An extreme form of fragility, that sphere must be defended. The attitude appropriate for such violent defense is ironic cynicism, a pose which demeans others and situates them as distanced objects. A deflationary stance, it hyperbolically reduces the value of others, transforming them into targets of literal violence. It is fitting, then, that the film alternates between scenes of cloying sentiment, as when Paul visits his catatonic daughter, and scenes of extreme objectification, when Paul kills muggers and blacks and poor people. Indeed, the entire narrative is dominated by a rather nasty irony. Paul's liberalism is ironized by the brutal treatment of his family by criminals; the liberal city government officials are ironized by the fact that Paul's exploits reduce crime, obliging them to want to squelch the story. The cynical rhetoric is evident in one aside particularly: a conservative woman says snidely to a man who complains that the vigilante's victims are primarily black that perhaps the number of white muggers should be increased by affirmative action "so that we'll have racial equality among muggers." Cynical irony is also enacted in the camera rhetoric. When Paul attacks his victims, the camera rarely places them both in the same frame. The literal distance marked by the editing is itself a correlate of the objectifying, demeaning attitude that is the public rhetoric of conservative sociality.

The sentimentalized domestic sphere in the film is associated with the concept or site of nature, which is represented primarily by the Sunbelt. Like the private sphere, it represents a place outside civility or urban civilization, a site associated with the male subject conceived as a private entity, the bearer of rights of property and propriety whose boundaries must be protected with violence. The exaltation of the male individual in conservative thought is always linked to nature for this reason. Nature is unconstrained. The privileging of male rights in nature is a noticeably conservative concept in that it eschews social responsibility altogether. The more "natural" Sunbelt is thus a metaphor for the conservative ideal of individual freedom, the exaltation of individual rights over collective responsibility. Over, that is, a metonymic social rhetoric of material contiguous connections between people. The metaphor of nature permits a separating out, an individuating of the self, which is also a denial of a rhetoric of connection and responsibility. For if Paul Kersey were really thinking, he would see his own role in the generation of the poverty which creates crime. But that requires a structural mode of thought, a metonymic rhetoric for constructing the phenomenal world and social reality which is alien to the subject-centered, personalized vision of this conservative film. Instead, Paul separates from others by exercising violence against them. What is at stake in the film, then, is as much a problem of establishing boundaries around the male self, of constructing the "individual," as it is an issue of crime. That construction requires a metaphoric mode which idealizes private thought by radically separating meaning from its material vehicle. The sense of private meaning in metaphor is inseparable from a concept of the self as private and separate from the material, literal social world around it. Such self-idealization and separation also entail a rejection of literal materiality, and this takes the social form of wanting to construct Sunbelt white havens apart from the material world of urban poverty. The more natural Sunbelt is a metaphor in several senses then,

Like all ideological metaphors, this rhetoric of social representation is undermined by a metonymic literality which displays its material basis. The metonymy underlying the natural metaphors in *Death Wish* concerns anality and retentiveness. Paul's Sunbelt friend, Ames, is careful to point out that one "can't even hear the toilets flush next door" in the southern enclave. And he refers to New York as a toilet. A literal or material connection is harbored within the metaphoric structure of conservative self-idealization. A turning away from something threatening or dirty or shameful motivates that ideal. Fear of bodily functions is a common trait of conservative psychopathology. But in addition, the sadism evident in the film is often associated with anal retentiveness. And one can at least speculate about the relationship between this fear, conservative defensiveness over property, and the conservative tendency to support violence against class enemies.

It is also noteworthy in this regard that the only strong "relationship" in the film is between men. The women are dispensed with almost immediately, and it seems that a flight from women's physicality is also a factor in the evident anal-sadism of the men. Conservative male misogyny is compounded with a strong sense of male alliance, of course, and it is probably fitting that Ames's gift to Paul is a gun in a red velvet box, a sign of an erotic attachment if ever there was one. But conservative homoeroticism can never be realized because of the conservative moral injunction against such things. Instead it is transmuted into its inverse, a pose of violence against other men. This is the price of a social structure of shared male power, one which requires homoerotic bonding yet enjoins it at the same time. Rather than assuming a healthily expressed form, those homoerotic energies become perverted into an entirely de-eroticized stance toward other men, a stance realized in Paul's gunmanship.

These arguments point toward a deconstruction of the two major metaphors which support the ideology of the film. The first is the isolation and elevation of the individual male subject, his anointment with sovereign powers that place him above the mass and beyond the communal constraints of liberal legality. An examination of the metonymic connections, the literal references, that surround that metaphor suggest instead that the conservative individual is a victim of a set of repressions and constraints which he cannot recognize. The second is the metaphor of a ground of self-evident, precivil value in nature which legitimates conservative class, race, and sexual social power. The counterforces in the film point to a reading which sees that ground as a perversion of natural tendencies like homoeroticism into sanctuaries of purity, guilt-free realms, purged of the taint of materiality, that assuage the anxiety regarding anal eroticism that necessarily inheres in an all-male power system.

Films display the material basis of their ideology, the violence underlying it, for example, at points that might seem marginal, moments of representation that seem tangential to the central argument. But if ideological values entail strategies of representing the world and are in fact effects of such strategies, then marginal points of representation are as essential or central as supposedly more conceptual matters. Thus, the anal sadism that energizes Paul Kersey's conservatism appears on a formal level in the distance that separates him, through scene composition and editing, from his victims. In Sidney Lumet's more liberal *Dog Day Afternoon*, the camera moves in what seems a random manner through a bank being held up by two inept robbers. The women employees make caring statements to each other, and they seem like asides in relation to the more central problem of the robbery. But one of them is also playing with one of the robber's rifles, and he is showing her how to drill with it. The pan shot that catches these marginal moments instantiates the liberal values of the film. Unlike the radically oppositional editing that separates Paul Kersey from his victims, the shot includes all of the characters in a way that suggests their commonality and their shared predicament. It has already been established that the robbers think of the women employees as people who are as much oppressed as they. The pan reinforces that sense of equality in its horizontal movement. Rather than isolate and elevate, it connects. One could say it is a metonymic as opposed to a metaphoric camera style.

Sonny (Al Pacino) and Sal (John Cazale) are trapped inside the bank by the police. After a long day of negotiation, they make a deal, but at the airport they are betrayed by the FBI, who kill Sal and capture Sonny. The ethos of the film is liberal, democratic, and egalitarian. Gays are portrayed positively, a fairly daring gesture in 1975. Sonny's motivation for the robbery was his need for money to finance his male wife's sex-change operation. Indeed, one of the tenderest scenes is between the two lovers, as they talk for the last time. Although Sonny is the focus, no individual is heroized; all the primary characters are flawed. Those who might be heroized in a conservative film—the police—are portrayed either as well-meaning boobs, unempathetic technocrats, or trigger-happy killers. "He wants to kill me so bad he can taste it," Sonny says of one. And the crowds that gather to cheer on the robbers shout "Attica," recalling the police murder of inmates and their hostages at the New York state penitentiary.

Against the strategy of rhetorical elevation, the film proposes a representational method which promotes a sense of empathy and common cause, even between the police and the robbers. Some of the most empathetic moments occur between Sonny and his hostages. They become friendly, almost intimate, and they express sympathy with each other's problems. The robbers are troubled by doubt, guilt, and remorse. It is not a rhetoric which would permit a simple opposition to be established between good and evil. No decisive moral meaning stands in as a metaphoric substitute which sums up the events and gives them a conceptual or ideal order. Most significantly, the hostages and robbers discuss working-class life, the difficulties of working for little to support a family. The film thus draws attention, in a liberal mode, to the social origins of crime. Rather than objectifying the criminals as opposites to a heroically conceived paragon of righteousness, the film's rhetoric situates the criminals in a context which prevents objectification. In *Death Wish* the audience remains external to the robbers; their murder is justified by a certain cinematic point of view. The isolation and separation of the male subject in the metaphoric mode of representation require a balancing isolation and separation of the world into an object to be treated coldly and unempathetically. In *Dog Day*, no such separation is possible; instead, a complex web of horizontal, material, metonymic connections links the characters and anchors them in their environment in a way that precludes either exalted subjectivity or debased objectivism. The two robbers are often drawn together in the same frame. The materiality of everyday life, that from which conservatives flee, is depicted in scenes where workers express a need to go to the bathroom and police stand about eating sandwiches. The same resolute everydayness is evident at the beginning when, during the credits, the camera moves about New York City picking up bits and pieces of street life. One could speak of this as realism, but it is more relevant to describe it as a specifically metonymic rhetoric of representation that constructs a certain sense of the world, a more egalitarian or horizontal and contextual phenomenal reality.

Death Wish enacts its moral ideology of purity on the representational plane. The narrative is fairly univocal; the cinematography is unsullied. The decisiveness of the isolated subject's will, the purity of his motives, is thus reinforced. We related this sense of moral purity to a fear of anality, of the homoeroticism which accompanies conservative male tribalism. In *Dog Day*, a certain undecidability of moral judgment is accompanied by a certain impurity of representation, as well as a thematic emphasis on the acceptance of social impurity, that is, of social difference and "deviance." The camera's attention to physical aspects of everyday life suggests a greater acceptance of the materiality of the world, less of a need to flee into self-exalting subjective visions which idealize one's own will and sense of moral righteousness as something which supposedly transcends everyday reality. Camera rhetoric and moral vision are indissociable.

Many liberal social problem films of this era pit a basically good individual against a fundamentally corrupt society (*Brubaker*, *The Border*, *Fort Apache, the Bronx*, *The Verdict*). Some show the corruption to be so overwhelming that change is impossible, while others validate the traditional Hollywood liberal notion that a good individual can make a difference (*Brubaker*). In films like *Fort Apache*, *Absence of Malice*, and *The Verdict*, Paul Newman has played tired, flawed heroes driven to decisive action and redemption by intolerable corruption. Although the actions sometimes have socially beneficial consequences, they primarily enact the moral redemption of the individual. In films like *Fort Apache* and *The Verdict*, the universe is so corrupt and fallen that no real social change seems possible. All that seems to matter is that individuals maintain their integrity. The liberal project of social reform is thus displaced in these films in favor of more individual alternatives. This development could be read symptomatically as a tacit acknowledgment on the part of liberals that more general social change was beyond their reach. They could no longer turn with pride to the accomplishments of the liberal programs of the sixties, since those programs were being blamed increasingly by the Right as the sources of economic decline and of crime. All that was perhaps left for liberals to cling to at a time when public politics was being successfully monopolized by the Right were more personal models of reformist hope.

That a large majority came to support capital punishment, which liberals had managed to neutralize in the sixties, suggests that the conservative cultural argument won out over the liberal one regarding crime. The one liberal film overtly critical of vigilantism—*The Star Chamber* (1983)—failed, while early eighties vigilante films like *Death Wish II*, *The Exterminator I & II*, and *Sudden Impact* were much more successful with audiences. But that development is indicative of a larger "social problem" that largely accounts for the general failure of liberalism. An essentially conservative socioeconomic system generates crime among oppressed poor people, especially during times of recession of the sort that occurred in the early and mid-seventies. It is part of the tautology of conservative power that liberal solutions to this problem inevitably fail, since they are based on altruistic assumptions about human nature that an essentially cutthroat economy refuses to permit to thrive and on a liberal individualist concept of "rights" which does not deal with the underlying structural inequalities that are responsible for crime. In such a situation, in the absence of socialist alternatives that address the structural sources of the problem in the capitalist maldistribution of wealth, only conservative solutions to crime will succeed politically, precisely because they offer images of power and just punishment to people rendered fearful, insecure, and resentful by the same unstable social and economic conditions that fuel crime.

3. Conspiracy Films

One of the primary arenas for liberal critiques of U.S. society during the seventies was a new genre of "conspiracy films."[5] These films are of interest because they reverse the polarities of earlier political thrillers, which generally affirmed American institutions, by suggesting that the source of evil was those very institutions. These films also permit an analysis of one of the major problems that led eventually to the failure of liberalism in the late seventies. Liberals often promoted causes (equal rights for women, opposition to nuclear energy, etc.) that were eventually embraced by the population at large, but they also eventually found themselves out of step with public opinion on several crucial social issues (welfare, affirmative action hiring, taxation, etc.) which the majority of people came to view negatively by the late seventies. In the mid-seventies, liberal filmmakers especially were very close to public opinion regarding government and business; the conspiracy genre accurately represents public perceptions after the revelations around the Pentagon Papers, the Gulf of Tonkin incident, Watergate, the ITT scandals, the CIA investigations, etc. But as the decade advanced and as the economy continued

The consumer and environmental movements helped focus public attention on corporate malfeasance, and many corporate conspiracy films transcode these discourses.

to decline, public needs changed, and the critical liberals found themselves out of sync with a broad popular desire for a more positive alternative.

We will argue that this is in part due to the failure of liberalism to live up to the populist expectations that it helped foster in the mid-seventies. In liberal conspiracy films, large institutions like the CIA are depicted as being corrupt, and such representations (in films like *Network* especially) appealed to populist distrust of big institutions and politicians. That distrust turned to more overt resentment as the decade progressed. Liberal federal taxation programs became targets of overt hostility in the late seventies as recession and inflation combined to diminish the earning power of lower- and middle-class people. Even populist Democrats like Jimmy Carter turned on the federal bureaucracy. Thus, liberals helped to promote the undermining of their own chosen instrument of social reform. Liberal filmmakers played to populist fears of big institutions, yet by the late seventies conservatives would turn those fears into a program for dismantling the liberal welfare state.

In a sense, liberals could not have done otherwise. The American cultural lexicon defines social reform in strictly individual terms. The liberal faith in individual, as opposed to institutional or structural, remedies or reconstructions limited the parameters of the liberal critique. Indeed, in order to play successfully to broad populist anxieties, it had to refrain from proposing structural change. The populist distrust of big institutions also took the form of a distrust of big institutional change. The same polls that reflected a crisis of confidence also indicated that while distrust of public officials and business leaders had grown, people continued to have faith in the institutions themselves. If the remedies offered were individual, it was in part because people perceived the problems in individual terms.

But in limiting the options for reform to noninstitutional remedies, liberals ignored the structural causes of the sorts of economic decline. Liberalism's philosophical commitment to the individual as the central social category prevented it from doing anything about the conservative individualist structure of the U.S. economy, while permitting the state to be represented as threatening and impersonal, the source of people's troubles. Liberalism's commitment to the state as an instrument of reform placed it at odds both with the anti-statism its own individualist ethic fostered and with the sort of radical neoentrepreneurial individualism that conservatives were beginning to mobilize against liberal statism.

Liberalism was thus in a quandary. Without a structural vision of how institutions like capitalism caused social suffering, it could not justify institutional change. Without a notion of class, it was limited to arguing that unrestrained capitalism was bad for individuals and that only individuals could change it by changing the bad individuals who run the system. But liberalism's commitment to remedying the negative consequences of capitalism through the only available instrument—the federal government—put it in contradiction with the rampant individualism of capitalist culture. In a culture in which the maintenance of artificial scarcity (in goods and jobs) was a necessary part of the economic system and at a time when inflation and unemployment were high, federally legislated equality, through such programs as affirmative action, was not likely to sit very well. Indeed, more and more people were blaming the federal government, not business, for inflation, a popular perception conservatives would successfully exploit. Thus, liberal politics set itself on a collision course with conservative economic reality, a collision that occurred in 1980.

One of the first political conspiracy films of the era, *Executive Action* (1973), concerns a right-wing plot to kill John Kennedy, the Democratic president of the early sixties. The film suggests that he was assassinated for being too liberal. The conservative plotters are afraid he is going to cut oil-depletion allowances, make peace with the Soviets, end the war in Vietnam, and strengthen the civil rights movement. At first, a powerful oil man refuses to join the conspiracy, but after seeing clips of Kennedy speeches in which he takes liberal positions, he joins in.

The film successfully transcodes the popular discourse of conspiracy around the Kennedy assassination that thrived in the early seventies, but it also instantiates a problem of the left-liberal conspiracy genre as a whole. The very premise of a conspiracy requires a prior assent on the part of the audience, one might say a generic assent, since it resembles the predisposition to believe that audiences must bring to formulaic film genres like the western. The ploy of the hidden conspiracy is socially critical in that it does dramatize a real aspect of power in the United States. Power must not present itself as simple power unmediated by democratic participation or by the rules of populist equality of participation or fair play. The democratic populist temper of American life obliges those in power to pretend they are not in power; they are merely representing the people and their interests. But the conspiracy ploy must turn the systemic concealment of real power structures into a personalized account of secret intrigue. Such intrigue can be shown to be for the defense of a class or of power (as in *Action*), but this strategy ultimately plays to the paranoid side of the populist imaginary, which conceives of evil in the world as personal and is incapable of conceptualizing the systemic character of power.

The discourse of distrust transcoded in *Executive Action* was extended in Alan Pakula's *The Parallax View* (1974), which deals fictionally with Kennedy-like political assassinations, and *All the President's Men* (1976), a key Watergate film. They form, along with *Klute* (1971), what has been called a "paranoid trilogy."[6] *The Parallax View* concerns a reporter's attempt to get inside an assassination bureau that operates for profit. *All the President's Men*, based on Bernstein and Woodward's book, depicts the uncovering of the conspiracy behind the Watergate affair.

Parallax depicts a society in which corporate powers kill with impunity. Joe Frady (Warren Beatty) changes from a skeptic, when a fellow reporter tells him that a political assassination was carried out by an assassination bureau, to a determined investigator of the bureau who is ultimately used by the bureau and killed. Film style and narrative structure reinforce the conspiracy theme by inducing a sense of unease in the audience, who are aware that a conspiracy is underway, though they do not know who controls it. The audience is first positioned in Frady's point of view, seeking to uncover the conspiracy, but by the end the audience is privy to the fact that Frady has been uncovered by the corporation, and by assuming the corporation's point of view concerning Frady, it in a sense participates in the conspiracy against him. Lack of knowledge is connoted by windows through which one cannot see well—at the beginning when a senator is assassinated and later when the Parallax men observe Frady from a glass booth. The word "view" in the title suggests vision or looking, and Frady shifts from someone looking for something to someone being looked at and controlled. Shifts of vision also occur in the plot; rapid reversal is a prominent narrative and editing device. A woman reporter is alive in one frame and already in the morgue dead in the next; a helpful sheriff tosses Frady a sandwich one moment and pulls a gun on him the next. Many of these events are initially presented opaquely; their causes are not evident. Low-key lighting and off-center framing make the audience aware quite literally that it is not being allowed to see or know what is really going on. The result is a sense of unease, and indeed, at the end knowledge is still denied; the viewer is left frustrated. The power of the corporation seems insurmountable. The traditional "emergence into light" convention, with its coded expectation of salvation, is inverted as Frady emerges from a darkened auditorium into bright daylight—and is shot point blank.

While *Executive Action* excessively personalized systemic wrongs, the rhetoric of *Parallax* can be faulted for exaggerating in the opposite direction. The members of the corporation are depicted as faceless businessmen, the dark lighting and extreme long shots of the concluding tribunal scene make the commission of inquiry into impersonal functionaries of corporate society. There is no recognizable enemy that the audience can identify as a nemesis or against whom negative emotion can be mobilized. In addition, architectural space and scene construction operate to make Frady seem overwhelmed by an impersonal environment over which he can have no control. Thus, the film is an exemplary rhetorical exercise in critique through negative representation, but it lacks the elements required to draw an audience into the sort of sympathetic identification with character that permits political films to be effective or to have an impact. *Parallax* may destroy the "American hero myth,"[7] but in doing so, it prevents an induction of the audience into its point of view. It is difficult to sympathize with Frady's death, because he too is depersonalized as a character. As in political allegories like *The Revolutionary*, *Parallax* may provoke the audience to think, but at the expense of making it feel. And some sort of identificatory feeling for victimization seems necessary if audiences are to be angry at the victimizers. At the end of *Parallax*, there are no victims; there are only bodies. It is not surprising that Pakula's more positive, resurrected hero film—*All the President's Men*—was more popular. That film also uses space and shadow to connote the systemic character of political corruption, but it poses against the corrupt conservative political system the brightly lit newsroom as well as the identificatory appeal of the enthusiastic newsmen.

In 1975–76, during a period when the Watergate hearings and revelations, the Rockefeller Commission, the Church and Pike congressional investigations, and reports of CIA wrongdoings were beginning to enter popular cultural discourses, Hollywood for the first time dealt critically with the CIA. Whereas *Executive Action* hinted at a secret CIA force, *Three Days of the Condor* (1975) explicitly portrays such a possibility. Robert Redford plays Joe Turner, a CIA researcher who is chased by killers because he inadvertently discovered the plans of a renegade faction within the CIA to invade the Middle East in order to protect the flow of oil to the United States. The film ends on a note of ambiguity characteristic of the mid-seventies. Turner tells his former CIA boss that he has given the story to the *New York Times*. But the man asks him if he's sure they'll publish it. The film concludes with a freeze frame of the look of uncertainty on Turner's face.

Condor adheres more closely to the conventions and formulae of the traditional Hollywood representational codes, and unlike the more intellectual *Parallax*, it situates itself within a populist framework. For these reasons, it is possible that it was more effective at promoting its ends; at least, it succeeded in being more popular (number 17 in box-office gross in 1975, compared to number 71 for *Parallax* in 1974). Like *Parallax*, *Condor* relies on uncertainty and reversal to motivate and structure the narrative. The popular attitude of distrust at the time is transcoded into a plot device; no one can be trusted in this world of double-cross and deceit (not even the *New York Times*!). What appears one way can easily be reversed. Yet, unlike *Parallax*, the narrative development along a line toward the clarification of uncertainty and a termination of reversals culminates somewhat more successfully in *Condor*. Turner, at least, finds out what's up. The all-American hero reaches a positive conclusion, even if, as is usually the case within the populist framework, institutions like the *Times* can't be counted on to come through on the side of truth and the American Way. A more conventional character construction also distinguishes *Condor* from *Parallax*. Turner's characterization is marked by down-home traits (he's out to fetch lunch when the killer first strikes), a traditional love interest, and the aura of the all-American ideal of the tinkering common man. In one scene, for example, he taps into the telephone lines of the CIA. Although at a loss at first, he is ultimately able to confound the telephone system, and the images of confused telephone circuits seem to connote the individual's triumph over bureaucracy.

Thus, the film operates within a more hopeful liberal outlook while playing to populist prejudices regarding big institutions, and the representational conventions it deploys (character, narrative, etc.) reflect that thematic. It is conceivable that the more traditional conventions helped make the film more accessible, more popular, and perhaps more effective. But the price of popularity is a diminution of radicality; the political vision of *Condor* (which includes a sympathetic portrait of a "good" CIA man, suggesting the redeemability of the institution) falls far short of the more extreme indictments of the corporate political power system found in *Parallax* and later films of the genre.

Indeed, as the decade advances, pessimism and distrust regarding the U.S. political system turn to overt cynicism. In Robert Aldrich's *Twilight's Last Gleaming* (1977), for example, a disgraced military officer attempts to disclose a secret document that reveals that the United States pursued the Vietnam War simply to maintain the "credibility" of the political and military establishment, despite authoritative intelligence reports that the war was politically unnecessary and militarily unwinnable. The president wants to disclose the document to the public, but his advisors have him and the renegade general killed. Eventually the political conspiracy genre became so recognizably generic that it gave rise to semiparodic excesses (*Winter Kills*, 1979) and to performances of the generic conventions (*Blow-Out*, 1981) devoid of the political critique present in earlier films.

Parallel to the political conspiracy films, a genre cycle of corporate conspiracy films emerged in the 1970s that critically question business institutions and values and show the interests of business to be antithetical to the public good. *Network* (1976), written by Paddy Chayefsky and directed by Sidney Lumet, is one of the first and most popular. It constitutes a cinematic extension of a growing scholarly and popular discourse about the power of the media as determiners of what will be perceived as "real" in American society. Like its predecessor, Kazan's *Face in the Crowd*, *Network* combines the styles of social realism and absurdist satire to attack both the media and corporate capitalism. A newscaster becomes an extremely popular "prophet of the airwaves," a populist critic of society who gets people to shout, "we're not going to take it anymore." Then he is converted to the ideology of corporate capitalism, the belief that "the world is a business . . . one vast and ecumenical holding company, for whom all men will work to serve a common profit, in which all men will hold a share of stock, all necessities provided, all anxieties tranquilized, all boredom amused." He preaches his new message and loses his audience. His ratings slip and he is assassinated by his corporation on the air as a promotion stunt.

Like political conspiracy films, *Network* shows the defeat of a resentful common man by impersonal large corporations, and thus, with films like *Blow-Out*, participates in the mode of populist tragedy which is pessimistic but which also operates to affirm the individual against the institution. Indeed, that representational strategy of affirmation-through-negation is a formal version of the dominant attitude of the film—populist resentment—which operates as an aggressive affirmation of the individual through a negative reaction to the corporation.

The popularity of *Network* suggests that liberals in the mid-seventies were successfully appealing to those populist themes of the culture (the small-guy hero, resentment against the system, distrust of power and big institutions) whose libertarian, individualist, traditionalist, and antiauthoritarian strains would be so well exploited by the Right later in the decade (in the form of the conservative attack on the federal government). In Michael Crichton's

By the late seventies, the traditional liberalism of the Democratic Party would cease to be able to provide answers to structural social problems.

Coma (1978), for example, the health industry is depicted as a conspiratorial and greedy monster that induces comas in order to extract organs for sale. The idea of corporate profit is successfully linked to traditionally fear-provoking elements of the popular imaginary like impersonal technology and the loss of power associated with medicine in general. Little guys are shown taking on the big guys and winning.

But liberalism also begins to falter during this period. Liberals could appeal to populist themes, but the social goals of traditional New Deal liberalism (social welfare, primarily) contradicted the populist theme of freedom from big government regulation (since social welfare required more government taxation and bureaucratic management). With the economy on the skids in the mid to late seventies, the liberals were in a jam. The limits of the populist outlook (such as its empiricism) meant that the government, not business, would be blamed for economic hardship. People could see (empirically experience) the government taking their money in the form of taxes, but the perpetrators of higher prices were invisible. And it was liberals who were most closely linked with the idea of big taxes for a big government. As a result, the Right successfully exploited the populist opposition to big government taxation to overthrow the liberals. One could vote for a new government and restore a feeling of power lost, but one could not vote for a new economic power bloc.

Something of the liberal quandary is evident in Stanley Kramer's seventies films. Kramer's work instantiates one of the problems with liberalism in general as a social program. It bases itself solely in political themes grounded in the individual conceived as an atomized, noncollective social agent. When the individual confronts the systemic character of corporate power, he will invariably be defeated; consequently, the only alternative to a naive individualist optimism for the liberal is a pessimism that is equally off-target, since it is predicated on the inevitable defeat of any individualist-based attempt to rectify systemic inequality, an inequality rectifiable only by nonindividualist structural change.

More generally, Kramer's conspiracy films evidence the limitations of liberalism that were becoming increasingly apparent in the mid-1970s. Kramer's earlier *R.P.M.* (1970) points to the inability of liberals to relate to the more radical movements of the 1960s in the story of a liberal professor's encounters with student radicalism. His next picture, *Bless the Beasts and Children* (1971) is a fantasy of children, surrogates for sixties radicals, who share values and engage in actions that a sentimental liberal can accept (i.e., fighting to preserve an endangered species, the buffalo). As the decade progressed, liberals became increasingly pessimistic about the possibilities of liberal programs and values in the political sphere. Thus, while Kramer's *Oklahoma Crude* (1973) depicts small guys triumphing over large corporations, in *The Domino Principle* (1975) large impersonal institutions win out over the individual. The ending of that film instantiates the predicament of liberalism at this time. As the hero walks alone along a beach whose expanse highlights his individuality and loneliness, he thinks about how one has to keep on struggling, never give up hope. The camera draws back to reveal a rifle pointed at him. The individual is affirmed, but the power of impersonal modern institutions (like the corporation) is also acknowledged.

Films that go further to the left point beyond the quandary liberalism got itself into in the late seventies and early eighties, when it found itself outmaneuvered by the Right in appealing to the population. For example,

The China Syndrome (1979) focuses on the corporate power structure behind the nuclear energy industry, and depicts it as putting profit before public welfare. The corporate executives are portrayed as ruthless and unscrupulous, but the film holds out the hope that a few good individuals can nevertheless make a difference against these bad individuals.

A popular film, *Syndrome* won the Oscar. It uses traditional conventions to make radical points. The narrative moves from naiveté to conviction, and the slow transformation of ordinary people into informed opponents of the corporate system probably appealed more to audiences than if the characters had begun as radicals. The model naive character is Jack Goddell (Jack Lemmon), an employee at a power plant that has almost suffered a nuclear disaster. He is encouraged by newspeople to investigate, and together they uncover wrongdoing on the part of the corporation. The film operates by situating the audience in a position of privileged knowledge. The narrative suspense that comes into play when the corporation tries to prevent that knowledge from emerging into public light is thus linked to a political position.

If our survey is to be believed, this rhetorical strategy works well: 37% indicated that their opposition to nuclear power began on seeing this film. But certain limitations need to be taken into account in interpreting this figure: 48% of our sample had not seen the film; a greater percentage of blacks than whites had not seen it; and 68% of those who had seen it earn over $30,000 a year. Clearly, the film appealed to white professionals. Still, of the 84% who, as a result of seeing the movie, believed business is willing to risk lives to make money, 23% come from working-class backgrounds. And 72% of the participants thought the movie's suggestion that business is unscrupulous was accurate; 93% of the working-class viewers chose this option as opposed to 63% of the middle-class viewers. Despite its white professional aura, then, the film still struck home with some non-middle-class viewers.

Nevertheless, *The China Syndrome* could be faulted for relying too heavily on traditional Hollywood stereotypes (the bad guys wear black). To a certain extent, the personalization of the corporate system is a necessity imposed by this particular form of narrative. It aids the enlistment of audience identification even as it misrepresents the reality. This strategy should be contrasted with that of a related film, *Silkwood* (1983), which portrays the effects of corporate malfeasance on workers without depicting the corporate bosses as ever-present, sinister, black-clad figures. The film thus conveys a greater sense of dread regarding the self-protective impersonality of corporate power. And while it offers a compelling picture of individual struggle, it does not suggest that the problems of capitalist life can be solved by such efforts. Indeed, it portrays the rather violent defeat of a purely individual initiative. Implicitly, it suggests that liberal solutions are not likely to succeed against a rapacious system whose fundamental laws are immune to liberal reform.

The one perspective that accurately represents that system—the socialist one—is itself a target of liberal criticism in a number of films like *The Formula* and *Network*. This seemingly marginal debunking of the radical alternative is in fact central to the cultural process that results in the political quandary of liberalism. For liberalism fosters the rejection of the one solution to the social problems which liberalism so unsuccessfully addresses. In so doing, liberals assure their own survival as well as their own defeat. In the American cultural context, where individualist values prevail, liberal filmmakers aid the acculturation of people to subjectivist outlooks that end up in the polling booth as votes for conservatives promoting individualist solutions to social problems. And this is indeed what would happen in the eighties, a time when a powerful counterattack by right-wing capitalists made it evident that liberal reform was a little bit like throwing a wet towel at a forest fire.

4. CLASS, RACE, AND THE NEW SOUTH

What we have called the failure of liberalism in the seventies helped undermine the Democratic Party and contributed to its overwhelming political defeats in the early eighties. Traditionally, the Democrats represent the lower income sector of the population, while the Republican Party is generally assumed to be the party of the rich and the economically powerful. The Democrats were defeated in the eighties because a large portion of their white male working class constituency shifted to the Republicans. Throughout the seventies, the old New Deal Democratic Party coalition of blacks, women, labor, and poor people had been put in disarray primarily by economic pressures that heavily affected workers and the poor. Inflation, unemployment, deindustrialization, a severe drop in productivity growth, and steadily rising net tax rates reduced the income of lower- and middle-class people, provoked increased tensions between Democratic constituencies, especially white workers and blacks, and undermined the basis of organized labor. The Democrats came to be viewed increasingly as the cause of the trouble; their tax policies, conservatives claimed, not only cut income, but also curtailed investment and jobs, while supporting unnecessary social programs funded by government borrowing (deficit spending) that increased inflation. Moreover, the Democrats were seen as incapable of handling the growing economic crisis. The party had been disunified since the 1972 candidacy of George McGovern, a left liberal who divided the party's fragile coalition of civil rights, labor, environmental, and feminist groups. The divisiveness was most evident in 1980 when Ted Kennedy ran against an incumbent Democratic president. Democrats themselves no longer seemed to have confidence in their leaders. While the Democrats represented a large coalition no one of whose members was large or powerful enough to define a single organizing agenda for the party, the Republicans, on the other hand, represented the exclusive interests of one powerful constituency—the rich. They therefore could offer a single-minded and firm program of economic renewal to increase income through tax reductions and cuts in social spending. That these programs would ultimately benefit the rich exclusively at the expense of the poor and the middle class meant little at the time. In 1980, many white working-class Democrats switched to Reagan and bought the line.

What most harmed the Democrats was the economic crisis of the period. It cut into the income of their traditional constituencies, and it made the traditional Democratic economic policy orientation toward equity and redistribution seem unreasonable. The economic crisis consisted of a persistent rise in the rate of inflation (meaning higher prices for goods) and in the rate of unemployment. Inflation went from 1.34% in the period from 1961 to 1965, to 9.68% in the late seventies, to 15% in 1980, while unemployment reached 11% by 1983. At the same time, the rate of earnings growth went from +1.8 to −1.4. People were earning less while having to pay more. Thus, between 1970 and 1980 the cost of basics rose 110%; between 1973 and 1980 there was an 18% decline in discretionary income; and between 1968 and 1981 there was a 20% decline in real standard of living among factory worker families. Moreover, the poverty rate rose above 15% for the first time in twenty years. If in 1973 most people thought things were not that bad in the United States, by 1976, after the major mid-seventies recession, polls recorded a sharp increase in fear of economic instability, and domestic concerns replaced international ones as a primary source of worry. By 1978, right in the middle of Jimmy Carter's term in office, one out of three people said things seemed to be getting worse. These developments eroded the base of the party and created hostility between its tax-paying constituents and its poor or non-tax-paying members, "hostility guaranteed to become directed against the party itself. . . . The economy was tightening like a noose around the neck of the Democratic Party."[1] Democratic "Big Government" thus became an easy target for Republican ideologues.

The Republicans' solution was a dismantling of the New Deal federal welfare state and an unleashing of a deregulated "free" market. Businesses by this time were already launched on their own solutions—destroying unions and imposing wage cuts to reduce costs and maintain profits. Those profits were going increasingly not into the maintenance of industry but into its demolition, as businesses packed up and moved either overseas or to the union-free South. U.S. economic power shifted significantly southward during the mid and late seventies as a result of the oil price boom after the OPEC agreements and the flight of northern capital to the Sunbelt. In general, business used the excuse of the recessions to impose new discipline on workers, reduce income, build opposition to government regulation enforcing racial equality, and make Americans pay for the cost of reconstructing the U.S. economy, away from the old smokestack industries of the North and Midwest and toward a service technology orientation increasingly located in the suburbs and the Sunbelt. While these changes increased the power of the wealthy by increasing their wealth (the number of millionaires rose significantly at the same time as more people entered poverty), they also eroded the support base of the Democrats in the North. And the previously Democratic South came to embrace the Republicans.

In this chapter we will look at films that deal with two major Democratic Party constituencies—workers and blacks—as well as at the development of "good old boy" New South films in the late seventies and early eighties. While

The mid-seventies witness the highest rates of unemployment the United States has seen since the Depression as well as the abandonment of America's old industrial base by corporations intent on finding profit overseas.

One immediate result of the mid-seventies recession and the unemployment and inflation it caused—a resurgence of racism by whites against blacks around such issues as affirmative action hiring and preferential treatment.

none of these films directly or explicitly represents the economic and political changes we have just described, many of them register the feelings of anger, fear, hope, and frustration that accompanied these developments. Others play to the audiences as political constituencies, offering metaphoric representations of escape that contain embedded political values. The "bad" IRS man in *Blue Collar*, the bad welfare regulators in a black film like *Claudine*, and the bad sheriff in *Smokey and the Bandit* all share one thing; they all belong to Big Government. And even if the filmmakers in each case did not intend it, those representations became part of a general cultural case that was being made by conservatives against government taxation, federal welfare, and state regulation of business.

1. The Hollywood Working Class

Working-class films are contradictory in character.[2] Most, like *Rocky, Saturday Night Fever,* and *Flashdance,* evidence a desire for transcendence of working-class life that potentially threatens the class system. But that desire to overcome the limited life possibilities which capitalism bestows on its bottom rung is generally limited to individualist forms, which tend to reinforce the founding values and the legitimating ideology of the class system. Nevertheless, the desire to improve one's lot, even in ways which reinforce the ideal of class mobility, is also indicative of more radical possibilities, for it suggests dissatisfaction with working-class life, with the limitations that capitalism imposes, and it points to the power of the need to overcome those limitations. Thus, it is the bearer of multiple, even contradictory meanings. It cannot help but reinforce the legitimacy of structural inequality, for it suggests that those who get out of the working class are better, more endowed individually, than their fellows. But it also signals the inevitability that a structurally unequal class system will generate an implacable material dissatisfaction that must be assuaged in some way if the capitalist system is to sustain itself.

Conservative films about the working class depict individual triumph, or they portray the working class world as a pigsty from which one should escape to a middle-class utopia, or they make arguments aginst unions. More liberal films question the myth of the ladder of success or show women and groups of workers rather than individuals struggling against oppression.

During this period, conservatives succeeded in convincing many white working-class people that blame for the miseries inflicted by inflation (corporate price gouging) and unemployment (forcing workers to pay for the inherent inefficiencies of capitalism) should be placed on the federal government, and in Paul Schrader's *Blue Collar* (1978), the negative protagonists are the unions and the government tax collector. While these representations seem to play to the sorts of prejudices that would conduct working-class votes away from the big government Democrats and toward the revivalist Republicans in the 1980s, the film also contains powerful images of interracial cooperation as well as of the use of racial strife to keep workers down. If the FBI did not have to be called in at the end to save a white worker from the union and from a black who sells out for a promotion, it might have been a more politically progressive film. But one thing that a sociocultural system cannot do in a sustained way is to question its operative premises. Not surprisingly, then, not a single film during this period suggests to the predominantly working audiences that there may be something wrong with a system that imposes wage labor for others' profit and one's own survival. The other conservative film about working-class struggle, *F.I.S.T.* (1978), does portray the great worker uprisings of the thirties and the brutal force used to suppress them. But it also suggests that organized labor is inherently corrupt, and in the credit sequence subliminally advertises "the right to work," a right-wing slogan of the period that referred to the destruction of unions.

While conservatives argued against unions and succeeded in bashing them into submission (union membership declined from 26% to 16% of the workforce during this period), liberals and leftists promoted unionization in such films as *Norma Rae* (1979) and *9 to 5* (1980). *Norma Rae* is significant because it depicts a union campaign then in progress against southern cotton mills; the issue was settled in favor of the unions shortly thereafter. It also gave a woman a lead role in a social melodrama, reflecting both the influence of feminism and the increase in women workers' activism during this period. Even more striking in this regard is *9 to 5*, since the three leads are women who use guile and deception to win reforms in their office. Yet this narrative ploy entails a certain political capitulation. The women's tricks would have failed if it were not for the intervention of the corporate boss, a benevolent, paternalist sort who straightens everything out in the end. "You have to keep the crew happy," he says, and the reforms the women have won have certainly made his crew happy for him. But they will also ultimately make him richer and keep the workers in their place. This collaborationist argument can be understood as an attempt to make progressive reform more palatable by suggesting that it also benefits business (as indeed it probably does). But power is left undisturbed by such tactics, tactics that characterize the labor movement as a whole during the early eighties, when givebacks and concessions were forced on labor and capital.

Even liberal working-class films thus take the world of class oppression as a given. They reinforce the assumption that it is natural and right for one small group of white men to own and control an immense portion of the wealth of a nation and to make the majority work for them. This implicit liberal capitulation to the values of capitalism and the prevalence of the individualist ethic helps account for the absence of a significant socialist alternative in the United States. The individualist ethic also accounts for the transmutation of resentment against class oppression into a desire for class mobility that ignores the structural causes of that oppression. The most common motif of conservative working-class films during this period consequently is the desire for class transcendence.

Liberal films question the template of success through individual effort, although their alternative seems to be a romanticizing of working-class life that fails to view it critically as a condition to be abolished structurally. Two films scripted by Steve Tesich—*Breaking Away* (1979) and *Four Friends* (1982)—both display the template and question it. *Breaking* seems an unabashed celebration of escape from the post–high school dead end of manual labor and meaningless marriage into the cosmopolitan world opened by higher education. But the camera lingers at the end for a moment on one of those who won't be lucky enough to "break in." *Friends* is a more overt critique of the attempt to rise on the class ladder. Those who do, disappointed by what they find at the top, return to their working-class world and their true friends. But that world is endowed with a sentimental aura that could take the conservative form of promoting contentment with oppression. The most striking example of this is *The Flamingo Kid* (1984), in which a young man charms his way into a private club, wins the heart of a rich young woman, and earns the patronage of a wealthy man. The young man almost rejects his working-class roots, but he ultimately discovers how corrupt the upper-class world is and returns to his home. Yet the film falls short of an indictment of the class system as such. It dramatizes one available instrument of those outside power who do not organize collectively—the refusal of the logic of individual mobility. The shortcoming of this necessarily limited alternative is that it must compensate for what is refused by idealizing working-class family life. The celebration of family and community has a strong appeal, but in its social context it is tantamount to putting daisies on the chains.

Conservative or populist films about individual mobility were much more popular during this period, a testament, perhaps, to strong desires to transcend an increasingly dull mid-seventies reality. The *Rocky* series offers a fantasy of transcending working-class life through individual initiative. *Rocky* (1976) depicts Rocky Balboa (Sylvester Stallone) as a palooka, a bum boxer, who gets a lucky shot at a title match against the black champion. Through faith, effort, and love from his girlfriend, he gets in shape and succeeds against tremendous odds. But the film is something more than a gratifying success story. Made during the second major recession of the decade, it transcodes white male working-class fears and desires, offering a vision of hope at a distressing time. Yet the edifying story of accomplishment just barely hides the spirit of resentful white working-class racism that motivates it. Rocky's attack against black power in the ring metaphorically mobilizes white working-class resentment of the sort that was prevalent throughout the seventies. One scene in which Rocky is obliged to give up his locker to a black contender suggests the literal, metonymic origin of that racism, at least as it appeared in the seventies, in fears of losing scarce jobs to blacks.

The subsequent *Rocky* films are indicative of changing cultural political configurations. *Rocky II* (1979) is a particularly good indicator of the pressures and growing resentments that would turn white working-class voters toward the Republicans in 1980. In it, Rocky is shown back in his old life, beset by money worries and unemployment. A black supervisor tells him that he must be laid off because of seniority rules (it was, of course, at this point in time that capitalist retrenchment for the sake of preserving profits was pressuring white workers to turn against affirmative action programs that gave blacks advantages over whites, despite seniority). Yet Rocky strives to succeed and does indeed triumph over the black champion in a rematch. As in all the films, he must overcome personal doubts, and he derives special reinforcement from family ties. The film displays the social psychological configuration which makes melodrama a favorite representational mode for many people. In melodrama, self-empowerment against strong odds seems easily available through simple faith. In a society that denies popular democracy and access to public debate, private problems assume exaggerated proportions. Thus, the sentimental tug of the melodramatic portion of the film is attached to the near-death of Rocky's wife in childbirth. The melodrama holds a magnifying glass up to the private sphere, and a similar hyperbole characterizes the fight sequence—rendered, as usual, as a mythic spectacle. Yet metonymic links tie the metaphor back to fallen reality. The material connection between the allegorized fight and the workaday world of lower-class people is signaled by the fact that Rocky goes off to the fight as if he were off to a day's work, kissing his wife goodbye. And on the way he drops in for a prayer from the neighborhood priest. Localism, a sense of territory and familiarity, is a characteristic of working-class life which the film accurately transcodes. And the fight consequently takes on the more metonymic meaning of being a defense against material threats that whites at the time were blaming on blacks, instead of on wage-lowering, price-raising capitalists.

The popularity of the *Rocky* movies (number 2 in box-office gross in 1977, number 3 in 1979, and all among the top fifty money-makers of all time) suggests that they appeal to widespread desires for class transcendence. Yet the films also indicate that such desires tend to get channeled toward the ideal of the accumulation of wealth, which merely reinforces the system of class oppression.

The desire for class transcendence frequently takes the form of physical activity like sports or dance. Working-class people in general are tracked away from intellectual power by the American educational system; consequently, physical activities like sports or dance are often their only way of breaking out of the cultural circle of class oppression. A version of the manual labor to which they are condemned is appropriately their one means of cultural escape. But the discipline required for such activities is also an internalization of guilt for one's class position, a way of telling oneself it is one's own fault and that one should work hard to overcome one's own failure and succeed. In a liberal individualist culture which denies the class character of oppression, class guilt is thus individualized, and the effort to overcome structural inequality is conceived in individual rather than collective terms.

Two major conservative films about the working class during this period— *Saturday Night Fever* (1977) and *Flashdance* (1983)—use dance as a correlate for the dream of class transcendence. Dancing, in film musicals, has traditionally served as a metaphor for the transcendence of everyday routine; it breaks through the constraints of realism, both aesthetic and social, that limit possible actions to a logic of propriety, and it inserts fantasy into the narrative of everyday actions. In contrast to everyday life, it is expressive rather than conventional. It puts in question the rule of necessity that regulates everyday life in the form of social codes of dress, work, movement, etc. For this reason perhaps, dance musicals have been traditional conduits for dreams of hope and the rise from rags to riches. Dance signals the possibility of the emergence of the altogether other within the everyday, the possibility of redemption from having to live with a reality of limited expectations.

In *Saturday Night Fever*, directed by John Badham, Tony (John Travolta) attains surrogate professional and personal gratification through dance. He is the king of the 2001 disco in Brooklyn. Content to work in a hardware store, he lives at home and passes his time with his small gang of buddies, dancing and chasing girls. Then he meets Stefanie, someone who can dance as well as he but who also has made the move across the class bridge to Manhattan, where she works in a talent agency. She makes him aware of just what a dead end his life is: "You got no class. . . . You're nowhere on your way to no place." He symbolically rejects his old world by refusing a dance contest prize he thinks was rightfully won by a Hispanic couple and travels over to Manhattan to seek her help in starting a new, class-mobile life.

For a Hollywood film, *Fever* is unusually rich in a sense of enthnographic detail. Its grainy, even seedy, urban texture and its use of high angle and long shots that bring the urban architecture into the frame, making it integral to the events, produce a sense of documentary accuracy that few other working-class films attain. Moreover, *Fever* allows one to read subcultural working-class practices like dancing both as cooptational diversions that merely support a commercial system which creates the need for such diversions in the first place and as strategies of resistance to the domination of life by that commercial system. In the film, dance is a subcultural communal activity that constitutes a temporary rejection of the imposition of the capitalist ethic of deferred gratification on the working class as well as a means of attaining a sense of self-worth denied working-class people under capitalism.

Yet *Fever* portrays working-class life negatively from the point of view of a critical cosmopolitanism. The word "shit" echoes in the working-class world of tawdry sex, violence, drunkenness, unemployment, dead-end jobs, family squabbling, disillusionment, and resentment. The film exaggeratedly portrays that world as something excremental, a waste without meaning. It is the lowest rung on a success ladder that leads through individual effort to middle-class life over the river. Color texture and cinematography elaborate this thematic. Stefanie wears white; soft light falls on her face when she and Tony first meet. She is an ideal, who even corrects her working-class English in order to make it. Tony in contrast wears the "fallen world" colors black and red, connoting sex and violence. When he finally joins her side and rejects his world, he too dons white and merits being bathed in the same soft light. When Stefanie and Tony walk in the street in the segment in which she accuses him of living a dead-end life, the symbolic bridge which connotes upward mobility looms in the background. Later, they will contemplate it together, in a scene in which he demonstrates his mental abilities for the first time, his potential for rising out of the excrement.

An ideological film of this sort works by establishing a set of oppositions between the fallen world and the redeemed world. The hero's movement from the former to the latter defines the trajectory of the narrative. If the fallen world is characterized by group loyalty, dead-end jobs, play with no external goal, family, neighborhood, incorrect English, animalistic sex, and meaninglessness, the redeemed world across the river consists of individualism, career jobs, work toward goals, deracination from neighborhood, alliances rather than family ties, corrected English, deferred sexual gratification, and meaning.

Working-class life is an end in itself; it doesn't point beyond to anything else that gives it significance. It remains bound to literality and materiality; it is unidealized. Tony's remark, "One day you look at a crucifix and all you see is a man on a cross," is important, therefore, because it suggests the evacuation of meaning from traditional working-class metaphors as well as from working-class life itself; all that's left is a literal, material thing that doesn't rise to a meaning beyond it. The problem of meaning parallels Tony's life problem. He doesn't rise to career goals; there's no ideal beyond toward which he moves and which gives his life meaning. His life is a series of episodes connected contiguously or metonymically, not a narrative moving toward a goal, a beyond that orients life into a meaningful line of development. Nonnarrative life is like literality; it has no ideal or metaphoric meaning.

Class-mobile life, on the other hand, has meaning in that, unlike the boys' life of play, it is not an end in itself. It is directed beyond its own activity toward a goal. The decision to go for a career is thus associated with metaphor, the elevation of literality and materiality to a meaning that substitutes for it and lifts it up to ideality. Tony's passage to Manhattan at the end is rendered cinematically in a highly metaphoric manner as a crucifixion and resurrection. He "dies" to his dance life, descends into the subway hell, and is resurrected into a Manhattan sunrise. An equation is established between the acquisition of career goals and the acquisition of meaning, the elevation of fallen, literal, end-in-itself materiality into an ideational substitute. A train ride is now a resurrection, but in a very real sense too, Tony must now see his life as being different, as having more meaning, as not being a dead end of play. It points beyond itself, and leaves that past literal, material, dead-end world behind entirely. The Saturday Night Fever must be doused and give way to Sunday morning brunch.

The film thus offers a lesson in the workings of ideology. Bourgeois idealization, which is associated with such metaphors as "freedom," "success," "career," and so on, operates by erasing the material underpinning of those metaphors; their literal meaning as venality, greed, exploitation, and outright murder is obliterated. The metaphoric substitution must be total, just as the cross cannot also mean something literal, like how brutal the Romans were to Jewish dissidents. So Tony's ascension to heaven cannot be allowed to be read as an exercise in crass materialist opportunism of the sort

Saturday Night Fever. Tony dies and is reborn. The idealization operative in metaphor is evident in the superimposition of the image of nature—the rising sun—on the working class boy.

being imposed as a general attitude on youth in the late seventies as the economy got worse and future prospects dimmed.

The film also displays why ideological systems are essential to social power. Metaphor is not merely an ancillary addition to a power structure that would remain intact without the metaphors. Power is inseparable from metaphor, the pervasive substitution in the culture of an ideal meaning for a literal thing. The exercise of greed and exploitation thus comes to be called "freedom" by an act of metaphoric substitution. Tony's ascension to careerism is inseparable from the elevation of literality to metaphoric meaning because buying into the system also involves believing in it, accepting its dominant metaphors and meanings, internalizing its ideological representations—that, for example, working-class life is excremental while upscale life is something higher, of a different order altogether. It is essential that the literal, material reality of the social system be substituted for metaphorically by meanings that are ideological in that they idealize the system and elicit belief in its justness. This is so because if exploited people believed the literal rather than the metaphoric version—that the upper class, rather than being better, higher beings who deserve more, are merely scavengers with an unjustifiable monopoly on wealth; that wealth is contingent, not a necessary endowment; that the working class is not a cause or ground beneath and below capital, but instead an effect of the operations of capital; that the ideological meanings of the system are opportunistic rhetorical manipulations as much anchored in materiality and literality as the provincial working-class world whose transcendence they advertise, not higher metaphoric truths emanating from the nature of things—the whole system would fall apart (or have to resort to overt force to maintain itself). Rulers can't afford to tell the ruled that they are a bunch of dumb shmucks for letting themselves be ruled so easily. The whole economic and political system depends on everyone pretending that things are otherwise.

Saturday Night Fever is interesting because it shows how this ideological process both does and does not work. It presents the ideological metaphor as if it were absolute, but it also shows the indeterminacy within the apparently uncontestable revelation of absolute truth. The bridge is the dominant metaphor of the film. Figuratively, it represents the transcendence of working-class life, the act of crossing over to the world of upward mobility. The film wants the audience to think of the bridge in that sense exclusively, as a means of getting from the lower to the higher, the material to the ideal, the static to the dynamic, literal meaninglessness to metaphoric meaning. But the bridge, in its literality, also indicates a problem in this metaphoric ideological system of thought and belief. For literally the bridge is a means of conducting working people to the drudgery of another day on the job. This literality must be sublated, excluded and replaced by an idealized substitute. That the bridge has both meanings at once, undecidably, is precisely the trouble and precisely the problem that the film overcomes by presenting the ideal or figurative meaning as the privileged one. The problem is exacerbated, however, by the boys when they play on the bridge. For in essence, they refuse both meanings;

for them, the bridge is neither a literal conduit to work nor a metaphor of class mobility. As a site of play, the bridge can mean anything; it comes to represent a potential for self-valorization, a refusal to go along with either the literal reality of work or the figurative ideal of mobility. For this reason the boy who most represents working-class "decadence" is killed while playing there. This very kind of play is most threatening to the work system and to its ideology, and it, especially, must be purged. For it troubles all systems of meaning, in particular the ideological system of meaning that endows the bridge with the higher truth of class universalism. The boys' play suggests that the meaning of the bridge is indeterminate, that one might use it for a number of different ends. But the discipline of work, like the discipline of ideological meaning, is at stake here, and in consequence, this undecidable possibility will be closed off by the main character's assumption of "responsibility" and by the imposition of the privileged metaphoric meaning. His choice of the career world confirms the ideal and ideological sense that the bridge does not lead just anywhere; it leads up.

But does it? Our deconstructive arguments so far have suggested that ideological metaphors always display their ungroundedness, much as they strain to appear grounded or absolute. What interests us about this film is that Tony's figurative class-mobile flight is hedged in by literal, material, metonymic connections, lines of dependency and reference that trouble the apparent unicity and absoluteness of its ideal meaning. His move is supposed to be purely individual, a confirmation of the individualist ideology of natural talent and entrepreneurial striving that sustains capitalism. Yet that move is a flight from something, and it is not entirely self-motivated. At one point, just before deciding to leave Brooklyn, Tony looks around the hardware store where he works. His boss has just promised him a long future with the store and given an account of how many years each one there has worked for him. They are all men in their late middle age, and Tony, confronted with the reality of his working-class future, looks appropriately horrified. His liftoff for Manhattan begins at that moment. What is striking is that it is motivated by a comparative connection to the communal fate of his fellows. This literal motive is in fact more important than the metaphoric meaning of mobility that the film privileges. It suggests metonymic connections that anchor that ideal meaning in a material reality which it pretends to transcend, but which cannot be transcended. Tony's rise to careerism supposedly leaves his working-class world behind, extracts him from the common mass and endows him with singular talents and a singular meaning, just as Christ's elevation from literal to spiritual meaning was supposedly in no way contaminated by contingent, literal historical references. Yet Tony cannot ride alone; like all escapees, the velocity of his flight is only calculable in terms of the world left behind. His escape is determined by its difference from the entrapment of his fellows. His ascent is as much a literal documentary of group oppression as a figurative elevation to ideal meaning. This duality or undecidability cannot be entirely reduced or removed. It suggests that the ideology of independence is constituted by hidden dependencies, connections to material reality that prevent the ideology from being what it claims to be. Those connections are metonymic because, rather than isolate Tony from his environment as in metaphor, they anchor him in that environment and see him as part of it.

Thus, a lateral or contiguous movement of metonymic reference operates against the vertical and elevating metaphoric idealization that the ideology of the film privileges. The attempt to negate class difference through the ideology of individualism merely affirms the recalcitrant structural character of class difference. Because escape has no meaning without a prison, the film cannot help but also point to the fact that for people like Tony to "rise," many must remain on the bottom, providing a measuring stick for tracking his ascent.

If the film displays the literality of the ideological figures of upper-class life, it also points to the figurality of what the film's ideology would like to be taken as literal or fallen—the working-class world. By representing the Manhattan world through metaphors of universal truth (death and rebirth, nature, the realization of self), it also by that very token points to the figural character of both worlds. We have seen how the trope of individual success is revealed to be a figure, not a revelation of truth, by virtue of being connected with the materiality and literality of class. It posits or creates the reality it supposedly depicts; it cannot claim to be a representation of a reality that preexists representation, that is not somehow shaped by the representations that supposedly derive from it. If the upper-class world is figurally constructed in this way, the same has to be said for the supposedly literal working-class world, which is only literal in relation to the supposedly higher ideal meaning of the upper-class world. If that meaning is nothing more than literality posing as metaphoric meaning, a construct made from rhetoric instead of an inherent natural reality, then the working-class world can no longer be conceived as a lower literal rung on that metaphoric ladder. Indeed, its presentation as a lower literal form of life must itself be seen as a rhetorical figure, a necessary construct or strategy which constituted the difference that defined the sanctity of upper-class ideals.

What we are left with is two material worlds which are undecidably figural and literal, shaped by a dominant ideological rhetoric while yet anchored in recalcitrant structured inequalities that belie the metaphoric ideals of that rhetoric. What is important is that the depiction of the working-class world in this film must be seen as a figure promoted by the upper class to justify itself. And the upper-class world, despite its metaphoric self-idealizations, is as much tied to a literality of material interests and desires as the working-class world that the rhetorical figures of upper-class ideology construct as debased for being tied to such materialities. The film, therefore, while it is an extremely successful exercise in ideological metaphorics, is also a lesson in the ultimate inability of such metaphors to transcend the metonymic literality they shape.

This is not to say that audiences, fresh from readings of Derrida, were able to call the movie's bluff. Most people responded to the film in precisely the way that the film responded to social reality—by personalizing it. When asked to select a statement that came closest to their own sense of the film, most participants in our survey chose highly personal meanings. For example, 44% (the highest percentage) chose "it's good to explore new arenas and to have a sense of direction in life." What is interesting about our sample is that it also confirms the very reality the film attempts to metaphorize into figural oblivion. Sixty-five percent thought the movie's depiction of a working-class boy's real chances was unrealistic, and this may be because of the class makeup of the audience. A larger percentage of those who had seen the film made less than $30,000, while of those who did not see it, most made over $30,000. People not only went or did not go to the movie along class lines, they also responded to it along such lines. Most of those who thought the film represented a real possibility of advancement for a working-class boy did not inhabit the working class, while almost half of those who thought it painted a false picture of class advancement made less than $30,000. Three quarters of the working-class viewers were also of this opinion, while only 24% of the upper middle class participants chose it. As one might expect, working-class people seem to have a better sense of the real limitations of working-class life than middle- or upper-class people. And the further away from that world one goes along class or income lines, the more likely is one to encounter personalized responses to films like *Saturday Night Fever*. The same can be said for political preference; 77% of the conservative participants felt the movie depicted a real possibility of advancement compared to 50% of the liberals.

By 1980, Hollywood, at least in its representation of union struggle, had clearly come a long way since 1953, when *Whistle at Eaton Falls* depicted unions as enemies of workers and advocated breaking picket lines. Hollywood does follow social trends; in the late seventies it turned a sympathetic eye on workers' problems in part because the economic recessions of the era made such problems a daily national concern. But the solutions adopted promoted a shift in the distribution of wealth in the country. As the number of poor people increased and as the country's wealth drifted upward, it was probably fitting that Hollywood should turn its attention away from working-class struggle to the upper class (*Arthur, Class, Risky Business, Trading Places, The Big Chill*). As cities became increasingly defined as black realms, whites predictably took up roost in pastel gentrified heavens, in reality and in Hollywood film. Urban realism gave way to suburban suprarealism. The self-advertisements of the rich relate very directly to the depictions of desires for class transcendence in working-class films, for they portray the goal of such desires. It is a curious conundrum of capitalist culture that the cause of middle- and working-class frustration (the shifting of wealth upward) comes to be presented both as the goal that justifies continued acceptance of the capitalist system of individualist aspiration and as the norm that evokes feelings of guilt at not having made it, of having failed as an individual. Moreover, the available political parameters limit the alternatives of action in such a way that the system manages to reproduce itself by advertising the fact that it is inegali-

tarian. But it must insist that the inequalities are individual rather than structural or class-based. This strategy is actually aided by films like *The Flamingo
Kid,* which reject individualism in favor not of class action but of family.
Thus, a romanticized and sentimental idealization of an institution whose
overemphasis in the working class is a defense against market predation substitutes for a perception of the structured character of class oppression.
Similarly, in the very popular *Karate Kid* films, which portray the overcoming
of an upper-class Goliath by a working-class David and play to populist resentment against Reagan's favored social group, tender and very liberal personal relations, as well as a fantasy romantic mediation of class differences,
resolve the structural backdrop against which the film's drama plays itself
out. Yet within the dominant, rather limited ways of addressing the issue of
class inequality in popular film culture, one can see the elements of an alternative discourse. For the desire for class transcendence, even in its individualist forms, does indicate dissatisfaction with the class system, and films
romanticizing family loyalty present images of community that are strikingly
at odds with the social ideals of competitive capitalism. These two ingredients,
we suggest, are the makings of a socialist discourse.

The subliminal presence (and potential popularity) of such a discourse
is evident in a number of youth working-class films of the eighties, when the
ideal of class mobility (the "yuppie" phenomenon) became the excuse the
Reagan era offered as a cover for a systematic demobilization of a large
number of especially young working-class and underclass people into low-
wage service sector and "temporary" employment. The obvious unfairness
of the skewing of wealth upward and the turning of expectations for lower-
class young people downward seemed to call forth films that made the conflict
between class sectors an overt theme. John Hughes's films (*The Breakfast Club,
Pretty in Pink, Some Kind of Wonderful*) make class differences the basis of
their romantic plots, and they seemed to mobilize persistent populist anger
against unjustifiable differentials in the distribution of wealth. In addition,
small "marginal" films (*Out of the Blue, Over the Edge*) continued to be an
important way of keeping alive in the popular cultural arena certain insights
regarding the problems and dissatisfactions that the cultural defenders of a
class society usually try to keep out of view or else render neutral. None of
these films overtly advocates a levelling of class differences, though one could
say that in the Hughes films particularly the metaphor of romance is undecidable to the extent that while it promotes the persistence of class differences
by suggesting that they ultimately make no difference (upper-class boy and
lower-class girl can after all overcome them as in *Pretty in Pink*), it signals a
desire for such levelling. While an effect of class oppression (the hyperbolizing
of personal/emotional over structural/rational perspectives) comes quite effectively to legitimate class distinctions, the youth working-class films made
evident that during this time the injuries of class would not succumb entirely
to conservative palliatives. If anything, their insistent presence was drawn out
even more by those very palliatives. Thus, if these films appealed to romantic
yearnings whose overwhelmingly conservative inflection in American culture

Black radical Angela Davis is a cause celebre of the early seventies. But the crucial issue of the mid-seventies in a time of recession is the harsh impact economic decline has on blacks, who suffer disproportionately high levels of unemployment.

was clear during the era, they also addressed real perceptions of the unjustifiability of class inequality.

2. Representations of Blacks

During this period, the black struggle for equality is marked by a turn away from the rhetoric of black power and toward a rhetoric of moderation. If early seventies films like *Sweetback* and *Spook* record the voice of black radicalism, mid to late seventies films about blacks come increasingly to espouse less militant, more moderate positions.[3] Some argue against radicalism and for an acceptance of the logic of capitalism as a way of improving the lot of blacks. Manning Marable has argued that the moderation of the black movement relates to the increased power of the black bourgeoisie during the seventies. Absorbed into the system as professionals, businessmen, and government officials, they turned against the more radical demands of an earlier era.[4]

The increase in moderation is accompanied by a new discourse of black pride which rejects white welfare patronage and instead calls for a push (as in Jesse Jackson's pro–black business Operation PUSH) to make blacks more self-reliant. Admirable as the ideal of self-determination might be, in the absence of communitarian values and institutions in U.S. society, and in a competitive capitalist context, the ideal easily becomes equated with "enterprise" and getting ahead on an individual basis through the acquisition of a "piece of the action." And the ideal of self-advancement in a white-dominated capitalist system must ignore the reality of structural inequality, which is unamenable to individual solutions. Self-advancement will necessarily be the privilege of the few. Black films of the seventies and eighties thus display a trajectory from Bread to Circuses, from the struggle for rights and equality to palliative comedies from which all rhetoric of struggle is absent.

The civil rights movement helped force Hollywood to address black issues in film, and the new liberalism opened up many possibilities for black directors like Ossie Davis and Gordon Parks. Along with the radical films of the era, the late sixties and early seventies witnessed the appearance of films about black life in America, some of them about the black family (*The Learning Tree*), others depicting the lives of strong black figures such as boxer Jack Johnson (*The Great White Hope*). Blacks also made their way into traditional genres like the detective film (*Cotton Comes to Harlem*) and the western (*Buck and the Preacher*). Many of these films are sardonically bitter statements against the systemic racism of American society. Some, like *Across 110th Street*, follow the rhetorical format of *In the Heat of the Night* by posing a competent black against a bigoted white superior who must learn to respect the black. Other films seek to affirm black dignity in the face of the enforced immiseration of blacks in the United States by positively portraying the everyday life of black ghetto communities (*Gordon's War*).

Eventually black films come to be dominated by the quest for dignity, and the attacks against racism disappear. This quest takes a number of forms, from the depiction of black cultural history, to urban social dramas concerning the struggle to survive, to "blaxploitation" films. In many of these films, structural racism is no longer blamed for the condition of blacks. Some even lay the blame at the feet of blacks themselves. These films are generally tales of heroic endeavor, yet some of them seem to be symptomatic of an internalization of guilt, of an assumption that in an individualist society only individuals can be blamed for not "making it." Cleaning up the effects of racism—drugs, prostitution, gambling, etc.—frequently becomes equated with eliminating racism itself.

The quest for dignity occasionally takes the form of hyperbolic or exaggerated representations of black power. Perhaps the most striking early seventies examples of this phenomenon are the blaxploitation films. They were clearly targeted for a black audience, and just as clearly they were attempts by Hollywood producers to cash in on the black movement. The films were nonetheless characterized by positive depictions of strong blacks—both male and female. For example, Pam Grier in the *Coffy, Foxy Brown*, and *Friday Foster* films is strong, efficient, and professionally competent. In *Shaft* (1971), directed by Gordon Parks, and *Super Fly* (1972), directed by Gordon Parks, Jr., blacks triumph over corrupt whites. In many of these films, however, success is achieved through extreme forms of violence. Shaft (Richard Roundtree) is a tough detective who is respected by white cops. He is hired by a Harlem crime boss to get back his daughter, who has been kidnapped by the New Jersey mafia. Shaft enlists the help of the Lumumbas, a black radical group, and carries out the assignment. The film is crucial for understanding the changes under way in the dominant cinematic discourses concerning blacks. A small businessman, Shaft argues against the radicals for a more moderate position. One could say he transcodes the emerging discourse of the black bourgeoisie for more cooperation with white capitalism. If *Shaft* points forward to the later assimilationist films that argue for an acceptance of the premises of capitalism as the basis for black dignity, *Super Fly* prefigures later films—from *Gordon's War* to *A Hero Ain't Nothin' but a Sandwich*—that depict blacks cleaning up their own house, getting rid of the drugs that frequently accompany poverty. Nevertheless, it and other blaxploitation films evoked protest in the black community, and the phenomenon quickly faded.

In the mid-seventies, the quest for black dignity was shaped by attempts to depict the everyday struggles of ordinary (as opposed to mythic) blacks and to portray black cultural history. Both of these strains evidence a desire to establish a separate black identity. While this desire results in the construction of historical narratives that connect the present with the black radical heritage and that advertise black cultural achievements, it also leads to arguments against white liberal patronage through the federal welfare system that resemble later white conservative positions. Yet the films are also generally more communal in character than films about whites. Banding together takes precedence over striking out alone. In these films one sees why blacks were more given to espousing radical positions during this era in general and why, in the U.S. Congress, the Black Caucus became in the seventies the locus of strongest resistance to conservatism and of support for socialist ideals.

The black cultural history films often recount the lives of famous black arts figures—*Leadbelly* (1976) and *Lady Sings the Blues* (1972)—or depict black sports legends, such as the black baseball leagues of the thirties—*The Bingo Long Traveling All-Stars* (1976). The absence of black radical figures from the past like W. E. B. DuBois and Marcus Garvey or Malcolm X is significant, although *Bingo Long* is distinguished by its use of an explicit, though playful, Marxist rhetoric to characterize the oppression of the black baseball players, and it refers positively to DuBois. One film—*Brothers* (1977)—breaks with the tendency by depicting the life of George Jackson, a black radical thinker who was murdered by prison guards in 1971. Nevertheless, the film assimilates Jackson's radicalism to a cultural historical format that places him in a mythic past. The film's refrain strikes a note of hopeless caution—"Any time a black leader appears on the horizon with any kind of charisma, he's cut down."

Films about everyday black life during this period espouse values of ethnic pride and self-sufficiency (i.e., *Black Girl*). The shift away from the earlier discourse of black power is highlighted in several of these films by the motif of the black radical figure who is either discredited or ridiculed. While these films did not receive the critical attention lavished on blaxploitation films, they are the fare most often shown on the Black Entertainment

Network, and thus are more likely to have an impact on black consciousness. Urban realism films like *Claudine* (1974) show blacks struggling to survive in a hostile environment. Claudine (Diahann Carroll) is a single mother who works as a housecleaner. She falls in love with a garbage man, but they cannot live together because the welfare laws won't permit it. The film argues for black dignity by demanding jobs instead of welfare. This moderate line is contrasted with the more radical position of Claudine's son, Charles, which is portrayed as self-defeating. While the film ends with a vision of black community, a happy wedding that heals all wounds, it also points forward disturbingly to what will happen to blacks later in the decade, as the heel of conservative social policy is brought to bear. For the film's argument is one that will be taken up by reactionary black economists like Thomas Sowell: welfare is bad for blacks, and racism will end only when blacks learn to accept the spur of poverty and play the game of capitalism.

The argument against black power is even more central to *Car Wash* (1975), a film scripted by a white—Joel Schumacher—which makes a moderate argument that black and minority workers should cooperate with white bosses and try to blend in with the system. The story focuses on Abdul, a black nationalist revolutionary, and Lonnie, an ex-con with kids who is trying to make good by proposing ideas to the white boss. The movie privileges his conservative approach and discredits Abdul's alternative. In addition, the film depicts how moderation is also induced by diluting politically radical resentment through cultural activities. One character ("TC") dresses nattily and adopts the persona of a comic-book hero. He demonstrates how cultural activities can become obsessive, focusing all of the person's energy on fantasy identities or on hedonistic pursuits that provide immediate satisfaction within a context of oppression. But TC also indicates how the conservative argument that blacks do not succeed because they seek immediate satisfaction instead of deferring gratification confuses a symptom with a cause. He pursues cultural gratification in response to oppression; hedonism is the result, not the source.

The film thus underscores the dual, contradictory character of cultural oppression. The vehicles of diversion that compensate for the absence of greater material wealth are not merely means of control; they can be appropriated for the sake of gaining a sense of self-worth denied by the larger society. It is a sign of the compensatory character of these activities that they are so exaggerated and fetishistic. But they are nonetheless indicative of an implicit revolt against oppressive circumstances, the laying claim to the right to an identity. TC's persona is extremely sexist, but such male self-exaggeration should be read as being symptomatic of the contradictory position of males in situations of oppression. The larger sexist society associates success with manhood, and in consequence the structural denial of success to black men particularly takes a heavy toll on their sense of self-worth. The only realm available for attaining it is culture or sexuality.

Car Wash shows mass culture to be a soporific drug, but it also points to ways in which such drugs can be catalysts—two quite contradictory things

Claudine. Righteous anger against the liberal welfare bureaucracy.

Claudine. Putting down black revolutionaries.

at once, both a cure for discontent and a poison that furthers it. Even as it provides an artificial self-identity and sense of self-esteem, it creates a sense of a right, a claim on such things. Yet increasingly in black film culture that claim was taking conservative forms. The principle of separate identity, bolstered by a narrative of a unique cultural history and allied to the principles of self-reliance that shunted aside radical positions blaming white racism, comes more and more to blend with the capitalist principle of individual self-advancement. This is particularly the case in the films of Sidney Poitier.

In his urban comedies—*Uptown Saturday Night* (1974) and *Let's Do It Again* (1975)—Poitier and Bill Cosby play working-class men who outsmart criminals to gain wealth. In *Piece of the Action* (1977) they play crooks who are obliged to help teach an unruly class of black teens and eventually aid them to become successful operators in the world of white capitalism. Undisciplined and unmotivated at first, the kids learn how to act politely, dress neatly, and get jobs. "That's what winning is," the Poitier character lectures them, "getting your piece of the action."

Thus, by 1977, a turning-point year in other sectors of American culture, the black radical rejection of capitalism seems to have given way entirely in film to an acceptance of the principles of the black bourgeoisie. Blacks should work within the system, accepting the logic of individual initiative and ignoring the structural inequalities of capitalism. One has only oneself to blame for not making it. This more positive and affirmative vision of black enterprise was probably motivated in part by the fact that during this recessionary period black youth unemployment sometimes exceeded 50%.[5] Yet the recalcitrant reality of such figures should also indicate that they depend little on individual initiative.

A further indication of this change in black cinematic culture is the work of Richard Pryor. Pryor's three concert films of the late seventies and early eighties touched on taboo topics whose repression is part and parcel with the apparent normality of racism. His comedy cut through the façade of politeness that helps cover over the realities of social oppression. Indeed, our survey found that 22% thought his concerts offensive rather than funny, and this included one-third of the white respondents and only two of the eighteen blacks who saw the films. He seemed at the time to be at the cutting edge of black cultural radicalism. Yet his later fictional films—*Stir Crazy* (1980), *Bustin' Loose* (1981), *The Toy* (1983), and *Brewster's Millions* (1985)—portray him as a reconciler of racial differences on personal terms. While these films provide positive representations of racial cooperation, they also ignore the increasingly brutal reality of life for blacks in a situation of recession and conservative economic retrenchment. Black liberalism, like all liberalism, displays its most severe limitation in that, incapable of conceiving of the world in structural terms, it resorts to personalist or individualist categories, and such liberalism is perfectly suited to the Hollywood narrative form, which privileges the personal outlook over structural representations. That Pryor has amassed so much power for making films is a positive development. Yet

The power and influence of the black bourgeoisie grows in the seventies at the expense of more radical black ideals.

it seems unfortunate that the only role for blacks in white culture is as co-medians—by now, one would think, a somewhat jaded stereotype.

In the eighties, Eddie Murphy's comedies replace Pryor's as the top money-makers. The homophobic, apolitical, hucksterish persona he projects was well suited to the active forgetfulness of significant social issues under way at the time. In a sense, there was too much suffering on the streets for anyone to want it on the screen. Consequently, Murphy's films are not al-together ideological. *Trading Places* (1983) does assume as natural a distinc-tion between black poverty and white wealth, and it seems to promote the values of capitalism. But it also enacts the illogical scenario of a black having economic power, and it thus offers both an enabling image and an implicit critique of the fact that blacks do not have such power. *48 Hours* (1982) takes for granted the legitimacy of the sort of police violence that during this time was resulting in an increased number of black deaths at the hands of police. Yet it also places a black in a position of power in relation to whites. And if classical narrative realism runs the risk of making worlds of oppression seem natural, then the comedy of *Beverly Hills Cop*, one of the most popular films of 1984–85, seems to make such worlds enjoyable. But like all ideological texts, the idealized image of racial harmony contains a counter ideological potential, since it projects a desire for a better world than the one blacks were being forced to accept by conservatives at the time.

Even though Murphy was stealing the comedy show from such whites as Dudley Moore, Hollywood was producing fewer and fewer black films by black directors. There seems to be at least a parallel between the return of conservatism to a position of dominance in American culture and the dis-appearance of the radical black position from the screen. At the same time, in films like *Breakin'* (1984) and a number of other break-dancing films, young blacks learn to do what so many of their ancestors did—dance for whites in order to make a living. One of the few significant films dealing with the issue of race—*A Soldier's Story* (1984)—was distinguished by being the only film with a predominantly black cast, but made racism seem a historical problem in the process of being overcome by setting the story in the 1940s, while Spielberg's *Color Purple* made poor rural black life seem positively suburban. The under- or nonrepresentation of blacks and other minorities, like His-panics and Asian-Americans, points to the way the "free market" of enter-tainment, like that of employment, tends to favor those with power. "Equal opportunity" simply means unequal reality, if "freedom" is the structuring rule of the social system.[6]

There are a few exceptions, like *The Killing Floor* (1984), a television film about black workers attempting to organize unions in Chicago at the turn of the century. Harry Belafonte's production *Beat Street* (1984), a sub-cultural urban hiphop musical, concerns a group of young ghetto blacks who have no future outside of music and dance. They are depicted as people with great artistic ability who are prevented by circumstances, especially lack of access to higher education, from realizing their potential. The film portrays cross-race friendships and suggests that blacks from different classes should help each other. The film is daring in that it is set in a New York City ghetto, an urban reality generally ignored in mid-eighties white cinematic fare.

Even if the earlier radicalism of the black movement seemed to have become submerged in American culture, the black movement as a whole contributed to a major shift in U.S. society at this time. It put pressure on the federal and state governments to provide welfare for poor people, including whites. That increased taxation demands on business, which was also confronted, especially in the North, by strong unions with their demands for regular wage raises for workers. The black and workers' movements combined provoked a reaction on the part of business, which pulled out of the North and fled either overseas or to the South. Thus, one could say that there is a certain deep structural relation between the working-class and black films we have examined in the last two sections and the New South films we will study in the next.

3. The New South

A major event in the post–World War II era in the United States is the "rise of the Sunbelt."[7] It has been an important factor in the rise to political power of a new, more right-wing, populist breed of Republican conservative in the eighties. When the old guard of Democratic liberals was swept aside in 1980 and 1984, bringing an end to the New Deal era of federal welfare, Keynesian intervention in the economy, and government regulation, it was executed by Sunbelt conservatives (Reagan from southern California, Bush from Houston) with the blessing of the New Right, which originated in the South (Virginia, particularly). This period also witnessed a transformation in Hollywood's representation of the South. The malevolent rednecks that populate the hills in *Deliverance* (1972) give way to happy-go-lucky good old boys like Burt Reynolds's "Bandit." We shall argue that these cinematic and socioeconomic developments are not unrelated.

The rise of the Sunbelt, which extends from southern California to Georgia, was a result of the flight of capital from the North to a southern climate with less taxation for social programs, fewer unions, and less government regulation. The rallying cry for this shift was "freedom." And what businessmen sought freedom from, frequently, was northern workers and blacks whose wage and welfare needs were a drain on profits strapped, especially in the seventies, by recession and international competition. The New South films, which often portray white individualists bucking the power of the state in the form of a sheriff, in some respects articulate the ideology of the region, the resistance to any state authority that interferes with the freedom of movement of white male businessmen in particular. But the films also clearly appealed to a nonregional population. Eastwood's redneck and Reynolds's Bandit films were some of the most popular of the late seventies. One possible explanation is that the shift to the Sunbelt itself placed such economic pressure on people elsewhere that films advertising either resentful aggression or limitless freedom had a certain therapeutic appeal. It is one of the par-

The rise of the sunbelt—a crucial factor in the shift of power away from northern liberalism and toward southern and western conservatism in the eighties.

adoxes of American film culture that the site most responsible for that hardship should become a locus of idealization for those beset by it.

Burt Reynolds's Bandit is the product of a long line of development
extending back to moonshine movies like *Thunder Road* whose most significant
change is marked out by the "Gator" films of the mid-seventies. In *White
Lightning* (1973) and *Gator* (1976), it is clear that the Old South will not be
able to resist the spirit of cosmopolitanism and modernization that accompanies the economic growth of the era and the shift in population from a
liberal North to the Sunbelt. Indeed, they point to an emerging contradiction
in American culture as a whole between a residual ideology of individualist
freedom, which permits conservatism to triumph in an economic sphere run
on competitive principles, and an emerging set of more liberal values regarding such social issues as sexuality. This contradiction will mean that even
though southern-based capitalist politicians can take control of the economy,
they will be incapable of turning back the process of social liberalization
initiated by the sixties. That contradiction is already evident in the Gator
films.

White Lightning and *Gator* both feature Burt Reynolds as Gator Mc-
Kluskey, a local good old boy who runs moonshine for a living but who
ultimately sides with the forces of the "progressive" New South against representatives of the corrupt and parochial Old South. In *White Lightning* Gator
agrees to help the feds get evidence against a corrupt county sheriff by
insinuating himself into the local moonshine business. The film's narrative
enacts the struggle between the Old and the New Souths. The sheriff is a
conservative throwback who was responsible for the death of Gator's brother,
a leader in the antiwar movement. The sheriff permits crime and profits from
it. One of his cronies insists "it can't be the way it was" any longer, but the
sheriff tries to make sure that isn't so. Gator represents an aspect of the Old
South emerging into the New. He rids himself of his localist loyalties and
takes sides with the federal government against states' rights, the principle
used in the southern states to justify continued policies of racism. He is also
a friend of blacks and is linked positively to the antiwar protestors.

The social liberalism of the film stands in contradiction to the implicit
male individualist ideology of the car-chase adventure format. That conflation
of a residual ideology and emergent liberalism on social issues is evident also
in the sequel, *Gator*. Like *Lightning*, the film is an argument against the Old
South, this time represented by a redneck crime boss who exploits blacks
and young girls. Gator is once again a transitional figure who is able to enter
the old world but who ultimately sides with the northern liberals. The tran-
sition from old to new is signaled by the two songs that open and close the
film. The opening song is a country and western anthem to Gator that glorifies
him as "the meanest man that ever hit the swamp"; none of the macho
imagery applies to the funny, sweet character Reynolds plays. The closing
song, a pop tune lacking the country flavor of the first, is about the fleetingness of modern love relationships—"I won't cry because you were mine

for a little while." Because his girlfriend wants a career, Gator and she split up in the end.

By 1980 Reynolds had left behind all the moonshine, swamp-boating trappings of the Old South which still were part of his persona in the mid-seventies and become the more modern good old boy Bandit, a driver of fast cars, a chaser of faster women, in some respects the prototypical New South figure: though somewhat cosmopolitan, he is nonetheless a defender of the country against urban elitism. He is also a populist individualist whose revolt against the state probably appealed to conservatives and whose disrespect for wealth probably struck a chord with "new collar" people. His tremendous popularity (both in the film and with audiences) seems due to his apparently limitless freedom. His folkloric reputation consists of being able to do what is forbidden others, most notably breaking the law and making fools of law enforcers. His life seems unrestrained by economic factors, and his sexuality is free from repression or domestic constraints. The Bandit is a narcissist who disregards social convention. Like so many folk outlaw heroes of the past, he can be interpreted either as a projection of desire that vents frustration or as a focus of popular resentment against public authority.

The *Smokey and the Bandit* films (1977 and 1980) are probably most significant as testaments to the importance of the Sunbelt as a cultural metaphor in the late seventies. As a result of the economic crisis devastating the North, the New South had become a site of escape, where workers could travel and seek jobs with the oil companies that had absorbed much of the nation's spare wealth after the early seventies Arab oil embargo (as in *Urban Cowboy*). And the illogical and senseless comic motifs of the films (racing across states to win a bet to deliver hundreds of cases of Coors on time) were an ideal entertainment mode for people burdened by the brutal logic and sense of necessity that were coming increasingly to dominate everyday life. They should be understood as twins to a film like *Take This Job and Shove It* (1981), about northern Rustbelt workers who take over and run their plant when it is threatened with shutdown.

Whereas the Bandit is a figure who combines a number of different ideological motifs spanning class differences, the sympathetic redneck played by Clint Eastwood in *Every Which Way But Loose* (1978) is a country proletarian who earns a living through bare-knuckled boxing matches in vacant lots. Yet he also is a figure of individualism, and whereas in Reynolds's southern films that ideology is characterized by a celebration of freedom, in *Every Which Way* it is marked by a defensive, bellicose, and resentful spirit. In Philo's world, loyalty and family are crucial as defenses against an aggressive and violent public realm. The little enclave of tenderness and compassion Philo shares with his family and his chimp is hemmed in by violence and betrayal.

This duality between public aggressiveness and private sentimentality is characteristic of the divided ethos of a culture riven by economic crisis. For this reason, the film is historically symptomatic. The resurgence of hyperbolically sentimental melodramatic and suburban fantasy films during this period is a cultural counter to the jungle survivalism of the emerging new conservative economic order. The sentimentalized private arena of family and romance is a balance to the public world where relations between people lose all emotional and trustful ties. The great popularity of *Every Which Way* (number 2 in 1979, right behind *Superman*) probably means that its dual vision appealed to over-pressured working people desirous both of a head to crack and of a lap to lean a world-weary head on. If the film did play accurately to the needs of the white male working class, then it is not surprising that it went for a Republican candidate in 1980, one offering both a bare-knuckled program for economic renewal and a set of sentimentalized ideals (family, faith, patria) that satisfied the sorts of emotional yearning that are central to this film.

Even within clearly ideological artifacts that seem to play directly into conservative politics, however, evidence of pro-socialist potentials can be found. Neurotic and skewed as the forms they assume may be, desires for community, trust, and cooperation still seem to be necessary counterweights to the brutality of the market. And the segregation of affection and aggression, the private and the public spheres, is shown to be tenuous in a film like *Every Which Way*. When Philo speaks of love, he uses the metaphors of the market (Royal gelatin). When he enters the market world, it is to find love, and he brings with him a surrogate companion in the form of the chimp. The high level of faceless aggression seems balanced equally by a high level of intimate interaction. And when Philo finally faces his ultimate challenge in the public market, he deliberately loses out of respect for and loyalty to his aging opponent. The firm boundary between two spheres (the emotive family and the aggressive market) that is crucial to a conservative social structure thus begins to seem more a tenuous construct than a reality. It testifies to the necessity of maintaining a non-affectionate, bare-knuckled attitude in a public world dominated by the conservative principle of survivalism; in such a world, communitarian altruism leaves one vulnerable to attack. Thus, the concentration of sentiment in the private sphere results from constructing the public world according to conservative principles; it is a defense against that world as well as a repository for all the emotions that must be purged from the public world in order not to be vulnerable in it. But the film also suggests that the public world attitude of bare-fisted aggression can be modified by the private sphere values of trust, loyalty, and affection. The film is less a celebration of the market than a depiction of the neutralization of its principles. It points to the fact that pro-socialist desires for community operate in a buried and unrealized form even in the most apparently conservative social and cultural forms. And it demonstrates how popular film often enacts a breaking down of the boundaries that maintain social order. Indeed, one suspects that without such therapeutic fantasy enactments of breakdown, social order could not be maintained consensually.

Every Which Way articulates the contradictory double politics of American populism, which evidences reactionary as well as progressive possibilities. It can breed fascism, but the fascism it breeds should be read as a symptom of desires for community and security that can also take socialist forms. In an

economic system that celebrates aggression, the insecurities fostered by economic downturns are likely to take aggressive, fascist forms. There is a logic
to the emergence of fascism out of capitalism in that the former is simply
the latter carried to its logical extreme. But this also relates to the socialization
of males to be the competitive aggressors in such a social system. If Philo is
threatened by other males, he is also threatened by a woman who betrays
him and makes him feel small. The insecurity of economic recession is also
a sexual insecurity, especially since male sexual power is socialized to be
equated with making it economically. Thus, the film puts on display the salient
psychological, economic, and sexual factors that account for the enlistment
of populist energies into right-wing politics. That the film appeared in 1978,
at a time when American culture was beginning to evidence more strikingly
conservative themes, is therefore important.

A study of New South films suggests why the Republicans triumphed
and why the Democrats fell apart in the eighties. If films at all register cultural
moods by appealing to audiences, then it is significant that on the eve of
Reagan's electoral victory (1979) the top three films were about strong white
males (*Superman, Every Which Way, Rocky II*). All three espoused populist,
ruralist, white male values and virtues; the latter two directly appealed to the
constituency of traditionally Democratic working-class voters that would assure Reagan's victory. The films record the cultural tendency that gave rise
to the political inevitability. They suggest that white male workers were angry
about something, frustrated in their world, seeking hope, deliverance, and
redemption. They got it.

Yet it would be a mistake to blame workers for the rise of the Right. If
they voted Republican in 1980, it was generally out of a desire for economic
recovery; the Republicans had captured the dynamic image of Keynesian
economic stimulation by inverting it in favor of capital, but they still promised
prosperity and growth, an appeal likely to resonate with those suffering from
the frustration of a Democrat-managed stagflation. Moreover, as inflation
put money in the coffers of conservatives, which they used to fuel their
political campaigns, it buckled and disabled the working class. As Mike Davis
argues in *Prisoners of the American Dream*, a minority of 26% of the electorate
was able to elect Reagan because of the "prior exclusion and disorganization
of the majority," not because of its "conversion to a new ideological agenda."[8]
And the Democrats, who themselves from 1978 on turned increasingly to
the right, forsaking their New Deal heritage and calling for "reindustriali-
zation" in a new corporatist social order, were themselves responsible for
ceding the political terrain to the Republicans. The victory of the Right in
1980 was really the result of a revolution on the part of the white middle
class against the one accessible prong of the double squeeze on their incomes—the liberal federal government. Workers and blacks suffered most
from the new hourglass income structure that resulted. Their wages were
cut, their social power demolished, and their work menialized.

Yet what should be underscored is that this middle-class revolution was
in part a response to gains made by the workers' and black movements in

Economic recession in the mid-seventies begins to pave the way for a right-wing resurgence later in the decade by generating resentment, fear, and anguish.

the sixties and seventies. If upper-class capitalists and the white middle classes who had tied their security to faith in the capitalist system were running scared by the late seventies—to the point of mounting a conservative revolution against social welfare, unions, and racial equality—it was because black militancy had put a strain on welfare taxation at the same time that worker militancy forced wages higher. A similar point could be made regarding the violent reaction against feminism that occurred during this period.

5. THE POLITICS OF SEXUALITY

One of the most powerful forces reshaping American culture in the seventies and eighties was the feminist movement. Initially characterized by radical gestures of rejection and separation from male domination, in its purest form feminism described all male sexuality as exploitative and turned to lesbianism as an alternative. As the seventies proceeded, the movement came to focus on issues of economic and political power, as well as on such sectoral concerns as rape and pornography which many feminists saw as essential to the exercise of male domination over woman. The movement found itself in the late seventies and early eighties divided between radical groups which were powerful in the world of intellectual culture (signaled best, perhaps, by such publications as *Ms.*, *The Woman's Review of Books*, *Signs*, and *Feminist Studies*) as well as in local subcultural arenas and a mainstream sector content to equate sexual equality with acceptance into the male professional business world. By the late seventies the phenomenon of the "professional woman" had eclipsed the earlier popular image of the feminist as avenging Amazon. The movement faltered somewhat in the early eighties in the face of conservative counterattacks, often violent in character (the bombings of abortion clinics), centering on abortion and the Equal Rights Amendment. Despite the conservative backlash, however, it was clear by the mideighties that feminism had succeeded in transforming American life. Like the civil rights movement and the student radical movement, it had shifted the parameters of public discussion, obliged conservatives to accept as givens certain rights and principles which had hitherto been denied or rejected, and established a strong presence in American public and intellectual life which had to be contended with.

Avoidance and denial were the first responses to feminism in a film industry dominated by men. The challenge to patriarchy appeared more in the form of an absence that defines the tenor of crisis-film metaphors than in the form of something actually present on the screen. Yet when men got the wagons together in a circle of buddy films in the early seventies, one suspected something was provoking their anxiety, although the band of bra-burning renegades remained below the Hollywood horizon—so threatening, apparently, they could not even be looked at. It was not until after 1977, in

The womens' movement bifurcates in the seventies into a more liberal or radical sector that promotes equality and opposes oppression, and a mainstream sector that favors integration into the male world.

the "women's film" revival, that Hollywood film came to examine some of the issues raised by feminism, although only a few of the films made could be called feminist. And no film, to our knowledge, dramatizes the feminist movement, although *Rich and Famous* presents a bourgeois version. Yet, as in crisis films, that movement is the object of reaction through indirection. Many neoromance and family films of the late seventies and early eighties project positive representations of mothering males while portraying women as in need of a strong male arm to lean on. At the same time, independent women are depicted negatively as neo-*noir* spider women or stigmatized as homewreckers. These representational reactions should be read, we would argue, in relation to the broader cultural backlash against feminism unleashed by the Right in the late seventies, a backlash that called for a defense of the traditional family, the abolition of abortion, attacks on gay rights, and the curtailment of government support of birth control for young and lower-income women.

1. The Position of Women

Women are constructed as subordinate subjects by cultural representations. In the seventies, feminist critics argued that women were positioned by cinematic representations as emotional, domestic, and dependent.[1] In addition, feminist film theorists argued that male cinema was inherently voyeuristic and scopophilic; women were positioned in the Hollywood tradition as objects of male pleasure. Male stereotypes paint women as unable to relate rationally to the world, an incapacity that takes the form of images that connote psychological immaturity and an inability to differentiate objects or to relate to the world objectively. If the fuzzy emotional world of domestic melodrama traditionally belongs to women, so also does the crazy, crossed world of the screwball comedy, as well as the extremely undifferentiated shadow world of the *film noir*. Women are portrayed as rule-breakers, crossers of legitimate boundaries. They are also positioned as fetishes of male desire, passive confirmations of male power. Some feminist critics noticed a deconstructive potential in these representational strategies. If women were depicted as boundary crossers, it was possibly because they threatened the order of legitimacy and propriety males needed to maintain if their social power was to remain intact. And if women had to be reduced to sexual fetishes, perhaps it was because they represented a threatening sexual power or difference (the absence of the phallus) which males needed to disavow if their narcissistic psychosexual integrity was not to be punctured.

When women have had access to the power of representation they have often represented their lives in ways quite different from the ways promulgated by men. The differences are marked out clearly in *Mildred Pierce* (1945), a celebrated "women's film" which was in part scripted by a woman. The woman's sections of the film consist of highly realist, well-differentiated, "mature" representations of Mildred as an independent woman who leaves her husband and becomes successful in business. But a man did the final script, and his major contribution was a *film noir* frame that associates Mildred's independence with a crime against patriarchy. The *noir* style blurs distinctions between objects, suggesting the breakdown of clear moral boundaries, and connotes immaturity on the level of representation by suggesting that women are excessively emotional, irrational, and immoral. Thus, what seems for women to have been a positive crossing of patriarchal boundaries, especially the separation of the private from the public spheres, is for men seen negatively as a transgression of the law.

Consequently, how women are represented and who does the representing are crucial political issues. We will take up the question by comparing a number of films about women's lives made during this era. Our focal concern will be the differences between male and female representations of women. And we will address some of the major issues of concern to feminist film theorists during the period—whether there is such a thing as a "patriarchal form," whether women employ forms that are by virtue of socialization significantly different from men's, and whether the traditional Hollywood forms used by men are appropriate to women's lives and issues, or whether women need to create altogether different forms appropriate to their own voice.

The seventies were distinguished by films about women's lives by male filmmakers, from Martin Scorsese (*Alice Doesn't Live Here Anymore*) to Paul Mazursky (*An Unmarried Woman*). By the eighties, more and more women directors, from Susan Seidelman (*Desperately Seeking Susan*) to Donna Deitch (*Desert Loves*), were making films that focused on such issues as lesbian love, domestic violence, and liberation from patriarchy. Men's films tend on the whole to impose either mythic or dichotomous schemes of representation on women's lives. If indeed men have been socially constructed to be rational and schematic, as opposed to emotive and contextual, then there is a symptomatic appropriateness in this fact. The dichotomy imposed most often on women by male filmmakers is that between career and marriage or love. The choice is usually either between work and children or between a vulnerable public life and male protection. Each of these oppositions is socially significant. The first is predicated on the allocation of child-rearing and domestic labor to women in patriarchal societies, and the second on the actual fact of male violence against women which in part results from the monopolization of the competitive public sphere by men. In the tradition, independent women are usually domesticated (with forties films like *Now, Voyager* being the most famous examples), and the thematic construction of an interior, domestic sphere as the one appropriate for women is frequently conjoined with certain formal (usually melodramatic) properties that execute a similar function. A sense of closure at the end of the narrative suggests that there is no beyond that need concern women; the plot and dialog generally revolve around personal rather than public issues; the spaces in which action occurs are usually circumscribed, suggesting domestic limits; camera framing portrays women as relational rather than independent; and the use of beautiful actresses and frequent intimate close-ups tends to reinforce a sense of women as objects of male desire. This history provoked feminist film theorists during this time to contend that the very apparatus of Hollywood narrative film form, the way it creates a sense of narcissistic continuity or unity between male spectator and film spectacle, actualized a misogynistic social structure, whereby passive women become the sites upon which male power is validated. Hollywood form is inherently patriarchal. If this constitutes a sort of visual violence, other film theorists, such as Joan Mellen, have pointed to the high incidence of acts of actual violence, including rape, against women in Hollywood films, especially in films made during the period of reaction against feminism in the seventies. Such renewed violence seems due in part to a reaction by men to women's escape from domesticity and subservience.

A number of films of the early seventies engage these themes, examining women's attempts to live in the public world. Made for the most part by men, they generally conclude with a restoration of traditional domestic order. One of the first films of the seventies to foreground a woman's life problems, *Klute* (1971) is symptomatic of its historical moment in that its title is the name of a male character, yet the film primarily concerns a woman. Jane Fonda plays Bree Daniels, a young woman who wants to make it as an actress and model but who chooses to be a prostitute in order to survive economically. She lives independently of men until she meets Klute (Donald Sutherland), a detective from a small town in Pennsylvania, who is looking for one of her customers who has disappeared. She helps him, and eventually gets sexually involved and falls in love. The killer of the man for whom Klute is searching is a businessman named Cable. He tries to kill Bree, but Klute saves her. In the end, they leave her apartment, which has become symbolic of both her independent life and her vulnerability as a public woman, apparently heading for hometown Pennsylvania, where they will presumably settle down together.

Despite its traditionalist and even prefeminist conclusion, *Klute* critically dissects the cultural stereotype of the happy suburban family and offers a somewhat positive picture of an autonomous and sexually independent woman. The clean, polite family dinner at the beginning of the film is shown eventually to harbor murderous desires and crimes and to be not all that distant from the urban nightmare that it seems successfully to keep at bay. Even if it is presented through the refracting filter of her role as a prostitute, Bree's open sexuality marks a breakthrough for the depiction of women in modern Hollywood film. Bree's sexual freedom and emotional honesty (which are made a verbal motif through the repeated and obsessional playing of a tape of her voice by Cable) contrast with the murderous repression of the businessman killer.

The motif of the taped voice points out an antinomy in the way women are positioned socially by men. Bree's voice placates male sexual anxiety; it is partly coaxing and partly soothing. Yet male violence is also elicited by it. This double character suggests the dual reality of women's social positioning. Their training in the soothing role of domestic caretaking is shadowed by the threat of male violence in the nondomestic sphere. The soothing voice on the tape brings together those two exclusive yet conjoined realities. It is a figure for woman's role as caretaker; yet it also is defensive in that the act of soothing placates an anxiety that threatens to become violent against the woman if she ceases to soothe and to allay male fear. What this suggests is that male public violence against women (in both its real and symbolic forms, rape as well as representational debasement in film) lurks within the private, domestic sphere, where it is soothed and allayed. Woman's role as caretaker is less a choice than the result of coercion, of the permanent possibility of violence that is embedded in her caretaking as the anxiety such caretaking assuages.

The symmetrical structuring of the characters in the film brings the point home, so to speak. There are two women and two men as primary characters. One woman is a wife who is missing a husband, who is lost in the public sphere. The other woman lives in the public sphere, also without a husband. But in the end she relinquishes the public for the private and finds a potential husband. At first untamed and isolated in the frame, in the end she is domesticated and subordinated within the frame. The two men shape the trajectory of her change. One represents male public violence against women. The other, who represents male protection, emerges from the private sphere into the public, removes the public male threat, and returns to the domestic world with a wife. Just as the two women seem minted from the same ore of female socialization, so also the two men seem to be two aspects of the same male project in regard to women. One punishes public independence while the other rewards the assumption of the proper domestic role with protection. But it is protection from essentially the same man.

Therefore, the film works from the perspective of an unstated opposition between independence and paternalist coupleship, and its rhetorical argument is in favor of the latter. Though Bree is more a victim than a failure, there is a note of failure in the final scene, when she abandons the apartment that symbolized her independence. A number of women's films of the era portrayed women as incapable of gaining independence or as neurotic and self-destructive (*A Safe Place, Play It as It Lays, Images, A Woman under the Influence*), and it is also possible to read *Klute* from this perspective.

Martin Scorsese's *Alice Doesn't Live Here Anymore* (1974) differs from earlier woman films in that it depicts a woman both struggling to become independent and being supported by other women. Alice (Ellen Burstyn) is left on her own when her husband dies. She decides to move away with her ten-year-old son to try to realize her dream of becoming a singer. The film details her attempts to live without a man. Although the film was directed by Scorsese, many women collaborated, and there is frequent evidence of their perspective in the film. For example, a major subplot is the developing friendship between women from different worlds who at first do not understand each other (the motif that becomes the basis for a successful TV show of the era).

The film, however, depicts Alice as failing in her attempt to live alone. Her first love affair turns out badly when she discovers the man is married and a violent brutalizer of his wife. She barely escapes attack herself. Finally, a fairy-tale rancher rescues and "conquers" her, while taking her to task for not disciplining her son properly. This ending is foreshadowed by the opening scene, a grandstand vignette of Alice as a young girl walking home along a country road singing. The vignette situates her dream of becoming a singer as an unreal fantasy. *Alice* concludes with mother and son walking along a neon strip toward a sign that reads "Monterey," the name of the place they had been striving for before being waylaid by economic necessity and hogtied by romance. This scene is, like the opening vignette, a sign of the artificiality of dreams. Both are situated outside the boundaries of the film's narrative, whose extremely realist style evokes an attitude of grim realism toward the world, which seems impermeable to a common woman's dreams of success.

The issue of career vs. love or marriage was so important during this era because women were increasingly moving into the workforce. Without a national daycare system or a rational social consciousness regarding male parenting, that move raised problems for many women. Entry into the work world also proved more hazardous than women initially might have expected. Women were generally given jobs that paid much less than men's jobs, so much so that "69" (cents for women for every man's dollar) became a common women's movement button, and the struggle for comparable worth (equal pay for equal jobs) became a major issue of the late seventies and the eighties. Moreover, the move into corporate life gave rise to a new phenom-

Alice Doesn't Live Here Anymore. The opening vignette sets the little girl's dream of being a singer within a fantasy landscape, the cinematic world of Dorothy in *The Wizard of Oz.*

Alice. The dream again at the end, its artificiality now reinforced by the fact that it has become a sign.

enon—the corporate woman who bought into the conservative male-identified system of capitalism. Images of "strong" women could no longer easily be equated with either feminism or political rectitude. Jill Clayburgh's strong women of the late seventies, in films like *First Monday in October*, in which she plays a conservative Supreme Court justice, or *It's My Turn*, in which she plays an upper middle class professional who "goes for it," are paradigms of this particular form of feminism. The phenomenon became more evidently questionable in the mid-eighties, as Elayne Rapping notes, in films like *Marie* (1985), in which a strong woman's success depends on the "successful" incarceration of black women welfare "cheats." The strength of such women often seemed to owe more to Ronald Reagan than to Betty Friedan or Kate Millett.

Not all men's films about women in the seventies oblige women to choose between career and love. *The Turning Point* (1977), one of the new updated melodrama revivals of the period, explicitly engages the issue by staging a conflict between one woman who sacrificed career for marriage and another who sacrificed marriage for her career, and the film attempts to resolve the issue in a way that does not privilege marriage. *Julia* (1977) also positively represents both a woman who chooses marriage and one who chooses public life. Yet each of the films evidences a male perspective. In *Turning Point*, the two women engage at one point in a clumsy "cat fight" that would have been high drama if it had involved two men, while *Julia* is marked by woozy flashbacks, hazy tones, and a lace-fringed emotionality in the voice-over narration that is equally "feminine" within the dominant cultural representational code for women.

Male representations of women, even well-intentioned ones, must necessarily look on women's lives from outside, and they often conceive of women's liberation as consisting of gaining (or deciding against) access to the traditional male realm of work and public endeavor. If early seventies male films suggested that women couldn't make it in the big world without male patronage, mid-seventies films began to permit women a bit more independence and power, although these films generally concentrate on upper-class women, ignoring the issues of daycare, abortion, and subsistence that faced many other, especially poor and black, women. Films directed or scripted by women do touch on such issues as domestic violence, and they also tend to show women more subjectively, less as objects of conquest and more as agents of life struggles. Comparing a male film like Paul Mazursky's *An Unmarried Woman* (1978) with a women's film—Claudia Weill's *Girlfriends* (1978)—also broaches the question of representational style or form—whether or not there is a woman's form that is distinct from the form men are socialized to practice. Is there a closure-oriented, voyeuristic patriarchal form that is opposed by a more open-ended, non-scopophilic form appropriate to women?

In Mazursky's film, Erica (Jill Clayburgh) is a happily married housewife whose husband leaves her for a younger woman. Although initially disabled and distraught, she manages to make it on her own. The early parts of the film sympathetically depict her struggle to survive alone, although her major concerns seem to be more romantic than anything. The group of women friends is portrayed as an empathetic enclave from a fairly mean world of sexual predation.

The male perspective of the film appears most clearly in its insistent focus on Erica's relations to men. All of her significant choices are posed in terms of men. It is indicative that the film's title situates her as out of wedlock to a man, not as being a subject in her own right. From the male perspective, the resolution of the "problem" of being "unmarried" and of having to go out with unhip guys is to meet a really hip guy, an artist played by Alan Bates whose mellifluous ruminations through the last quarter of the film turn Erica into a silent, slack-jawed gawker at his brilliance. While he paints and talks, she cooks breakfast. In the end, she decides to live alone, although in this too a male model of nonrelational, decontextural independence seems to prevail. In part, Erica's feminism consists of adopting certain male postures. She is not represented as confronting any of the everyday life problems that non–upper–class divorced or independent women face—daycare, work, unequal treatment, etc.—and she certainly is not shown struggling for something like equality. The male perspective also displays itself in the voyeurism and objectification of the scenes where Clayburgh prances seminaked through her apartment.

An Unmarried Woman successfully expunges all radicalism from feminism and repackages it as a "new woman" or "corporate" feminism which equated liberation from patriarchy with enlistment in its ranks. It is significant that the film appeared in 1978, since, as we have noted, around that time an important shift seems to occur in American culture; just as more movie theaters moved to white suburbs beyond the reach of the carless urban underclass, so also films themselves became more concerned with suburban dwellers, or those who lived high above the city streets. Erica's version of angst is to gaze down from her penthouse, pensively sipping white wine.

Claudia Weill's *Girlfriends* is quite different in style, characterization, and theme. Weill made her film as an independent, and whereas Mazursky's film reflects the high production values of mainstream Hollywood, Weill's displays all the roughness of a low-budget production. While this has its drawbacks (characters walking out of the frame and almost knocking the camera over), the film's lack of slickness also lends it a greater sense of proximity to lived experience. It is much less continuous in its image construction and less oriented toward drama in its narrative than *Unmarried Woman*. It catches the episodic quality of life, with all of its metonymic disjointedness, as well as the lack of firm dramatic boundaries between those episodes. Thus the economic power of men makes a significant difference on the level of style, but Weill seems to derive advantages from that shortcoming. Indeed, it becomes a playfully reflexive motif at one point when the electricity fails in an apartment and the soundtrack music conks out.

Girlfriends also suggests that women do indeed represent the lives of women differently from men. The story concerns two young women, one of whom, Susan, is an aspiring photographer, while Linda is a writer who marries and has a child, to the detriment of her work. Unlike Erica, who hangs out with artists (all men), Susan is an artist. Thus, the woman filmmaker accords a greater subjectivity to her character. Moreover, unlike the women's group in *Unmarried Woman*, which discusses primarily romantic concerns, women's friendship in *Girlfriends* focuses primarily on issues of work and survival. One woman friend advises Susan on how to succeed in her work by advising her to be more aggressive. And Susan and Linda discuss their feelings for each other, not for men. Finally, Weill refrains from ending on the sort of false note of hope and optimism that concludes Mazursky's film (Erica's decision to live alone). Linda's husband returns to break up the friendly encounter and reconciliation between the two "girlfriends." Men represent an outside, an other that intrudes, rather than a secure peg one can finally hang one's wayward life on.

Weill's film invites comparison with *Independence Day* (1982), an exceptional "minor" film scripted by Alice Hoffman that explores a scarcely-ever-represented reality of domestic violence. *Independence Day* concerns a young woman who decides to leave her small-town home to go to an urban art school. Portrayed as sexually independent, she actively pursues a young man, who becomes her lover, then befriends his sister, a housewife who is brutally mistreated by her husband. The film emphasizes the young woman's relationships to others—the dying mother she does not want to leave, the housewife whose plight she tries unsuccessfully to alleviate, the boyfriend she loves but whose desires she won't let keep her from her artistic goals. And it dramatizes her sense of entrapment between a feminist-age desire to have an independent career and her desire to stay with her family. A negative parallel is established between the independence of the young woman and the brutalized dependence of the housewife. The film suggests that the housewife's victimization is in part the fault of her own fear, in part the fault of a social system that obliges women to accept domestic domination because they are "one husband away from the poverty line." It ends with parallel acts of redemption: the housewife blows up her husband, using the symbol of her torment—a match—and the young woman escapes and proves she is strong enough to live alone.

The film is distinctly metonymic in its approach, and, along with *Girlfriends*, it raises the issue of whether or not female socialization gives rise to a representational form that differs significantly from the dominant patriarchal forms. Both films seem to represent women in ways closer to female socialization in that their drama relies on the exploration of relations, and both seem to appropriate traditional male self-representations (autonomy, activity, etc.) for women. If *Independence Day* suggests that women conceptualize women's lives differently, more metonymically, *Girlfriends* suggests that traditional "patriarchal" forms such as meaningful resolution, narrative closure, and nonrelational character construction can be given feminist inflections. To a certain extent both films transcend these distinctions. The young women of *Girlfriends* and *Independence* are presented as capable agents who lay claim to an identity separate from that the culture imposes and who presume the same rights as men regarding sexuality and careers while never-theless maintaining their sense of relationality. Narrative resolution works in favor of this appropriation in *Independence* when the boyfriend gives in and joins her in the city, and in *Girlfriends* when the two friends are reconciled. A traditional representational form—narrative closure—is thus recoded to promote alternatives—female dominance, female friendships—to the patriar-chal ideology such closure usually fosters.

But the films also display formal traits that reflect feminine socialization patterns. Women are generally considered to be field dependent—that is, contextual, relational, dependent, etc.—while men are considered to be field independent in that they are socialized to be autonomous, less relational, more objectifying, etc. However ideological that polarization may be, it prob-ably reflects real socialization patterns. The character in *Independence Day* is depicted in relation to many people; her camera does not objectify; it puts her in contact. She is moved by a spirit of support and solidarity in relation to other women. In *Girlfriends*, the narrative establishes a deep context for the little "action" that occurs. Compare these representational modes to those of a consummate conservative male film like *Dirty Harry* in which context and character relations are kept to a minimum to facilitate narrative closure and action development. Women's films about women tend to show women involved in a number of parallel, contigously connected relations. More field independent men project images of women who are mirrors of their own socialization—more autonomous, less dependent on contextual relation-ships—and this, of course, accounts for the male tendency to objectify (sco-pophilically), since independence is a way of separating from others, reducing their subjective attachment to oneself and constituting them as separate ob-jects. To use our rhetorical terminology, one could say that the women's films are more metonymic in their representational form. Rather than promote decontextualization and the transcendence of relations, they anchor singu-larity in community and social context. Indeed, if one compares a woman director's film about a group of people—Joan Micklin Silver's *Between the Lines* (1977)—and a male director's—Lawrence Kasdan's *The Big Chill* (1982)—one notices that the woman's sensibility is one which equalizes relations, while the man's is one which establishes a superior male center around which all the other characters revolve.

Yet representational form does not seem to be gender specific in any biological or ontological sense, although one strategy of male ideology re-garding women is to impose such a fixed identity. No form seems to be appropriate to a nature or being of femininity, and women's use of patriarchal forms suggests that the putative nature of masculinity is itself a construct posited by the forms or representations it supposedly underlies. Different representations do, therefore, posit or construct different natures for men and women. And the mode of representation each practices seems to be influenced by the socialization that occurs during immersion in a culture in which certain representational forms are assigned exclusively to one gender group. What is interesting about the mix of appropriated male representational forms and socialized feminine forms in the women's films about women is that it opens up the possibility of gender positions that are neither "male" nor "female." The women are represented acting like "men" in some respects, like "women" in others. This is more possible for women because they are in the process of taking over a traditionally male-monopolized set of representations and socialization patterns, and although the taboo against feminine traits in male socialization makes that more difficult for men, traces of such a move are also evident in a film like *The Kiss of the Spider Woman* (1985). One could even say that women's films by men, ideological as most are, also reflect similar subliminal desires.

All of this would suggest that what one sees emerging in the seventies, as more and more women move into filmmaking and as women become more realistic, rather than voyeuristic objects of cinematic attention, is a deontologized gender reality, one that points forward to the possibility of a world without gender oppositions, one in which sexual characteristics and traits would circulate freely without being anchored to one sexual position. Indeed, one can speculate that this possibility is partly what motivates the right-wing backlash against feminism and the new sexuality in the eighties. If representations are what pin down gender positions, then it is important that male and female filmmakers during this period have begun to develop alternative representations which underscore the indeterminacy of such positions. The "other" world to patriarchy toward which female forms seem to point might not so much indicate a different being or nature of femininity as the possibility that the resolute and determined male forms may merely be ways of defending against the inherent indeterminacy of sexual positions. The alternative to patriarchy which female filmmakers seem to indicate may be less another female nature than the possibility that all sexual nature is merely a social and cultural construct fabricated out of reigning representations. This is why it is so important that women have begun to toy with the dominant gender representational system. Rather than an epiphenomenal gesture, it gets at the root of the construction of gender positions.

Threats to the dominant system of gender construction have been most evident in films by liberal and radical filmmakers that deal with the instability of gender positions. Both Robert Altman's *Three Women* (1977) and Susan Seidelman's *Desperately Seeking Susan* (1984) concern women who undergo or undertake changes in socialized gender position. While Altman's film tends to recuperate this potentially radical insight into the constructed nature of such positions by ontologizing an ideal of feminine nature, Seidelman's film goes further toward elaborating an alternative to the reigning sex gender oppositions.

Rather than associate women with myth, mysticism, motherhood, and the irrelevance of social roles to women's true being as Altman does, Seidelman emphasizes the malleability of woman's psychology and "being," the way the adoption of different representations can transform what only appears to be "natural." It employs the traditional representational form of the fantasy romance comedy of self-transformation whereby an ordinary per-

son changes magically into someone new (and better) to argue that different
representations posit different "natures."

In *Desperately Seeking Susan*, a New Jersey housewife who reads the personals finds herself living the life of the character in the personals who most
fascinates her—a punk ne'er-do-well whose romantic free life is very different
from her own boring suburban existence. Entering the life of her fantasy
through a knock on the head, she is restored to her senses at the end only
to recognize that the fantasy life is more real than the real world she left
behind. She decides to leave her husband for a young man in Manhattan. It
is a fairy tale of rebirth with all the traditional elements—magic (a talismanic
jacket), doubling (housewife/punk queen, as well as a sawing-in-half scene),
witchery (Madonna in black), death and rebirth imagery (being knocked out;
emergence through a window into a costume room that reinforces the idea
of the malleability of woman's social roles—so many changeable costumes),
etc. The narrative follows the conventional romantic format by moving from
a place of social restriction, to a midsection of confusion in which the previous
identity is broken down, to a final liberation from confusion (of identities,
in this case) that entails a reconstruction of society (the housewife's decision
to leave her husband). The playful and inventive style of the film stands in
contrast to the ponderous, mythic style of Altman in *Three Women*. Rather
than posit a stable women's nature, the film suggests that what passes for
nature (passivity, dependence, etc.) is an internalized representation or role
that can easily be exchanged for an alternative one—just as the film itself
adopts the traditional male stylistic costume of romantic adventure and recuts
it to suit a woman's figure.

Seidelman's film points to a deontologized indeterminacy of sexual positions which lies beyond the opposition between male and female. The alternative to partriarchy is not an exaggeration of the "feminine" into a mystical ideal, it suggests, but rather an appropriation of the realms of
representation that have served the ends of male power in a way that turns
them against themselves. The film signals the possibility of a deconstructive
recoding of supposedly patriarchal representational forms into feminist ones.
Rather than being scopophilic, the film depicts a moment of voyeurism, but
it defuses its power; the man is fearful, and the woman at that moment is
departing on her own. And after having been an object of male sexual pleasure, Susan rips the man off, stealing his money and his jewels. These feminine
men and male women are probably closer to what psychologists during the
era were discovering to be the actual range of social gender possibilities in
both sexes. And the film's own appropriation of patriarchal forms and its
depiction of shifting gender identities indicate the extent to which form or
representation plays a role in occluding that broad differential spectrum of
possibilities and in constructing simple oppositional gender positions. Within
that oppositional system, with its psychological structures of oedipal desire,
castration anxiety, and disavowal, what motivates the fetishism of patriarchal
form is sexual difference, but our analysis suggests that behind this fear lies

another—the fear of sexual indeterminacy. And it is that indeterminacy which increasingly obtrudes in the cinematic culture of sexuality.

Not all patriarchal forms can be appropriated by women, and the feminist search for alternative, uncontaminated, specifically women's forms is motivated in part by the recognition that male narratives of radical individuation through power and violence pertain to a pathological worldview derived from occupying a position of domination in a system of oppression and inequality. Yet because of the interconnectedness of gender positions, their interconstitution, the feminist alternatives transform male patterns of representation, sometimes in progressive directions, sometimes in regressive ones. As women move more and more into the traditional male world, as they dress, look, and act increasingly like men, the boundaries between the two break down. Men no longer seem like men in the traditional sense, and women, as they mix tradition with modernity, seem less and less like either men or women.

Most women's films deal with middle- or upper middle class white women. Women of color are still outside the expanding limits of Hollywood, and it is symptomatic that a white male (Spielberg) directed the film of Alice Walker's *The Color Purple*. If white women have been cultural products rather than cultural producers up to this point, nonwhite women scarcely make it even as products. It is unfortunate, since that excluded position has generated powerful literary statements during this era that are enabling models for all women, and one suspects that cinematic statements by women of color would be equally empowering. This is underscored by the changes wrought by the emergence of white women filmmakers like Weill, Seidelman, May, Silver, Deitch, and Hackerling during this period and the sorts of alternative representations they developed. It all points to the importance of gaining access to the power to determine what the dominant cultural representations will be. It is an important concern for those who have been excluded from public power, both socially and culturally, since it in part determines what the substance of their lives will be.

2. From a Male Point of View: Men's Movies and the Return of Romance

Most Hollywood movies are "men's" movies in one way or another; it could not be otherwise in a patriarchal society. Yet just as the assumption that the word "race" means "nonwhite" presumes the centrality of a nonracial white subject, so also the traditional Hollywood category of "women's films" acknowledges that the male subject occupies the central position in the cinematic world, the one that is not named as a genre, because it is the nongeneric norm. Because men dominate the public realm, however, it would be difficult to narrow down a specific genre of films that deal with men's issues without including most public issue films. Yet the late sixties and early seventies witnessed a surge of "buddy films" that deal with the friendship between two men. And other film cycles exemplify a specifically male point of view—the romance films that began to appear in the late seventies reposition women as objects of a male quest, and the *film noir* revival films participate in this process by designating the deviations from the norm the romance films seek to reestablish.

Feminism troubled the system of cultural representation that imposed male norms on women, and thereby troubled the construction of male sexual identity, inasmuch as that depends on idealized representations of males as agents and of women as passive objects of pursuit and as tokens of male prestige. For this reason, men's movies of this period are marked by high levels of self-protective bonding and, eventually, overt rage against women.

The sort of tight bonding between men that characterizes the buddy genre (*Easy Rider, Midnight Cowboy, Butch Cassidy and the Sundance Kid, The Sting, Papillon, Thunderbolt and Lightfoot, Scarecrow, Mean Streets*) can be found in many earlier war, musical, western, and comedy films. What distinguishes the buddy genre is the absence of a romantic interest. Women, in fact, are sometimes absent altogether, but if they are present, as in *Butch Cassidy* (1969), they are in secondary roles; the real romance is between the men. Because this era was also characterized by the resurgence of the lone, neo–Natty Bumppo frontier male films (the "Dirty Harry" tendency), one could read this development as an initial, excessive reaction to feminism, a projection of male representations that suggest that male-male friendship could replace an increasingly troubled arena of intergender relations. To cite *Butch* once again, it is of note that the woman is a schoolteacher, an independent woman, and that she ultimately abandons the two men to their fate.

The films can also be read as compensatory fantasies of a male union unavailable without the taint of stigmatic fear in a world in which men, because of sexual socialization patterns, are not permitted the sort of close friendships permitted women. But the constraints are still operative even within these fantasies. Men in these films are always engaged in quests or tasks that face them forward. They stand side by side, not face to face, as women do in films like *Girlfriends*. The constraints still operate because the fear of homosexuality is still at work in these films. Occasionally it is waylaid by one male's mock adoption of a "feminine" role, as in the bar strip scene in *Scarecrow*. The reality of the fear is metaphorized in a film like *Deliverance*, in which a group of men set out down a southern river and are sexually assaulted by rednecks. The homosexual attack can be interpreted as a projection of the fear that inhabits such male-on-male group relations. It is fitting that the film should end with a man in bed with his wife, having a nightmare of the return of the repressed, a clammy hand that emerges from the water of the river.

In male/male buddy films, women also appear as tokens of exchange between the men. Women are ways of securing a homophilic bond of the sort that is the basis of male social power. The other male's desire for the same woman allows her to function as a link between the men. The first male in part desires the desire of the other male as a confirmation of his own power and status. This assures his male identity by validating his desire in comparison to another male's desire, and it allows the males to bond without fear of homosexuality, since the mediating female reassures both of their male sexual identities. Moreover, the structure also assures male power because the threat of subjective equality that is always there in a male-female relationship is defused by the fact that the woman cannot escape the objective position which allows men to compare their desires and to establish a bond. She cannot share in their desire for her and must remain outside the alliance.

In *Butch Cassidy*, for example, the woman is the Kid's lover, but she relates closely to Butch and circulates between the two. After she leaves them, they choose to die together, and death is both a traditional metaphor for sexual union and a literal apotheosis of bonding as mutual self-sacrifice. The establishing of an alliance around a shared female object is critically examined in *Carnal Knowledge* (1971). Two college men compete for a coed; one marries her, although it becomes clear later the other had an affair with her. One ends up divorced and with a much younger woman, while the other ends up alienated entirely from equal sexuality. Their regression is symptomatic of the more general law of regression operative in the buddy film phenomenon, a desire to return to an earlier, less threatening phase of mutually validating comradeship before the encounter with the troubling difference of another sex, an object that turns out to be a subject.

Yet the buddy phenomenon can also be given a somewhat more affirmative reading. If the changes of the sixties and early seventies broke down boundaries between hitherto hermetic social arenas, they also lifted repressions that had previously been in place around sexuality. The era saw the birth of the modern gay and lesbian movements most notably. The general air of cultural liberalism at the time permitted a variety of desires to be expressed. The prevailing heterosexual cultural system was in part neutralized, and this allowed nonheterosexual urges to emerge. The buddy genre could be read in this way—as the expression of a natural homoeroticism which a pervasively heterosexual culture does not permit to flourish but which did get articulated in the liberal climate of the time. In this light, Redford and Newman are the most important romantic couple of the period.

However the phenomenon is interpreted, it must be placed in relation to another major development of the early and mid-seventies—the decline of romance. We interpret this as an effect of the critical pessimism of the era. Romance is a traditional representational mode for sanctifying fairly limited heterosexual possibilities; it is conservative to the extent that it enacts male power fantasies and legitimates the positing of the patriarchal family as the one normative sociosexual ideal and institution. The decline of romance as an ideal, unproblematic, always successful model can therefore be seen as an effect of the critique of conservative institutions during the era.

Following the love high of 1971, when three of the top four films were romantic melodramas (*Love Story, Ryan's Daughter, The Summer of '42*), many films of the early seventies portrayed a decline in the traditional model of romantic love. For one thing, men seemed to prefer men, as the buddy genre attested. The homophilic boisterousness in *Butch Cassidy and the Sundance Kid* scarcely matches the torrid exchange of glinty, blue-eyed glances in *The Sting*, one of the most popular films of 1972. In addition, romantic melodramas like *The Way We Were* (1973) were ending in separation. Ethnic dramas like Scorsese's *Mean Streets* (1973) suggested that it was becoming more difficult to choose between the guys and the girl next door. The travails for men of the new singles scene were evident in Allen's *Everything You Always Wanted to Know about Sex* (1972). The ironic narrator in Malick's *Badlands* (1973) captioned the young romance in deadpan terms that rendered it thoroughly comic. Nichols's *Carnal Knowledge* concerned men on the make who come to hate the "ballbusters" on the other side of the sexual battlefield. The ante of male cynicism was raised by *Shampoo* (1975), a film that portrays the erosion of romance and the trading in of love for money. The trend had become so obvious by 1973 that David Denby remarked, "Romance is just about dead in our movies."[2]

On the surface, this decline was due to changes in U.S. society. Divorce was on the rise, and marriage seemed less likely than ever to be a guarantee of romantic happiness. Easier birth control and a relaxing of traditional restraints separated sexuality from the marriage career track and made possible a singles life that entailed greater experimentation, frequently without romantic involvement. In addition, feminism meant that more women were striking out on their own and supporting themselves through work; they were less dependent on men for their well-being. The traditional model of romance (active male/passive female) suffered in consequence. It was put in doubt by the emerging difference between the prevailing representations of personal romantic bliss promoted by film and the media and the reality of interpersonal violence, marital failure, and alienation unearthed as part of the social critiques of the late sixties (evident particularly in films like *Who's Afraid of Virginia Woolf?*). The disparity between image and reality even became a theme of certain films like Allen's *Play It Again, Sam*, in which a man tries to imitate Bogart, and *Badlands*, in which a couple play out a James Dean fantasy.

The liberal critical spirit that motivated the decline of romance is strikingly articulated in *Shampoo*. Written by Warren Beatty and Robert Towne and directed by Hal Ashby, it concerns a hairdresser named George (Beatty) who sleeps with all of his rich women customers while trying to maintain a steady relationship to which he isn't committed. Set on the eve of the Nixon electoral triumph of 1968, it is also a satire of the Republican style of political sleaze as well as being a post-Watergate "I told you so" that presupposes the subsequent revelations of Republican corruption as an ironic context for Agnew's moralistic pontifications. Though critical of conservative attacks on "permissive attitudes," the film nonetheless is itself critical of sexual promiscuity. At least, George loses everything, including the woman he realizes too late he really wants. She goes off with a wealthy man.

The film's deflationary rhetoric can be said to presuppose an audience that did not need to revere political leaders, businessmen, and the holy family. The shocks which would later make those institutions important psychological anchors had not yet occurred. Consequently, the film offers no metaphoric idealizations. Its rhetorical mode is more metonymic. Rather than pretend to reveal a moral truth, it constructs meanings through the juxtaposition of material worldly elements (an Agnew speech on TV about morality with a rankly downbeat and ironic discussion of sexuality between a Republican fund raising powerhouse, who speaks of getting his "gun" off with his mistress, and a philandering hairdresser, who remarks that women know that men are all trying to "nail 'em"), or the satiric displacement within the narrative of the same event so that the various contexts transform its meaning (George's various and numerous performances, for example, as he ambles amiably and compliantly from bed to bed). These debunking strategies prevent idealization, and they point toward the material basis which leads a woman to choose one man over another. In this film then, an ideal of a genuine romance serves as an implicit criterion for judging both female opportunism and male cynicism. The failure of romance is associated with the success of conservative capitalism and the undermining of human relationships by the cash nexus.

As *Shampoo* illustrates, the undermining of romance is linked to the shearing away of self-delusion and pretension regarding the materiality of social life. If conservative delusion and idealization are based on the suppression of materiality, liberal and radical critiques of those delusions promote a counterideological awareness of the power of materiality in determining social interaction, especially such fragile, delusion-fraught dimensions of social life as romance. Woody Allen's mid-seventies films are notorious for displaying the rampant amorality of desire, its refusal to adhere to proportion or propriety. One of the most important critical films of the period, *Annie Hall*, appears in 1977, the last year of the preceding era of liberal and radical cultural ascendancy. The film is typical of that outlook. Allen's character, Alvie, recounts his affair with Annie Hall, a neurotic midwesterner coached by him into self-confidence and independence who then leaves him to pursue her career. The film signals that part of the problem with romance was feminism. As women became increasingly conscious of their rights to independence, the social institutions reinforcing dependence became more and more suspect. Romance stood high on the list. But it is also interesting to note how the critique of such an institution is based in certain representational revisions. Allen's narrative consists of discontinuous displacements that suggest life's seriality and contingency. The sense of necessary development toward a resolution which characterizes conservative narratives is absent, and consequently the world posited by the film's rhetoric is more open-ended and negotiable.

The delusions of romance continue to be a topic of Allen's films from *Manhattan* (1979) and *Stardust Memories* (1980) to *Zelig* (1983), *The Purple Rose of Cairo* (1985), and *Hannah and Her Sisters* (1986). If human beings, in Allen's vision, are eminently fallible, they are also preeminently malleable. Isaac in *Manhattan* is betrayed in love, but manages himself to redeem his betrayal. If romantic delusion ends painfully in *Rose*, in *Hannah* it is absorbed into the ongoing, open-ended process of life. If this social and cinematic rhetoric strikes us as being metonymic rather than metaphoric, it is because it presents the world as a material construct that can be remade. Life as represented neither rises to idealist values like home and country nor moves toward apocalyptic conclusions. Instead it develops, varies, changes course, and alters meaning, in a series of nonteleological displacements. Again, to use the category of realism to describe this is to miss the point that realism pertains to cognition, while rhetoric includes the material practices of constructing the phenomenal social world. Rhetoric implies a choice of values, not "truer" description. Allen's "vision," then, is ethical rather than moralizing in that its locus of value is not the individual subject depicted as a source of righteousness, but instead the relations that obtain between people. And part of that ethic entails reflecting on the rhetorical categories which shape social attitudes as well as on the cinematic rhetoric which shapes the phenomenal world of life experience. For example, in *Zelig* images are superimposed, the frame of fictional illusion is broken in *Annie Hall*, the boundary between film and life is shattered in *Rose*. An ability to reflect on the cinematic illusion in this way is usually associated with a concomitant ability to reflect on the illusionarily absolute values that constitute social life—romance, the patriarchal family, etc. It seems that the sort of sensibility shaped by metonymic as opposed to metaphoric representational capacities is one that is given to a materialist and reconstructive understanding both of the social world and of the representations which construct it.

In the films of Altman, Scorsese, and Alan Rudolph during this time, romance is also either satirized or held at a cool ironic distance. Altman's *Nashville* (1975) concerns large numbers of people involved in varying degrees of romantic delusion (see chapter 10). Rudolph's *Remember My Name* (1978) is a critical depiction of one woman's romantic revenge on a man who betrayed her. She elaborately seduces him, then abandons him, leaving him in the very position in which he had left her. Romance is realistically depicted as a realm of patriarchal violence, but it is also shown being transformed into a weapon of revenge. In Altman's films particularly, distancing devices preclude audience identification with characters.

A similar sort of disidentification is operative in Scorsese's films of the period. They generally portray romance as an at least troubled terrain. And they are also usually critical examinations of male psychopathology. *Who's That Knocking at My Door?* (1969) and *Mean Streets* (1973) are male coming-of-age films that depict the socialization of lower middle class Italian men into the rituals of misogyny, male-bonding, cock-fighting, and violence. *Raging Bull* (1980) constitutes a more critical examination of male rage. It is the story of a white boxer whose violence outside the ring leads to the breakup of his family. The film is shot in an austere black and white, which aids the distancing of the character as someone to be looked at critically rather than identified with. Moreover, the boxing sequences depart from the traditional sports film code by forestalling any arousal of emotions over the spectacle. The alienation effect is especially effective in the final scene of the boxer, aged and fat, practicing a comedy routine in front of a dressing room mirror.

No other filmmaker during this time has gone so far in exploring the social determinants of male pathologies.

One could say that it is in the nature of ideology in general to exclude self-irony, and this is perhaps why romance, the least ironic of the genres, is revived at the same time that ideology (as patriotism, conservative economic values, and so on) is reasserted in American culture. Conservatives have always sought to exclude irony from the city-state or from the "great" cultural tradition because conservative social values of piety, reverence, and obedience cannot withstand the sort of critical reflection associated with it. It is in the nature of a self given over to ideology and weakened by reliance on external instances of authority in a conservative patriarchal society to seek secure grounds of truth and power as compensatory anchors. Reflection on the conventionality of values is thus difficult to sustain. Under an ironic gaze, male self-aggrandizement becomes impossible. Allen's counterideological significance resides in this minimalist cultural gesture. All of this pertains to the critique of romance in that romance is that generic code which is most sustaining of male ideals of sexual power, the least tolerant of assaults on narcissism. This is so because romantic union, under conservative, patriarchal auspices, is essentially a reunion with a maternal ground of security. It is the ultimate way of overcoming the sort of shame a patriarchal family structure, with a male authority figure at the center, engenders in young men. Shame has sexual roots, and it is overcome through fantasies of female adulation. They firm up the male ego, purging the sense of embarrassment and shortcoming which patriarchal authority necessarily instills, and purging as well the ability to reflect critically or ironically on oneself or on the representational conventions that construct one's world.

The search for psychological stability is also a search for representational stability and this is why the return to order after 1980 is accompanied by a revival of romance movies. Indeed, psychological stabilization consists of the ability to represent clearly, to internalize an image of what is absent, and thereby to accept loss, insecurity, and separation without anxiety. The conservative inability to accept change and reconstruction is linked to a failure to develop a power of representation which does not require the images of fusion made available by romance. An inability to reflect on representation inheres in a psychological disposition that longs for a return to the maternal unity of primary narcissism. To this extent, contemporary film theory is perfectly correct to notice a relation between reflection on representational conventions and an ability to escape from patriarchal sexual structures. Not surprisingly, then, when male-centered romance is revived as an ideology it assumes familiar, generic, and traditional representational forms. They recall the past, instead of reconstructing the future. And this is so because romance itself is the enactment of a return, a fusion that purges insecurity and restores what is lost—the stability and constancy of an object both in the world and on the level of representation.

Predictably, the resurgence of conservatism in U.S. social life coincides with a revival of highly patriarchal and narcisstic forms of romance. If con-

servative male social power necessarily entails and is dependent on the subordination of women, then this cultural alignment is indicative of a certain
internal necessity. Neoromance films like *An Officer and a Gentleman, Grease,*
and *Flashdance* seem in part a response to feminism since they self-consciously
strain to position women in traditionalist roles. Yet conservatism had more
to deal with than it might have thought, and in consequence, many romance
films of the late seventies and early eighties—from *Head over Heels* to *Eye of
the Needle*—depict new, stronger heroines. Marsha McCreadie points out that
these new women are more rational and capable of controlling their emotions,
while their male counterparts succumb to emotional weakness—a reversal of
the traditional gender stereotypes.[3] The new, stronger women seem, however,
also to be eliciting appropriate responses from men. In several films of the
era the woman is depicted as a source of power in order to facilitate a more
empowering male quest. In both *Zelig* and *The Man Who Loved Women* (1983),
for example, women psychoanalysts, who occupy uncustomarily powerful
positions in relation to prone men, are overcome and domesticated by their
male patients. In neoromance films like *The Natural* (1983) women are also
positioned in traditional stereotypes of the witch and the angel. An "evil"
woman wounds a promising baseball player, but with the love of a devoted
woman he is once again able to raise his bat high and hit one for the zipper.

The abreactive character of the portrayals of many strong women is
signaled particularly in the *noir* revival. In such *noir* remakes as *The Postman
Always Rings Twice* and *Body Heat* (both 1981) strong women are the occasion
of the fall of an innocent man. In *Body Heat* the woman is depicted as a
greedy seducer and manipulator. In *Against All Odds* (1984), a remake of *Out
of the Past*, the female figure from the original is recoded from witch vamp
to weakling. Thus, while many of the neoromance films play to the new
feminism by portraying strong women, they also are direct attempts to cir-
cumvent the feminist rewriting of the script of patriarchal power by reacti-
vating traditional male models of femininity.

Male-centered romance was revived during a period of reaction against
feminism, high unemployment, shrinking job possibilities, political instability,
and potential war. Read diagnostically, the phenomenon seems to indicate
felt needs for structures of reassurance in a time of increasing uncertainty
and insecurity. By 1985, the cynical reality would emerge more clearly and
unromantically in American culture. Madonna would sing of material girls
seeking boys with cash in their pockets, and surveys would reveal that young
upscale "yuppie" women were increasingly choosing mates on the basis of
income. Nevertheless, the struggle to redefine intergender love relationships
through cinematic representations would not be entirely pacified. Critiques
of romance would appear in Allen's and Rudolph's films and in others like
St. Elmo's Fire. In these films romance appears less as a solution to all life's
ills than as one of their major causes. Certain Robert Altman films of the
period (*A Wedding, Health,* etc.), portray romance as a terrain of exploitation,
cynical manipulation, and easily broken dreams that are frequently depicted
as naive illusions. Alan Rudolph's *Choose Me* (1984) ends with a just-married

woman displaying an array of facial expressions ranging from hope to despair in the final shot. It sums up the uncertainty that the critique of romance had introduced into the old, secure scenario of marital bliss.

3. The Family and the New Sexuality

Women's struggle for liberation from male social power and for equality directly affected two arenas in which male power was particularly felt by women—the family and sexuality. Control over women in the family included control over their sexuality. Thus, feminism in its early stages in the modern era was often associated with liberated sexuality (the Erica Jong/"Happy Hooker" phenomenon). In conjunction with feminism, a movement developed to loosen strictures around youth sexuality (evident particularly in such excellent youth films as *Foxes* and *Fast Times at Ridgmont High*), and at the same time the various gay and lesbian movements began to redefine the boundaries of permissible sexual behavior. These movements also affected the family, since they offered alternatives to the traditional male-dominated reproductive couple.

As the seventies developed, women came increasingly under attack for destroying the family. In a number of films, images of loving, nurturing fathers are contrasted with prejudicial images of selfish mothers. *Kramer vs. Kramer, The Champ, Ordinary People, Hide in Plain Sight, Author! Author!, Table for Five, The World According to Garp*, and *Mr. Mom* present new images of loving, nurturing fathers, focus on the impact on children of divorce, and idealize relations between fathers and children. In *Kramer vs. Kramer* (1979) Ted (Dustin Hoffman) is an advertising executive whose wife, Joanna (Meryl Streep), leaves him unexpectedly. He must cope with parenting his child, Billy, alone, while working. Ted puts his child before his work and loses his job. Then Joanna returns to claim Billy, and the court awards her the child. Eventually, she decides not to take him, because she realizes Ted is now the "real" parent.

Kramer, an extremely popular film, is an astute rhetorical exercise. The scenes of interaction between father and son are endowed with charm, and their relationship is worked out narratively as a series of crises mixed with a growing sense of intimacy. It is a love story of sorts, and its tremendous sentimental appeal easily allows the other tale, that of the wayward mother, to be shunted from view altogether. Indeed, the positive portrayal of the father-son relation is a way of indicting the mother for a crime against the family. In the end the general audience is fully prepared to accept that she should give up the child.

Throughout the film, camera rhetoric, image composition, and framing all work to position Ted as a superior being and to situate Joanna as a silent, cold, and neurotic presence who ultimately seems inferior and undeserving of the child. Ted's righteousness is established several times through dialog. More than once he silences a woman with a self-justifying and accusatory remark. The camera lingers on her face as she absorbs the great truth. More-

The era witnesses the rise of single-parent families and a shift in male attitudes toward parenting.

over, as Rebecca Balin notes,[4] he is usually situated high up in buildings, and he appears in the frame as an active, moving figure. Joanna, on the other hand, is often positioned at the bottom of buildings, hiding behind windows. Her presence is usually cool and distant; she is a motionless observer rather than an active agent in the frame. In addition, the narrative is structured in such a way that she is silenced by it. She leaves at the outset, and by the time she returns such a harmonious rapport has been established between father and son, and so much audience energy has become invested in their struggles, that her reemergence occurs narratively as an intrusion, a violent act against something warm and good. When she finally is given a chance to explain why she left, it makes little difference that her desires were justified, that Ted did indeed give too much time to work and too little to her. Yet even this structure of justification assumes that less time given to work and more to the little wife is a plausible improvement. Part of the film's seeming effortlessness at accomplishing ideological ends is due to its shifting of fairly basic questions about the patriarchal division of labor into axioms or taken-for-granted assumptions. The working out of the film's equation is therefore in terms of values that are never interrogated. The positive resolution thus occurs within an essentially patriarchal frame, which the resolution reinforces. Another word for this strategy is reform. Patriarchy in this film is saying that it can reform, but it is doing so in a way that leaves intact the structuring assumptions of a patriarchal social system. It is saying that a man can both mother and work successfully. The question it poses implicitly is, "Why can't a woman do the same?"

Camera rhetoric is particularly important for studying the way woman is indicted by the film. In the opening scene Joanna leans over her child, and the pastel colors and lighting tones suggest a madonna. The scene establishes the norm that she breaks. In contrast to this ideal image, her actions seem violent and irrational. She leaves without explaining why, behaving in an apparently neurotic manner. The intercutting of this scene with images of Ted working serves a dual function. It suggests the source of her unhappiness, but it also sets up a situation of betrayal. Ted is portrayed as hardworking, yet while he's out in the world his wife is preparing to leave him. His return to abandonment thus establishes him as the wronged party. And the film pursues this assumption throughout. The indictment of the woman is literally enacted in the trial. When Joanna is being questioned by the attorney, as Balin points out, the camera moves in on her, suggesting her guilt by its intimidation.

Our survey confirms that these stragegies worked: 61% felt that the depiction of Joanna was fair, and 44% (the highest group) thought the most important meaning of the film was that it showed a father acting as a caretaker. Women had different reactions to the film, however. Of the 18% who chose the meaning "a woman finds herself" as the most important for them, 74% were women, and of the 40% in our sample who felt the film was negative in regard to independent women, 64% were women.

Scapegoating of women as destroyers of the patriarchal family is especially pernicious in view of the fact that the abandonment of women by men is responsible for the majority of broken marriages.[5] To be sure, some films do depict men abandoning their wives and families (*Shoot the Moon* or *The Four Seasons*, for example), but these films tend either to present the male's dilemma sympathetically or to resolve the family's problems comedically. The prototypical film of the era was probably *Ordinary People* (1980), a tale of an upper-class family in which the mother is a neurotic who was semi-incestuously attached to a dead son and who does not care for her living son, who in consequence suffers a breakdown. Eventually, she leaves the home, and the father and the son discover a new bond. To get a sense of the perniciousness of this sort of cinematic misogyny, one needs to ask how many films are made about neurotic fathers who act seductively toward one daughter while ignoring another and who need to be banished from the home so that the mother and the daughter can finally relate without the old bastard around. Moreover, not all families can afford joint psychotherapy sessions or, as in *Shoot the Moon*, to have a new tennis court built in the backyard to make up for heartbreak. If family films tend to scapegoat women, they also tend to ignore the tremendous hardship many divorced working women of the era were undergoing as they tried to raise a family alone.

As part of the reassertion of traditional family models, the late seventies and early eighties witnessed what has been termed a "return of melodrama" in Hollywood film.[6] Films in this trend are *The Other Side of Midnight* and *Bobby Deerfield* (both 1977), *Slow Dancing in the Big City* (1978), *Ice Castles* and *Voices* (both 1979), *Shoot the Moon* (1982), and such women's films as *Rich and Famous* (1981). Frequent themes in these melodramas are disenchantment with the false happiness of wealth; an affirmation of the goodness of the simple, down-home family values of trust, duty, loyalty, and devotion; the priority of feeling or sentiment over worldly rewards like money or career; the obligation to pay through punishment for transgressions against middle-class family morality; the role of sickness or death as a reminder of the need to accept one's lot and to reconcile oneself to what one has, no matter how limited, etc. Although the new melodramatic tendency as a whole can be read as a symptom of the increasing self-concern of an ascendant white upper middle class that no longer wants to be bothered with questions of poverty or inequality, it can also be read against the grain as an indicator of a need in audiences for representations of the security of strong emotional and familial attachments in a time of economic and social insecurity. Where real social security is absent, emotional security will be sought out.

A major melodrama of the period is *Terms of Endearment*, one of the most popular, Oscar-bedecked films of 1983, which celebrates the traditional family and argues that family bonds are the most enduring form of support in a difficult world. A mother, Aurora (Shirley MacLaine), and her daughter, Emma (Debra Winger), remain close over a thirty-year period until Emma dies of cancer. Emma tries to be a devoted wife and mother, but her husband persists in having affairs, and she ultimately takes a lover herself. The strife between husband and wife is depicted as damaging to their children. In a parallel plot, the mother falls in love with a promiscuous and rambunctious neighbor, Garrett (Jack Nicholson), who tries to leave her but who comes through in the end as a surrogate father in a reconstituted family.

Terms promotes a modernized traditionalist model of sexuality and the family. Through the narrative process wayward males are transformed into potentially good fathers. Independent women, on the other hand, are depicted as herpes-ridden harpies. Yet extramarital relations for women are also presented positively; an older reclusive widow learns to come alive sexually and emotionally; and matriarchal relations are privileged. The film draws on the representational codes of television (the director, James Brooks, crossed over from TV)—painting characters with single strokes that are almost caricatural but which make viewing and understanding easy, using a quippy comedic dialog that incorporates a sexual explicitness characteristic of the women's talk shows of the era, and employing a concentrated bright lighting in almost every scene that makes even the exterior scenes seem like television stages. Thus, the film has a kind of modernized middle-class liberal glow to it.

Critically diagnosed, however, the film is revelatory of several ideological mainstays of the softcore brand of conservatism. One is the opposition between women, conceived as caring mothers, and men, conceived as uncaring philanderers who need to be tamed for domesticity. The purpose of this naturalization of socialization patterns is to legitimate the relegation of women to domestic labor and child breeding, since that is their "natural" function. At the end, however, the film inadvertently displays the socialization process that underlies this "nature." The mother tells Emma's daughter to sit closer to her on the steps of the home, while the male neighbor/surrogate father takes the male child off to show him his pool, turning him outward toward a male world of activity. In addition, the film demonstrates how the general conservative value system rests on a dichotomized way of conceiving the world defined by an internal/external model that is closely bound up with familialism.

The family is a haven of intimacy, a world folded back on itself, a place of face-to-face proximity that admits of no intrusion from "outside." Outsideness is defined as the breaking of familial proximity, and it is linked to a number of things conservatives project as threatening in society—divorce, singles life, sexual diseases, abortion, women working, etc. But more crucially, family "endearment" is a necessary bulwark against the sort of unendearing market jungle that conservatives fostered at this time. The two presuppose each other necessarily, although they seem to have a firm boundary between them. (We noted this earlier in our discussion of *The Godfather*, and *Terms* clearly is the internal correlate to the male survivalist external world evident in that film. It is in a certain way *The Godfather Part Three, The Motherdaughter.*) Yet the conservative family and the conservative market world are exchangeable. Their traits pass over into each other, and the market/family dichotomy deconstructs and becomes undecidable. That world opposite and outside the

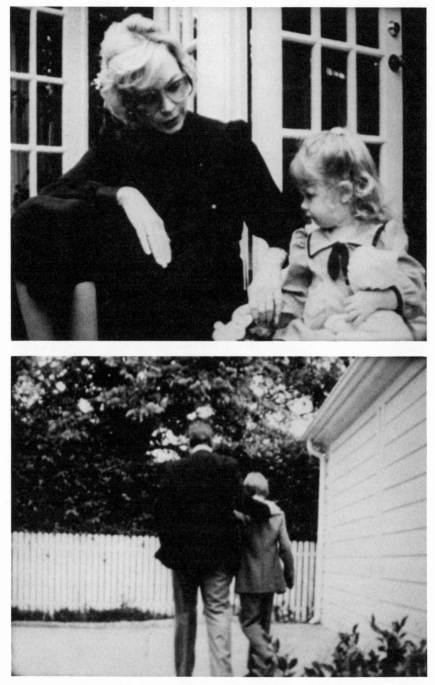

Terms of Endearment. Conservative gender socialization.

family is defined by nonintimate relations of contract and money exchange that enforce obligations, relations from which the family is supposedly free. The difference between the family and the market is demonstrated in the supermarket checkout segment when Emma has insufficient money to pay for her groceries. Emma's lover-to-be, Sam, saves the day by offering help without any demand for equal compensation; he behaves, in other words, in a family manner and keeps the cold market world at bay (an opposition coded as rural/urban when he accuses the checkout girl of being from New York). Yet the purpose of a contract is to make the market world behave like a family, to create the obligation for face-to-face exchange, whereby people give equally. And the family is not immune from contract. Indeed, in some ways it is the model for contractual obligation. This is why the title of the film is so significant, for "terms of endearment" are also the "terms" of a contract.

This reading is suggested in the scene in which Garrett tries to break out of the relationship with Aurora—he says he's beginning to feel an "obligation." As he should, since beneath all the family endearment, certain "terms" of obligation are spelled out, terms Emma's husband doesn't meet, even though she does (without much protest, she follows her obligation and follows him to his new job), and this is why the film punishes him so unrelentingly. The gender social contract that emerges out of the inside/outside, female/male, family/market opposition stipulates that women will do domestic labor if men will support them. This film is to a large extent about the quandary of a woman whose husband is not fulfilling the terms of his contract. And the fact that women undertake his punishment is indicative of the extent to which a certain class of women are indeed active defenders of patriarchy; it is in their interest. (We have in mind primarily the Phyllis Schlafly/Eagle Forum phenomenon of the era.)

Thus, the conservative model of a strict inside/outside opposition between family and world harbors a differential structure of complicity between the two. Contract gives the market world the semblance of a heart, the honoring of obligation, yet the hearty family world can only be a successful haven against marketplace heartlessness if all adhere firmly to the terms of obligatory endearment. The family, too, has its contracts, its structures of construction and enforcement; only they are concealed ideologically as structures of feeling. The implications of this deconstructive analysis extend beyond hermeneutic highjinx. It shows why conservatism must defend both the disciplinarian model of the family (and Emma is a real disciplinarian) and the public marketplace model. They presuppose each other to the extent that each is the norm for the other. Yet the ideology of the film demands that the two be made to seem absolutely exclusive, and this justifies defending the family as the one haven of endearment in an otherwise cruel world. This accounts for the incredibly emotive aura of the film. The viewing of the film is itself a way of carrying out this justification, since it bathes family life in bright light, melancholic music, gentle sentiment, and pleasing humor. Moreover, the tremendous popularity of the film confirms the conservative agenda, but only to the extent that flight to the family is a result of the conservative marketplace world. In other words, the depiction of the family as the sole locus of care makes sense only in the context of a heartless market. A different world, a world in which the opposition between the emotive family and the hyperrationalized market world was broken down, so that "endearment" was distributed more differentially throughout the social system, including the economic system, might make such hyperemotive implosions of familial "endearment" less necessary. Such a world is not a utopia, something altogether outside the current world. A deconstructive analysis of the ideology informing a film like *Terms* suggests that it already lurks within the reigning conceptual and institutional oppositions.

Our survey found that the movie's modernized middle-class ethos endeared it to audiences. 82% felt it was not antifeminist. 71% felt Emma was not a victim, and 85% felt she grows through the course of the film. While the film came out with a distinct white middle and upper middle class representation in its viewers (a greater percentage of blacks were nonviewers than viewers, and a higher percentage of nonviewers earned less than $30,000 a year), the working and lower middle class viewers were markedly more critical of the film. For example, concerning the representation of Emma's New York women friends, a higher percentage of these viewers felt it was directed against independent women (57% and 63% respectively) than did middle and upper middle class viewers (33% and 18% respectively). In addition, whereas 47% of working-class viewers perceived Emma as a victim, only 26% of the middle and upper middle class viewers did. Finally, 67% of the working and 88% of the lower middle class viewers felt the film made them question conservative roles for women, while 52% of the middle and 47% of the upper middle class viewers reported similar responses. The closer viewers came to the film's class fix, the less likely they were to be critical of its sexual politics. What this seems to suggest is that upper-class people tend to be more accepting of the sort of personalized, melodramatic vision of the world which the film offers. And they are distinctly less critical of films that deal with their own social stratum. People lower on the class ladder tend to look at certain issues more in terms of the social position of the characters involved, whether or not they have a fair shake.

While most of the family films concern upper middle or upper class families, they were very popular, and their popularity (*Kramer* was second in gross in 1980; *On Golden Pond* was third in 1982; and *Ordinary People* won the Oscar in 1981) suggests that there is a strong need for communal, supportive social arrangements in a post-1980 world where marketplace brutality reigns supreme. That the only available support system in a capitalist culture of the sort restored to full viciousness in the early eighties is the family may account for the popularity of images of redemptive care and empathy during the period. Thus, while the family films demonstrate the extent to which the personalization of class in American culture succeeds in occluding structural inequalities between people of different positions, they also point to the necessity of images of community at times when the very anticommunitarian dimension of capitalism is particularly felt. The family films become noticeably more popular at the same time as do fantasy adventure and romance films, a time when Americans' loss of confidence in the economy and in politics probably reached its nadir. The economic function of the family, as a stabilizer of social relations and as a means of survival, is explicit in *Places in the Heart* (1984), for example. But the film also makes clear the ideological service the personalization of class through family images accomplishes. The strong farm woman character survives; the local capitalist is shown to be a good soul after all; the film concludes with a fantasy of social unity; and Almendros's cinematography bathes the whole undertaking in a subdued and pacifying blue. It would have been hard to tell that at that same time farmers out of frustration over bankruptcy were murdering bankers and taking their own lives. Yet it is precisely because that was the reality of the eighties that such sweet images of family happiness were in demand. In the face-to-face encounter of family life, fear of the knife in the back in the marketplace could momentarily be put aside.

As part of the conservative attempt to restore the dominance of the traditional patriarchal family, the sexual revolutions of the era—abortion, gay rights, birth control—were combatted on a number of fronts. The conservative drive to restore the family was in some respects merely a pretext for reimposing sexual discipline on youth and for curtailing independent feminine sexuality. Conservative male socialization to aggressivity and competitiveness—in the economic marketplace, in military matters, in politics—required a concomitant female socialization to subservience. Thus, the feminine move toward independence touched on something much deeper than sexuality; or, to put it another way, feminism revealed that conservative male sexual socialization underlay the principles of the market, the military, and most other patriarchal public institutions that are dependent on male socialization patterns. And conservative women spearheaded the drive for moral reasons, but also because the new feminine models upset their own self-idealizations as virtuous wives untainted by sexual desire. The conservative war on the new sexuality, therefore, relates to the fundamental power dynamics of a society that programs one half of the population to be aggressive and domineering and the other to be passive and weak. At stake in the issue of sexuality is the division of the world between a public and a private sphere.

Hollywood took both sides of the issue. Some films explored the origins of male violence against women in media fantasies (*Lipstick*), while others brutalized women for being sexually independent (*Looking for Mr. Goodbar*). A breakdown in the restraints on pornography was provoked initially by films like *Deep Throat*, and later in young male fantasy films like *Private Lessons*, *Porky's*, and *Risky Business*, one of the most popular films of the summer of 1983, in which a young man enlists the help of prostitutes to help repay a debt. Male teen sex films like *Animal House* (1979) feature fairly regressive intergender relations and promote the restoration of prefeminist attitudes. If young males were being moved toward more exploitative and cynical attitudes toward women in the arena of sexuality, the new liberalism permitted young women to be represented as having greater agency and choice in the sexual arena. For example, unlike fifties family dramas like *Rebel Without a Cause*, in which Natalie Wood's "wild" sexuality is tamed into family domesticity, in *Fast Times at Ridgemont High*, directed by Amy Heckerling, women high school students are depicted as independent subjects who exercise some control over their own sexuality. In the opening scene, two friends counsel a young woman on how to make a pass at a man. Jimmy Dean never would have stood for it.

Independent sexuality took its hardest drubbing during this time in the work of Paul Schrader, the Cotton Mather of contemporary Hollywood. In *Hardcore* (1979) a devout midwestern Protestant sets out to the big city to find his daughter, who has been kidnapped and turned into a porn queen. The search consists of a moralistic tour through the porn industry which polarizes the fallen city and the homey family world back home. The film does not study the exploitation of women through pornography, and it avoids analyzing the clear link between pornography and violence against women. Instead, it dramatizes the issue of child kidnapping for sexual exploitation, but it uses this more as a plot device than as a social issue to be examined for progressive ends. And although the religious world is not portrayed idyllically, in the end the restoration of the young girl to her repressed father is positively valorized. For Schrader, there seem to be only two sexual possibilities—total licentiousness or austere repression. In *American Gigolo* (1980) the representation of sexuality is divided between negative images of homosexuality and prostitution and positive images of transcendental romantic love which redeems a male prostitute. Family monogamy seems to be the implicit norm of these films, which are laced with racist stereotypes and which seem to articulate an anxiety that the clean, white world of fine, upstanding Americans is somehow being corrupted by moral decadence, minorities, and wealth. We will suggest later (8.3) why we think this mind-set tends more to the right than the left.

But despite resistance, post-repressive sexuality was here to stay, and its presence was probably nowhere more clearly felt than in the arena of gay and lesbian sexuality.[7] Hollywood continued to make prejudicial films about gay life up until 1980, when both *Windows* and *Cruising* appeared (and generated countrywide protests). But in later films like *Making Love, Personal Best* (both 1982), *Lianna* (1983), *Kiss of the Spider Woman* (1985), and *Desert Hearts* (1986), gays and lesbians are portrayed positively and sympathetically, although in some of them (like *Personal Best*) gay life still appears as a steppingstone to more "mature" heterosexual love. The new sexuality was also felt in films dealing with transsexuality, like *Victor Victoria, The Rocky Horror Picture Show*, and *Tootsie* (the second most popular film of 1983). *Tootsie* is a good example of the accommodation of mainstream culture to some of the new sexual issues. A man dresses up as a woman in order to land an acting job, and in his new female persona becomes a nationwide sensation. He also shows women a thing or two about how to stand up to sexism. In this curious argument, men prove to be better feminists than women. Nevertheless, the film is the bearer of a submerged desire. As fantasies of class transcendence testify to desires for a non-work world, so fantasies of gender transcendence (men mothering, women pursuing male careers, sexes changing) testify to desires for a post-gendered world of greater equality, in which the traits and privileges now assigned to men and women on a dichotomous and unequal basis would circulate more freely without attaching to fixed gender positions. Thus it is that within ideology, within the imaginary resolution of the fissures in old forms of thought and behavior, the emergence of the new can be glimpsed.

Not all of the new sexuality films were as restrained or ideological. *The Kiss of the Spider Woman* is probably the most significant departure from the Hollywood trend. An independent production, it concerns two prisoners, one gay, the other a heterosexual Marxist, who come eventually to exchange traits and to become lovers. As the boundaries between them disappear, so do the boundary markers between their "real" lives and the films they discuss constantly. The power of representation has rarely been so foregrounded as a thematic issue in a film. And the term "a figure of a man," as a sexual reference, takes on a tropological dimension, underscoring the representational construction of sexual identity, when in the end the Marxist comes to internalize the representations of cinematic femininity his now dead transvestite cellmate bequeathed him. Sexuality is figural, the film seems to suggest, a matter of representational conventions, both social and rhetorical, even cinematic.

6. HORROR FILMS

Horror films were one of the most popular genres of the seventies and early eighties.[1] Cycles of occult, demonic possession, slash and gash, psychotic killer, werewolf, and vampire films appeared, a phenomenon seemingly related to the prevalent temper of insecurity, distrust, and lack of confidence. The films indicate heightened levels of anxiety in the culture, particularly with regard to the family, children, political leadership, and sexuality. A central motif of many contemporary horror films is violence against women. Rather than merely condemn this violence, we shall argue that it needs to be situated within a broad cultural system that includes the representations and socialization patterns central to both the military and the capitalist economy. Such violence is in some respects merely an extension of the institutional violence that a male-dominated capitalist culture accepts and promotes as part of its "normal" operations. Thus, an analysis of violence against women in horror films points out the centrality of a seemingly marginal cultural phenomenon to the normal operations of a social system run on principles of aggressivity, competition, domination, and the survival of the fittest.

During times of social crisis, several sorts of cultural representations tend to emerge. Some idealize solutions or alternatives to the distressing actuality, some project the worst fears and anxieties induced by the critical situation into metaphors that allow those fears to be absolved or played out, and some evoke a nihilistic vision of a world without hope or remedy. If Dirty Harry is an idealized solution, the shark in *Jaws* is a metaphoric projection of fear, and the end of *Chinatown* is a realization of cultural pessimism. The process of idealization and projection is a way of reconstructing psychological identities dependent on social codes and cultural representations that have been disturbed or even destroyed. Idealization offers new, compensatory models to alleviate a sense of psychological loss, while metaphoric projections allow fear to be dissipated and a sense of security to be attained so that damaged subject constructions and the social codes that sustain them can be rebuilt. For example, in the late eighteenth and early nineteenth centuries, during what is called the Romantic period, political and industrial revolutions destroyed old cultural orders of all kinds. The changes threatened to herald in an entirely new social world, and they also provoked a dual process of idealization and fear projection. Nature and feeling were idealized in relation to the ascendency of Enlightenment rationality, urban industrialization, commercial calculation, political modernization, and science. At the same time, the rapid changes in political and social life (the French Revolution and the Napoleonic period of anti-aristocratic reform) provoked fear projections in such metaphoric modes as the gothic and horror genres. If nature was a site of ideal feeling, it was also a site of extremes that sometimes took monstrous forms. This was when Frankenstein's monster was created, and the era eventually included those continental writers (Hoffmann especially) whose work would inform the first great wave of horror films during the German Expressionist era of the 1920s. The nihilistic possibility is evident particularly during this later era. At the extreme edge of fear, hope is eclipsed altogether. But visions of a total destruction of social order can also be a way of refusing conservative principles of stability. The refusal of healing, especially of conservative healing, can be a progressive tactic.

The radical changes that occurred in American society from the sixties to the mid-seventies provoked a similar set of responses that seem part of a cultural process of reconstructing stabilizing representations of self and world that were broken down by those changes. Compensatory idealizations occur around romance and the family, as we saw in the last chapter, and also through representations of the male hero (see chapter 8) and military power (see chapter 7). There is even a sort of neoromantic revival of sorts during this period as in Spielberg fantasy films (see 9.3), that idealizes feeling and nature. It is in the horror genre that some of the crucial anxieties, tensions, and fears generated by these changes, especially by feminism, economic crisis, and political liberalism, are played out. Unlike the last great wave of horror films in the 1950s, the contemporary horror film articulates a greater level of social anxiety as well as, frequently, a higher degree of pessimism and even nihilism. The male sexual fears addressed by at least certain of these films are often such that they require a displaced and metaphoric representation. Indeed, the very need for such indirection is symptomatic of the sort of psychological disposition (anxious, insecure, intolerant of cultural liberalism, incapable of expressing itself directly about troublesome issues) that gives rise to such negative reactions. Not surprisingly, many of these films were targeted at low-income, less educated, and less articulate audiences in rural and urban underclass areas. And the nihilistic vision of hopelessness, while it has radical versions, is often also a way of eliciting calls for authority and strength as answers to the dissolution of order. Only the strong can endure the total loss of meaning.

But if the horror metaphor provides a medium for expressing fears the culture cannot deal with directly, it also provides a vehicle for social critiques too radical for mainstream Hollywood production. Some of the critical energies of the sixties did not so much go underground as under cover of metaphor during this period. It was a commonplace among film students of the era that some of the most radical statements in criticism of American society were to be found in the low-budget monster films that played the drive-in circuits. Indeed, one of the most important radical statements against American conservatism at this time is George Romero's "Living Dead" trilogy.

1. The Occult

Films featuring occult motifs frequently use demonic or supernatural figures to represent threats to social normality and the existing institutional order. Such use increases during periods of internal social disorder or when external threats to the society are especially feared. The great cycle of German Expressionist horror films appeared at a time of tremendous social crisis in the Weimar Republic, and the classical Hollywood monster films first appeared during the Depression. Horror films were revived during the fifties as metaphors for both the Red threat and for internal enemies (like teenagers). They reappear in the seventies during a time when the United States suffered a combined crisis of legitimacy in its dominant institutions and the economy.

At such times, the occult appears as an efficacious ideological mode which helps explain seemingly incomprehensible phenomena. It suggests that what seems meaningless has meaning. In a society run on irrational principles of unequal work and reward distribution, the need for such meaning structures will be augmented the more the system enters dysfunction—an unavoidable possibility and a recurrent reality of market capitalism, as this period proves. Thus, the occult should be read as a projection of fear, but it is also a way of attaining meaning of the sort denied in "real life" under capitalism. A sense of meaning provides security by describing the origin and function of seemingly irrational phenomena, like the breakdown of the economy. The occult provides a narrative that posits a subject of evil (the devil), as well as a logic that situates events within a predictable order. Thus, the occult has an extremely rational function—the restoration of the sense of security undermined by the dysfunctions of capitalism and the crises of political confidence that corrupt leadership in an underdeveloped democratic context provokes. It is less an irrational phenomenon than a way of dealing with the irrationality of the American social system.

Sixties romanticism and mysticism fostered an interest in the occult that went so far as to include the demonic. This was first evident in *Rosemary's Baby* (1968), but it reached the center stage of American culture with *The Exorcist* (1973) and *The Omen* (1976). The strain of occultism blended with the strain of religious fundamentalism that appeared in the seventies. If the former generated the *Amityville Horror* trilogy (of which the first was the fifth most popular film of 1979), the latter gave rise to a demonic occult cycle, the *Omen* trilogy (third most popular in 1976), which played to religious fantasies about the devil taking over the world.

Like religion in general, these films should be read as metaphoric representations that fulfill emotional needs whose satisfaction is not available anywhere else in the social system as it is constituted. They are also symptomatic of fear reactions to the tremendous social changes and crises of the

The rise of irrationalist accounts of the world become popular at a time when no rational answers are offered by the country's leaders and thinkers.

period. One major negative impact of those transformations is the provocation of anxiety responses that appear as fantasies of evil in the world. Those whose feelings of self-worth and psychological identity depended on idealized representations of the nation, the country's leaders, and a sense of one's proper role in relation to others in the patriarchal family had those feelings undermined by loss of war, the dishonoring of a president, and the youth, sexual, and feminist revolutions. It is noteworthy that the *Omen* trilogy, the story of a young devil who uses corporate and military power to try to take over the world, begins a year after the "loss" of Vietnam, the public discrediting of national icons such as the CIA, and the triumph of liberation movements against U.S. interests abroad. A year prior Nixon had been unseated, and the year before that, the Arab oil embargo had brought the United States to its knees. During a time of seemingly permanent recession, uncontrollable inflation, and consistently rising unemployment, the sense of loss that resulted from the deprivation of identity-conferring cultural representations gave rise to paranoid projections, combinations of defensive aggression transposed into external nemeses and genuine fears of forces in the world that had dethroned the public cultural representations whose internalization had secured personal identity in the past.

The dislocations of social crisis can also provoke critical perceptions, and if the *Omen* trilogy plays to crisis-induced fears it also plays to resentment against those who remained unaffected by the inflation and unemployment ravaging the white middle class in the seventies—the upper class. The films resonate with a sense of fascination with the social unseen, the hidden brokers of economic and political power. It should not at all be surprising that those invisible powerful people should be associated in the popular imaginary with the devil, that other great unseen force of "evil." At this time, moreover, secret wrongdoing on the part of those in economic and political power was very much in the air; the public had been made keenly aware that the powerful who hid behind closed doors did so for good reason. Even if the devil was not in the board room or the Oval Office, corruption was—as invisible as any spirit. Fittingly, then, the third film in the *Omen* trilogy (*The Final Conflict*, 1981) begins with a film clip about the economic crisis of the past decade, a "great recession" called "Armageddon" which seems due to demonic causes. The devil is an evil corporate chief and political broker who arranges coups and natural disasters for profit. In the second film, *Damien* (1978), the devil is associated with big business malfeasance (the artificial creation of famine in order to sell pesticides) and militarism. Thus, the occult motif is in some respects a magnet for popular resentment against the economically and politically powerful in the mid to late seventies. It is also an example of the populist imaginary at its most potentially critical extreme, a point where resentment, while veering into the traditional irrationalism of that outlook, also gives rise to searing insights into the nature of unjust power.

If the occultist films seem to transcode public anxieties, they also pick up on more private ones, especially around the family, sex roles, and generational relations. *Amityville*, for example, concerns the "horror" of a young man who murdered his parents, a horror that resides in a house, a familiar metaphor for family life. The localizing of fear projections in the family is understandable given the enormous changes in family roles during this period. The sexual revolution that liberated young people from traditional morality and the feminist revolution that allowed women to trade their traditional places for new roles also dislocated male identities dependent on other fixed points of reference for their map of self-meaning. This might help explain why children appear as demonically possessed in many occult films of the period (*The Children, Patrick, The Godsend*, etc.).

The cycle of demonic or evil children films is one of the most striking developments of the contemporary horror film. Previous representations of children in Hollywood film had, with few exceptions (like *The Bad Seed*), been positive; children were idealized as innocents. Contemporary monster children do rather nasty things to adults, however, and, not surprisingly, polls at the time suggested that parenting was becoming a less and less desirable occupation in a postindustrial culture of increased leisure and an expanding singles life.[2] It was as if the kids were catching on to what the grown-ups were thinking. Moreover, the children of the rebellious subcultures of the sixties and early seventies, who rejected parental authority, must have seemed fairly monstrous to an older generation of more conservative Americans.

The intersection of public and private occult thematics is particularly evident in Stanley Kubrick's major work of the era—*The Shining* (1980)—a

With the rise in external economic pressures, there is a concomitant rise in violence against women and children within the family.

critical horror film that maps a story of family violence onto an occult narrative. Kubrick uses the occult story as an instrument for analyzing the sort of breakdown that occurs when interpersonal structures like the family are forced to absorb the negative feelings of aggression and resentment generated by an economic system that unequally distributes success, gratification, and a sense of self-worth. Jack Torrance (Jack Nicholson), an unemployed teacher and aspiring writer, is employed as caretaker of a mountain resort; as the winter progresses, he becomes psychotic, eventually attempting to kill his wife and son before he freezes to death outside. The son has psychic powers that permit him to see the murderous past that is still very much alive in the haunted hotel. Jack is absorbed into the occult world, and it is to preserve its secret under orders from the ghostly former caretaker who had murdered his own family that Jack attempts to kill his family, so they can all live there with the other ghosts "forever and ever and ever." The occult motif brings together a number of social themes—male rage against wife and child resulting from economic failure, the emergence of violence from past guilt, and the more conservative idea of the inefficacy of civil institutions in the face of the evil in human nature.

Jack's failure as a writer seems to inspire his madness, a theme highlighted in the Stephen King novel. Indeed, the line he types over and over—"All work and no play makes Jack a dull boy"—is a sardonic comment on the work ethic. The close relation between work and family violence is indicated by his wife's account of his first act of violence against his son. He is angered because the boy disturbed his papers. Moreover, when he first attacks his wife in the hotel, he speaks of his "responsibilities" and his "contract," things he claims she doesn't understand. The hotel can thus be read in part as a metaphor for the isolation of the family in a cold and bleak economic landscape. It is a troubled garrison into which external market pressures of work and contract easily insinuate themselves, with violent results.

The hotel is also a metaphor for the psyche, both for the unconscious and for the repressed past that returns to haunt the present. Jack's descent into madness is a descent into his own unconscious, a scene of guilt and repressed impulses. The previous caretaker's murder of his family can be interpreted as a figure for Jack's own past violent desires. And indeed, the historical past is represented as a kind of fate that determines the present just as personal history lies under present behavior. The unconscious also harbors utopian desires for escape from repression, family responsibilities, and the constraints of polite behavior which induce the curtailment of urges. For example, in the haunted bar, Jack, who has promised to refrain from drinking and who clearly has money worries, is able to drink without paying. The double nature of the unconscious, as a site of both utopian and fearful desires, is signaled in the green bathroom fantasy, when a beautiful, naked woman Jack embraces suddenly turns into an ulcerous old hag. Descent into the unconscious permits a liberation from restraint, but it also is represented as a potentially dangerous pathway that unleashes repressed horrors—in this case, the fear of woman's sexuality.

Finally, the occult narrative figures the theme that beneath the platitudinous patina of liberal civility lurks a murderous and vile human nature. This theme was particularly evident in Kubrick's other films of this era—*2001*, which argues that there is little difference between primitive life and humanity's most advanced achievements, *A Clockwork Orange*, which depicts attempts to reform criminals as doomed, and *Barry Lyndon*, a film based on a novel by Thackeray, the nineteenth century English satirist, which depicts social life as a charade for predation and opportunism. *The Shining* is linked to these other films by the theme of fate and by its ironic style, which suggests that polite liberal society is little more than a decorous cover, a theater concealing more primordial violent impulses. The theme of primitive fate appears in *The Shining* as the occult past which determines Jack's behavior, and the ironic style of presentation consists of contrasts between a civil world that is shown to be empty and a frightening, more powerful world of primitive aggressivity. Jack cites the platitudes of civilized family life—"Wendy, I'm home!"—as he breaks down the door with an axe. In the end, he is represented as a grunting neanderthalic hunting animal, a figure of the conservative vision of human life.

Kubrick codes these themes chromatically, so much so that few scenes fail to be inflected along the lines of a semiotics of color. The most prevalent color opposition is between red and blue. Blue is the color of civility, platitude, and polite behavior. It is associated with the empty chatter of television,

The Shining. Desire and repulsion from female sexuality.

scenes of decorous family life, stereotypical repetition ("all work . . ."), and Jack's wife, Wendy, who is represented as something of a space cadet. Red is the color of horror and violence, everything from the blood that flows from elevators to the bright red walls of the bathroom in which Jack receives instructions to kill his family. Kubrick uses filters to make certain color tones dominant in certain scenes, and the device is especially noticeable in contrasting scenes, as when there is a cut from a dominant blue family/television scene to a dominant red scene in which Jack enters the occult world. In the end, when Jack breaks down the bedroom door with an axe, the alternation is between a blue exterior and the red interior, as if the external world of civility were being set off from an inner world of primitive blood violence. When Jack is in between the two worlds, still behaving civilly, not yet mad, he wears both red and blue; when his son, Danny, begins to enter the occult world, he is shot against a red carpet and he starts to wear a bright red sweater; and when Wendy finally passes over into the occult world, she too shifts from predominant blues to red. Moreover, intense yellow to gold coloring in the fantasy bar connotes a world of leisure and wealth, a world from which Jack is excluded in reality. The same color is associated with his work, the medium of his attempted rise on the class ladder.

The color coding instantiates the theme of the violence of human nature underlying the patina of civilization. It is significant that the film ends outside the house "in nature," but nature appears metaphorically in the house in the form of the recurring bathroom motif. In one, Jack encounters the ulcerous woman; in another he receives his murderous instructions from the previous caretaker. There also Wendy hides from him when he begins his rampage. The bathroom suggests interiority, and it is comparable to the unconscious to which Jack descends and to the past into which he retreats. If the house is a metaphor for the psyche, then the bathroom comes to figure as a site of bodily guilt and disgust. It signifies gross materiality (the hag), the compulsive fated horror of the past (the previous caretaker), and the violence lurking beneath polite family life (the attack on Wendy). Its significance as the gross secret (excrement) that underlies polite civility is especially clear in the scene in which Jack and Wendy sit on the bed to one side of the frame. On the other side of the frame is the open bathroom door through which one sees the toilet and above it a bright shining light. Earlier, light is associated with civility, and here it is shown in contrast to the toilet, which underlies it quite literally within the frame. Jack, who is linked to "shining," is parallel to the light, while Wendy is parallel to the toilet. The ulcerous woman was also found in a bathroom, and one senses that revulsion from feminine bodily functions (and from materiality in general) informs the horror theme. That, in fact, would explain the recurring images of blood pouring forth through elevator doors like an uncontrolled menstrual flow. Thus, the bathroom is the site of that "nature" of gross materiality which drags down all the pretensions of civil behavior. It is important, then, that the bathroom in which the horrible woman appears is a bright green, the color traditionally associated with nature.

The Shining. The parallel between the woman and the toilet.

The motif of "shining" or preverbal communication is a further elaboration of the opposition between civil and natural life. It suggests a truth that shines forth without the mediation of representation. The film is a visual rather than a verbal text. That is, it makes its point primarily through images and color coding, not through a discursive elaboration of its meaning. Language signifies civility, and at the level Jack comes to inhabit, language is no longer operative. Thus, "nature" seems to stand outside language and civilization altogether.

But the colors are themselves metaphors, civil institutions rather than natural substances. The nature of primitive desire can only be presented by civilized means, and it can only stand forth as the effect of a differential contrast, a juxtaposition with civility. Like the mountain mirrored symmetrically in the lake at the beginning of the film, or the maze which mirrors the straight civilized lines of the hotel, nature can only be posited from within civilization as its inversion—from platitude to murder. This is so because "nature" is itself a projection of a conservative worldview onto nature and a product of conservative socialization. It is a metaphor for conservative social institutions and values, which are in fact the inversion of liberal ideals. Where liberals see the possibility of rational arrangements, conservatives see an irrational and violent world that cannot be redeemed by ameliorative measures. But conservative "nature" can never shine forth as such, outside of representational mediations which foreground its origin in a particular sort of civil arrangement.

Kubrick's film thus examines the sexual psychopathology of right-wing disciplinarianism and primitivism. The conservative social theme of the necessity of discipline to control an uncontrolled, disorderly, and violent nature is embodied in the film's style, which is itself highly controlled. Such fastidiousness in form (rituals of behavior, extreme attention to detail) is associated in psychoanalytic theory with anxieties regarding uncontrolled impulses as well as a desire to control and retain what threatens to depart. Such desires connote a fixation on anality, and they are linked with sadism—hence, perhaps, the importance of the bathroom, where Jack encounters both a horrifying mother and a disciplinarian father. If mothers are associated with the horror of gross physical processes, then it is fitting that the paternal figure or superego should represent control over those processes, the power of the mind to supersede involuntary physicality. But the father (the previous caretaker) also is a figure for the violent separation from a female horror that threatens to engulf the "boy" Jack (as in the green bathroom sequence where Jack's attraction to the woman/mother gives way to repulsion). Appropriately, the bartender tells Jack—"Women, you can't live with 'em, you can't live without 'em." These points help explain the disciplinarian, sadistic, and sexist orientation of conservative social thinking. It is based in a horror of materiality coupled with a desire for control over it, and in a fixation at an immature level of psychic development that is anal retentive and sadistic in orientation. They might also explain the conservative attachment to the past, that which cannot be let go and which must be clung to. Fittingly, Jack's final descent is both into a figure of intestines (the maze) and into a frozen past (the photograph in which he appears magically in a 1920s setting). It is as well the historical world of the father-caretaker, and one senses that the conservative desire to retain, never to let go, is linked to a desire to restore the father, to lay claim to his disciplinary power (over the child and the mother). At the origin of the conservative model of "nature" seems to lie a certain authoritarian family form whose configuration provokes the sort of socialization we have been describing, one oriented above all toward restoring paternal discipline that is somehow a source of pleasure.

For, in the final photograph, Jack for the first time appears happy and free. The image of pleasure at escape from family responsibility and guilt stands in contrast to the painful means employed in its attainment. At a certain point in the conservative psychological scenario, sadism seems to ally with a masochism which turns pain into pleasure. The converse of the disciplinarian father is the obedient son, whose obedience is a means of waylaying pain, of converting parental punishment into pleasure. The internalized correlate of patriarchal discipline is self-control, pleasing through obedience and therefore avoiding pain. That, of course, is the key to the replication of the conservative psychopathology through family socialization. Its negative side is the reproduction of the desire to retain and control as a model for society. Such thinking easily legitimates retentive greed, a jungle survivalist psychology, and social discipline. Yet it contains a progressive dimension. For the need to convert the pain of conservative socialization into pleasure suggests that such social forms (discipline, obedience, etc.) survive only at the expense of their internal subversion. It is as if conservatism evidenced a desire ultimately to escape from conservatism.

2. Monsters

Monster figures can be used to affirm the existing order in that they represent threats to normality which are purged. The release of narrative tension is often identified in the tradition with conservative institutions. But monsters can also be used critically and deconstructively if they draw attention to particularly monstrous aspects of normal society, as in monster tragedies like the "Creature" films of the fifties. The leftist use of the monster motif in the modern era is thus not altogether unprecedented. Indeed, an argument could be made that all monster figures are immanently critical of reigning social norms, since what cultures project as "monstrous" in relation to "normality" is frequently a metaphor for unrestrained aggression and unrepressed sexuality of the sort upon whose exclusion the maintenance of civility depends. The viewing experience of such films often also elicits feelings that a purged civil life cannot by definition afford, and this probably helps account for their popularity both with young people, whose sexuality is restrained in bourgeois society, and with underclass people who live under the gun of a class society that must for its survival keep their urges as controlled as possible. Even the classical monster films often elicited sympathy for the monster figure, though conservative social authority ultimately had to triumph. The plight of the spurned groom in *The Bride of Frankenstein* was more likely to appeal to lonelyhearts than to conservatives on the lookout for something to repress.

In classical monster films a reassuring social order is restored through the successful operations of conservative institutions and authority figures. In most contemporary monster films no reassuring vision of restored order is affirmed. And the monster is often a figure less of an external threat to an essentially good social order than of an exaggeration of the most normal features of that very order. While many fifties monster films rehearsed scenarios of ecological or nuclear disaster from a liberal point of view, few blamed corporate greed or uncontrolled militarism for the problem. The new critical monster films often do so, and this motif seems a direct result of the radical movements of the sixties and seventies. The culture became sensitized to the real possibility of such disasters as a result of the environmental and ecological movements. In addition, during this period the increased power of American corporations and conservative political forces led to an increase of arrogance regarding such issues as toxic waste, nuclear power, and pesticide poisoning. When the discovery of toxic poisoning at Love Canal and of nuclear industry malpractice at Three Mile Island brought that arrogance to public attention, one result was an increase in the level of public skepticism regarding the virtuous interests of such institutions. Those public attitudes are transcoded and addressed in numerous monster films of the period.

Among the most important socially critical monster films of the era are the three "Dead" movies made by George Romero: *Night of the Living Dead* (1968), *Dawn of the Dead* (1979), *Day of the Dead* (1985). By depicting normal

Many revenge-of-nature monster films render in figurative form the literal fears of pollution and radiation which entered public consciousness and public discourse during the era.

people becoming monsters, Romero subverts the line demarcating normality from monstrosity and suggests that much of what passes for normal life is in fact quite unseemly. Romero established the lexicon for the contemporary monster film in *Night of the Living Dead*. Operating as an independent outside the Hollywood mainstream, he was able to explore themes (incest) using dramatic modes and representational strategies (cannibalism rendered literally) without restraint from the reigning Hollywood conventions. The premise of *Night* is that dead people walk around in a zombie-like stupor attacking and eating living people, who in turn become "living dead" that prey on others. A group of people hiding out in a farmhouse are besieged and overrun by the Dead. In this film the Dead can be read as externalizations of tensions and conflicts internal to the family and patriarchal social relations. Robin Wood writes: "The zombies represent the suppressed tensions and conflicts— the legacy of the past, of the patriarchal structuring of relationships, 'dead' yet automatically continuing—which that order creates and on which it precariously rests."[3] The farmhouse group is as much destroyed by internecine bickering and by the surfacing of suppressed desire and violence as by the zombies. It is important, therefore, that the horror that emerges to destroy the good middle-class family comes from the basement of the house (their own daughter, who becomes a zombie and kills her mother). If the house is the traditional symbol of family life, then the basement signifies the family's hidden subconscious dimension of repressed desire and violence.

The film also evokes more political and social themes. A middle-class white who represents the capitalist values of survivalism is almost more threatening than the Dead, and one suspects that an equation is being made between his unethical anticommunal selfishness and the consuming threat outside the house. When he is shot by Ben, the black central figure, the audience is positioned to approve, an audacious gesture in a film of the period, since, as Tommy Lott points out to us, no filmmaker had dared allow a black to kill a white for justifiable reasons in the Hollywood tradition. Moreover, Ben's death at the end of the film at the hands of the redneck posse is depicted as mindless and brutal, and another equation seems to be signaled between the white hunters (who are reminiscent of southern sheriffs as they appeared on television during the period as persecutors of black civil rights marchers) and the Living Dead. It is difficult to decide who is more dangerous (a point underscored more forcefully in the later films of the trilogy). Indeed, the stills at the end of the film, which portray the posse using meat hooks to hoist Ben's body onto a bonfire, recall news photos of southern lynching parties. Finally, the posse is portrayed in a manner which points to the way U.S. soldiers were operating at the same time in Vietnam (they use helicopters and call their work a "search and destroy" operation).

Thus Romero criticizes a number of conservative values and institutions, from the police to the patriarchal family to white supremacism. And he suggests that conservative order is as monstrous as the Living Dead, who in fact are presented as victims of radiation. As in his later film, *The Crazies* (1973), the authorities are depicted as more interested in covering up the disaster than in acting for the social good.

Throughout the trilogy, cooperation (between races, sexes, family members) is privileged as an alternative to the mindless, self-indulgent greed of the Dead. The zombies gain a different inflection from their historical context in each film. During the Nixon era, the Dead suggest the "Silent Majority" who blindly follow conservative leaders. By *Dawn of the Dead*, the zombies have come to represent programmed compulsive consumption. A shopping mall now serves as a metaphor for an America of material goods. Without knowing why, the Dead come to the mall out of habit. Again they are represented as blindly violent and selfish, but in this film intergender and interracial cooperation saves some people. The Freudian night has given way to a more Marxist dawn, and a positive image of salvation or at least hope is offered in the end. A black policeman relinquishes his rifle to the Dead in order to escape with a white woman. *Day of the Dead*, made at the height of Reagan's power, is a more specific political statement against militarism. The Dead have overwhelmed the living, and a few scientists work on ways to domesticate them. The scientists—the most important of whom, as in *Dawn* is a woman—represent civility and tolerance, but they are guarded by a group of intolerant, uncivil, racist, and sexist militarists. By this point, the Dead have come to appear more as victims than as victimizers. And they acquire the additional meaning of being a force of retribution and punishment of evil. In the end, the good values of the scientists are rewarded with escape, while all the militarists are served up for an afternoon snack.

Metaphors always harbor metonyms in ways that permit a deconstruction of the idealizations to which metaphors lend themselves in conservative ideology. In radically critical films like the *Dead* trilogy, a similar process is at work. The Dead are clearly metaphoric, and they also contain literal, material and metonymic connections to aspects of an unidealized social world. What is striking about this metaphor is its lack of distance from that reality and that materiality. Indeed, the metaphor of the Dead is almost directly metonymic, since it is a figure for mindless materialism, the crass, spiritless consumption of goods. It signifies a literal hunger that destroys and leads people, under consumer capitalism, to destroy others. But the metaphor is not singular in meaning, and to this extent as well it is metonymic. Rather than hypostatizing a single universal meaning, the figure shifts meaning according to context and time. In the early eighties it means something quite different than in the late sixties. From being a figure for the mindlessness of conservative culture, it shifts to a figure for the radical resistance to conservative power. In addition, like metonymy, the figure of the Dead materializes rather than idealizes; that is, it produces associations with material dimensions of social life, rather than exalting a single aspect of that life into a transcendental ideal. The figure is open-ended and future-oriented. No narrative conclusion offers redemption. The possibilities of permutation are open, and no ideological paradigm or ideal resolution commutes the sentence of material existence.

Romero's films helped launch a strain of socially critical independent monster films depicting monstrous aspects of "normal" American life. They are usually referred to as "exploitation" films because they exploit topical events like sensational murders. In the early films of Wes Craven and Tobe Hooper particularly, Americans are portrayed as monsters who are capable of engaging in fairly violent behavior. Hooper's cult classic *The Texas Chainsaw Massacre* (1974) is probably the most notorious of these. In it a demented family murders a group of teenagers to process them for their barbecue business. Although the rural family is totally crazed, their behavior parodies "normal" capitalism and "normal" family relationships.

Displaced by mechanization which forced the closing of the slaughterhouse where they worked, the family turned to cannibalism as a mode of survival, substituting people for animals in their meat business. Their horrific behavior is thus a consequence of economic immiseration and the displacement of labor by mechanization, and their situation allegorizes the destructive psychological effects of forced unemployment. In Mary Mackey's words: "The unemployed family, showing true American self-reliance, hasn't gone on welfare. Instead the father has set up a small roadside barbecue stand, and the two sons and the grandfather have proceeded to provide the meat. The meat, in this case, is tourists—a class of people that, as far as the family is concerned, is no different than any other breed of cattle. In this film the poor in order to survive literally eat the rich."[4] In fact, the family members, and the father in particular, have internalized the ethos of capitalism, which puts profit above people, production above human life, and self above others. For instance, the father, while kidnapping a girl for slaughter, comments: "Gotta remember to turn off the lights. The cost of electricity is enough to drive a man out of business." The film thus represents the very real contradictions between capitalist efficiency and social ethics.

If the Romero and Hooper strain of exploitation films suggests metaphorically that capitalism is monstrous, another series of "mutant monster" or "revenge of nature" films argues more literally that capitalism and science can have harmful effects on nature and humans. Many of these films—*Night of the Lepus* (1972), *The Island of Dr. Moreau* (1977), and *Piranha* (1980), for example—concern monsters that result from scientific or military experiments or industrial pollution. In some of these films, conservative figures and institutional practices are targeted as the cause and the direct object of the rampaging monsters. In others (*Nightwing, Prophecy, Wolfen*), corporate malfeasance and modernization are criticized for destroying Native American life.

Perhaps the most significant of these films (and certainly the most successful with popular audiences—number 4 in 1979) was Ridley Scott's *Alien*, in which a monster invades a corporate space vessel. The spaceship world is characterized by sexual repression, hierarchial social relations, the exploitation of labor, and the sacrifice of life for corporate profit. The monster that encroaches from without seems in many ways merely a displaced and projected emanation of the negativity produced by the normal operations of that world. In a deconstructive vein, the film seems to say that capitalist normality is monstrous, and for this reason it is significant that the monster literally emerges at one point from inside one of the crew. The real nemesis is the corporation that programs the ship to investigate dangerous alien beings and to sacrifice the lives of the crew members if necessary in order to bring the findings back to earth. This critical thematic is instantiated in the form of the film, which attempts to create a more materialist or nonidealized atmosphere than usual by muddling dialog, leaving out romantic relationships, deflating heroism, and portraying flagrant bitchiness among crew members.

It is in comparison to the purist efficiency and pure self-interest of the corporation that the film's cluttered style and anarchic society assume a radical significance. Indeed, the film is structured as a conflict between a mode of organization that is hierarchical and authoritarian and a mode that is communal and egalitarian, and this difference also takes the form of a difference in modes of representation. The two workers (one of whom is black) complain about wages and threaten (good-humoredly) to strike. They are positively portrayed and seem the only ones who have empathetic relations. They are also more material or humorously crude in comparison to the stuffy professionals, who bicker over command structures and the division of labor on ship. For much of the first section of the film, the narrative focus shifts back and forth between the workers and the managers, and this establishes a sense of equivalent importance. The camera rhetoric also communalizes and contextualizes, denying the sort of individualist privilege of conservative camera rhetoric. Initially the camera travels through the ship, establishing a sense of material context, setting, and environment; it shows a world defined not by an individual subject's experience but by material place, social setting. The characters appropriately will be defined by their institutional roles—science officer, etc. At the circular mess table the camera moves around in a full circle drawing all the characters into the frame equally. In later framings three characters are placed in close-up, thus stressing the ties and tensions between them. It is a world of social subjects, the camera seems to suggest. But it is also a world of great material clutter, an aspect deliberately emphasized in contradistinction to the pure, clean, white, and eminently efficient corporate authority source—the master computer. It is as if, once again, a more mature radical attitude toward the world entails a representational logic that can encompass undecidability, indeterminacy, and complexity, a crossing of the clear boundaries that a fearful and defensive conservative representational structure requires. The character who represents corporate order on ship is Ash, the android officer who admires the "purity" of the alien. It is, he says, "a survivor, unclouded by conscience, remorse, or delusions of morality." A good contemporary conservative, in other words. Ripley, the woman survivor, on the other hand, is associated with liberal values of care and empathy. "We have to stick together," she urges the others. And she goes so far as to take the trouble to save a cat (although this has invited charges of sexual stereotyping, a charge reinforced by the small strip scene she must undergo—Scott's movies are admittedly contradictory in regard to feminism). The film thus depicts corporate capitalism as a predatory, survivalist machine; self-interest takes precedence over community. The alien is a projection of the principles of the capitalist system. Against the alien, the film proposes a counterprinciple of community, which it draws out most noticeably in the camera style. The camera rhetoric is reconstructive; it emphasizes the materiality, hence the non-natural malleability, of the corporate world. Similarly, the crew continually devises machines for combating the alien. The tools of the enemy can be recoded. The system offers the means of its own deconstruction.

Alien struck a critical, anticapitalist chord with lower-income viewers, its primary audience. While only 38 of 153 in our sample had seen it, of those, 57% thought the critique of the corporation was accurate, and most of these were in the under $30,000 income bracket; the percentages declined as income rose. Again, however, personal meanings outdid structural ones; only 16% felt the primary meaning of the film was that corporations put profit before human life, while 52% chose the meaning "humans can triumph over impossible situations."

The format of *Alien* recalls that of many "discovered alien" films of the fifties, including Hawks's celebrated *The Thing*. Fittingly, at this time a number of classic monster films, including *The Thing* and *Invasion of the Body Snatchers*, were remade. *Body Snatchers* (1978) revives the pessimistic ending of the original (dropped by the producers), and *The Thing* remake (1982) likewise ends on a much darker, more pessimistic note appropriate to the contemporary era. Instead of banding together to watch the skies, the men have to watch each other, since anyone might be "it."

If conservatives use the figure of the monster to demonstrate that in the jungle world of conservative psychopathology no one can be trusted, everyone potentially is a monster, left-liberals use the metaphor of the American-as-monster to criticize bourgeois normality and to suggest that American life harbors monstrous impulses that conservatives claim are moral and good. The werewolf and the vampire have traditionally represented the possibility that normal people might become monsters, and both are revived in this period, frequently in socially critical or camp parodic ways. Camp werewolf films like *The Howling* drew out the sexual meaning of the animal-human metaphor. Similarly, in numerous vampire films of the period (between 1970 and 1977 alone there were over two hundred new films)[5] sexuality and power are often explicitly identified. One of the most critical, Romero's *Martin* (1977), depicts a young vampire who sedates women, rapes them, and drinks their blood. Rarely has the fact that rape is an act of violence been made more explicit. Yet while Romero's film critically examines the violence against women that is institutionalized in American culture, many other horror films of the era promote such violence.

3. Brian De Palma and the Slash and Gash Cycles

We have suggested that metaphoric representational forms permit both radical critiques and conservative projections of the sort that might normally be too extreme for mainstream Hollywood to reach the screen. In Paul Schrader's remake of *Cat People* (1981), for example, a woman "animal" is tied to a bed with rope so that she won't get out of control, and the audience is cued to think this is good for her. If the image had not been framed by a fantastic horror narrative of a woman who becomes a panther during sex and eats her partner, it might have evoked justifiable criticism as a gross exercise of male power that should, certain radical feminists would argue, have been censored. But even as a horror metaphor the image and the film can tell us something about what was literally going on in American culture during this time in regard to the new independence women had gained around sexuality. For one thing, female sexuality is represented in the film as a threat to men; in one segment, a man has his arm ripped off by the panther woman. (Get it?) Therefore, woman's "animality" must be controlled. In the last chapter we studied the sorts of metaphoric violence this attitude can generate. *Cat People* and the films of De Palma tell us a bit more about why women were being punished. That punishment was not limited to metaphoric violence. It also took the form of overt violence, often executed with a sharp kitchen knife, as if to emphasize its domestic origins. The place where that literal, social violence against women was most easily exercised was the horror genre, with its covert metaphors. Shades of that violence emerge in social realist films earlier, for example in *Looking for Mr. Goodbar* (1977). But the ending of that film, in which a sexually independent woman is brutally murdered by a bisexual male already indicates the need for a metaphoric medium of representation for such violence. A flashing strobe light interrupts the realist style with a garish and naturalistic set of stills. It was as if conservative filmmakers realized that they could only get away with so much within the confines of realism. Otherwise it would appear that their representations indicated what they really thought should be done to women, instead of simply metaphorizing a male rage at insubordination, betrayal, and abandonment and indicating a possibility of punishment, a threat to restore order, like a knife to the throat or the point of an ice pick touching the iris of an eye.

The horror films that are most often associated with such violence are the slash and gash cycles and the work of Brian De Palma,[6] in whose films women are generally represented as sexy dumbbells, slashable victims, or threatening witches.

Both stylistically and thematically De Palma's films manifest a high level of anxiety about independent feminine sexuality and women in general. They display the sort of doubling we have noticed already, whereby women are represented either as threatening nemeses or as compliant and submissive ideals. If the splitting of an object on the level of representation is a symptom of fear regarding that object, then *Sisters* (1973), one of De Palma's early horror films of the era, is a particularly good example of this. A liberal woman reporter, a figure of "feminism," witnesses a murder; she "meddles" in the investigation, and as a result is herself driven half mad. It turns out that a doctor has separated siamese twin sisters, but the "bad" one returns to inhabit her good sister, emerging at inappropriate times to commit murder and, eventually, to castrate the doctor. If one sister is a figure of male fear, the other is a figure of male desire for a caring and submissive woman.

What is interesting about the terror that seems to motivate the narrative is that it also seems to give rise to a disorder of representation consisting of exaggerated lighting and editing effects, jarring camera angles, and fantasy dream segments shot in an entirely different color medium from the main narrative. Perhaps the most symptomatic device is the split-screen technique, which could be read as a literal rendering of psychological splitting as a result of anxiety over male sexual identity. Male sexual anxiety in particular seems due to a double attitude toward the primary caretaker, usually the mother. To attain a male sexual identity the boy must separate from the hitherto dominant sexual pattern of his life, which is a dependent "female" attachment to a powerful woman. If not entirely successful, that process can lead in later life to anxiety over sexual identity and violence against independent or strong women who are perceived as threats because they place the man once again in a dependent, passive, "castrated," "feminine" position and to desires for compliant, weak women who make the man feel "male." If the first attitude toward the mother is to fear her power, the second is to require her presence as a confirmation of maleness. Her withdrawal or absence can confuse the male child, make him feel passive and weak, not sufficiently powerful to retain her attention. If the father is perceived as the one who receives that attention, then a desire will set in to obtain the father's power (his phallus). The double attitude therefore consists of a contradictory desire for separation and difference conjoined with a desire for fusion and presence.

The development of representations which internalize an image of maternal presence is the precondition of being able to live separately without having either to yearn for fusion or to repel oneself aggressively from relationships with others that threaten to engulf one. The failure to develop the capacity for such representation can result in such yearnings and fears. Thus, the disorder of representation in De Palma's films can be read as a late version of an early failure to develop healthy modes of mental representation. The result is an inability to represent women as nonthreatening or independent and self-sufficient—different from the man.

Male anxiety can also arise around "feminization" in the form of homosexuality. In De Palma's mid-seventies occult horror film *The Phantom of the Paradise* (1974), for example, a gay rock star is made the target of homophilic humor as well as of a fatal electrical charge. The story concerns an independent music composer whose music is stolen by a corporation run by a demonic figure who also steals a woman the man loves. Finally, the "phantom," disfigured by a record press, destroys the corporation but is himself killed. The film contains scenes of voyeurism (already evident in the opening segment of *Sisters*) that will come to characterize De Palma's films. Voyeurism is a form of objectification, an exercise of scopophilic power, although in *Phantom* it is associated with a weak male's envy of a strong male's (father's) power. It constitutes an attempt to gain power over the woman in a way that reassures a man's sense of being male. *Phantom* also establishes a link between sexual power and economic power, a theme fully realized in the later *Scarface* (1983), in which gaining power over the boss's girl is coincident with the actual displacement of him from a position of economic superiority.

Of De Palma's next two films, *Carrie* (1977) extends the occult concerns while *Obsession* (1976) reprises the theme of splitting. *Obsession* (co-scripted by Paul Schrader) concerns a man who falls in love with his own daughter, who looks exactly like his dead wife. He doesn't realize it is his daughter until the end, when, instead of killing her, as the audience expects, he embraces her. Symbolically, the wife is killed off in favor of the daughter, someone more liable to control and devoted worship of the husband/father. *Carrie* is a fairy tale of an ugly duckling teenager who uses her telekinetic powers to intimidate her sexually repressed mother and those who harass her. The link between telekinesis and sexuality is established by Carrie's discovery of her power when she is menstruating for the first time; later she is doused in blood as a practical joke at the prom and retaliates by destroying the gym and killing most of the people present. *The Fury* (1978) also associates telekinesis with youth sexuality, and it divides women into either evil whores or mothering helpers.

Indeed, De Palma's scheme of punishment for sexually threatening women is repeated with obsession in his eighties films—*Dressed to Kill, Blow-Out*, and

Body Double. Dressed to Kill (1980) is an oedipal fantasy in which an overly independent woman/mother is slashed to death for being a "cock-teaser." The film understandably elicited great hostility within the feminist community. It begins with a woman's fantasy of being raped in the shower; she surrenders to the attack. In the next scenes she fakes orgasm with her husband and makes a pass at her therapist. She then picks up a man at an art gallery, allows herself to be raped by him in a taxi, and goes to his apartment, where she discovers he has veneral disease. As she leaves, she is slashed to death on the elevator. The killer, it turns out, is the psychiatrist, who is a transsexual in conflict with himself over his sexual identity. With the help of a prostitute her son finds the killer, and ends up in bed with the prostitute because his father is "away." In the structure of the fantasy an "independent" woman is traded in for a more pliant one, and the son takes the father's place in relation to the woman in the house. Thus, male sexual identity is established through the acquisition of the father's role in relation to the mother, and through the replacement of a mother who abandons by one who makes the male feel powerful. The wayward woman is punished, moreover, by a figure of male sexual uncertainty—someone who doesn't want to be a woman—and the prostitute is tormented in the conclusion by a dream in which her throat is cut by the same killer, a symbol of the threat of punishment that situates her in a subservient position and keeps her there.

Thus, the film is about the proper positioning of sexual subjects. Uncertain males are represented negatively, as are inappropriately independent women. But the film also concerns the alleviation of male sexual anxiety and uncertainty. In the symbolic sexual scenario, the son is made to feel uncertain by his mother (who moves from a scene of sex with her husband to a sexually teasing scene with her son where she alludes to his masturbation). The mother is further positioned as someone who casts doubt on male sexual identity in the subsequent scene with her therapist, where she criticizes her husband's sexual skill. She then seeks out an alternative, the man she picks up at a gallery, and her punishment for undermining male sexual identity begins immediately. That the son is the instrument of salvation who purges the figure of sexual deviancy and redeems the mother (by finding the killer and by finding a replacement for her) is indicative of the oedipal character of the symbolic scenario. It is important, therefore, that the resolution of the symbolic narrative consists of the son's installation in the place of the father and of the restoration of a more confirming mother to the house.

It is also noteworthy that the instrument of the son's power is a camera which he places outside the psychiatrist's office, since visual power, the mental power to represent the world, is in part what is at stake in the film. Insecurity over sexual identity is associated with a failure of mental representation. When the transsexual psychiatrist is watching a TV show interview with a man who has undergone a sex change operation, the film image is split and divided. On the one side is the "feminized" psychiatrist and the TV screen, and on the other is the narcissistic prostitute and a mirror into which she looks while putting on makeup, signaling a relationship between his passivity

Dressed to Kill. The split screen.

and sexual confusion and her self-absorption (a figure for a mother who does not attend to the male child, thus provoking anxiety over her absence and over the male child's sexual identity). Anxiety over sexual identity of the sort projected in such images is due in part to a failure to develop a capacity to represent the world as a coherent, objective, and differentiated phenomenal space. The anxiety has to do with feelings of passivity and helplessness, feeling like a "woman." And the anxiety is overcome by the development of an extremely exaggerated power of private representation, cut off entirely from a threatening object world and withdrawn into narcissistically gratifying and reassuring fantasy images. For good reason, the male fear of "castration," of being a "woman," is associated with vision and its failure.

All of this seems to be played out in De Palma's film. The son is abandoned symbolically by the mother, and the vehicle of vengeance is someone associated with anxiety over passive or "feminine" feelings as well as with a failure of representation, an inability to differentiate phenomenal elements. The means of overcoming both, by attaining a power of mental representation, is an instrument of visual or representational power, the camera. Yet something of the fear that motivates the film is still evident even as power is attained. The murderer and a woman detective in masquerade are confused at one point, and this lends the narrative a hysteric quality similar to that evident in films like *Psycho*. That confusion is at the moment of capture linked to a failure on the part of the boy to see properly. Thus a case of mistaken identity turns on a case of anxiety over sexual identity. And that anxiety emerges as narrative confusion, as the nondifferentiation of fantasy from realist segments at the beginning and end of the film when the audience is positioned to see dreams as real events, and as the visual theme of representational dysfunction and power.

De Palma's films make clear the extent to which style is crucial to male sexual identity. And the style of many of these films is defined by baroque excess. One aspect of narcissistic unity with the mother is a sense of meaning in the world; a meaning-filled world is secure, predictable, nonthreatening, recognizable. Meaning affords a sense of well-being akin to that provided by the presence of the (m)other, a predictable supplier of needs. The baroque world, in contrast, is unpredictable; it is a world of anxiety projections, threats potentially coming from anywhere, because the secure presence of meaning has withdrawn from it. If signs of affection do not lead to a predictable and secure maternal presence, then signs in general cannot be trusted. Signs might mean anything or nothing. Indeed, that they might mean nothing is the worst sort of anxiety, since that implies the absence of a confirming presence, a comforting semantic plenitude. This, we would suggest, helps explain the occult motif in De Palma's films. It represents an attempt to give meaning to the world by infusing it with hidden significance that is of the order of a private insight not available to others, a token of mental representational power. This also would account for the prevalence of the metaphor of te-lekinesis in his films, since it also connotes a private mental power, and for the young man's use of his own visual technology in *Dressed to Kill* to catch the murderer.

The fantastic, exaggerated, baroque style is thus essential to the sexist vision of the films. That style constitutes a representational performance that indicates power over the world, an ability to manipulate it at will. If the child sees himself as not cared for, he will grow up not caring about the world, converting his resentment against his abandonment into a calculating, cynical, unempathetic manipulation of that world (evident particularly at the end of *Blow-Out*, when the recording of a murdered lover's scream is inserted into a B horror film soundtrack). Moreover, if the world cannot be trusted, then security can only be gotten in a private, artificial world of one's own making. The vulnerable male withdraws from a threatening world into a private world of mental representation where split screen collages take on meaning from their artificial arrangement within a fantastic plot that is already one removed from a confirming reality. The prevalence of segments in De Palma's films in which dreams or fantasies are indistinguishable from and meant to be mistaken for realist segments (*Body Double* is based entirely on this premise) is therefore important; they recall the inability to differentiate self from other and subjective vision from objective reality that gives rise to an incapacity for complex, articulated, or differentiated objective representation. Only in the artificial realm of the baroque style, where the parts of the meaningless world can be juxtaposed and played with in split screen images, is his power realized as the ability to do what he will with the world, as he desires to do with women. This is Walter Benjamin's baroque tyrant become a petit bourgeois family man.

We disagree, therefore, with the suggestion that De Palma is a progressive filmmaker whose work reflects critically on issues of morality. While his films are critical of aspects of American society, these critiques are limited to a traditional populist suspicion of big institutions (government in *Blow-Out*, corporations in *Phantom*). In his interviews, he does voice some sense of the reality of feminism, but his films speak more loudly (and perhaps more unconsciously) than his words, and they stand as symptomatic expressions of a misogyny so endemic to American culture that it passes as normal.[7]

Less baroque but equally obsessive male fantasies of violence against women are evident in the "slash and gash" or "slice and dice" film. In these films, which thrived in the late seventies and early eighties, women and teenagers are brutalized, generally for being sexually independent (although other narrative motivations come into play as the cycles develop). The films are characterized by a conservative moralism regarding sexuality and frequently feature occult elements. The cycles begin in 1978, the year that also witnessed a conservative turn in films dealing with blacks, the Vietnam War, male heroism, teen sexuality, and a number of other social issues.

John Carpenter's *Halloween* (1978) launched the cycles. It turned a $300,000 budget into a multi–million–dollar profit and led to a rash of spinoffs, sequels, and imitations. The film establishes the template for the series: Young teens, especially girls, are shown engaging in "immoral" activities like sex and drugs. They are killed.

The style of slash and gash films is as exploitative as their themes. Perhaps the most striking device is the use of point of view shots from the killer's perspective using the new steadicam cameras. In this way, the audience helps stalk the victims. More so than in other films, then, male scopophilic tendencies of the sort fostered in American culture in the age of visual advertising and mass pornography are directly addressed, and the relation between such voyeurism and an objectifying violence is made explicit. Moreover, particularly in *Halloween*, the musical accompaniment (characterized by a high level of repetition) works to cast the events in the realm of the fated and to give them the meaning of a supernatural moral retribution. The same scenario was repeated in *Friday the 13th* (Parts 1, 2, 3, 4, and 5) and *Prom Night*. The template became so rote after a while that it was easily parodied in films like *Student Bodies, The Slumber Party Massacre*, and *Pandemonium* that frequently featured body counts flashed across the screen after each murder.

The slash and gash films invite calls for censorship, yet they also depict the questionable character of the censorial mentality at work in the films. That mentality seeks to repress because, perhaps, it arises from repression. Incapable of incorporating sexuality into its own life, it attempts to blot it out from the world. But it also betrays a fascination with what it opposes. For films that evidence such a high level of conservative moralism around sexuality, these films are surprisingly prurient. There is a contradiction between the explicitly erotic scenes and the puritanical messages of many of the movies. Perhaps they are simply symptoms of a culture which is fascinated with sex but which still thinks of it in terms of guilt and transgression. One senses, however, that if sexuality were incorporated into everyday life in healthier ways it would not provoke such perverse pornographic excrescences or such moralizing hostility.

The slash and gash films can also be said to relate to the problems that the new culture of sexuality in post-sixties America brought with it. Birth control, liberalized abortion laws, and greater sexual permissiveness changed the character of male-female relations, giving women more power and independence while scuttling the old rules of male responsibility that mediated sexual interaction. Out of the intersection of aggressive independence and irresponsible predation hostility was probably certain to emerge. With increased sexual activity came increased guilt, tension, and confusion around such issues as commitment, a key word of the era. All of this was compounded by the discovery of the spread of traditional and new venereal diseases.

Although these films deal primarily with sexuality, they also have consequences for other social issues. As David Thompson suggests, their portrayal of psychopathic killers fosters intolerant attitudes toward the "mentally ill and the criminally deviant" while supporting the most reactionary theories of criminality and law enforcement.[8] Moreover, they project the "mean world" syndrome which George Gerbner and his colleagues found to be a distinctive feature of U.S. television, and which they claim produces fears in the audience that could be manipulated by right-wing politicians.[9] Indeed, the strategy of the conservative rhetoric of these films, like the projection of nihilism in certain horror films that seems to imply a call for a strong antidote of meaning and leadership, is to represent the world as a paranoid's paradise of fear and distrust that is beyond rational redemption. What is most significant about this world is that violence seems unmotivated. It is faceless and without rational cause, as in *Halloween*. The world thus appears irrational, a jungle governed by no logic or law. It is only in such a context that the conservative view that the world cannot be redeemed makes sense. What is irrational cannot be dealt with rationally; instead, it should be controlled or repressed. Consequently, narrative illogicality serves the ends of a very conservative logic.

The conservative slash and gash cycle can therefore be said to accomplish two tasks. It carries out a metaphoric attack on feminism and on wayward youth, and it paints a world as in need of paternalist power. Read diagnostically, of course, these highly metaphoric films also therefore display what conservatism is literally all about—the projection of repressed aggression onto the world in a way that justifies the exercise of insufficiently sublimated aggression against the world. This broader possibility relates to the sexual theme of the films. The sanctification of aggression as a social principle (of the market, for example) in the conservative ethos is linked to violence against independent women because the counterpart of aggression (presumed to be a male trait in conservative thinking) is submission. Aggression as a social principle must at some point become domination; it presupposes someone else's submission; otherwise, the social system would become permanently unstable. The locus of submission and domination that secures stability in the conservative framework is the family. One could say therefore that while the slash films evidence a direct reaction against independent women's sexuality and against feminism in general, they also are part of an attempt to restabilize the patriarchal social system as a whole, by reasserting discipline over youth and by repositioning women as the submissive other of a primary, aggressive male subject. To a certain extent these films must be read as violent reactions to a violence feminism and the youth sexual revolution have done to traditional patriarchal prerogatives. As such the films enable a deconstruction of the opposition between the functional stasis through violent aggression that is assumed to be normal in U.S. society and the abnormal horror of these films. There is a certain documentary exactitude to these films that is revelatory of the attitudes and propensities fostered by a culture predicated on survivalist market principles of competition, aggression, and "devil take the hindmost." In many horror films, the devil does indeed take the hindmost (usually women, blacks, or the least powerful of survivalist society), but his occultist mask should not prevent one from deciphering the grim face of a conservative businessman beneath.

7. VIETNAM AND THE NEW MILITARISM

Halloween and *Dressed to Kill* appear around 1978–80, at the same time as *The Deer Hunter* and *Apocalypse Now*, two major conservative Vietnam films. All four are distinguished by regressive portrayals of women combined with assertions of male power and right-wing violence. That ideological conjunction, we suggest, is not accidental. It is symptomatic of a turn occurring in American culture at that time, a turn whose trajectory intersects eventually with the rise of the New Right as a force in American politics and with the renewal of militarism during the Reagan eighties. It is also symptomatic of the necessary connection between representations of paranoid projection in the horror genre as a reaction to feminism and representations of revived military might as a result of threats to national self-esteem. The psychological source was similar in each case as was the representational violence that emerged as its solution.

In American culture, film representations of military prowess seem inseparable from national self-esteem. For conservatives especially, greatness as a nation means the ability to exercise military power. In war, the strength and courage of the soldiers who represent male national prestige are tested and proven. In post–World War II cinematic representations of this ritual, proof of manhood was accompanied by a nationalistic idealism that pictured the American fighting man as a heroic liberator of oppressed people and as a defender of freedom. This ideal legend was justified by World War II, when American forces did indeed help defeat right-wing fascist regimes. After the war, however, the defense of political freedom against the right-wing corporatism of the fascist movement was replaced by a defense of free enterprise capitalism against both Soviet communism and national liberation movements throughout the world, from Latin America to Southeast Asia. The legend of the freedom-defending U.S. fighting man soon began to be tarnished by the frequent sacrifice of political freedom and democratic rights that the defense of capitalism entailed. While the overthrow of democratic leftist governments in places like Guatemala and Iran could be tolerated in the Cold War climate of the fifties, in the sixties a new generation, nurtured in a more liberal cultural atmosphere and faced with having to risk their lives in the defense of capitalism overseas, began to question the right of a corporate controlled

194

1978. The conservative turn in American society begins to occur around such issues as abortion, gay rights, government spending, affirmative action, and the Soviet Union.

U.S. government to suppress democracy and socialism throughout the world in the name of "freedom." The equation of "freedom" and "democracy" with capitalism became increasingly strained because antidemocratic military dictatorships were more often than not U.S. allies in policing Third World liberation movements. During the 1960s, the Vietnam War became a focus of popular contestation. American youth refused to fight an unjust war, and by the early seventies, a majority of the people came to oppose the war. In addition, the army began to look increasingly incapable, undisciplined, and demoralized. In 1975, the United States suffered its first military defeat in its history with the liberation of Saigon. The loss created a lesion in the sense of national prestige, and it provoked a heated debate over American foreign policy.

We shall argue that Hollywood military movies of the seventies and eighties need to be read, first, in the context of the national debate over Vietnam, and, secondly, in the context of the "post-Vietnam syndrome," which was characterized by the desire for withdrawal from "foreign involvements" after the debacle in Vietnam and epitomized by the Clark Amendment forbidding intervention in Angola.

In the decade following the end of the war, America's military posture shifted from doubt to assertiveness, as the liberal tide of the mid-seventies receded and a rightist current came to dominate American political life. Films during the period articulate the arguments that led to this change and point the direction American culture was taking regarding the war long before actual political events confirmed the shift. Around the issues of Vietnam and war in general, the failure of liberalism took the form of an inability to transform the widespread antiwar feelings of the time into a permanent institutional change in foreign policy. Once again, in this regard as in economic policy, the liberals were victims of historical circumstances. As Carter and the Democrats staved off new military programs like the B-1 bomber, the Soviets invaded Afghanistan, the Sandinistas overthrew a U.S.-supported dictator in Nicaragua, and Iran's revolution led to the taking of American hostages all in 1979 and 1980. The American empire, which had lasted from 1945 to 1970, was crumbling, and the triumph of conservatism around military policy resulted from the ability of conservatives to take advantage of these circumstances to promote the sort of military buildup they favored. Many films of the period argue the conservative position.

One major factor in the conservative triumph was the social psychology of shame that was a significant motif of American culture after the military defeat in Vietnam. It is for this reason that the returned vet motif is so important in contemporary Hollywood film. Those whose self-identity is in part constructed through the internalization of representations of the nation as a military power no doubt felt a loss of self-esteem as a result of the nation's failure. That sense of loss generated resentment as well as a yearning for compensation. One aspect of the failure of liberalism is the inability of liberals to provide a redemptive and compensatory vision that would replace military representations as a source of self-esteem. Conservatives, on the other hand, managed successfully to equate self-restoration with military renewal.

1. Debating Vietnam

The posture Hollywood initially adopted toward Vietnam is best summed up in the title of Julian Smith's book—*Looking Away.*[1] With the exception of *The Green Berets* (1968), a jingoist war story, no major films dealt directly with the war until the late seventies. Nevertheless, war itself was a topic of great debate in films of the late sixties and early seventies, and many of these touch covertly on the issue of Vietnam. Blacklisted screenwriter Dalton Trumbo's thirties antiwar novel *Johnny Got His Gun* was made into a film in 1971, a time when opposition to the war was peaking, and films like *M*A*S*H* and *Soldier Blue* of the same period indirectly criticized Vietnam era militarism. A similar sort of indirect message from the conservative side was delivered in *Patton* (1970), a promilitarist film scripted by Coppola that supposedly helped inspire Nixon to bomb Cambodia. Indeed, Patton's opening speech, shot against an immense American flag, which exhorted Americans never to give up the fight, probably had a subliminal topical resonance for many prowar hawks.

The first major 1970s Hollywood film to deal directly with the issue of the war was the independently made feature documentary *Hearts and Minds* (1975), directed by Peter Davis. If *Patton* demonstrated that the conservative militarist pathology is inseparable from male self-aggrandizement, an authoritarian model of social discipline, and the skewing of the personality away from a composite of affectionate and aggressive traits and toward a hypertropism of violence, *Hearts and Minds* by combining clips from war films with scenes of football games, shows how militarism emerges from a culture that promotes aggressivity in young men and furthers a racist attitude toward the world. The film juxtaposes defenders and critics of U.S. policy, and the accompanying documentary footage of the ravages of war positions the prowar speakers as being arrogant and cruel. For example, General Westmoreland's remark that Asians do not value human life is juxtaposed to long and painful scenes of the Vietnamese mourning their dead.

The film is also significant for attempting to establish the historical context and social system out of which the war emerged. Unlike later fictional narrative war films, *Hearts and Minds* adopts a multiple perspective that undermines the power and the blindness of a monocular subjective position. What other films pose as an object (the Vietnamese), this film grants some subjectivity, as when the Vietnamese themselves express their anger and suffering. And it situates the war in a historical context that displaces the conservative concern for violent redemption or the liberal focus on the fate of individual (usually white, male) characters.

It was not until the war was over that fictional films began to appear that dealt directly with or were explicitly critical of the war. The first films to appear concerned returned veterans, frequently portrayed as dangerously

alienated or violent (*Black Sunday, Stone Killer*). Later films take a more sympathetic point of view; films like *Cutter's Way, Who'll Stop the Rain?*, and *Some
Kind of Hero* portray the vets as confused and wounded victims. Another
strain of returned vet films use the motif as a springboard for justifying the
kind of violent and racist disposition that initiated the war in the first place
(*Rolling Thunder, First Blood, Firefox*). And finally, the vet motif in the eighties
(*Uncommon Valor, Missing in Action, Rambo*) becomes a means of affirming the
militarism of the new era.[2]

Liberal vet films focused on personal issues at the expense of the historical and global systemic concerns of *Hearts and Minds*. They criticized the
war for what it did to good, white American boys, not for what ruin it brought
to innocent Vietnamese. The first major liberal vet film—*Coming Home* (1978)—
was also the first major Hollywood feature film to deal seriously with the
issue of the war from a critical perspective. It skillfully manipulates the personalist and emotive codes of Hollywood to elicit sympathy for a wounded
antiwar vet and to generate an empathetic yet critical stance toward a gung-
ho soldier who is driven suicidal by the war experience. The scenes of the
military hospital filled with the victims of war lifted a veil of silence, yet at
the same time the film reproduces the traditional, Hollywood, sentimentalist
vision of postwar experiences (as in, say, *The Best Years of Our Lives*).

Both *Who'll Stop the Rain?* (1978) and *Cutter's Way* (1981) use the figure
of the returning vet to engage in social critique. In *Rain* a vet tries to help
a buddy's wife who is victimized by drug dealers with whom her husband was
involved. He is killed, and his death is cast in such a way as to evoke a sense
of victimage. In addition, the fact that the final fight takes place in a carnival
atmosphere suggests a critical parallel with the fruitless struggle in Vietnam.
Passer's *Cutter's Way* is even bleaker. A bitter disabled vet becomes obsessed
with revealing that a wealthy capitalist has murdered a young girl. He associates the man with the class he feels sent him to Vietnam to do its dirty
work. Again, the vet dies, while riding a white horse through a lawn party
on his way to have justice done. Such liberal vet films are distinguished by
the hopeless vision they project, a vision reinforced in *Cutter's Way* by the
use of somber color tones and confined spaces that suggest desolation and
despair. Yet both direct the violence of the vet against groups or elites who
clearly profited from the war at the expense of ordinary working-class soldiers.
Conservative vet films turn shame into violent affirmation, but to do so they
direct violence against the Vietnamese, in an attempt to win the lost war.

Rolling Thunder (1977) is an example of an extremely reactionary representation of the veteran issue. A veteran returns home to find his wife
having an affair (a familiar cultural motif at the time expressed in the popular
song "Ruby," concerning a woman who betrays a wounded vet). In this
reprise of the post–World War II classic *The Blue Dahlia*, the wife and children
are brutally murdered, and the veteran seeks out and kills the perpetrators
with the aid of another veteran. Male bonding heals female betrayal, and
violence, as usual, cures all ills. The wife's murder could be seen as a symbolic
projection of the husband's revenge (his hand is mangled by the attackers,

and the two events seem interrelated). And the rest of the violence is directed against non-whites. In this vision, the Vietnam War is not left behind; it is brought home to roost.

The film depicts the psychological basis upon which post-Vietnam Americans are enlisted into the new militarism. The hero is depicted as being shamed ("castrated"), and his reaction is to become violent against non-Americans. The shame associated with sexuality in the film is linked both to military defeat and to being deprived of money (the attack on his family is a burglary attempt). Thus, the denial of self-esteem around economic matters is also in part signaled as a source of resentment.

Returning veteran films range from the critical vision of films like *Coming Home* and *Cutter's Way* to the military revivalist vision of *First Blood, Firefox,* and *Rambo*. Films directly about the war experience itself are equally mixed, although, as in the returning vet subgenre, none adopts an explicitly oppositional posture toward the war.

Go Tell the Spartans (1978) and *The Boys in Company C* (1978) both criticize the U.S. involvement in Vietnam while forgoing more radical critiques of the military, U.S. foreign policy, or the values that support militarism. *Spartans* shows the army blundering deeper into the war during its early stages, and it stands as an allegory of the futility of the war effort as a whole. A small group of U.S. soldiers in a provincial outpost are ordered to occupy another, even more obscure position. They are overrun, and many are killed in the senseless action. Nevertheless, the critique of the war is executed against the standard of the "good war," which reproduces a traditional trope of critical Hollywood war films in that it criticizes a specific war while celebrating military values in general. *The Boys in Company C* suffers from a similar drawback. The story follows a platoon of young marines from boot camp through combat in Vietnam. Along the way, they discover that their officers are corrupt and only interested in high body counts. The film points to the futility and misguidedness of the American war effort. It criticizes both the U.S.-supported Vietnamese bourgeoisie and the Army high command that treated genocide against Vietnamese as a numbers game and as an excuse for using fancy high-tech weaponry. The common soldiers, in alliance with the Vietnamese people, symbolized by the children, are pitted against these two groups. They and the children are slaughtered in the end. *The Boys in Company C* constitutes one of the few overt statements against the war to come out of Hollywood, yet it resorts to the traditional Hollywood convention of valorizing "good grunt soldiers" over officers, and avoids criticizing the military as such.

Vietnam combat films like *Spartans* and *Boys* share the same limits as the liberal vet films. Liberals usually avoided the broader implications of the war, its origin in a desire to maintain access to Third World labor, markets, raw materials, etc., and to forestall the rise of noncapitalist sociopolitical systems. The traditional liberal focus on individuals implies a personalistic account that easily permits larger geopolitical issues to be displaced. And the sorts of self-replicating identifications that such an account invites usually evoke sentimentalist reactions to individual suffering rather than outrage at national policies of genocide. What needs to be determined is whether or not such personal evocations can translate into broader systemic lessons.

The rhetoric of liberal films nevertheless marks an advance on that used in conservative films. In simple thematic terms, the liberal films are critical of figures of authority, while conservative films like *Patton* metaphorically elevate such figures to an ideal position. There is a singularity of focus in conservative war films that is lacking in liberal rhetoric. *Boys* concerns a multiplicity of characters, and no one point of view is privileged. The "other" in *Patton*, a German officer assigned to study the general, is there simply to instantiate the implicit narcissistic male (self-)gaze, which takes the empirical form of the German's adulation for the great American hero. *Boys* draws Vietnamese into the narrative and grants them empathy not as admirers of the Americans but as their victims. Finally, *Patton* resorts to overwhelmingly metaphoric rhetorical strategies, while *Boys* is more metonymic in its approach. *Patton* assumes an ideal purity of character, and it even intimates a rather silly sort of universalism in the male militarist spirit. The trope of elevation and subordination fits easily with an authoritarian ideology in this film. In *Boys*, on the other hand, a representational strategy which emphasizes the equality of terms and their material, contiguous interconnections prevails. One soldier reprimands another for endangering all their lives; on the material level at which the soldiers are obliged to operate, metonymic connections are very real.

By the late seventies Vietnam was no longer an explosive issue. Conservatives decried the slow erosion of American international power in the face of Third World liberation movements, and in response to what they perceived as an expansionist USSR, they called for an end to the "post–Vietnam War syndrome." What began was a period of resurgent militarism, and Vietnam films of the time take part in the conservative backlash. They do so in part by rewriting history.

If, from a conservative political point of view, the period of the "post–Vietnam War syndrome" was characterized by national self-doubt, military vacillation, and a failure of will to intervene overseas, then the appropriate counter in the "post-syndrome" period of national revival was a triumph of the will, a purgation of doubt through action, and an interventionist military stance that brooked no restraint of the sort that led to the United State's first military defeat, tarnished national prestige, and shamed American military manhood. Both *The Deer Hunter* and *Apocalypse Now* contribute to that revival by incorporating Vietnam not as a defeat from which lessons can be learned, but as a springboard for male military heroism.

The Deer Hunter, directed by Michael Cimino, won the Oscar in 1978. The film is more about the accession to leadership of the seer-warrior-individualist hero, Michael Vronsky (Robert DeNiro), than about the war. But this turning away from defeat, loss, and responsibility to an emblem of male strength might itself be symptomatic of a denial of loss through a compensatory self-inflation of the very sort that helped initiate and prolong the war.[3] Nevertheless, the film is multivalent politically. It appealed to working-class

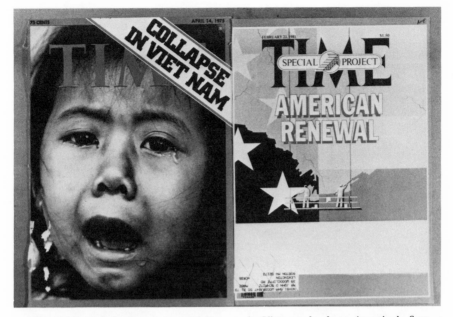

The withdrawal from a neocolonialist war in Vietnam leads to America's first military defeat and to calls for a renewal of American power abroad on the part of the Right.

viewers who saw in it an accurate representation of the dilemmas of their lives. Radicals praised its implicit critique of certain male myths. And its bleak, ambiguous ending inspired many to read it as an anti-Vietnam-War statement. We respect all of these positions, but we read the film from the perspective of the critique of ideology, and in that light, it seems less progressive.[4]

The story concerns three steeltown buddies—Michael, Steve, and Nick—who are shown united in the first part in a highly ritualized wedding scene that conveys a sense of strong community. The church steeple, a symbol of unreflective faith, spontaneous adherence to hierarchy, and paternalistic authority, rises above the community as its guiding axis. It is returned to repeatedly by the camera, and the gesture underscores the church's centrality as a locus of social authority and an anchor securing community cohesion. All three men go to Vietnam, where they are reunited as prisoners of the Vietcong, who force them to play Russian roulette. Michael outsmarts the VC and saves his buddies. But Nick, apparently unhinged by his experience, remains in Vietnam playing roulette for money. Steve, now confined to a wheelchair in a stateside hospital, refuses to leave and return home. Michael returns to establish a relationship with Linda, Nick's old girlfriend. He forces Steve to overcome his shame, to be a "man" and leave the hospital. Then, Michael returns to Vietnam at the time of the fall of Saigon to witness Nick kill himself in his last roulette game. The film closes with Nick's funeral and the group of surviving friends singing "God Bless America."

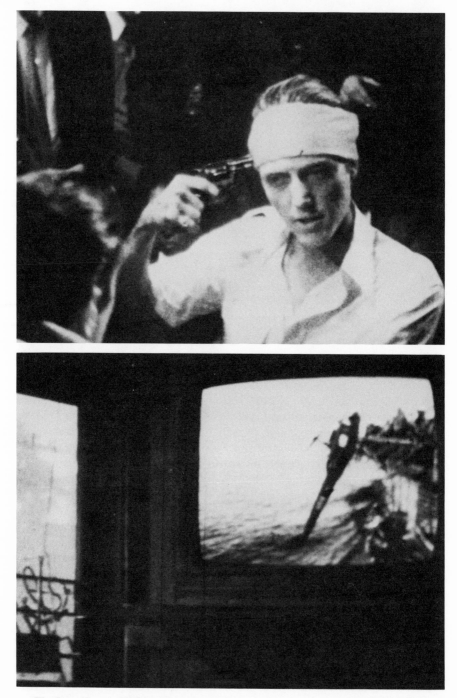

The Deer Hunter. Nick's suicide is associated with the U.S. defeat in Vietnam.

Like so many films of the seventies, *The Deer Hunter* offers as a solution to complex political and social problems the exercise of power by a male individualist who is charged with saving a community through strong leadership. The community is patriarchal; women are present to be fought over, as bossy mothers, and in the role of not altogether faithful, weak, yet at the right moment supportive partners. War breaks the community, and its worst effect is the transformation of men into will-less weaklings (Steve) or addicted obsessives (Nick). It falls to Michael to exercise his natural power of leadership to restore the communal cohesion and order at the end of the film. That restoration requires the sacrifice of Michael's weaker counterpart, Nick, with whose funeral the film ends. The reaffirmation of male military power in the character of Michael is predicated upon the purgation of weakness, vacillation, and the obsessively suicidal behavior in which the country was engaged in Vietnam, all of which seem embodied in Nick. It is important that in the scene immediately following Nick's suicide, the audience sees documentary footage of the U.S. Army's "disgraceful" flight from Saigon. The juxtaposition associates Nick's weakness and self-destructiveness with the military defeat of 1975. The film, then, can be said to work in two dimensions. It concerns the restoration of community through strong patriarchal leadership. And it offers an allegorical solution to the problem Vietnam poses by symbolically purging the source of defeat and proposing a way to renewed national strength and patriotic cohesion.

The call for strong leadership as a solution to historical crises is a political version of the aesthetic transformation in the film of actual history into a moral allegory. Just as the warrior-leader-savior resolves vacillation into a triumph of heroic will, so also the romantic, allegorical form of the film attempts to resolve the contradictions, meaninglessness, and ambiguity of the actual historical war into a meaningful and apparently noncontradictory quest narrative executed in a synthetic style that balances the unity of the individual leader with a formal or aesthetic unity. It is not surprising that a political ideology of the superior individual subject should seem inseparable from an aesthetic of romantic, quasi-mystical exaltation, since both are forms of empowerment. The romantic aesthetic overpowers history and incorporates it into highly subjective fantasy representations. The problem of realistically depicting history, which is linked to the political problem of acknowledging responsibility and loss as a nation, is solved by sublimating history into a stylized, ceremonial fusion of color, sound, and theme that elevates contingent events to a moral allegory of redemption and an ordinary human to secular divinity. It is important that the most stylized and allegorical representations appear while Michael is hunting. The aesthetic transformation of the mountains into a mystical temple (replete with choir) parallels the political and ideological elevation of the member of the gang into the strong, mystical leader, naturally destined to lead the lesser mortals around him. It is also, of course, a means of attaining the sorts of separation we have described as necessary to the more pathological forms of male sexual identity. Heightened mental representations of the sort evident in the mountain scenes are themselves ways of denying connection to the world and to others who might transgress the boundary between self and world which a reactive male sexual identity must establish. It is significant, then, that Michael is most alone in the mountain scenes, most separated from others, and most protected from them by a representational boundary that makes him seem transcendent, unique. Those scenes are also, of course, the most metaphoric.

Yet affirmations of transcendence are necessary only when the actual world is fallen (meaningless, hopeless, unhappy). "My country right or wrong" makes sense or is necessary only if the country can be or is frequently wrong. The quest for transcendence, for turning the everyday into the grandiose, the monumental, and the meaningful, presupposes the absence of the empirical equivalents of these spiritual ideals in the actual world. Indeed, the actual world has to be a positive negation of such things as fulfillment, self-worth, and significance for the quest for other-worldly, transcendent meanings to be activated. The metaphor exists in necessary tension with a more metonymic or worldly and material set of constraints which bring the metaphor into being as a reaction against them.

The transcendent moments of the film can thus be read either as successful enactments of the attainment of a spiritual ideal just short of the clouds that are the floor of heaven, or as the neurotic symptoms of this-worldly victimization, attempts to secure a sense of self-worth against a world that denies it nine to five and only allows a few leisure-time pursuits, like the male rituals of drinking and hunting, as metaphoric alternatives. The film depicts both, and our point is that its progressive potential resides in the fact that it cannot avoid this undecidability. The transcendental moments can only appear as such in contrast to a detailed description of a fallen everyday reality. This is why the film is so incredibly dense with ethnographic detail from everyday life, from the long marriage celebration to the scenes inside the industrial workplace. It is important, therefore, that the film opens in the factory, with an establishing shot from under a viaduct at night that makes the factory world seem enclosed and oppressive. The colorful mountain scenes of transcendence gain their meaning from their difference from the darkness of the workplace and the squalor of ethnic neighborhood life. And Michael's individuation is defined as a separating out, a denial of "weakening" social links of the sort that characterize his less strong male cronies.

Thus, the film permits a deconstruction of the premises of its idealization of Michael as the seer-leader. His elevation occurs through the metaphor of the deer hunt, which transforms a literal leisure-time activity into a higher ideal meaning that transcends literality, just as Michael comes to transcend the literal and material social texture, to rise above it. He must do so if he is to give it order, but the metaphor cannot fully rise above the literality that is its vehicle. Part of its literality is that it exists in metonymic or contiguous relation to the opening factory scene of fallen fire, confinement, and darkness where the men seem all alike. Michael's distinction as the superior individual who can read sunspots, like a shaman, or who knows the mystical meaning of a bullet ("This is this"), or who takes down deer with one shot like a true hunter has meaning only in differentiation from the other men, from their sameness in the factory. And the metaphor of transcendental leadership takes on meaning only in distinction from the workaday world; without that contrast, that determining difference, it makes no sense. Yet the film's ideology depends on the assumption that the metaphor subsumes the literal event into an ideal meaning which transcends wordly materiality and meaninglessness (nondistinction) entirely.

The film thus puts on display the interconnections between wage labor oppression and white male working class compensations for that oppression. In this film, a mythic idealization of the individual counters the reduction of all the men to faceless and impersonal functions in the industrial machine at the beginning of the film. An idealized meaning substitutes for the fallen reality of everyday life. The powerful emblem of the church, the extremely ritualized wedding, the mythologized hunt, and the strong bonding between the men should thus be seen as ways of counteracting the banality of life on the bottom of capitalism.

Like many populist films, this one therefore has a double valence. Its depiction of the accreditation of right-wing political leadership points to the way pre–class–conscious working class men can have their resentment against oppression channeled into conservative, even fascist forms in a highly individualistic and patriarchal cultural context that limits the means of attaining communal cohesion to strong male individual leadership. Yet it also points to potentially radical desires to transcend the cruel material conditions to which working class people are reduced (or were being reduced, in the late seventies particularly), conditions that deny a sense of worldly meaning or worth to people, who, as a result, overcompensate for those lacks by turning to either religious or political idealizations.

If both *Deer Hunter* and *Apocalypse Now* (see 8.3) indicate the reactionary way of dealing with the Vietnam War, they also testify to something amiss in the country's prevailing conception of itself. The need, demonstrated in these films, to repudiate the war as history and to transfer it into an allegory of militarist manhood is itself symptomatic of a wound, a sense of shame, that seems resistant to the sort of healing these films attempt. And the films merely reproduce the desire to realize a totality of American will in the world that reveals its own problematic anchoring in a web of serial, contiguous nontotalizable relations with other people the more it asserts itself so hyperbolically and hysterically.

By the mid-eighties, the Vietnam syndrome had been at least partially overcome, and conservatives once again felt a pre-Vietnam license to exercise U.S. military power overseas. Yet the country remained convinced by the experience of Vietnam, and it refused to back full-scale interventions that might lead to wars in places like Central America. Our poll suggests that American viewers tended to turn even conservative war films like *The Deer Hunter* into antiwar statements: 69% felt that it portrayed the war as a mistake, and 93% said that it confirmed their opposition to the war. The ending made 27% feel patriotic, while it made 51% feel disheartened. Perhaps the most

In 1980, the United States begins to adopt a more belligerent posture toward the world.

disturbing result we found was that 74% felt that the representation of the Vietcong in the film was accurate. Even if Americans had learned some lessons regarding foreign wars, they still seemed to need to learn lessons regarding foreigners. And this perhaps accounts for the fact that, although they continued to oppose interventionism on a large scale, they overwhelmingly approved Ronald Reagan's strikes against Grenada and Libya during this period.

2. The Military Rehabilitated

One consequence of the Vietnam War and the draft that supplied it with men was an undermining of the U.S. Army. By the end of the war, soldiers were "fragging" (deliberately killing) their officers, rather than obeying orders to fight. As a result of this, as well as of the widespread opposition to war that the draft helped inspire, the draft was eliminated, and the army was transformed into an all-volunteer force. That new force was heavily minority, since nonwhite minorities in a retrenching capitalist society dominated by whites had few other career opportunities. Advertisements for the army began to appear on diversionary television shows (sports and MTV especially) that might attract working-class, unemployed, and minority viewers. The restoration of the army became a more pressing concern in the late seventies, when events such as the Soviet invasion of Afghanistan and the taking of U.S. hostages in Iran made it clear that American imperial interests were no longer going to be taken for granted or allowed to go uncontested in the world. Hollywood joined in the effort, and a number of early eighties films "humanize" the army by turning it into a scene for family melodrama, liberal ideals, and humor. The link seemed so overt that one suspected that some Hollywood filmmakers had not heard that culture is supposed to be at least relatively autonomous in relation to political power and the state.[5]

These films are generally liberal in tone; their humanization of the military is laudable in contrast to the more conservative exaggeration of the worst traits of the military—violence, discipline, intolerance, masculinism, etc.—in such films as *Rambo*. Yet these films appear at a time when the country, in the hands of conservatives, was adopting increasingly militarist poses in the world theater and when a "culture of militarism" was developing (in the form of toys, magazines, TV shows, and films). Whatever the intention of these films, their political valence was reinflected in a conservative direction by their historical moment and their social context. Moreover, the liberal vision takes for granted the necessity of an institution like the military. Liberals fail to see the deep structural roots and systemic relations that link the military per se as an institution to the patriarchal socialization patterns that are partly responsible (as we have argued) for war. It is in light of a broader radical critique of the military itself that the liberal position must be judged. Such a critique would see the military as an instrument of class defense, as well as a machine for producing a model of a general social discipline of the sort capitalism (or any work-oriented, inegalitarian society) requires. In addition, the military from this perspective is less a protection than a threat. In the modern world especially, the very existence of the military poses a danger, and it is no longer possible, because of modern weapons, to justify the military as a defense against aggression. Defense and a war of total annihilation are no longer separable concepts.

The format of humanized military films like *Stripes, Private Benjamin*, and *An Officer and a Gentleman* consists of the transformation of an unsuccessful person into a very successful one. Thus, an affirmative personal narrative is laid over an attempt at institutional reconstruction, and, like the ads for the army on television ("Be all that you can be"), the films identify personal achievement with military life. In this way, the films seem to participate in an attempt in the culture to restore the army to its pre-Vietnam credit and, in certain instances, to reintegrate it with a lost patriotic vision of the United States.

Private Benjamin (1980) incorporates feminism into this process. It recounts the transformation of a dependent and ineffectual woman who is at a loss when her husband dies on the night of their wedding into a strong, independent figure. The change is marked by the difference between the first wedding scene, in which she is little more than a sexual servant of her husband, and the last, when she socks her husband-to-be on the jaw because he is a philanderer and stalks off alone. The ideological dimension of the film consists in intimating that the army is what has made her strong. Thus, a very antifeminist institution is made to appear an ally of feminism.

Stripes (1981) and *An Officer and a Gentleman* (1982) both concern the transformation of ne'er-do-wells into successful soldiers and "men." But more important, both are allegories of the metamorphosis of the Vietnam generation, with its anti-bourgeois and antiauthoritarian dropout values, into the fighting machines of the eighties, who believe in patriotism, nationalism, and militarism. In *Stripes* an underemployed goof-off whose girlfriend has left him is transformed by the army into a good soldier who becomes a leader of his squad as well as a sexual success.

The most popular humanized military film, *An Officer and a Gentleman*, is neo-forties in outlook and tone; advertisements made it seem like a story out of the past, but that attempt to step back into the generic form and style of an older, more innocent male military ethos was very much a statement about the present. The film recounts the transformation of Zack (Richard Gere) from an undisciplined, motorcycle-riding, down-and-out tough guy into "an officer and a gentleman." Brutality saves, the film says, as the hammer shapes steel. Foley, Zack's black drill instructor (Lou Gossett), brutalizes him until he renounces his selfishness and becomes a team player. Zack stops treating women badly and does the honorable thing by carrying off his working-class girlfriend (Debra Winger) at the end. And he sacrifices his chance to set a new obstacle course record by returning to help a female classmate. The film elicits audience sympathy (even applause) at points like this. It plays on human, even liberal sentiments (integrationist and token feminist), but it does so in order to reinforce the military institution. Zack's military training seems to make him a better man, a "gentleman." We would argue that the film should be understood, then, as an allegory of a transformation being promoted by the Right in contemporary U.S. society. Zack represents a generation of youth who grew up disaffected with traditional institutions like the military. Through Zack, we see that generation overcome its alienation and accept such values as military honor and team play. The price is submission to discipline, authority, and brutality, but the prize is self-respect and love.

The love story is sweet and reassuring; its retreat from modernity to the sort of "torrid romance" of early Hollywood films invests libidinal energies into militarism—soldiers get the "girls," the film suggests. In a film where men must learn to be "men," it is fitting that women's goal should be portrayed as "getting a man." The love story, in fact, depicts the real state of affairs of many working class women in a society that fails to satisfy real human needs and that makes women's survival often depend on men. Such romance has a double edge. It permits a hothouse closure to be established which reinforces the film's masculinist-militarist ideology. But romance also testifies to structural differences between male power and female dependency that could never be fully sublated to an ideological closure and are underscored, even as their reality is denied in a film like this. They remain outside such closure always, for they are the very things that make ideology necessary in the first place.

Films like *Officer* were some of the most successful ideological narratives of the era. Yet for that very reason, they are some of the most interesting for understanding the rhetorical procedures of ideology as well as the social system of militarism. They are open to deconstruction precisely because they seem such perfect exercises in ideology. Strong personal needs for romance or family are transferred metaphorically or by analogy onto the military. And by virtue of metaphoric substitution, the military stands in as the answer for the personal desires. Yet this exercise in metaphoric closure also signals literal connections between the realms which are joined metaphorically. The films do not merely compare male-dominated romance or the patriarchal family to the military; they inadvertently dramatize the real material or metonymic relations between these realms of socialization.

For example, in *The Great Santini* (1982), a narrative of intergenerational strife between a gung-ho old-style military man and his son is mapped over a justification of the military. The narrative proceeds as a movement toward a moment of recognition when the children finally see that the father was a good man despite his excesses. He becomes a locus of sympathy when he dies sacrificing himself so that a town will not be destroyed by his crashing jet. The son, who seemed to reject his father's values, dons his flight jacket, assumes his father's position at the driver's wheel of the family car, and begins to act like him. The gesture is indicative of the patriarchal character of the military. It is passed from fathers to sons, bypassing women, who serve in this film as breeders. If the family is not just a legitimating model by metaphoric analogy for the military, but also a literal seed-bed of militarist values, then this division of labor is not accidental. The socialization patterns of the two seemingly separate domains form a continuum.

Liberal films like *Taps* (1981) and *The Lords of Discipline* (1983) criticize military excess in the name of a humanized military, one in which militarism must be tempered by restraint and respect for life. Indeed, *Taps* thematizes this very position. Cadets at a military academy, in order to defend the existence of the academy, engage in an armed revolt, which results in the deaths of several of them. The most fervent apostle of military honor, an aging general, also dies, and his disciple, the young cadet who leads the revolt, learns that militarism must give way to good judgment. Yet the military itself is affirmed.

Films like this display the crucial ingredients of the failure of liberalism to develop a program for significantly transforming American society. Liberalism operates from within patriarchal presuppositions, which, like the similar procapitalist presuppositions liberals hold, limit the ability of liberals to see beyond the walls of the ideological prison in which they operate. Militarist patriarchs are okay, these films seem to say, though we'd be better off with nicer ones. But in a world in which one trigger-happy fool can send everyone to happy vaporland, even nice militarist patriarchs must be seen as pathological. It is such a shift of vision, whereby the most everyday assumptions of patriarchy and capitalism, especially the assumption that strong, rambunctious men are needed to lead and defend us, are relinquished forever, that lies beyond the capacity of liberals. Indeed, liberals should probably be defined as people incapable of such structural conceptualizations.

Liberals do not see the military as a social problem that must be eliminated, in part because they accept the patriarchal logic of the Cold War—that the only way to keep peace with an antagonist is through the threat of aggression or annihilation. Yet this position is itself a product of a patriarchal socialization to competition and power. In other words, if you only look at the world with sunglasses, you'll never see anything but a dark world. In order to perceive the military itself as an unnecessary and potentially dangerous institution, liberals would have to step outside their own socialization, exit from the structure they inhabit, question the very words that come automatically to their lips.

A more radical position would argue that the outlawing of armies and weapons is not a utopian dream; it is a precondition of the modern world's survival. Beyond patriarchal and capitalist socialization to competition, aggression, and domination reside alternative socialization possibilities, and alternate ideals of cooperation, demilitarization, and peaceful communal existence. But that would require a different set of structuring assumptions, as well as a different set of social institutions. If the problem of the military is wedded to the social institutions that justify it metaphorically, then it is not likely to change until they are changed. Indeed, one could say that something of that potentially emergent reality is signaled by even the ideology of some of the humanized military films. For by comparing the military with the family, they indicate the possibility of a breakdown of the boundaries that separate the two realms. The family is a patriarchal form, and for this reason, it can successfully legitimate the military. But it is also a communal form. The very "humanity" that it lends the military also threatens the military. The price of analogy is comparison. And in comparison to the family, the military can only ultimately appear as being inhumane. For if the family breeds children, the military murders them. *Taps* and *Lords* at least point this out. They just don't follow the point to its logical conclusion. And they couldn't, because of the very patriarchal assumptions which underwrite the military, assumptions which also limit any critique of the military by immediately branding accurate critiques as unreal, utopian, or, worse, not manly enough.

3. The New Militarism

Liberals succeeded in stemming the growth of the military in the mid to late seventies, but they were incapable of turning the loss in Vietnam into a permanent structural reform of U.S. militarism. This was so in part because of historical events that made a renewed defense of the American empire necessary. That empire consisted of a network of client states overseas, in places like the Philippines and Iran, that were tied into the imperial economic and military system by treaty and corporate investment. These states helped assure that leftist or anticapitalist governments would not come to power in areas American corporations deemed necessary to their interests. Usually they brutally repressed liberation movements, in places like Indonesia and Chile, for example, and they protected the flow of raw materials and the supply of

The new militarism of the eighties is evident in the revival of traditional imperialist adventurism, the rehabilitation of the CIA, and the engagement in illegal wars against leftist Third World countries.

cheap labor for American firms. Military buildups within the United States were thus closely related to the status of the imperial client states, and they both have an economic dimension. In the late seventies and early eighties several client states fell to liberation movements (Nicaragua, Iran, the Philippines), others (South Korea, South Africa, El Salvador) were troubled by incipient liberation movements or unrest, and other U.S.-supported military regimes (Argentina, Brazil, Peru, Chile) were subject either to internal disturbances or to overthrow by democratic forces repulsed by the exercise of state terror in the name of defending capitalism. At the same time, several previously "secure" colonial nations became socialist—Angola, Ethiopia, Mozambique—as a result of revolutions. The empire was trembling, and the Iran hostage crisis of 1979–80 heated up jingoist sentiment enough in the nation to give the new conservative power bloc the support it required to begin carrying out a momentous military buildup decked out in militarist and anticommunist rhetoric.

Yet public sentiment was not entirely homogeneous on the subject of militarism. Polls indicated that in general people opposed foreign interventionism. For this reason, perhaps, there was a cultural offensive to enlist support for the conservative ideals of an aggressive, combative defense of imperial interests. If the public didn't need to be whipped up, there would not have been so much whipping going on in the early to mid-eighties, especially in films.

The revival of militarism was not spontaneous, however. Conservative groups like the Committee on the Present Danger campaigned throughout the seventies for greater "defense" spending and for a firmer foreign policy. The new militarism is not an effect of the Reagan era; rather, Reagan himself is in part an effect of the culture of militarism born in the late seventies, with some help from Democrats like Jimmy Carter. *The Final Countdown* (1979) is an example of a film that prefigures the conservative military buildup of the early eighties. It concerns an aircraft carrier that travels through a time warp to emerge on the day before Pearl Harbor. The captain has to decide whether to intervene and change the course of history. The purpose of this historical displacement is to suggest that the United States needs a powerful military in order to prevent another Pearl Harbor. Indeed, in a number of new militarist films, the Vietnamese, the Russians, or the "enemy" are decked out in uniforms that markedly resemble Japanese and German World War II battle gear. This evocation of the notion of the past "just war" in the contemporary context recalls the American Right's persistent equating of communism with German Nazism, a movement which was in fact conservative and rightist in character as well as being devoted to the eradication of communism.

Militarism in the United States is inseparable from anticommunism. Although anticommunism has been a staple of post–World War II culture, after the late sixties, during the period of détente, it faded somewhat from American consciousness and from Hollywood film. But in the late seventies and early eighties it was revived and promoted in conjunction with the new militarism. It ranged from military revival allegories like *Firefox* to dance musicals like *White Night*. The new anticommunism worked either by projecting its own aggressive animus onto the "enemy," thus justifying itself as a "defense" against a hypothetically offensive Red Terror, or by dehumanizing the ideological adversaries of the United States through the use of racial and social stereotypes in such a way as to excuse the use of violence against them. For example, *Megaforce* (1982) was a Pentagon-supported advertisement both for military hardware and for elite military manpower. It concerns an elite group of fighters known as "Megaforce" (who look and taste like the Pentagon's Rapid Deployment Force). They use some of the most sophisticated military technology available to fight Castro-like, south-of-the-border bandits and their communist allies, who overthrow governments like dominoes, not for social ideals, but out of greed for money. The film presents social revolutionaries as venal criminals. And this criminalization and dehumanization of foreign people struggling for liberation from capitalism and feudalism seems to be essential to the promotion of weapons designed for their liquidation.

Perhaps the most audacious anticommunist film of the era was John Milius's *Red Dawn* (1984), about a hypothetical Soviet invasion of the United States. A group of youngsters hide out in the mountains and become a successful guerrilla unit. In the end, they are all killed. Along with the usual right-wing themes (the Soviets are subhuman concentration camp guards, Latin American revolutionaries are merely their agents, the United States is the last bastion of justice and freedom), the film is distinguished by certain ideological motifs that hark back to fascist and national socialist ideologies of the twenties and thirties. At one point, an intellectual liberal and a jock conservative fight over how to proceed in the group. The liberal's call for democracy loses out to the conservative's assertion of his right to command the others. The authoritarian leadership principle is linked to the assumption that those with greater force or power should prevail—not those with the best principles or rational arguments. Such force derives its authority from nature, from what the Nazis called "blood and soil." The blood motif in the film appears as the ritual drinking of a deer's blood as proof of one's warrior manhood; it refers to the Nazi fetishizing of powerful animals, and it elaborates the conservative idea that human life is primitivist, a struggle for survival in a civil society that is no different from nature. The soil motif appears at those moments when Milius's camera meditates on nature, positioning it as a still, immense, unmoving presence. The existential loneliness of the individualist warrior leader is associated with expansive fields and high mountains, fetishes of power and strength.[6]

Thus, the film displays the close relationship between contemporary American right-wing ideology and Nazism. Indeed, one curious dimension of the film's argument is that what it poses against communism, depicted as totalitarian domination, is a social model of authoritarian leadership. The authoritarian camp in the mountains is not much different from the totalitarian "camp" in the town. At this point in history, conservatives like Jeane Kirkpatrick argued for a distinction between totalitarianism (authoritarianism for the sake of communism) and authoritarianism (totalitarianism for the sake of capitalism). The film shows why such a distinction might have been necessary to avoid confusion.

While films like *Red Dawn* were not particularly successful at the box office, they are shown repeatedly, for months on end, on cable television. In fact, this phenomenon points to the breakdown of the distinction between film and television as well as to the eventual erosion of the importance of box-office figures in the determination of the potential effects of films. Since blockbusters must be kept off the market in order to maintain their scarcity and value, lesser films arguably acquire a greater ability to influence audiences by virtue of saturation showing on TV.

In the late seventies and early eighties, the "world communist conspiracy" becomes associated with "terrorism," the use of non–state–sanctioned violence to gain political ends. Conservative fantasists like Claire Sterling made careers out of tracing all violent opposition to U. S. interests back to an "international terrorist network" emanating from Moscow. Numerous Hollywood films transcode this discourse, from Stallone's *Nighthawks* (1981) to *The Final Option* (1983), which suggests the peace movement is communist-inspired, and Chuck Norris's *Invasion U.S.A.* (1985), in which terrorists invade the United States. Norris and Stallone were also involved in promoting fantasies of veterans who return to Vietnam to free American POWs—*Missing in Action (I* and *II)* and *Rambo.*

In *Rambo* (1985), a veteran, who is depicted mythically as a super-killer, is enlisted to rescue missing POWs in Vietnam. He succeeds through heroic effort and a display of primitive violence that kills off numerous Russians and Vietnamese. The film satisfies several contemporary conservative prejudices. Asian communists are portrayed as subhuman. The film rewrites history in a way that excuses American atrocities against the Vietnamese. And it portrays Americans, not the Vietnamese, as the ones fighting for liberation. The overall significance of the film seems to be to try to make certain that the Vietnam War would be won in Nicaragua. It is less about an event than an attitude. The theme of betrayal that characterized the conservative attitude toward the liberal critics of the war (Reagan's remark that the army did not lose the war but was prevented from winning it)—and that is also reminiscent of post–World War I German attitudes that aided the rise of Nazism—appears in the way Rambo is misled by a Washington bureaucrat who wants him to fail in his mission so that the book can be closed on Vietnam. Yet we suggest that a film of this sort needs to be read as a symptom of victimization. A paragon of inarticulate meatheadedness, the figure of Rambo is also indicative of the way many American working-class youths are undereducated and offered the military as the only way of affirming themselves. Denied self-esteem through creative work for their own self-enhancement, they seek surrogate worth in metaphoric substitutes like militarism and nationalism. Rambo's neurotic resentment is less his own fault than that of those who run the social system, assuring an unequal distribution of cultural and intellectual capital.

We read the new militarist phenomenon as being both a psychological problem of patriarchal society and a problem of a threatened and defensive capitalism. Reagan's "hard line on defense," his stubborn hewing to a stern, punitive, and intolerant attitude toward the world, is symptomatic of patriarchal pathology, as much a matter of socialization as of social organization. *Rambo* is important because it displays the roots of that pathology. The male need to feel singular, to separate out from dependence on initial caretakers, is metaphorized in Rambo's mythic isolation. Because the social world is necessarily interdependent, such isolation is necessarily aggressive. Aggression separates, whereas affection binds and makes one dependent. The isolated male is therefore without affectionate ties. Freedom of action is his norm; it requires the repudiation of anyone who threatens his space or his sense of singular importance, from the communists to the federal bureaucrats—both enemies in the film. War is, as we have argued, in part a matter of representation, images that people identify with and internalize which mobilize action. Loss in war can in consequence be experienced as self-diminution, damage done to internal representations that have become inseparable from the self. Given the prevailing socialization patterns, such loss draws out male dependence and vulnerability, male "femininization." It is the rejection of this possibility, of its intolerable shame, that results in the sorts of hypertropic representations of violence in *Rambo*.

Yet within this problem lurk the rudiments of a solution. For the need for a confirmation of manhood signals a broader need for a feeling of self-worth of a sort that can only be provided by others. It depends on others' affection, just as all singularizing metaphors depend on contextualizing metonyms. To a certain extent, Rambo's violence is simply an expression of such a need. Such a radical compensation for lost self-esteem is in some respects a demand for a return of the other's recognition. If we call such needs "socialist" it is because the ideals of socialism are communal support, mutual help, and shared dependence. Even the male militarist's pathos articulates needs for such social structures. Even as he rejects dependence as shame, he affirms its necessity as the need for self-worth. And such unrecognized dependencies and unrealized desires cannot be recognized or realized in a patriarchal and capitalist social context. Indeed, this film is a testament to that reality.

One major consequence of this argument is that it is not only male sexualization that is at stake in militarism. Women, as they are socialized to be passive, to need strong men in order to survive, are complicit in the socialization process of men for war. This was made particularly clear to us at a viewing of *Rambo*. Women in the theater were especially loud in their demands for blood and vengeance. We were reminded of the housewives of Santiago de Chile who beat their pots at night to help bring down the leftist government. The sort of male self-display evident in *Rambo* requires an adulatory other in conservative women whose applause validates male violence. Thus, a reconstruction of male psychology is inseparable from a broader reconstruction of the patriarchal socialization system that produces both sexes.

The new militarism did not go uncontested. Films like *War Games, Wrong Is Right, The Dogs of War, Blue Thunder, Full Metal Jacket*, and *Platoon* opposed certain forms of militarism in the eighties. And several films like *Testament* and *Countdown to Looking Glass* during the same period criticized nuclear war policy. This cultural mobilization, in conjunction with public protests, had an effect. Reagan moved from statements regarding the feasibility of limited nuclear wars in the early years of his tenure to a defensive and somewhat disingenuous call for the avoidance of all nuclear war in his later years. Comedies also contributed to the continuing liberal critique, especially such Chevy Chase vehicles as *Deal of the Century*, a satire of the arms industry, and *Spies Like Us*, a satire of Reagan's "Star Wars" program (the "Strategic Defense Initiative") and of the militarist-Americanist mentality in general. In *Spies*, two trickster figures (played by Chase and Dan Ackroyd) overturn the military's plan to initiate a nuclear attack by the Soviet Union in order to use a new space defense system. The system fails, and one character remarks: "Such a short time to destroy a world." In the film's carnivalesque vision, military authority figures are little worthy of respect, and the irrationality of conservative nostrums ("To guarantee the American way of life, I'm willing to take that risk" [of nuclear destruction]) is underscored. What is noteworthy in this and other antimilitarist films is the attempt to depict alternative social attitudes (toward gays or sexuality, for example) that are necessary correlates of a post-repressive, post-militarist social construction. What the comedies underscore is the importance of irony and humor to such a process, since so many of the militarist films are distinguished by high levels of self-seriousness and an inability to engage in the plunge into indeterminacy that the carnivalesque inversion of hierarchy entails.

What all of this points to is that if militarism is a public projection of private or personal human relations and attitudes, then its reconstruction is something more than a matter of foreign policy. Liberal antimilitarist films like *War Games, 2010, Testament*, or *Platoon* frequently contain images of nonauthoritarian, nonexploitative, equal relations between people. Many conservative films offer just the opposite sorts of relations, and the positive relations are frequently oiled with sentimentalism, a form of alienated positive affect that often accompanies an equally alienated aggressivity that takes authoritarian and militarist forms. What this suggests is that one necessary route to a world free from militarism is a reconstruction of the alienated and skewed affective structures feeding the distrust and enmity that operate behind militarism. Militarism is a collective neurosis, not just a foreign policy alternative. The micrological or interpersonal dimension of human existence, therefore, is not apolitical, nor is it entirely distinct from the macrological dimension of political interaction. A different nonantagonistic structure of international relations, one purged of genocidal impulses, would be predicated in part on a different psychology and a different social construction of interpersonal affection and aggression.

8. THE RETURN OF THE HERO: ENTREPRENEUR, PATRIARCH, WARRIOR

Representations are as much a part of power as the actual occupation of institutions. Idealized self-representations (on the level of both the individual and the nation) help hold a society together; internalized, they guide thought and behavior in certain ways, while braking them from going in others. Cultural representations of male heroism, which fetishize male "power" and provide idealized objects for male behavior modeling, have been a traditional way of reproducing male dominance in the political, economic, and domestic spheres. That strategy is given a specifically conservative ideological inflection in the late seventies and early eighties.

By 1980, conservatism would be triumphant in the American political sphere; feminism would have been at least institutionally defused by the defeat of the ERA; civil rights for minorities would be under attack from the Right in the form of court decisions like the Bakke case; the Iran hostage crisis of 1979 would help revive a pre-Vietnam sense of patriotic jingoism and militarism; the New Right (a mixture of fundamentalist religion and conservative economic and military thinking) would through massive mail order campaigns have organized a powerful social bloc; well-financed conservative political action committees would have successfully dethroned liberal politicians like George McGovern and Frank Church; a Democratic president would have proved inept at handling domestic problems and foreign crises; recessionary inflation would have provoked a white middle class reaction against state taxation for social services and against affirmative action programs that gave scarce jobs to minorities; the truce between capital and labor of the New Deal era would be broken by a successful capitalist attack against unions like the Air Traffic Controllers; the shift of wealth and economic power away from the Northeast to the Sunbelt would mean a destruction of the membership base of the liberal industrial unions as well as an increase in the power of southern conservatism (signaled in a tepid manner by Carter, and more grossly by Bush and Reagan). By the early eighties, the failed hero of *Midnight Cowboy* would have become the beer-guzzling, wife-beating, "I'm jes' happy to have a job" chump of *Urban Cowboy*. The country had changed.

217

Three wounds that conservatives reacted against in the late seventies—feminism, military defeat, and economic recession.

The cultural terrain that led to the rise of conservatism was already being prepared in the mid to late seventies. Not that one caused the other; rather, both were part of the same general historical movement. We will argue here that the revival of the hero in Hollywood film of this period, after such heroes had been put in question in the liberal climate of the late sixties and the seventies, plays an important part in that cultural mobilization. The strong male hero allowed an affirmative vision to be deployed by conservatives of the sort that liberals seemed at this time incapable of generating. The American economic system is such (based on a "free" market of competing individuals) that only conservative ideals and methods could convincingly offer themselves as solutions to its ills. The liberals offered the state, taxes, affirmative action, and welfare generosity to a society suffering from price inflation, intense job shortages, and foreign competition. The liberal program emerged as in contradiction with American economic "reality," that is, the real material constraints generated by an economy based on conservative principles of the market, cost-benefit efficiency, and competitive individualism. Thus, the situation of the New Deal, in which twenties conservative individualism had to be cured by thirties statism, was reversed; sixties and seventies statism would be cured by eighties conservative individualism.

1. The Triumph of Individualism—From Man to Superman

We have argued that a yearning for redemptive leadership on the part of the white middle class is evident throughout the seventies in American culture. In the late seventies, images of strong heroes appear on the scene in apparent answer to that yearning. What is particularly noteworthy about these heroes, from Indiana Jones to Luke Skywalker, is that they often respond directly to the economic, political, sexual, and military issues that were the motivating sources of that psychological need. If representations in the psyche direct the person toward satisfactions that alleviate needs, these cultural representations respond to needs by guiding people toward certain social policy choices. More often than not those policy choices are conservative, and we will argue that the heroes of the late seventies and the eighties aided the triumph of conservative individualist models of social action during this time. The new hero is usually an individualist who combines three essential components of the contemporary conservative social agenda; he is a warrior, an entrepreneur, and a patriarch.

These three components are necessarily interdependent, both on the level of cultural representation and on the level of social policy. The new heroes are often entrepreneurs who buck government power and stand up to state tyranny. This scheme would be innocent enough if it were not advanced in a historical climate that witnessed a successful conservative revolution against the New Deal federal government whose rallying cry was "freedom to choose." Conservatives complained of "excessive" state regulation and taxation of business, and as an alternative they proposed the unleashing of the "free market" in the hands of capitalist entrepreneurs who would generate enough wealth through their activities to make up for the loss in tax revenues. Tax cuts and a rollback of regulation would spur capital investment and unleash a new entrepreneurial spirit in America. The real agenda of this program, as we have argued, was to compensate for international competition, lower foreign wage rates, and reduced domestic profits by imposing a new sense of discipline on American workers and reducing their wages substantially. This could only be done if government protections were put aside and regulatory agencies were handed over to business—as indeed they were in the Reagan era.[1]

This war on Detroit was carried out in necessary conjunction with a war against leftist opponents of capitalism abroad, in places like El Salvador and Nicaragua. Conservatives argued for a transfer of funds from social spending like welfare (which only made workers and blacks immune to the harsh discipline of the "free" labor market) to military spending, a strategy which greatly enriched Ronald Reagan's defense industry backers in southern California. It also aided the drive launched by these white men against nonwhites in the Third World who threatened to disturb white male world rule. Callousness and a return-to-the-jungle, survivalist mentality of the market in domestic matters were linked with brutality and murder in foreign affairs. The new conservative hero (both on the screen and off) thus combines entrepreneurial power with military power; he is also a warrior.

Finally, the new hero is often a patriarch, someone who dominates women. The conservative revolution was also a counterrevolution against feminism. It sought to return women to more traditional social roles, and it attempted to reimpose male discipline and control on women's sexuality. If peasants were to be bombed, so were abortion clinics. But the new conservative economics also aided the anti-feminist drive. More women were subject to impoverishment as a result of the rollback of federal welfare programs. Poverty was "feminized" during this period. George Gilder, a conservative ideologue whose book *Wealth and Poverty* was adopted as a secular bible by the Reagan White House (copies were handed out to the staff), makes clear the interrelations between male entrepreneurial economic power and the redomestication of women. He argues that the unleashing of creative entrepreneurial economic energies depends on a reassertion of male sexual power and of male dominance in the family. "The male impulse to compete and the need to dominate affects all relations between the sexes." Women must remain at home and serve as caretakers for the new entrepreneurs, who must fight like warriors all day in the jungle marketplace. It is in this image of the conservative male capitalist that one sees most cogently joined the three ingredients of the new hero—the warrior, the patriarch, and the entrepreneur. And it is also here that one notices the tendency toward authoritarianism and fascism in this particular form of conservative individualist social agenda. Gilder writes: "It is only individuals who can be original . . . , and material progress is ineluctably elitist." Male domination over women in the family is the prototype for male rule over the social family, and male "freedom" to act without

One major target of the right-wing movements of the late seventies and early eighties is the federal government, whose liberal policies of taxation and regulation of business were seen as antithetical to the ideals of "free enterprise."

The third recession in a decade assures the defeat of the Democrats and the victory of the Right in 1980.

restraints as individualists is the seed out of which the imposition of an authoritarian will on society grows.[2]

This vision of society is clearly very primitivistic; it attempts to reduce social life to primary process thinking, that is, to the assertion of the power of natural instinct over rational arrangements. In many of the new hero films, metaphors of nature and primitivism abound, and the great enemy is often an image of extreme rationality, science, intellect, or technology. Nature is the primary metaphor in the hero films because the ideal of the free individualist which the hero seems to promote is itself based on the assumption that individualism is more "natural" than something like rational state planning, which is too distant from nature. The entrepreneurial individual is free precisely because he follows his "own" natural instincts, rather than rational imperatives which come from outside. The metaphor of nature implies interiority, the "private" self-identity of the individual as well as the self-regulating mechanism of the market. Left to itself, the market works naturally to maintain a healthy economy, one that tends to distribute wealth according to natural patterns, with more going to the more endowed and less to those who don't deserve it. Similarly, according to the ideology, in nature the patriarchal family is intact, unbroken by the rootlessness of modern urban life. Women and children obey fathers; the race is pure; and life follows naturally ordained rhythms. Nature also justifies the warrior ideal of conservative social policy which is embodied in the new hero. In the primitive jungle of the market, the naturally superior win; distrust reigns because marketplace competition cuts both ways. The line "trust me" is a recurring motif of "movie brat" films for good reason.

Clearly what is at stake in this social policy as well as in this social psychology is the issue of boundaries—boundaries around property, the home or family, and the individual self. Those boundaries, like the metaphor of nature, designate an interior realm which is self-identical or proper to itself, in no way dependent on or related to anything or anyone else. This psychology is noticeably pathological but also extremely powerful. Indeed, it derives from a need for power and control. White middle class males in particular, after having been out of control for so long in the seventies for all the reasons we have elaborated, were probably ready by 1978 to respond to images of renewed power, and what those images offered was a means of psychologically attaining control over a threatening environment. The high degree of representational power in the new hero films (most are fantasies characterized by extremely dynamic metaphoric images bearing little relation to an accurate or metonymic picture of the world) permitted a difficult material reality to be overcome. Threatened boundaries could be reestablished through the use of representations whose extremely high level of formal resolution marked out a distance between the self and the world and offered a sense of a private representational power that aided the realignment of male sexual identity. Not that these films appealed to males exclusively, but they do offer predominantly male idealizations. Like mental representations which accomplish a similar task on an individual level, these highly developed cultural representations allowed a boundary to be erected which severed a sense of emotional connectedness with the world. The world could no longer threaten or harm if it was kept at bay. Indeed, that separation enabled the placing of the world and of others in a purely objective position, one that permitted manipulation. That severing of metonymic connections and that objectification may account for the use of the term "meanness mania" to describe this era. In studying the new hero films, therefore, we will be concerned both with their social references and with the way their representational dynamics function to secure a psychological disposition appropriate to the conservative white middle class political bloc which came to dominate the country in the eighties.

Like all cultural events, the revival of the hero after a long period of anti-heroism has a history. We have noticed its negative preparation in crisis films of the seventies. It is prepared for more positively in the films of Sam Peckinpah and John Milius.

Peckinpah is a transitional figure who links traditional American individualism with the new ideological heroes of the late seventies. More populist in orientation, Peckinpah favors common types, lone men who stand up to adversity with taciturn good humor or who rebel against the authority of large institutions, including business. Yet in his films as well can be found an edge of reactionary resentment which takes violent forms. Peckinpah's early seventies heroes are more concerned with the disappearance of the past and with their own status in a changing, modernizing world than with fighting communism or with keeping an urban underclass in its place. Nevertheless, his individualism is elitist, and it is informed by a belief in the greater sexual power of the heroic individual that is in keeping with the sexual psychology we outlined above. In *Cross of Iron* (1977), for example, the hero is an elite Nazi soldier whose enemy is an effeminate, aristocratic officer. While the film is in some ways critical of war (it opens with a quote from Bertolt Brecht), it is also a potentially fascist anthem to elite warriors. The Peckinpah film that points most clearly forward toward the later ideological heroes of the conservative revolution is *Convoy* (1978), in which Kris Kristofferson plays a trucker who rebels against state authority, represented by the police, and leads a convoy in protest against government policy. The trucker is a populist individualist who speaks out against big institutions that curtail freedom. As usual, the populist ideology cuts two ways. The convoy of truckers voice quasi-radical resentment against big corporations and big government, and they act in concert to save a black buddy, but they are also organized as a group under a single great leader in a structure with recognizable right-wing features.

Peckinpah's truckers indicate the influence of economic realities on the figure of the hero as he emerges from the anti-heroic era of the late sixties and early seventies. But John Milius's films of the mid and late seventies are better indicators of the conservative character of the new heroes. In *Dillinger* (1973), for example, the authoritarian gangster hero voices opposition to the New Deal and beats up women. His major concern is that his elite outlaw force be perceived as superior to all others. In *The Wind and the Lion* (1975), the story of a Berber chief who kidnaps an American woman and her children, Milius eulogizes the passing of the era of great robber barons and ballsy leaders like Teddy Roosevelt. The film celebrates U.S. imperialism, and it suggests that force is the only way to conduct foreign policy, a conservative theme of the era. The style of these films is congruent with the ideology of radical individualism in that it promotes awe at the majestic power of nature and of the warrior leader. Awe is the correlative of the political attitude of obedience superior individual leaders must inspire and require if they are to succeed. Moreover, the style draws attention to the level of representation itself, which is highly resolved and in color tone qualitatively superior to an image that merely records an objective reality. We have argued that the ability to separate out from the world of primary caretakers requires a capacity for mental representation which permits the child to retain an image of the caretaker even in its absence. A too radical separation, of the sort prescribed by a conservative patriarchal gender socialization system, will give rise to hypertropic mental representations that are detached entirely from any contact with the real world—or with the mother who prevents the child from attaining a patriarchal male identity. They do not so much represent as stand in for, and one could compare this to the structure of metaphor as we have described it. The metaphoric comic book imagery of *Wind and the Lion* is significantly most hypertropic at those moments when the young boy is gazing in awe at the Berber chieftain who serves as his paternal identification. When the chieftain kills off lepers who have kidnapped the boy and his mother, or escapes on horseback from heavily armed Germans, the scenes are shot from the boy's point of view in a slow motion that emphasizes the almost super-human quality of the action. The film dramatizes the process of identification as an internalization of idealized representations of the father which permit a separation from the mother. The exaggerated quality of the representations points to the excessive nature of that separation, its possible source in an anxiety over attachment to femininity. To be identified as a man is to be purged entirely of the maternal, and the hypertropic representations of Milius's individualist hero are themselves means of accomplishing that identification.

It is in Milius's next film, *Big Wednesday* (1978), that the principles of the coming conservative revolution find one of their first explicit cinematic articulations. Set in a golden age prior to Vietnam and the sixties, it concerns three surfers who are always on the lookout for the big wave which will allow them to prove their manhood. They react negatively to modernity as the sixties unfold; of urban riots, one remarks, "People don't know what's good for them." (Strong leaders? the police?) The boys weather the storms of progress with only a few scars (caused, of course, by untrustworthy women), and the film ends with a celebration of their elite surfing power and of the sanctity of male bonding. Shot in a bombastic style that emphasizes the prim-itive power of the sea, the film resembles *Wind* in that its representational surface correlates with the themes of male individuation, the rejection of women, and individual superiority. Hypertropic imagery exercises a cognitive separation as the lusty boys are elevated above the world around them and become true fascist "knights." The more contemporary conservative agenda of the film is signaled in a subplot concerning a friend of the boys, a small businessman, who builds a surfboard business from scratch into a thriving concern until "taxes" do him in and he is reduced to nothing. In this 1978 anthem to right-wing male herodom the material motivation of the cultural mobilization is strikingly evident.

In *Conan the Barbarian* (1982), it is more submerged, although the values it provokes are amply on display. A conservative fantasy projection, the world of *Conan* is a jungle where no one can be trusted and where one must fight to survive. Other people are either bonded allies who act as satellites to the male individual's will or violent enemies who threaten one's existence. In the plot, Conan's parents are killed by an evil necromancer; Conan is sold into slavery, but grows up to find the necromancer, kill him, and free the people the necromancer held in thrall. Another way of describing what we are char-acterizing as the need in conservative male socialization to adopt represen-tations of the father and to purge traits of the mother is to speak of castration. The boy, in order to avoid feeling castrated, that is, being a woman, must compensate by internalizing exaggerated, even fetishistic representations of male power. We mention this because *Conan* is full of castration imagery. Phallic power seems to be at stake in the struggle between Conan and the necromancer. Conan wins by hacking off the necromancer's head with the broken stump of the sword his father made and which the necromancer used to behead Conan's mother. One senses a sexual anxiety—a fear of impotence, femininity, or castration—underlying all of this; hence the almost hysterical counteraffirmation of macho power as an antidote. Bully men are still only half-grown baby boys underneath. Moreover, the necromancer's high priest is distinctly gay, and the priest's followers are hippieish and effeminate. They engage in a swarming sexual orgy in which no one seems to belong to anyone else, and eat a cannabalistic stew containing severed hands. To be dominated or part of a collective, rather than "free" as an individualist, is to lose one's masculinity; to be a right-wing small businessman in loincloth is to be sexually potent. If Milius's film underscores the sexual anxiety underlying conservative individualist social thinking, it also points to the pervasive theme of resentment against government control. The tyrants of the loincloth hero films are icons of a state power which can only be represented as unjustly domineering. And indeed, from a right-wing business perspective, excessive federal government was the real evil of the modern era, second if at all only to the Soviet Union, that other emblem of a state gone out of control.

While Peckinpah articulates the populist individualist resentment against class or power elites, Milius articulates the rootless, nostalgic conservatism of the petit bourgeois, the lower middle class sector whose lack of a stable class or economic fix motivates an anxious yearning for stable order, simpler times, and a powerful authority to dispel the multiple fantasy threats that are the paranoid projections of economic and social insecurity. Deprived of a secure populist ground, this ideology compensates for its instability by projecting exaggerated images of male power and by idealizing its past. Whereas Peckinpah asserts an aggressive male individualism that is dynamic, rebellious, and resentful of power (thus displaying some of the potentially radical components of populism), Milius demonstrates the regressive and passive side of conservative ideology, the longing for maternal security even as it yearns for representations of a powerful male figure to provide a stable identity. Conan is saved ultimately not by a man but by an idealized woman.

There is a continuity between Milius's romantic individualist films of the mid-seventies and the more fantastic films of the later period. As romance or fantasy, both carry out a rejection of the constraints of social reality, a representational dynamic appropriate, we suggest, to the ideology of individualism. The celebration of the individual hero is also an inflation of subjective power over objective reality or over society's collective limitations (the tyrant state). There is in consequence a tendency in the hero films toward styles that deny history or ignore contemporary reality. The inflation of the individualist's subjective power seems to be carried out through a hypertropic representational form which is itself antisocial, in the sense that the images draw attention to themselves and are not merely transparent representatives of an external reality. They are more metaphoric than metonymic, tropes of substitution not connection. The depreciation of social realism, the inflation of romantic style, and the escalation into heroic fantasies of power are the aesthetic or representational correlates of the social theory of conservative individualism.

During this time a number of conservative stars (Eastwood, Norris, Stallone) parlayed success at the box office into power in the industry, and the films they wrote, produced, or directed generally espoused the new right-wing values of the era. All the films feature the stars as strong heroes who save the United States from invasion, provide leadership to threatened communities, or obliterate underclass threats to white middle-class life. Norris's and Stallone's films are particularly integral to the new culture of conservatism. In Stallone's *Rocky IV*, the ex–working–class hero stands up for the consumer society and wins against a Soviet mechanical man. The usual nature metaphors (wood chopping, mountain climbing) supply the needed index for distinguishing the good American from the overly technological Russian who, nevertheless, converts to the creed of "for me"-ness and himself rebels against his masters before being drubbed into submission by his natural superior. The film suggests the strong link between middle-class ownership and the ideology of the self. Property is a confirmation of the individual self inasmuch as goods are gotten through one's own effort, one's own faith in oneself. But resident in this ideal is a violent reality: an individualized society is one in which people necessarily compete rather than cooperate. So it is that one of Stallone's characters remarks, "We're the warriors, and without some war to fight, the warriors might as well be dead." Bring on the night.

Norris initially made a name for himself by translating the Bruce Lee martial arts film craze into an American idiom. But Lee films like *Fists of Fury* contain a class dimension that is absent in Norris's films; Lee plays a member of a working-class family whose members are killed off by a corrupt boss, and the significant battle scenes are between workers and the boss's goons. In contrast, Norris in films like *An Eye for an Eye* (1981) and *Code of Silence* (1985) tends to play resentful loner cops who buck authority in order to go after aristocratic drug dealers, demonstrating the curious mixture of antiauthoritarian individualism and extremely conservative law and order moralism that characterizes the populist American male. Norris is also featured in *Invasion U.S.A.* (1985), a movie produced by Cannon Films, which made a cottage industry out of right-wing hero films during the early eighties. The movie is distinguished by a sadistic style of violence and a rhetoric of neofascism. In it Norris plays a gator-wrestling redneck retired from the CIA who is called upon as the only one capable of saving the country from a terrorist invasion, led by a Russian. Constitutional freedoms are presented as weakening America ("they are their own worst enemy"), and the terrorists are so bad they turn Americans against themselves, "and even worse, against authority." Leaders are necessary, the film argues, because without them groups would be disorganized and undisciplined. During this era, such right-wing thinking was linked to the exercise of state terrorism against leftists in the form of torture or disappearances, and the film contains several scenes of sadism. This is the extreme of the distancing, separating, and objectifying procedure which establishes the individualist's identity. Purged of socialized female traits such as empathy, attachment, and dependence (Norris's hero, of course, lives alone), the individualist becomes hyperbolically independent, detached, and unempathetic. Torture is the logical consequence of conservative socialization, the true face of extreme individualism.

The hero revival films were among the most popular of the late seventies and early eighties. *Star Wars* was the leader in 1978, *The Empire Strikes Back* in 1980, and *Return of the Jedi* in 1983. *Rocky II* was third in box-office gross in 1979; *Rocky III* was second in 1982; and *Rocky IV* was third in 1985. *Raiders of the Lost Ark* led the take in 1981, while *Indiana Jones* was second in 1984. And the one conservative *Superman* film, the second, finished second in gross in 1981. All of this is not to say that the era was dominated by conservative hero-revival fare. Liberal films were also extremely popular: *9 to 5* was fourth in 1981, while *Tootsie* was second in 1983, followed by *War Games* at number four and *Superman 3* at number five. Yet one should also bear in mind that the conservative hero films grossed much more than the liberal ones, with the exception of *E.T.* (1982), though, as we shall argue, the sentimentalism of the film is in some ways in curious conjunction with the ideology of the hero films.

2. George Lucas's Strategic Defense Initiatives

George Lucas's *Star Wars* series has clear roots in the sort of nostalgic populism we noted in Peckinpah, but the series also espouses values of individualism, elite leadership, and freedom from state control which are congruent with the principles of the new conservatives of the eighties.

In Lucas's early films—*THX 1138* (1971) and *American Graffiti* (1973)—the mixed political possibilities of libertarianism are evident. *THX* is an individualist quest set in a futuristic totalitarian society which has overtones of both right-wing dictatorship and communist egalitarianism (see 9.1). *Graffiti* is a more communitarian movie, but it also implicitly privileges one superior heroic individual, and the community is bound together by a paternalist figure—the DJ Wolfman Jack—a secular deity who, like the Force, unites the disparate individuals in a quasi-higher mode of being. The film is set in pre-sixties Southern California, and it is infused with a sense of a world about to fall. In keeping with the sentimental evocation of a past golden community, the young hero longs for an older woman who remains inaccessible. It is a story of failed sexual maturation, and it ends appropriately with a nostalgic review of the futures of the young kids which suggests that the earlier, pre-pubescent period was better. The threat of modernity provokes in this instance a desire for a restoration of an earlier state of union with a maternal and gratifying source of care. And what this evokes, of course, is an anxiety over separation and loss. That maternal union is lost, and the problem is how to accept that loss through the development of mature mental representational patterns. The regressive character of the film, its indulgence in a fairly gratifying fantasy, suggests that Lucas's films will not be distinguished by such representations. While this will provoke both increasing nostalgia or

Films like *Star Wars* offered what many white middle class Americans were seeking in the late seventies—"A New Hope."

longing and increasingly fantastic attempts to attain the fused security the lost maternal union used to provide, it also will give rise to extremely gratifying cinematic experiences, since part of that process of psychological compensation will consist of heightened representational effects which in themselves fulfill the psychological need.

The *Star Wars* series is probably the most popular film series of all time in part for this very reason. The representational dynamics are appropriate to the story of the rise of a young man from humble origins to the discovery that he is in fact a knight, to quests which prove his manhood and power. The films pit "good" rebels against the "evil" Empire, which is controlled by a demonic Emperor and a former Jedi knight, Darth Vader, who has fallen prey to the "dark side of the Force . . . anger, fear, and aggression." In *Star Wars* (1977), the first film of the series, Vader pursues Princess Leia (Carrie Fisher), who has secret information about the Empire's new death ship that can destroy planets. Luke (Mark Hamill) joins her forces when he discovers that Empire troops killed his foster parents. He receives training in Jedi knighthood from Ben Kenobi (Alec Guinness), and they hire an adventurous merchant and smuggler, Han Solo (Harrison Ford), to transport them to the Princess's planet. The group eventually rescues the princess and destroys the Empire Death Star as it is about to destroy the home planet of the republican freedom fighters.

The rhetoric of the film promotes individualism against the state, nature against technology, authenticity against artifice, faith and feeling against science and rationality, agrarian values against urban modernity, etc. The Empire represents the destruction of an agrarian trade-based market economy; it disturbs the natural order of the patriarchal family; and it breaks down the simple ground of faith that binds small "republican" communities together. It is also associated with technology, artificiality, urban life, and facelessness. The film thus displays the ingredients of the dominant American conservative ideology that makes U.S. culture so resistant to urban-based, rational socialist ideals. In that ideology, such socialism will appear as a faceless threat, a state bureaucracy of tyrannic control against which must be mobilized a combination of agrarian, spiritualist, and patriarchal values. The threat can only ultimately be defeated by that ideal that is most at stake in this ideological conflict—freedom. And the symbol of freedom is the male individual. It is significant, therefore, that Han Solo is a small capitalist entrepreneur who outruns the state's police ships. More important, the hero of the epic—Luke Skywalker—is a figure of individual freedom who brings together all of the ideological motifs, from the agrarian to the spiritualist, that undergird the ideology we are analyzing. The peculiar alliance between the antistatist, antirational individualism of that conservative ideology and an ideology of corporatist discipline, authority, and elitism also emerges in his character.

Luke Skywalker is the son of an elite Jedi knight who proves himself a natural warrior and leader. His name suggests spiritual transcendence as well as the western movie hero myth. He is also in touch with a cosmic spiritual force that is a source of power and that makes elite military leadership seem natural, almost divinely sanctioned, thus legitimating the rule of supposedly superior white males in a vision of elitist corporatism. The notion of a naturally chosen elite leadership coheres with a kind of corporatist social organization in right-wing thinking. But Luke is also a champion of freedom against tyranny. Thus, his figure combines both traditional conservative (elitist) and newer (libertarian individualist) motifs.

The combination of ideological motifs is evident also in the dually regressive structure—historical and naturalist—of the narrative. *Star Wars'* myth cites the code of the heroic period of the birth of capitalism when the great struggle was for mercantile "freedom" against feudal "tyranny." It is significant in this regard that Darth Vader is a "lord," that Luke is a "knight," that the enemy is "Empire," and that the rebels are "republicans." The discourse of early capitalism's war against feudalism is transcoded and allied with the terminology of capitalism's just war against Nazism and its Cold War against Soviet communism. The Empire troops are referred to as "Imperial Storm Troopers"; they look both Germanic and Slavic, and their generals wear World War II Soviet uniforms. All in white and all the same size, the troopers represent collectivization and massification, what conservatives fear and project onto socialism. Luke, on the other hand, is an individualist, a hero born to be distinguished from others.

The return to the historical roots of capitalism coincides with a return to its ideological roots in the concept of nature. The rural family scenes are endowed with an aura of simple virtue, while the city is depicted as a site of vice where monsters gamble, kill, and listen to jazz. Moreover, salvation lies in trusting one's natural instincts and in ignoring reason. In the key battle scene, when Luke is attacking the Death Star he turns off his computer and trusts his instincts to hit the target, using skills he learned in his rural home. The romanticism of feeling and submission to irrational "force" thus intersects the agrarian and naturalist ideology of the film.

The antirationalist romanticism tends to reinforce values of submission to duty and reverence for authority, and it is also related to the pro–free–market sentiments of contemporary conservatism. Natural forces prevail in the free market; the trouble with urban liberals and rationalist socialists is that they try consciously to control nature too much. Their "imperial" planning interferes with the natural arrangement of things (the "Force"). It is better to trust, as Luke does, what is (super-) natural, what is outside one's conscious control, the irrational force of nature, with quiet obedience and a sense of duty.

The individual leader is also naturally selected, someone with privileged access to the ground of natural power and authority that allows born leaders to emerge spontaneously (without having to bother with democracy). The authority of that ground is linked to the idea that nature is unarticulated; it is an incarnation rather than a representation, a revealed truth rather than an artificial act of figuration, a matter of feeling, not thought. This "republican" elitist political philosophy is, of course, extremely antidemocratic. And that attitude is embodied in the way subordinates to the elite are represented in the film. They are either robots or dumb beasts, most of whom cannot speak.[3]

But the film also inadvertently questions its own grounding metaphor. The authority of the ideology of individualist elitism depends on the metaphor of nature being taken for a literal expression, something that is in no way contaminated by the artificial rhetoric associated with urban culture. Yet especially in the later films, that which must be controlled for the Jedi knight to attain his destiny is also natural—aggression. In some respects, the villains are bad because they have not learned to control nature. The shift in the function of the figure of nature—first as a sign of goodness, then of evil—draws attention to its figurality or artificiality. It is a trope of artificial comparison, not an expression of an unarticulated incarnation or revealed truth, a figure that takes on different meanings in different narrative situations rather than the instantiation of an inherent or natural meaning. The figure of nature is chosen by conservatives because it suggests inherence and authority, what is pre-figural and self-evidently true, something that stands before and outside all discourse and negotiation. Yet its self-contradictory use in this film suggests that such terms are always rhetorical figures, the products of discourse rather than primordial truths which underlie discourse. That the elite individual stands out only in differential comparison to the mass, and that the figure of nature which sanctions his selection changes meaning in order to differentiate him from those who cannot control nature, suggests that the ground of the ideology is put in question by the very rhetorical equation that establishes it. What becomes clear is that such ideology depends on rhetorical tropes like metaphor whose figural character must be overlooked in order for the ideology to operate successfully.

In *The Empire Strikes Back* (1980) Luke undergoes a ritual of initiation into Jedi knighthood and confronts Darth Vader, who cuts off Luke's hand in combat. He is taught the mysteries of the order by Yoda, a dwarfish Jedi master. The episodes emphasize the irrationalist and romanticist basis of the films' ideology. Yoda teaches a prereflexive faith, and reflection or intellectual activity—with its propensity for criticism—is antithetical to romantic sentiment and faith. He is childlike in shape, and this embodies a desire for regression to a world of preoedipal symbiosis, prior to the complex world of adult responsibility. Yoda's cave is a fantasy space, outside of social reality, a figure for a regressed world of childhood, where all one's male narcissism can be fulfilled, all one's wishes answered. Yoda imparts to Luke the power to alter and control the objective world through thoughts. This omnipotence of mental processes is related to the fantastic representational dynamics of the films, which are themselves antidotes to a fear of castration (Luke's severed hand), or more generally, a fear of an uncontrollable adult world of negotiation, sacrifice, and compromise where male childhood narcissism must give way to a more interactive and dialogic psychic orientation, one capable of tolerating loss without resentment or a sense of "castration," of a diminution of power.

In *Return of the Jedi* (1983) Luke completes his rite of passage, finally acts as a knight, and defeats the Emperor. He also saves his father, Vader, from the dark side of the Force. In this film, evil is associated with materiality and sexuality (in the figure of Jabba the Hut), while good is given the added meanings of ascesis, discipline, and self-control. Luke's Jedi robe is markedly monastic, and he is separated from sexuality altogether by discovering that his potential romantic partner—Leia—is his sister. Thus, a relationship emerges between the spiritualist and elitist ideology of the film and a repulsion from the material world that could be traced to the protestant Christian ethic of capitalism. This separation of realms is reinforced by the recognition that, in this world of boys' struggles against tyrannical paternal figures, the mother and all that she represents in regard to socialization (care, empathy, etc.) are absent. Heroic marketplace individualism and male militarism require a purgation of that maternal or feminine sphere, a sphere associated with materiality and sexuality, as well as with the tempering of male violence. It is for this reason, perhaps, that conservatives so often justify their worldview with spiritualist and idealist ideologies.

Thus, the *Star Wars* films put on display the internal psychological and interpersonal circuits that give rise to such public institutions, policies, and values as aggressive male individualism, the privileging of "masculine" attributes of competition and domination in the market, and the patriarchal scheme of power inheritance, whereby male socialization seems "naturally" to lead to the rightful assumption of social power by men. The seemingly personal biography of the hero is a template for the institutionalized values that sustain patriarchal capitalism, inasmuch as that social system is predicated on male individualism as its operative principle. The narrative of training for knighthood and privilege is a temporalization of the founding structures of patriarchy. The films suggest why the patriarchal family is indissociable from the capitalist principles of individualism and of freedom (which should not be confused with democracy and equality). In that family form, the authority of the father (first represented in the films by Vader and later by the Emperor) evokes rebellion in the son, simply because the internalization of the image of the father as the basis for forming a masculine identity (rendered literally in the film as Luke's adoption of his father's Jedi role and his acquisition of his father's laser sword-phallus) implies a conflict with the actual limiting power of the father. This is why conservatism always is a peculiar combination of authoritarianism and rebelliousness, the exercise of discipline and the refusal of any communal constraint on individual "freedom." The male child's rebellion takes individualist and individualizing forms; that is, the assertion of one's own power aids separation from the primary caretaker (usually the mother in the patriarchal family) and the adoption of a masculine sexual identity. It therefore also consists of attempts to differentiate from the way women are represented in the patriarchal family as passive, dependent, and subservient. The internalization of the representations of paternal power by boys thus occurs in ways conducive to the requirements of capitalism and of conservative political institutions, that is, to a social philosophy of constant male individualist deviation from the threat posed by the paternal instance of the state or the threat of engulfment in an undifferentiated mass signaled by the metonymic connections of communal relations and responsibilities.

Yet the *Star Wars* series shows as well how this process of patriarchal reproduction rests on an irreducible anxiety. That anxiety is the result of a fear of feminine sexuality and of the threat to male sexual identity it represents. The films swerve away into the past, as well as into the regressed world of fantasies of mental power and into the fantasy of elite privilege. But the series also swerves away from women, and because women are so absent, one can only deduce this anxiety from the form of the films. If male sexual identity hinges on the ability to construct mental representations, that retain the mother as a metaphoric image which also distances her literally, in these films, that ability assumes hypertropic forms. Not only are the films themselves about the ability to develop mental power (Luke's training by Yoda), but their form is an exercise of such power. If representation is a way of attaining individuation, then it is fitting in these exaggeratedly individualist films which deal so much with sexual power struggles with paternal figures that the representational style is itself so hypertropic and idealizing. Normal events are endowed with transcendental significance by martial music; ordinary people are represented as infused with spiritual power in the action sequences; the images are highly resolved, full of nonrealist detail and color, and shot in a way that heightens a sense of being apart, separated out from the world of mundane events. The idealization of the male individual as a separate and privileged agent is accompanied by an idealization of formal visual properties, which signals a sort of mental power appropriate to a male who wishes to deny the material power of the mother, to separate himself out from communal connections, and to align himself with the paternal instance of power in the patriarchal family. Yet that idealization is excessive, a sign of an anxiety that troubles the resolution of the crisis of sexual identity. Indeed, as in genres, the repetitive character of the series (no doubt in part due to opportunism but also planned before the films were successful) testifies to an inability to resolve that anxiety. What the films demonstrate, however, is that it could never be fully alleviated. For it is in the nature of patriarchal socialization (the turning away from the maternal and the literal toward the paternal and the metaphorically ideal) to be structured in such a way that male sexual identity is always precarious, founded as it is on an assertion of prerogatives that are not natural and that in fact must deny the reality of a rather large body of material nature.

Like the realist hero films, the *Star Wars* series point to two elements of American culture that help explain the failure of liberalism and the success of conservativism during this period: the power of heroic male individualism as a cultural representation that resonates with the way men are socialized or constructed as subjects in a capitalist society, and the ease with which the state (either the liberal government or the socialist state), because it represents the curtailment of individual self-control and freedom, can be turned into a figure of evil. The films are successful ideologically in fact precisely because their conservativism is "revolutionary" rather than passive. The ideology is one of rebellion against power and domination. The films point forward in a dynamic mode, and conservatism during this period was so successful for precisely this reason. It gave people something to fight against (the state) and something to fight for ("freedom") at a time when recession was making people feel passive, frustrated, and constrained by forces beyond their control.

To that extent, *Star Wars* is the paradigmatic conservative movie series of the period because it also makes conservatism revolutionary. It presents a conservative past (both temporally as a prior, premodern era and morally as a set of simpler, more "natural" values and institutions) as something to be fought for in the present and future. And it associates that agenda with dynamic self-assertion and simple self-trust of the sort needed to help people transcend the mid-seventies malaise of economic recession, military defeat, and distrust of leadership. The films also project a model of a corporatist social structure that includes all groups—women, blacks, small-businessmen, leader-executives, the military, even "Third World" people (the Ewoks)—in a fantasy of renewed consensus after the discord of the sixties and early seventies. This model, emerging as a compensatory reaction to the mid-seventies dissensus, seems to transcode the new conservative discourse of social reunification both domestically and as a foreign policy necessity.

In our survey, given a choice of meanings for what the heroes stood for in the first film in the series, 57% chose "being true to oneself" while 17%

felt they promoted American values like individual freedom and capitalism. 53% chose to see the Empire as an embodiment of "evil," as opposed to 24% who saw it representing right-wing dictators or 12% who saw it representing communism. In our oral interviews, the most common description was that the heroes represented the "underdog" in a struggle against "big institutions" or "imperialism" or "dictators." Several people compared the heroes to the American revolutionaries in their fight for independence, and for some this description carried more contemporaneous patriotic meaning, in the sense that it meant a struggle between American "democracy" and communism or a call for the United States to stop letting itself be "bullied by other countries." Nevertheless, others said the heroes represented freedom of thought and self-determination, and the word used most often for the Empire was "tyranny." On the whole, the highest percentage of the survey sample (30%) felt the film represented liberal values, yet, as so often in this survey, people also seemed to hold several quite distinct political positions at once. For example, when asked if the film supported the conservative ideal of peace through strength, 54% said yes, and 74% thought the heroes more resembled conservative "freedom fighters" than leftist revolutionaries, yet 67% also felt the film supported the liberal idea of political self-determination "even as say in Nicaragua." But, once again, it should be noted that a much larger percentage of conservatives than liberals (76% as opposed to 46%) chose the conservative ideal as a meaning, while the largest number of liberals (43%) felt the film promoted liberal values on the whole.

Star Wars seems to be a neutral enough adventure story in some respects to evoke a variety of responses. The struggle against tyranny does to a certain extent transcend political demarcations. Yet, we would still maintain that in the historical context of the late seventies the privileged meaning of the film ("being true to oneself") was likely to fuel a conservative rather than a liberal political and social agenda. For at that time what conservatives were promoting was an individualist ethic which equated self-fulfillment with capital accumulation, and as conservatives succeed in the eighties in imposing that agenda and that ethic on U.S. society, "being true to oneself" would come increasingly to mean "going for it" and "saving one's own hide."

The series is politcally significant in one other way. It demonstrates why the capitalist principle of freedom is incompatible with democracy. That principle emphasizes individualist will over social cooperation of the sort democracy presupposes. Democracy is a matter of negotiation, the curtailment of one's own will for the sake of respecting the will and needs of others. Freedom is a principle of self-assertion, regardless of its effects on others. The capitalist version of freedom is particularly antisocial, since it assumes that capitalists have the right to do what they want regardless of the social consequences. The films also depict how the capitalist ideal of individualist freedom tends to become a leadership principle. The singular individual is validated for leadership by virtue of being singular, separated out from and thus elevated above the democratic mass. Patriarchy, which promotes a male socialization that occurs as a separating out or a singularization of the self,

thus hinges with a paternalist political form. Freedom and fascism, as the
rise of conservatism in the eighties demonstrated, are thus understandably
found in frequent alliance during this era. The Reagan war to restore "freedom" (the right of male capitalists to accumulate wealth and power) to the
United States was often on the side of a war to impose authoritarian regimes.
We will examine this question further in the next section.

3. The Leadership Principle—From Movie Brats to Movie Moguls

Lucas belongs to a group of young filmmakers who in the seventies were
labeled "movie brats"—Coppola, Spielberg, Milius, Schrader, De Palma, Cimino, and Scorsese. During this period several of them acquired tremendous
power in Hollywood as a result of successful films like *The Godfather, Star
Wars, Close Encounters of the Third Kind*, and *Raiders of the Lost Ark*. With the
exception of Spielberg, whose work is liberal in character, and Scorsese,
whose sensibility is more film buffish and technical than ideological, they on
the whole promote conservative ideas in their films. Milius, as we have noted,
is an overt neofascist; Schrader and De Palma are sexual reactionaries; Cimino
and Coppola seem to advocate a white male leadership principle in films like
The Deer Hunter and (as we shall see) *Apocalypse Now*. What is interesting is
that, Milius aside, these directors do not see themselves as being political. In
this they are very American, for American culture is characterized by the
belief that its values are "pre-political." Indeed, avoiding contamination by
artificial, urban politics is one of these values. Such contamination characterizes the "sophisticates," a term Coppola and Reagan both use to describe
liberal intellectuals. The conservatism of many of these filmmakers is pre-
political in this sense; it is not articulated in recognizably Left or Right discursive forms. And inasmuch as it is occasionally populist, its political valence
is indeterminate. It contains elements that are potentially either Left radical
or Right radical.

That duality is striking in Cimino's films. *Heaven's Gate* (1980), a leg-
endary disaster for United Artists, is a story of immigrant farmers struggling
against cattle barons in the late nineteenth century. The choice of characters
and of historical setting avoids more politically valorized urban industrial
class struggles of a later era. The combined immigrant and agrarian motifs
suggest the rooted homogeneity of ethnic communities, which is capable of
generating fairly conservative values. Yet the film takes the side of the popular
masses against ruling economic elites, and a woman leads the fight at one
point. Thus, a more radical possibility exists within the same ethnic, populist
ideology. (It is probably worth noting that Cimino made *The Year of the Dragon*,
a film that provoked praise by radicals as well as denunciation for its affirmative representations of bovine patriotism and sexist violence, as well as its
questionable images of Asian-Americans as gangsters,[4] and that he has said
he would like to do a remake of Ayn Rand's reactionary celebration of conservative individualism, *The Fountainhead*.)

The taken-for-granted or pre-political values these filmmakers hold are predominantly conservative in part because they favor individualist solutions to public problems, and such solutions usually implicitly work against liberal statist or socialist alternatives. We have noted how, in hero-revival films, the heroic male individual is invariably posed against figures of public state authority. The hero's freedom consists of being his own leader, and the defeat of an impersonal, unjust state authority creates a need for a more genuine, just, and authentic leadership that only the male individual can provide. The individual can do so because liberal bureaucratic institutions are either inefficient or misdirected. They rely on artificial means rather than on the natural intuitions of the genius leader. In this way, the pre-political principle of individualism contains the seeds of a political leadership principle. For individualism is founded on the notion that one's own private intuitions are sufficient for social action. They take precedence over negotiation, bureaucratic procedure, and democratic processes. In its extreme form self-leadership becomes so intolerant of interference from others, of the democratic need to share decision-making or to negotiate policy, of the curtailment of its will by "tyranny," that it assumes the form of authoritarianism, of leadership over others. This development is usually presumed to be benign, since the self-leader is also a self-lover, a narcissist who believes others will respect his decisions as much as he does. Moreover, the leader becomes a mirror for all the "individuals" in the society, someone who mediates the reality of mass society with the fantasy of individual distinction. In its rightist forms, the leadership principle is thus associated with the ideal of society as an organic whole, a corporate order where all obey a leader unquestioningly because they venerate him. And they venerate him because they venerate themselves as individualists in him. What is striking about Riefenstahl's *Triumph of the Will*, for example, is that Hitler is portrayed not as a cold, impersonal tyrant, but as a beloved individual leader and father who draws people together in a community in which all alienation is overcome. The alienation and impersonality of modern democratic urban life dissolve into a neoagrarian ideal of community where personal ties, among people in the community and between them and the leader, replace the cold bureaucratic ties of impersonal liberal state forms. Thus, in this way, the seemingly apolitical principle of individualism can produce a highly political social structure of leadership. It is for this reason, perhaps, that many of the values espoused by the contemporary Right in the United States so much resemble Nazi ideology. The Republican platform of the early eighties sounded like a translation of "Kinder, Kuche, Kirche," even though the free market ideology of individual freedom seemed at odds with fascist statism. What it really opposed was liberal statism, and in its place it espoused an authoritarian use of the state to restore a conservative order.

We have already noted the conjunction of individualism and hero-leader worship in several movie brat films, like *The Godfather* and *Star Wars*. It is particularly striking in Coppola's *Apocalypse Now*, in which Kurtz's renegade behavior is in part motivated by his desire to be his own boss. We suggest a relationship between this and the small-business or petit bourgeois psychology, which sanctifies individualism and is usually as well connected with an orientation toward political models of authoritarian leadership. The film centers on Willard's (Martin Sheen) successful pursuit of his assignment to assassinate Walter Kurtz (Marlon Brando), an officer who has set up his own command in Cambodia during the Vietnam War. Willard travels upriver in a patrol boat, encountering situations that portray different aspects of the war—from an Air Cavalry attack on a VC-controlled village to a USO show replete with Playboy bunnies to the accidental killing of peasants to a besieged and leaderless U.S. outpost. Finally, he arrives at Kurtz's camp, a grotesque scene of severed heads, hanging bodies and servile natives. At this point, the degree of ritual escalates, and Willard is put through a process of initiation into Kurtz's secrets. In the end, he slays Kurtz in juxtaposition to a ritual sacrifice of a bull by the natives.

The narrative focus is on Willard's progressive identification with Kurtz's power and ruthlessness and on his concomitant transformation into an effective warrior. The point is made through Willard's increasing disgust with the ineptitude of the leaderless army and his admiration for Kurtz that Kurtz's brand of authoritarian warrior leader is needed as a solution to the disarray of the war. The film translates all the metonymic contingency and complexity of actual history into a metaphoric quest narrative that resolves confusion and doubt into certainty and authority. And the resolution of that narrative coincides with Willard's blending with Kurtz and with his assumption of Kurtz's leadership position over the natives. In the beginning, Willard himself is a metaphor for the disarray of the American Army in Vietnam. He drinks, he cries, and his wounded hand suggests a symbolic castration. In his voice-over narration, he thinks of how tough the Vietnamese are in comparison. His inverted head later becomes significant in contrast to the Buddha's upright head, perverted in the film into a metaphor of Asiatic ruthlessness, which connotes the uprightness and power he will acquire from Kurtz. At the end of the film, after Willard has rectified himself by undergoing an initiation into Kurtz's mysteries, learning the truth of why it is necessary to kill ruthlessly in war, the two heads appear again, both upright, and merge. This signifies Willard's acquisition of Kurtz's power, his identification with him.

Willard has learned that one must identify with what the film describes as the Vietnamese way of killing without conscience. If Kurtz dons black greasepaint in order to kill one of Willard's men, Willard dunks himself in a swamp and emerges black in order to kill Kurtz. Each symbolically assumes the color of what the army general at the beginning calls the "darker side" of humanity. And each also adopts the tactics (Kurtz's hit and run) and weapons (Willard's machete) of the native Vietnamese, thus enacting Kurtz's supposition that we might have won the war if only we'd had "ten divisions of those men." After the killing, Willard stands with half his face in light and half in darkness. He seems to have successfully combined the two sides of humanity as it is described in the film—the overly bureaucratic, rational, and conscientious West and the supposedly ruthless, irrational, and primitive East—

into a warrior king. It is revealing, then, that Coppola originally wanted to end the film at the moment when Willard emerges from the room in which he kills Kurtz to find the natives bowing down to him as the new leader.

The film celebrates individualism, and its individualist theme is indissociable from the idea that there exist "right" leaders. Willard and Kurtz are posed against the army generals, who are characterized as an inefficient, bureaucratic "corporation." Kurtz goes "for himself" instead of joining the corporate ranks, and he becomes a leader. His natural intuitive genius is made evident by his decision to execute suspected spies, bypassing a trial. As a result, there are no more harmful leaks. Willard exhibits a similar disregard for liberal procedures and institutions, cutting through bureaucratic red tape at a gas depot with a show of individualist violence that produces immediate results. And when he simply executes a wounded peasant woman who was holding up the operation, he immediately feels closer to Kurtz.

The film thus privileges an individualist rebellion against liberalism, bureaucracy, and large corporate organizations that conjoins with the assumption that powerful individuals are natural leaders. That Milius wrote the original script for the film probably accounts in part for the quasi-fascist inflection of this conservative ideology in the film. But the film also displays the origin of this ideology in conservative male pathos. Kurtz complains of the generals at one point that they won't even let flyers write "fuck" on their airplanes. Brando's whine is appropriate for the idea, since it evokes a young boy's resentment of the power of a disciplinary father. The escape from that power takes the form of its assumption, a self-modeling that rejects paternal (or, by implication, corporate or liberal bureaucratic) limitations in order to establish oneself as one's own boss. It is interesting that *Apocalypse* enacts this scenario, since Willard is Kurtz's son, who offs the old man only to don his crown.

The term "leadership principle" sounds rather frightening, but, as we have explained, it is a logical and natural derivative of the individualism that is endemic to American culture, and it usually assumes very benign forms because it is linked to paternalism, the principle of male care and family authority. The identification with the hero-leader is a rememoration of fathers, as well as an identification with oneself. Through the leadership principle the pleasure of narcissism is transposed onto a public figure who is the locus of one's own pleasurable feelings about oneself. Fascism is a way of making people feel good through patriarchal political forms. It is also, of course, a way of rectifying class struggle in favor of capitalists and conservatives, but as a system in which most people participate as a mass voluntarily, it should not be confused with right-wing military putschism of the sort rampant in places like Chile and Turkey. What we are getting at is that the leadership principle can be found in very "fun" cultural artifacts, and the fun is part of the system of leadership. The combination of rememoration (harking back to a romanticized patriarchal past), narcissistic individualism, incipient authoritarian leadership, and fun is evident in *Raiders of the Lost Ark* (1981), a film Spielberg directed for Lucas, who claimed full responsibility

Raiders of the Lost Ark. Indiana Jones paces above his workers.

for the project.[5] Indiana Jones is an individualist who struggles against his "competitor," Belocq, for gold in South American jungles. Entrepreneurial risk, the film seems to say allegorically, is the source of wealth, not something as mundane as collective labor. In fact, groups of people are shown to be mindless in comparison to the individual entrepreneur. They function only by taking orders from the leader and acting as a mass.

In one scene, while Egyptian workers pick and shovel, Indy walks back and forth above them. They are shot against the sunset, and while only their upper torsos are visible, one can see his entire body. It is significant that they work manually while he provides intellectual management. This scene seems to constitute a metaphor of the division of labor between manual workers (who are spatially lower and non-white) and mental managers who stand above, directing things. The executive leader is a powerful, distinct individual; workers form an undifferentiated mass. The film thus points to the relation between entrepreneurial individualism and elitist corporatist leadership.

The distinguishing of the individual-leader and his association with such power fetishes as mountains (as in the opening shot) is significant. He is the source of power in this cinematic world, and his power is a mark of distinction. Distinction is always comparative, however. Something in its very constitution or coming-into-being detracts from its purity. For example, Indy is distinguished in comparison to non-white laborers, his male competitor, women, the government bureaucrats who hide the ark away in a huge, impersonal warehouse at the end, and himself. It is the last distinction which explains the others. Indy-as-adventurer is distinguished from Indy-as-archeology-professor. His change of roles is akin to the change Luke Skywalker undergoes in *Star Wars* in that it entails acquiring power and attaining a new public identity. The change is a direct rendering of the male sexual socialization process we have been describing as at the root of many of these male power films. The "feminine" role of passivity and weakness is sorted out from a truer, hidden role of "masculine" identification. The character of Indy dramatizes the segregation of a personality into different traits, one set of which become dominant. By the end of the film Indy is once again a professor, but now he is powerful, and a once-powerful woman leans dependently on his arm, a token of the difference that is the real constituent of his identity.

The isolation of an individual, which leads to a sense of singularity and superiority, very clearly relates to male narcissism of the sort that motivates the desire to accumulate more than one needs in male-dominated capitalism. Such accumulation permits a freedom denied others, a narcissistic sense of total power that is an effect of exploitation but that comes metaleptically to justify it by substituting an effect for a cause. The economic and psychological are intertwined, and they are bound up with representation, the representation of oneself that one holds (as a singular individual) and the representation of the individual in a culture (as a natural leader because singular). Indeed, we would argue that the cultural question of representation is crucial to an understanding of the politics of the male leadership principle (both as an ideology and as a set of practices and institutions). In order for it to work, men must be represented in a certain way in the culture, as superior individuals who rise above the democratic mass (Kurtz, Michael Vronsky, Indy Jones, Luke Skywalker). And, as we have noted, this elevation of the superior individual male is frequently carried out through a stylistic elevation that blends synecdoche—the part standing in for the whole—with metaphor—the lifting of the literal or everyday into something more idealized or meaningful that stands in for it. While left-liberal films like *9 to 5*, *China Syndrome*, and *The Boys in Company C* establish a chain of equivalence whereby each one can stand in for the other in the narrative, no one stands out as the natural leader of all, and all are connected contiguously or metonymically, rightist films obliterate the chain of democratic equivalence and subsume it to a vertical hierarchy whereby one element of the chain becomes a paradigm that stands in for all the rest as the leader-hero through metaphoric substitution. This political structure is carried out through cultural representations which secure legitimation for it. And those representations operate in much the same way. This is what we mean when we say the the representational dynamics of films like *Apocalypse* provide clues to the workings of right-wing politics in general, inasmuch as such politics are founded on notions of how communities should represent their interests in the political arena. These films advertise those politics using the same sorts of representational devices and assumptions (separation, substitution, subordination, exaltation) that define the politics.

A similar thing could be said regarding the very surface of representation, as we have noted, and this bears crucially on the sexual agenda of the leadership films. It is significant that *Apocalypse*, like *Deer Hunter*, resorts to a highly metaphoric style at those points where the hero-leader begins to separate out from a world charged with images of "effeminacy."*Apocalypse* is also characterized by an allegorical and romantic form that fuses color, sound, and narrative into an apparent synthetic unity (the Wagnerian ideal), apparently an aesthetic correlative of the political theme of unity under a single leader. Allegory and metaphor are the aesthetic modes of transcendence, since the materiality of the worldly object is annulled and replaced by a higher, ideal or spiritual meaning. It is a fitting form for a politics of transcendence, whereby a strong leader overcomes worldly constraints through a supreme exercise of seer-like or intuitive mental ability that does not rely on worldly forms like language or discussion. In Michael Vronksy's shamanic insight, in Kurtz's warrior intuition, and in Luke's mental power, one sees versions of the power of mental representation which establishes a boundary between the superior individual and the mass, which, like the mother, threatens to engulf the individual, to destroy his boundaries. It is noteworthy, then, that the films themselves are characterized by representational dynamics which seem to mimic that heightened mental power.

We have contended that this turning away both politically and formally from something threatening or constraining into a transcendental vision of leadership and mental power has its roots in sexuality. *Apocalypse* is laden with castration imagery for good reason. The question of the marginal representation of women in these films is therefore more important than the films want it to appear. Willard, the professional killer in *Apocalypse*, separates out increasingly from the "effeminate" regular army as he comes to identify more and more with the more masculine, powerful, and paternalist Kurtz. If Kurtz writes to his son instead of to his wife, Willard decides to return to Vietnam and to sacrifice his marriage. In *Deer Hunter*, Linda is a token whose attainment proves Michael's superiority to the weaker Nick. In that film as well, male love constitutes a significant alternative to the female world, and it is not at all unimportant that only a jump-cut separates a homoerotic scene in a playground (in which Michael lies naked and prone next to Nick) from the battlefield in the film. It is in part the anxiety caused by that cut that provokes the aesthetic and political compensations (authoritarian, allegorical, and narcissistic) that characterize both films. The homoerotic bond between Kurtz and Willard or Michael and Nick can be maintained only by being denied. Violent assertiveness separates men from women, but it throws the men together, a situation as threatening as femininity to the male ideal of masculinity. The all-male club is necessarily homoerotic, but that homoeroticism must be denied if the criterion of membership—masculinity—is to be salvaged. It is perhaps for this reason that the weak must be purged in each film. Nick goes, as does Kurtz, sacrificed so that the stronger can survive and affirm heterosexual manhood.

The desire for separateness is related to the desire to dominate women. Yet such excessive assertions of independence betray a certain dependence. In *Deer Hunter*, Michael's heroics must be validated by Linda at the end as she looks at him, confirming his grandeur. When Willard executes Kurtz, a silent Vietnamese woman watches, confirming his accession to leadership. These marginal moments are more telling than the grandstand "perform-ances" of the men, because they suggest that the boys are acting, that they need something that only women can provide—a certain look or gaze that says they are what they pretend or would like to imagine they are. Male assertion (politically, economically, militarily) is a way of eliciting that gaze, but it is also a way of deflecting the male's dependence on it.

The tendency toward authoritarianism in the small business or petit bour-geois social sector whose ideology permeates the work of rightist filmmakers like Milius and Coppola seems to derive from the competitive capitalist mode of the post-studio, "let's make a deal" film industry, which fosters a psy-chology appropriate to its structure. Movie brat films frequently promote the paranoid, distrustful, aggressively competitive outlook of the industry where they were the fittest to survive. And their rise from movie brats to movie moguls is a material justification of an elitist leadership ideology. The strong-est, those with the most savvy and will to succeed, do probably deserve to rule this knaves' paradise. The system is such that expansive individualism does lead to power. Perhaps it should not be surprising that Coppola has demonstrated authoritarian tendencies in his work practices, or that he evi-dences a fascination with hero-leader films like Gance's *Napoleon*.[6] It is prob-ably also telling that he and Lucas produced Schrader's *Mishima* (1985), a film about a right-wing Japanese writer who committed suicide when his bid to overthrow modern Japan and to restore the samurai elite failed. The film is characterized by an aestheticization of its violent subject, a fastidious height-ening of formal effects which points to the motivating source of the con-servative male quest for a leader-father. It derives from fear, an anxiety at a felt lack in the world, as well as in oneself. What is missing in the world is a secure anchoring point for one's sexual identity, and what is missing in the self is security-providing mental representations of the sort that would permit one to live in the world without the need for patriarchal leaders.

The hero films have a historical value in that they help explain why conservatism succeeded and liberalism failed in the late seventies and early eighties. If the hero films indicate how males are socialized under capitalism to be individualists, guided more by self-serving opportunism and a survivalist mentality than by altruism, then they also show why the Right appealed more to the popular imaginary than did liberals. It is a tautology of power that those most responsible for the misery of recession also benefit most from its effect on people, especially men. For recession induces desires for compen-satory images of self-worth and self-empowerment, and desires that privilege the individual over the collective, a self- orientation over an other-orientation. And of course, such an orientation is more likely to be of use to a social philosophy based on individualism than to one linked to collective ideals. Thus, one could say that liberalism did not so much fail as find itself in an irresolvable quandary at this time. When capitalism makes survival a primary imperative, then it is the ideology of survivalism which is most likely to thrive.

9. FANTASY FILMS

The triumph of conservatism made itself particularly felt in the fantasy genre, in large part because the sorts of representational dynamics afforded by fantasy were peculiarly well suited to the psychological principles of the new conservatism. Nevertheless, fantasy was not an entirely uncontested terrain at this time. In such major fantasy genres of the period as technophobic films and dystopias, a struggle between right-wing and left-wing uses of the fantasy mode is evident. And the major fantasist of the period—Steven Spielberg—consistently promotes liberal ideals through his films. If conservative filmmakers used the motifs of technology and dystopia to project terrifying images of collectivization and modernity, liberals and radicals used them to launch covert attacks against the conservative ideals of capitalism and patriarchy. The flight into the future in many fantasy films is often a flight into the past, toward a world of more traditional values. But it is also often a flight toward more radical alternatives than the constraints of "realism" (both as an aesthetic principle and as a principle of social control) allow to be elaborated. Detachment from the constraints of realism allows fantasy to be more metaphoric in quality and consequently more potentially ideological. Fantasy replaces an accurate assessment of the world with images that substitute desired ideals or feared projections for such an assessment. But such detachment from realist reference also permits the development of alternative constructions of social reality which might otherwise be smothered under hardnosed conservative realist injunction against being "utopian." If fantasy is given to metaphor, it is also an open terrain which permits the deployment of more metonymic rhetorical forms. Indeed, it is in the future-fantasy genre that one finds some of the most radical critiques of American society during this period.

Moreover, the fantasy mode became a locus for projected idealizations of empathetic social relations of the sort more and more unavailable in a public sphere increasingly dominated by conservative principles of survivalism. The fantasy genre is especially revealing in this regard, since, as a result of the conservative occupation of the public sphere, the society's dominant institutions less and less satisfied people's sense of idealization, their sense of being "good." Meanness and venality are not particularly cherishable traits. The rise of economic realism (the triumph of criteria of efficiency over criteria of welfare) in the public sphere in the eighties put a burden on the private

244

sphere (the family particularly) as a locus of idealization. It should not be surprising, then, that Steven Spielberg's family fantasy films became tremendously popular during this era. Displaced from the public sphere, liberal ideals of empathy, tolerance, and care tended to retreat to the private sphere.

This shift is telling because it indicates that the new conservatism was not entirely in sync with what most Americans believed. Even if the Republicans succeeded in playing to resentment against taxation, welfare, and affirmative action hiring in order to enlist support for a procapitalist economic program, by the mid-eighties most Americans were expressing distrust of the Republican economic agenda. The majority correctly saw it as unfair. Moreover, Republicans were incapable of attaining hegemony in the social sphere of the sort they held in the political and economic spheres. Thus, as much as liberalism, conservatism found itself in a dilemma during this time. It could seize political power on the basis of economic doctrine, but it could not transform American culture in a way suitable to its social ideals. What one could call an American quandary developed in the eighties. In the face of entrenched social liberalism, conservatives could not impose their values on the private domain, but liberals faced with entrenched conservative power in business were powerless to reform the economy and to make it more humane.

1. Technophobia

Fantasy films concerning fears of machines or of technology usually negatively affirm such social values as freedom, individualism, and the family. In the seventies technology was frequently a metaphor for everything that threatened "natural" social arrangements, and the conservative values associated with nature which we examined in the last chapter were generally mobilized as antidotes to that threat. But technophobic films were also the site where the metaphor of nature which sustains those values was most saliently deconstructed. From a conservative perspective technology represents artifice as opposed to nature, the mechanical as opposed to the spontaneous, the regulated as opposed to the free, an equalizer as opposed to a promoter of individual distinction, equality triumphant as opposed to liberty, democratic leveling as opposed to hierarchy derived from individual superiority. Most important for the conservative individualist critique, it represents modernity, the triumph of radical change over traditional social institutions. Those institutions are legitimated by being endowed with the aura of nature, and technology represents the possibility that nature might be reconstructable, not the bedrock of unchanging authority conservative discourse requires. Indeed, as the figure for artificial construction, technology represents the possibility that such discursive figures as "nature" (and the ideal of free immediacy it connotes) might merely be constructs, artificial devices, metaphors designed to legitimate inequality by positing a false ground of authority for unjust social institutions.

In the early eighties, conservative economic policies helped create a new class of well-to-do white professionals as well as a larger underclass of impoverished and homeless people.

The significance of technology thus exceeds simple questions of mechanics. It is usually a crucial ideological figure. Indeed, as the possibility of reconstructing institutions conservatives declare to be part of nature, technology represents everything that threatens the grounding of conservative social authority and everything that ideology is designed to neutralize. It should not be surprising, then, that this era should witness the development of a strain of films that portray technology negatively, usually from a conservative perspective.

The technophobic theme is most visible in the early seventies in Lucas's *THX 1138* (1970), a quest narrative set in a cybernetic society where all of life is regulated by the state. Individuals are forced to take drugs to regulate sexual desires; thoughts and individual action are monitored by electronic surveillance devices. A sense of mass, collectivist conformity is connoted by shaved heads, the assigning of numbers instead of names, and starkly lit white environments. The lack of differentiation between individuals is suggested by the limitless quality of space; everything lacks boundaries, from the self to the city. The libertarian basis of the film's value system cuts both ways politically—liberally, in that recorded messages allude to the McCarthyite repression of dissidents, and conservatively, in that they also refer negatively to socialism ("Blessings of the State, blessings of the masses. We are created in the image of the masses, by the masses, for the masses"). Against undifferentiated totalitarianism, the film valorizes the differentiated individual. THX flees the cybernetic society, and the last image depicts his emergence into freedom and nature. His liberation is associated with a bright orange sun that strikingly isolates him as he emerges. The bright sun is a metaphor for individual freedom, for the departure from a world of contrivance and artifice into nature. The sun literally singularizes THX by giving him a distinguishing boundary. He is no longer one of the intersubstitutable mass. In addition, the sense the image imparts is of something literal, the thing itself, nature in its pure presence. Indeed, nature is supposed to be just that, something outside contrivance, artifice, technology, and the sort of substitution which rhetorical figures (the very opposite of what is literal) usually connote. The grounding of the ideology of liberty in nature is tantamount to grounding it in literality, since literality implies things as they are, unadulterated by the sort of artificial intersubstitution of people which prevails in the egalitarian city. Visual style connotes political attitudes, and given a choice between the deep white frieze of equality and the warm orange glow of liberty, one suspects what people are likely to choose.

The rhetorical strategy of many technophobic films, therefore, is to establish a strong opposition between terms (liberty vs. equality) that does not permit any intermediation. The elimination of the middle ground is an essential operation of this ideology. A major mid-seventies film that executes this strategy is *Logan's Run* (1976), in which a policeman named Logan is induced into fleeing a cybernetic city by a young female rebel against the city's totalitarian regime. The representation of the city evokes all the negative traits in the conservative vision assigned to the figure of technology—the

THX 1138. The masses and the free individual. A symbolic bird flies past.

destruction of the family, the interchangeability of sexual partners so that feeling is destroyed by rationality, enforced mass conformity that places the collective before the individual and effaces individual differences in an egalitarian leveling, the power of state control over the freedom to choose, and so on. The city is a mid-seventies liberal pleasure dome where one can summon sexual partners at the touch of a button or periodically receive a new identity. Population size is regulated, and no one has parents. This lack of self-identity is associated with hedonism and collectivity. Logan and the woman rebel get caught up in an orgy at one point, and the colors suggest hell. When the two are separated (divorced, one might say, to emphasize the ideological motif), they almost lose their identities in the teeming crowd. In such a sexually permissive, hedonistic world, clearly no social hierarchy or subjective boundary can be established or maintained. Collectivity is thus associated with a loss of self-identity and a lack of sexual discipline that breaks family bonds.

One of the first things that Logan says upon emerging into nature is, "We're free." In nature one knows who one's mother and father are, whereas in the city of collectivism and sexual hedonism no one knows his/her parents. Thus one can only be an individual, a self, within a society of monogamous marriage, in which sexuality primarily serves the "natural" function of reproduction rather than pleasure. In the film's conservative ideology, the restoration of the traditional family, the preservation of individualism, and the curtailing of nonreproductive sexuality seem to be interdependent, and they all depend on the rejection of everything technology represents—mediation, equality, intersubstitutability, and so on. In this vision one catches a glimpse of the actual ingredients of the emerging conservative movement whose values the film transcodes.

Outside the technological city, the rebels discover nature as well as supposedly natural social institutions like patriarchy and political republicanism. The woman ceases to be an equal of the man, a structure of equivalence generated in the city by representations, primarily wide-angle long shots of crowds, that place everyone on the same plane in the same frame and imply their equality. In nature, she assumes a subordinate position, both socially and within the camera frame as they sit by a crude campfire. Close-ups connote an unmediated spontaneity of "natural" feeling, a literality of social structure uncontaminated by liberal revision. This is the real thing once again, not a technical substitute or an artificial contrivance. One senses why empiricism is often the best recourse of ideology. At the level of empirical literality, equivalences cannot be established of the sort that thrive in the technological city, where the possibility of infinite copies annuls individual differences. At the level of social literality, everything is radically individuated, incapable of comparison. Appropriately, then, Logan kills his police partner, who has followed the rebels out of the city. He is a double or copy who is Logan's functional equal, and his death individuates Logan. He renounces his identity as a cybernetic functionary precisely because his intersubstitutability means he has no identity as such. The death occurs at the moment in the narrative when the rebels have come to Washington and rediscovered the United States's republican political system. With it, they rediscover the predominance of liberty over equality, the individual over the collective.

The peculiar twist of this ideal of liberty, therefore, is that it is a social theory that rejects the social (being other than oneself, mediated by social relation, a copy or technological robot). The choice of nature, as an alternative to technological collectivity, is thus appropriate, since nature is what is entirely nonsocial. What conservatives ultimately want is a ground of authority that will make inequalities that are in fact socially constructed seem natural. This is tantamount to saying that such instituted inequalities must seem to embody the literal truth of nature, things as they are and should always be. For this reason, the strategy of ontologizing, of making technology and technological constructs seem as if they possess a being or essence in themselves, independent of context and use, is crucial to the conservative ideological undertaking. Technology must seem to be intrinsically evil, and this is so if the natural alternatives to technological society—the family and the individual especially—are to seem inherently good, ontologically grounded in themselves and not subject to figural comparison or connection to something outside them that might possibly serve as a substitute or equivalent. What is literal cannot be transported, as in metaphor, out of itself and made to stand for something else. Thus, technology represents a threat not only to self-presence in the sense of individual freedom in the conservative frame, but also to presence as the criterion of the ontological ground, the nature and the literality that anchor conservative social institutions.

A deconstructive analysis would point out that what is posited in this ideology as an ontological and literal cause that gives rise to social institutions—as well as to derivative, secondary, and unauthorized deviations of the original intent of nature through technological simulation and figural substitutions—is in fact an effect of those very things. The nature of ideology is the product of technology; literality is an effect of rhetoric. One notices this at those moments when nature and the literal are shown forth in films like *THX* and *Logan*. Nature takes on meaning as such within the films only as the other of urban technology. Its immediacy is mediated by that against which it is posed, just as the individual is necessarily mediated by society. Moreover, the supposed literal ground of social institutions is the effect of the metaphoric comparison of those institutions to nature. In order to call them natural, one has to engage in precisely the sort of metaphoric or figural comparison, the sort of rhetorical "technology" that is supposedly excluded by that ascription. It is a case of innocence by association, and as a result, those institutions are guilty of being something they must claim not to be, that is, rhetorical constructs, mere technology. Thus a deconstructive reading points out the extent to which representation plays a constitutive role in the making of social institutions, because the metaphors and representations that construct the ideal images of such institutions are also models for social action.

The ideological character of the conservative technophobia films stands in greater relief when they are compared to more liberal or radical films that depict technology not as in itself, by nature, or ontologically evil, but as being subject to changes in meaning according to context and use. For example, the figure of technology is given socially critical political inflections in *Silent Running* (1971), which opposes nature and individual freedom to corporate misuse of technology in an ecological vein, representing the corporation as putting profit before the preservation of the environment. In *Star Trek* (1979) a human actually mates with an astral body born of a space probe, proving that humans and machines can get along more intimately than conservatives ever imagine. And in *Brainstorm* (1983), the story of a technological invention that can be used either for war or peace, the family is shown falling apart, then mending with the help of the invention. Through this narrative motif the family is depicted as a constructed institution, itself an invention reliant more on negotiation than on naturally given laws.

Perhaps the most significant film in regard to an alternative representation of technology that takes issue with the ideology deployed in conservative technophobia films is *Blade Runner* (1982), directed by Ridley Scott. The film, based on the novel by Philip K. Dick, concerns four androids ("replicants") who revolt against their "maker," the Tyrell Corporation. A policeman, Deckard (Harrison Ford), is assigned to "retire" them. Deckard falls in love with Rachel (Sean Young), one of Tyrell's most advanced replicants. With Rachel's help, he manages to kill three of the rebels and fights a final battle with the fourth, Roy (Rutger Hauer), who allows Deckard to live because he himself is about to die. At the end, a fellow policeman allows Deckard and Rachel to escape from the city and flee to nature. The film offers a mediation between technology and human values. "Replicants are like any other machine. They can be a benefit or a hazard," Deckard says. And the film concludes with a happy marriage of humans and machines.

Blade Runner deconstructs certain ideological oppositions at work in more conservative technology films. The marrying of human and replicant undercuts the posing of nature as an opposite to a negative technological civilization. The film also deconstructs the conservative romantic opposition of reason and feeling. In the film, reason is represented by analytic machines that dissect human and objective reality. The police detect replicants with analytic instruments that observe emotional reactions in the eye. When Deckard analyzes the photograph of a room, he breaks down the reality into small parts until he captures what he seeks. The analytic gaze is thus represented as an instrument of power. Posed against this power is feeling. But the film suggests that feeling is not the polar opposite of reason. Rather, feeling, especially in the replicants, is the product of technology. And these machine humans are shown to be in many ways more "human" than their makers. Analytic rationality is depicted as irrational and anti-human when used instrumentally in a policed, exploitative society, but it is also the instrument for constructing a more communal ethic. Thus, the film deconstructs the oppositions—human/technology, reason/feeling, culture/nature—that underwrite the conservative fear of technology by refusing to privilege one pole of the dichotomy over another and by leaving their meaning undecidable.

Blade Runner also calls attention to the oppressive core of capitalism and advocates revolt against exploitation. The Tyrell Corporation invents replicants in order to have a more pliable labor force, and the film depicts how capitalism turns humans into machines, a motif that recalls Lang's *Metropolis*. Indeed, German Expressionist features are evident throughout. The bright pink and red colors of the huge electric billboards contrast with the dark underworld of the streets, and this contrast highlights the discrepancy between the realm of leisure consumption and the underclass realm of urban poverty and labor in capitalism. In addition, the neo-Mayan architecture of the corporate buildings suggests human sacrifice for the capitalist god, and Tyrell is indeed depicted as something of a divine patriarch.

Although the film contains several sexist moments (Deckard more or less rapes Rachel), it can also be read as depicting the construction of female subjectivity under patriarchy as something pliant and submissive as well as threatening and "castratory." (The female replicants are sex functionaries as well as killers.) Similarly, the flight to romance and to nature at the end of the film gives rise to at least a double reading. Romance is escape to an empathetic interior realm from the external realm of public callousness in a capitalist society. Although it promotes personalization and atomization, the final flight also creates a space of autonomy and compassion which can be the basis for collective and egalitarian social arrangements. If the film privileges privatism, it may be because in U.S. society of the time, it was possible to locate humane values only in the private sphere.

The film implies that even the supposedly grounding, ontologically authoritative categories of conservatism like the individual, nature, the family, and sentiment are indeterminate. They have alternative political inflections that revalorize their meaning according to pragmatic criteria of context and use. It is important, then, that unlike the conservative films that end with a move toward (cinematic as well as ideological) literality that supposedly reduces constructed social institutions to a natural or ontological ground of meaning, this film ends in a way that foregrounds the construction of alternative meanings from the literal through the figural or rhetorical techniques of substitution and equivalence, especially the equivalence of human life and technology (of Rachel the machine and Deckard the human at the end, for example). Figurality is foregrounded through juxtapositions that are not justified by the literal logic of the narrative. For example, Roy suddenly carries a white dove that soon becomes a symbol of charity and forgiveness. He himself in fact becomes a figure for Christ as he lowers his head and dies. The dove he releases flies up into a blue sky that also appears out of nowhere for the first time in the film, for no literal reason. The figural or rhetorical quality of these images is thus underscored by their narratively illogical emergence. The same is true of the origami doll the other detective leaves for Deckard as he and Rachel flee; it signals that the detective allows them to escape and becomes a figure for charity. And the wry, ironic comments

Blade Runner. The replicant Roy with peace dove.

Deckard makes at the end about his new relationship with the android woman foreground a figural doubleness or undecidability of meaning.

All of these figures place literality in abeyance, and they underscore the fact that the metaphors conservatives employ to create a sense of a natural or literal ground are irredeemably figural. Indeed, the reconstituted family at the end is working on such a high level of constructedness and figurality, an open-ended relationship between a human and a machine, that it could never touch ground with any literal authority of a sort that the closing images of nature might have conveyed in a conservative or ideological film. What rhetoric, like technology, opens is the possibility of an ungrounded play with social institutions, simulating them, substituting for them, reconstructing them, removing them from any ground of literal meaning that would hold them responsible to its authority. Perhaps this is why technology is such an object of fear in conservative science fiction films of the current era. It is a metaphor for a possibility of reconstruction that would put the stability of conservative social institutions in question.

But the longing for literality and nature in conservative technophobic films might also be indicative of an antinomy of conservatism in the modern world. As conservative economic values became ascendent, increasingly technical criteria of efficiency came to be dominant. In addition, conservative economic development emphasizes the displacement of excessively costly human labor by machines. The increasingly technical sophistication of the economic world and the shift away from industrialized manufacturing to tertiary sector "information age" production creates a hypermodernization that is at odds with the traditionalist impulse in conservatism, the desire that old forms and institutions be preserved. Yet the new technologies make possible alternative institutions and lifestyles, as well as the reconstruction of the social world. Perhaps this accounts for the desire for a more literal, natural world in conservative films. It is a reaction to the world they themselves help create through an ideal of efficient economic development. One antinomy of conservatism is that it requires technology for its economic program, yet it fears technological modernity on a social and cultural plane. This can be read as a sign of the dilemma conservatives faced in the eighties. In control of political and economic life, they could not gain power in the private realm of social values that on the whole continued to be more liberal.

Although in the mid-eighties there was a marked decline in the number of conservative technophobic films, those fearful of technology do not give up easily, as might be suggested by a film like *The Terminator* (1984), in which androids continue to look and act like Arnold Schwarzenegger. Indeed, the film is about a punitive robot that just won't give up. It keeps coming on, not having seen *Blade Runner*, unaware that it is supposed to forgive and forget.

2. Dystopias

Films about the future might seem to be the most aloof from contemporary social problems. Yet they frequently are characterized by radical positions that are too extreme for Hollywood realism. In some respects, the genre that seems most distant from the contemporary world is the one most free to execute accurate descriptions of its operations. Fantasies of the future may simply be ways of putting quotation marks around the present. They carry out a temporal displacement that short-circuits the implicit ideological censors operative in the reigning realist narrative regime of Hollywood.

Future films on the Right dramatize contemporary conservative fears of "terrorism," or socialism, or liberalism as in *Logan's Run* or *Escape from New York*. Left films (*Outland, Blade Runner*) take advantage of the rhetorical mode of temporal displacement to criticize the current inequalities of capitalism. These films display what we have called the American quandary. Conservative films evidence fears of liberal modernity, while Left films advertise the tremendous power of conservatism in economic matters even as they criticize it. The films put on display the split that runs through American society between a civil sphere dominated by liberals and run on quasi-democratic, pluralist principles, and an economic sphere, dominated by conservatives and run in a feudal manner, in which workers are essentially slaves of capital. As such, however, these films delineate a salient antinomy of contemporary capitalism. The principles of political liberty and self-determination that informed the bourgeois revolutions from the seventeenth to the nineteenth century have been successfully blocked from making incursions into the economic sphere, which has continued to operate on two levels. The liberal principle of "freedom" governs the intercourse between capitalists as the principle of marketplace competition, while the intercourse between capitalists and workers operates according to the preliberal principle of domination and exploitation. Freedom, in the liberal sense of self-determination, has yet to reach that level of society, and one function of capitalist ideology is to prevent it from doing so. But the strategy of defense, like all such strategies, indicates a danger and a potential even as it successfully deflects them. The capitalist civil sphere must adhere to "democratic" principles of operation because by so doing the ideological illusion is fostered that the whole society, including the economy, operates according to such principles. It is not accidental that capitalists now refer to their national fiefdoms as "industrial democracies." But the capitalist attitude toward such liberalism will always be only tentatively supportive. To prevent the incursion of the principles of political liberty into the economic sphere, capitalists will reserve the right to impose the neofeudal principles of the economy on civil society as a whole, revoking liberalism entirely. The prevalence of capitalist "states of siege" in the world, from Pakistan and Turkey to South Korea and Chile, is an indicator of this reality, as is indeed also the undeclared state of siege carried out against workers and poor people during the Reagan years. But they also point to a threat; a siege indicates an embattled position. And this is the progressive possibility embedded in the American quandary and in the antinomy between liberal civil society and neofeudal, conservative economic society that became strikingly clear in the eighties. The threat is that the principles of liberty and self-determination will finally enter the economic sphere, and one could interpret the hypertropism of capitalist self-justifications at this period in film (the hero phenomenon) as an indicator of an increase in that threat.

Signs of the threat emerge clearly in the imaginarily liberated space of the future film, especially in what are called dystopias. Dystopias, or negative utopias, predominate in the future-film culture of the seventies and eighties, in part as a result of the era's crisis of confidence. Dystopias generally project into the future the fears of the present, and their themes often transcode the sorts of anxieties that characterized that crisis—uncontrolled corporations, untrustworthy leaders, a breakdown of legitimacy, rising crime, etc. They are vehicles for populist and radical critiques of the capitalist ethic and of capitalist institutions (evident particularly in the popular *Road Warrior* films, which pose an ecological vision of liberal hope against the brutal primitivism of competitive capitalism). The dystopia films can therefore be seen as indirect, displaced articulations of progressive forces and desires that constituted a resistance to conservative hegemony in the eighties and that pointed forward, literally as well as figuratively, to alternative futures.

In the mid-seventies, populist fears were directed at the power of large corporations in films like *Soylent Green* (1973) and *Rollerball* (1975). Values of nature, family, ecology, and individuality are posed against statist domination, characterized by massification, modernization, and the destruction of family life. The destruction of the family, a locus of personal attachments, is equated with the impersonality of corporations. *Rollerball* concerns a sports hero named Jonathan (James Caan) whose world is controlled by a cartel of corporations and characterized by the breakdown of the family. Jonathan's wife is taken away by a corporate executive. In keeping with the populist ethos of the film, he in the end engages in an individualist rebellion against the corporations that rallies the people to him in a kind of revolution. As in so many films, the choice of literal examples is relevant to metaphoric meaning structures. The team against which he has to contest in the end is Japanese, and of course at this time the Japanese were beginning to undercut American world economic power. The radical edge of populism is evident in the film's critique of capitalist domination. Yet a conservative potential emerges in the privileging of traditional male-dominated family life and of individualism conjoined with a leadership principle. *Rollerball* operates ideologically by dichotomizing the world of social alternatives into two possibilities—either individual freedom (linked with male property right over women) or totalitarian domination. No middle ground is allowed in this equation, no middle term. And anything that departs from the ideal of pure individual freedom (corporations, but also socialism) is by implication lumped under domination. Audience sympathy is thus potentially channeled toward support for small business individualist capitalism, since everything else—from socialism to corporate liberalism to the welfare state—is made to look bad by being subsumed under the polar opposite of individualism. The success of such representational strategies in popular culture helps account for the absence of a socialist alternative in the United States.

    If the mid-seventies are characterized by populist dystopias that articulate the growing feelings of resentment against corporations in American culture, in the late seventies and early eighties, a number of left-liberal and radical dystopias (*Quintet, Blade Runner, Outland*) appear that negatively represent the basic tenets of capitalism (the right to exploit labor, competition, etc.). In Altman's *Quintet* (1979) postholocaust life consists of playing a brutal game in which the goal is to kill the other players through a complex system of alliance and betrayal. It is a market world; no one can be trusted; and kisses frequently precede slit throats. This disturbing allegory of capitalism was too bleak for late seventies audiences desirous of more romanticized visions, and the film flopped.

    Peter Hyams's *Outland* (1981) was more successful, perhaps because it was an obvious pastiche of *High Noon*, the story of a sheriff betrayed by his fellow townspeople who must stand up to outlaws alone. But the film is also one of the most accurate representations of the reality of labor exploitation under capitalism that has appeared in Hollywood. At a space mine, workers are given drugs to make them more productive, but as a result they become psychotic and commit suicide. The drugs eliminate the boring and oppressive features of work. "When the workers are happy, they dig more; when they dig more, the company is happy; when the company is happy, I'm happy," the manager tells the sheriff of the mine town, who attempts to end the practice. The company sends killers to prevent him, and he defeats them with the help of a woman scientist.

The conservative ascendancy of the early eighties seemed to invite more radical counterattacks than Hollywood had hitherto seen. What is striking about films like *Outland* and *Blade Runner* is that in a future fiction mode they depict the present reality of capitalist labor exploitation, a reality usually kept off the Hollywood screen. Indeed, the harshness of that reality in part accounts for that absence, since it makes it necessary for the leisure world of post-work entertainment to be something that alleviates the boredom, lack of fulfillment, and pain of wage labor exploitation. It is a commonplace of radical cultural criticism to say that many Hollywood films can in fact be characterized as the real world equivalents of the drugs of *Outland*. But what this suggests as well is that such drugs are indicators of very real pain, potentially threatening diseases.

These radical future films point out the feudal character of the wage labor system and attempt to mobilize traditional representational forms (the western, the hard-boiled detective), as well as traditional liberal humanist ideals (freedom, charity) as critical weapons against that exploitation. The use of traditional representational codes is especially significant for drawing out the contradiction between the political ideals of liberty and the feudal reality of the economy. For those codes—especially the detective and the western—are associated in the tradition with the principles of liberalism. Even if they do so in an individualist manner, they promote the liberal value of freedom or self-determination. And they frequently argue as well for community cooperation and social responsibility. The antiwealth ethos of the detective is especially marked by this trait. However, the dominant procapitalist ideological system of American culture has succeeded in limiting the applicability of those ideals to capitalist entrepreneurs, and, as we have seen, that ideology is refortified during this era.

Because the western and the detective genres usually serve the ends of that ideology, their very narrative form suggests the liberal value of self-determination. The detective acts alone; the cowboy usually rejects community (as in *Shane*) for the open road. It is part of the critical strategy of films like *Outland* and *Blade Runner*, then, to apply those forms to the critique of economic exploitation. The use of such forms dramatizes more strikingly the discrepancy between the values of freedom and self-determination on the one hand and the realities of mass exploitation on the other. On a formal level, they draw out the antinomy between a capitalist ideological sphere that justifies itself with ideals of freedom and a capitalist economic sphere that belies those ideals. In so doing, the films suggest that the reason for this segregation is that a revolution of the sort *Blade Runner* enacts metaphorically would probably result were those ideals allowed entry into the world of labor.

The American quandary we have described is thus one that promises to be more threatening to the Right than to the Left. For one senses that the Right can only be on the defensive, given the distribution of forces and of possibilities. Our argument has suggested that their hold on economic power is not firm; it is defensive, and it probably cannot forever withstand the incursion of liberal principles of self-determination into the economic sphere that dystopian films either imagine or suggest. Indeed, the growing prevalence of liberal principles in the civil sphere would seem to indicate that the current tendency is for liberal values to spread and for conservative ones to contract. This seems confirmed by the dominant defensive and resentful attitude toward non-economic matters that is evident in conservative dystopian films. In John Carpenter's *Escape from New York* (1981), for example, the metaphor of the "fallen city" covers a lot of modern liberal terrain, from punk subcultures to feminism to liberal politics. The city is a conservative nightmare of minorities and criminals rampant. It is a case once again when the literal vehicle of the metaphor is a direct representation of conservative fears. A pro-détente president is about to sell out the United States to the Soviets, but he is kidnapped by terrorists. Only a tough, conservative, martial arts, military hero named Snake can save the day. In the last scene, he walks away contemptuously from the buffoonish president and the press as an American flag looms behind. (Will the real Führer please step forward?)

The edgy, resentful mood of the film characterizes conservatives faced with the increasing power of liberal modernity (in social relations, sexuality, and politics) and the increasing threat (reflected in a negative mode in current life and in the film as underclass crime) that the liberal principles which conservatives cannot quell in the private sphere might spread to the public economic sphere. If, at this time, liberal ideals tend to be reclusive and sentimentalist, confined to the private sphere, conservative social ideals tend to be hostile and resentful, in part because they are so much at odds with a modernity they cannot turn back. If liberal dystopias are either tragic or whimsically metaphysical and ironic in the early to mid eighties—modes appropriate to a value system out of power—conservative dystopias evidence the brutal and resentful edginess of those anxious to turn the dystopia of modernity into a utopia of brutality. Yet we see something progressive in this situation. When the Nazi said that whenever he heard the word culture he reached for his revolver, it was because the radical Jewish culture of Weimar Berlin was indeed a threat to the Right. If conservatives seemed to be reaching for their guns a lot in this period, it was probably for a similar reason.

3. At Home with Steven Spielberg

It is in Steven Spielberg's films that the American quandary we have described appears in its most dramatic form. In Spielberg's cozy home world of cuddly beasts and warmhearted social relations, liberal ideals thrive of a sort that elsewhere in American society and Hollywood cinematic culture were being shunted aside in favor of a brutish, quasi-fascist cinematic and economic realism. Spielberg's fantasy films of the late seventies and early eighties—*Close Encounters of the Third Kind* (1977) and *E.T.* (1982)—always seem to be keeping something at bay, much like the white suburban world where most of the action of the films takes place. It would be relatively easy to excuse liberal fantasies of ideal communities and spiritual transcendence from an examination of contemporary conservative culture. But classical music played at Auschwitz has a different meaning from its performance in prewar Vienna. And any affirmation of white middle and upper middle class culture during the era of the conservative revolution must be judged in relation to what the white middle class and its political representatives accomplished during this period. White liberal sentimentality becomes criminal when it is measured against the rise in the black infant mortality rate provoked by the Reagan domestic budget cuts or the increase in deaths among workers affected by reductions in federal safety standards or the numerous killings perpetrated by bombs and death squads in Latin America as a result of the foreign policy of the white conservatives in power in the eighties. Spielberg's family fantasies can be understood as symptoms of the banishing of liberal values from the public sphere and their retreat into private visions of at least domestic charity and care. But they must also be understood, we suggest, as strained attempts to close ears to the sound of suffering elsewhere in the social system, outside the bounds of the suburban tracts his films endow with such a warm glow. To a certain extent, what one witnesses in these films is a cranking up of the classical music so that the screams of the doomed won't be heard.

Unlike other "movie brat" filmmakers like Coppola, Lucas, and Milius who relish celebrations of a conservative male socialized public world of aggression and violence, Spielberg is distinguished by his emphasis on the family as an embattled sphere of empathy and care, threatened by external forces. Frequently those forces are associated with such things as the state, bureaucracy, science, rationalism, and capitalist greed. The mixture of antistatist and anticapitalist motifs, conjoined with a neoromanticist affirmation of ecologist and spiritualist values, situates Spielberg within the arena of "New Age" politics that developed after the sixties in places like California (with Jerry Brown being the most famous avatar). Both liberal federal bureaucracy and conservative capitalism are rejected from this ecologist point of view, which favors decentered social forms as well as more benign economic arrangements. The immense popularity of his films, especially *E.T.*, suggests that resistant liberal forces existed in American culture at odds with the dominant conservative value system.

In his early films—*Duel* (1972) and *Sugarland Express* (1974)—Spielberg depicts working and middle class people struggling against threatening impersonal forces. In *Express* particularly, the family is defended against the forces of the state, which threaten to break it up. The family is a central concern of his first major fantasy film, the enormously successful *Close Encounters of the Third Kind* (1977), an allegory of escape from the travails of everyday life in the mid-seventies—unemployment, divorce, cynicism, lack of confidence. Yet the film inverts the order of causality by presenting the supernatural as the cause of unemployment and divorce rather than depicting the quest for spiritual relief as a symptom of such social travails. Roy Neary (Richard Dreyfuss) encounters an unidentified flying objective and becomes so obsessed with making contact with it again that he is fired from his job and his wife and children leave him. He is portrayed as an unappreciated, childlike genius who clings with faith to his intuitions and eventually finds the spaceship again. In the final scene, in which the UFO lands, he climbs a mountain, an obvious symbol of spiritual transcendence, and is taken away by the benevolent, childlike space creatures.[1] That happy conclusion is coded as a mystical encounter and is also associated with the reconstitution of an ideal family. Neary encounters a young mother and her son who share his mystical insight. Thus, while the film obviously plays to the sort of religious revivalism rampant in the mid and late seventies, it also is a male fantasy of the transcendence of all the troubles and responsibilities of family life, a life increasingly harried in the recession-ridden mid-seventies when the incidence of divorce, suicide, and mental illness among working people rose.

The film cites some of these social problems, but it does so only in order to justify a flight from them. And that flight is toward an idealization of certain aspects of reality which afford comfort. Those aspects are predominantly private, like religion and family, and are associated with feeling and nature, while the state is linked with science, skepticism, and rationality. The private world of individual insight shared by a special family of idealized common people stands in contrast to the technological world of the scientists, who in the opening scene seem incapable of understanding a mystical occurrence which a common man grasps naturally and intuitively. Not surprisingly, the aliens communicate through music and images implanted in the minds of chosen people, not through words, which in romantic ideology are thought to be too artificial and rational. The film thus offers the possibility that ordinary people can feel special; indeed, it is a story of election, the choosing of a special person who attains private bliss. His commonness permits him to be an object of universal (well, at least white male) identification. The film enacts as narrative the very structure of identification which allowed it to be so popular. For that identification is with a retreat from public concerns to a purely private experience (reinforced once again by heightened representational dynamics), and the story is also of such a progress. While it would be possible to read this congruence as yet another symptom of the compensatory operation of culture, it is also necessary to situate it historically. The white middle class actually did retreat from the troubled public world into privacy in the late seventies, and as it is enacted in this film that retreat has benevolent consequences. But it also needs to be read as a means of saving one's own hide. Roy Neary gets away scot free, and, to a certain extent, so would the white middle class in the years following this movie. They too would seek a purely private salvation from economic recessions for which blacks, the poor, workers, and women would be obliged to pay. And they would imagine themselves to be special enough to deserve it.

Spielberg's *E.T.*, released in the summer of 1982, quickly became the highest grossing film of all time. The long lines around theaters testified to its enormous appeal, an appeal due, we would argue, to the film's idealization of a harmonious and romantic sentimentalist private sphere at a time when the public sphere, in the hands of Republican conservatives, was given over to a vicious program of economic apartheid that gutted support systems for the poor, menialized labor, and allowed the brutality of the market to pauperize those least empowered to resist its harsh logic. If the white middle class turned away from the world in *Close Encounters*, in *E.T.*, that class covered its ears.

The story concerns a suburban family, from which the father is absent, which encounters a friendly lost alien in its backyard. They care for it, but their house is invaded by bureaucratic government officials and scientists who almost kill the cuddly little beast. The children help the alien to escape, and this happy conclusion is associated, like the ending of *Encounters*, with a reconstituted family. A sympathetic scientist who believes in unscientific things like feelings and space critters is positioned as a new father in the family, taking the place of the alien.

Like *Encounters*, *E.T.* idealizes nature and feeling over scientific rationality. Yet whereas conservative films link such romantic motifs to the market and militarism, this liberal film associates them with such positive interpersonal attitudes as tolerance, empathy, and acceptance. The adult world of harshness and competition that so many conservative films celebrate is looked on from the children or E.T.'s perspective, through frequent point of view shots, in a way that portrays it as menacing. The real aliens in the film are all over thirty or over three feet tall. The style of the film and its use of cinematic conventions are also romantic and generically nostalgic. Elliot's first encounter with E.T. in the backyard is shot through a filter that bathes the scene in a warm, gauze glow reminiscent of a Norman Rockwell painting. And the tradition of Hollywood child fantasy films, from Peter Pan to Pinocchio, is consistently cited. The film is thus cinematically coded as harking back to an ideal of social reintegration, and this is paralleled by a formal motif of reintegration with a lost cinematic tradition. One notices this dual nostalgia in the way suburban life is depicted. It is endowed with the cinematic characteristics of the mid-American small town as it was represented in earlier Hollywood films (the Hardy Boys, Capra).

Such nostalgia can be read as further evidence of audience responsiveness to the possibility of fleeing a troubled present into an untroubled past. Indeed, in Spielberg's production *Back to the Future* (1985), an escape into the past rectifies it and permits white upward mobility to occur successfully. A young man leaves for the past, where his actions bring his parents together and change the future, so that when he returns his family has jumped several income notches. The explicit economic theme of this film bears retroactively on the themes of *E.T.* The escape into an untroubled generic past serves an obvious therapeutic function. The broken ego (or family) is reintegrated through the fantasy of regression and enabled thereby to engage once more with the world. But in *E.T.* that regression occurs in a nature just adjacent to the suburban tract, and while this placement has a metaphoric ideological intent, it is also literally indicative of the fact that the white suburb is at the very edge of white middle-class civilization, as far as you can go to get away from the urban underclass. It should be remembered that this is also the time when comedies like *Trading Places* and *48 Hours* about the integration of blacks into the white middle-class world were becoming popular.

The fantasy of regression in *E.T.* cannot be separated from a literal distancing of other realities, especially the reality of what was being perpetrated in the U.S. economy at the same time. Indeed, the incursion of those realities is itself rendered literally in the destruction of the white suburban house by the forces of the state who invade in search of the alien. At stake in the film is the very integrity of the white middle-class home, threatened from without by the logic of the world. It is appropriate that it is saved by an entirely private measure—feeling—and a purely familial instance—the restored father. For the film does through these recourses successfully keep the world of harsh economic and political realities at bay. What the film displays, therefore, is the cohesive interiority and boundaried impermeability of the white middle-class worldview. The enactment in the film of the restoration of family and ego integrity alike is in keeping with its implicit public position, which is that there is no public, only a threatening other which must be repelled, kept out of sight entirely. Only in this way can one go about living one's life of private concerns, within earshot of the urban underclass camps but far enough away within oneself not to hear.

Spielberg's world is a dichotomized one. The same oppositions recur repeatedly—science and feeling, reason and spirituality, the beast of repressed sexuality (*Poltergeist*) and idealized family life (*Gremlins*). This set of oppositions seems to transcode the larger split that came increasingly to define American culture at this point in time, the division between a public world of conservative cynicism and a private world of liberal idealization. It is indicative of the extent to which the public world had been purged of empathy, feeling, and community that the private idealizations of these traits take on such exaggerated forms in the popular imaginary of Spielberg's films. Indeed, one could say that a film like *E.T.* is merely the logical correlate of a film like *Rambo*, the other side of the same social psychological coin. Everything that is purged from the white male heroes of the eighties, all the attachments and dependencies which must be removed if the cinematic version of the conservative revolution was to be carried out, have to be pushed into the private sphere, where they become exalted and hypertropic.

Yet the great popularity of the films can also be read as testifying to the presence of strong needs and desires denied in the public world for community and empathy. In other words, the very escapism and privatism of these films are interpretable as indicators of progressive potentials in American culture. By sentimentalizing the family, Spielberg's films play along with the contemporary conservative conversion of the public sphere into a survivalist jungle to the extent that they assume abdication from the public world. Yet they can also be said to indicate that despite the best efforts of conservatives, desires still exist for something better. The imbalance of fantasy desire and public reality is also due, we suggest, to the fact that capitalist modernization has outrun the traditional institutions (the family especially) that accompanied and sustained the economic system. The "critical" edge of films like *The Godfather* is sharpest at those points where they depict how capitalist modernization undermines institutions that once held communities together. What is interesting about films like *E.T.* is that they show the demise of old family forms and the reality of divorce (and this is the difference between a liberal reconstructive attitude toward change and a conservative one, like Coppola's, that clings to old forms and resents the encroachments of the new). Yet they also suggest the possibility that a new stabilization can occur; another man enters the family. Such order is shown to be provisional and unstable, not a fixed order of the sort conservative films seem to establish. The low level of even these liberal reconstructions is indicated, however, by the fact that patriarchy still provides the model for reconstruction. In a few decades perhaps we'll be ready for a cuddly female or even androgynous alien who will teach us new forms of community support and broad group care that won't require the restitution of a "man" to the "family." With any luck, we won't even know what those words refer to.

By the mid to late eighties, it was becoming clear that the tensions be-tween traditional conservatism and the newer brands were working to the detriment of the conservative forces that assumed power in 1980. If 1971 signaled the onset of that edgy rightist tone that would characterize the conservative movements of the late seventies and early eighties, 1986-87 signaled the end of conservative hegemony. Ronald Reagan finally began to lose power, Congress passed into the hands of the Democrats, rendering him even more harmless, and the Iran arms-for-hostages/Contra-supply scandals ruined his credibility and his popularity as well. Within his own ranks, divisions had been evident throughout his reign between the hardline New Rightists and the more traditional conservatives. It was already evident by the mid-eighties that the Right's united front would no longer hold. And the major factor working against the Right was capitalism itself. Because competition and self-interest are its operative principles, coordination and cooperation are inherently alien to its psychology. If a metonymic vision is impossible for the Right, so also is metonymic action which paratactically coordinates rather than hypotactically subordinating its elements. If Hitler served a certain func-tion for all of German capital (only to get out of hand), Reagan served a function for all of American capital but could hand on power to no one with as universal (as metaphoric, one might say) an appeal. He supervised the gutting of old industrial capitalist sectors and the fueling of newer techno-logical defense oriented forms of capital, but what is good for one branch of capital is bad for another. While finance capital thrived during the eighties, productive capital withered; New York became one immense Wall Street, but major production shifted overseas. Multinational productive capital saved its hide in Singapore but scorched the earth of mid-America in the process. The result was division rather than unity. Right-wing capital came into power proclaiming the gospel of fiscal responsibility, but it left the country in hock to Japan, and that hurt major production-oriented sectors of the American economy, which began to fight back in the form of trade laws. Moreover, the popular abstention which permitted Reagan to succeed in 1980 gave way to resistance as more and more people realized what that success produced in the way of social misery. And the tremendous accumulation of wealth which permitted the Republicans to become so powerful (through the infusion of great amounts of money into the media and mail campaigns) was by the mid-eighties slowing down. Once-mighty Texas almost went into receivership as oil prices fell, and the stock exchange index zoomed up and fell alternately as speculation tried to resolve the evident and deep dilemma of a system at odds with itself. At the same time, insider trading scandals on Wall Street revealed the cesspool of illegality lying under Reagan's public philosophy of greed. And the religious evangelical Right, which had promoted the conservative revival of the era, was wracked by sex scandals and fraud.

In the midst of all this, the vision that was likely to appeal to Americans was not the Rightist one which called for a rejuvenation of capital; that worked in 1980 at the tail end of a recessionary decade. Rather, the communitarian theme of the social family (evident in part in Spielberg's films) stood to gain from the misery the Right had inflicted on large sectors of the country. Each social movement generates a new level of composition in its adversary, and if the movements of the sixties in part generated the reaction of the eighties, that reaction itself created the terrain on which a more liberal social vision was likely to succeed. It was difficult to argue that "welfare cheats" were robbing the country blind when they were dying of starvation on the streets. It was easier to suggest that the rich had gotten rich enough and that it was time once again to care for the needy. By filling its coffers while emptying the welfare rolls, corporate capital had set itself up as a target. And in the short run, the only one capable of exploiting that possibility was the Democratic center, which, because it is slightly more sensible than the Right, knows better than to push the poor too far into penury.

We will conclude by suggesting that other things are possible. The United States is not without its Left alternative, although its parameters are limited, its power nonexistent. Nevertheless, its agenda is not entirely unrealistic. Egalitarian possibilities exist in American society, as they must in any unequal social system. For example, in our poll we asked if people thought the American economic system was just; 60% said no. The answers followed class lines, as one might expect: 72% of the working class participants, 60% of the middle class, and 49% of the upper middle class participants answered negatively. And 90% of the blacks, compared with 54% of the whites, responded with a no. We also asked if people would prefer a society in which wealth was divided equally, and 50% responded affirmatively, again along class lines (71% of the working-class respondents, 46% of the middle, and 47% of the upper middle class participants). Of those who make under $30,000 a year, 65% would prefer such a society, as opposed to 43% of those who make over $30,000. For blacks, the figure was 82%. Women more than men also felt the society was unjust, and a surprising 42% of the conservative respondents expressed a desire for an egalitarian society. We do not hold out these figures as indicators of revolutionary possibilities. What they do suggest is what one would expect: inequality, especially if you are on the receiving end of it, generates desires for equality. But it also generates desires among the Haves for things to remain the same. It is a simple and understandable difference. What we do take away from our poll results is the conviction that ideology is not entirely successful. It can't be, in situations of real material inequality and injustice. It is for this reason that we will argue in conclusion that the Left should attend more to the counterideological impulses and possibilities which reside within the apparently seamless system of conservative cultural power.

10. THE POLITICS OF REPRESENTATION

The revival of militarist, racist, patriarchal, and capitalist ideologies in post-1977 Hollywood films would seem to suggest that the United States had turned significantly rightward. There is evidence to the contrary. Indeed, one could say the virulence of contemporary conservatism is itself ample evidence that something very nonconservative was still active in U.S. society.

We have described the power of the individualist ideology in American culture. As a result of the residual appeal of that ideology, the socialist possibility, of the sort that would address certain pre-political popular desires we have noted throughout this book, is denied any general availability in public debate. That ban is fostered by longstanding, carefully manufactured antisocialist prejudices that equate socialism with statism and play to populist anxiety regarding the impersonal power of big government. The overwhelming power of capitalist interests in promoting their anticommunitarian philosophy of social life also accounts for the almost total silence on the issue of socialism in the media as a whole and in film particularly. With the exception of British filmmakers like Ridley Scott and Americans like Peter Hyams, John Sayles, and Warren Beatty, few filmmakers criticize capitalism itself, and none overtly suggests that a socialist alternative might be better.

This implicit ban is aided by the dominant representational codes of Hollywood, codes shaped in the same cultural climate of liberal individualism that fosters the uncritical acceptance of the entrepreneurial capitalist model and the unquestioned popular prejudice that all socialism is "totalitarian," a denial of individual freedom. Because those codes are inseparable from the perceptual codes that frame audience experience of the world, it is difficult to rework them in ways conducive to the development of a more critical attitude toward capitalism or a more positive attitude toward socialism without promoting a negative audience reaction, a mismatch between representational strategy and audience receptivity—in film lingo, a flop.

In this chapter we will consider the work of several filmmakers who have tried to operate from a leftist perspective within Hollywood, and we will compare it with the work of radical independent filmmakers. We will be concerned particularly with the ways in which progressives attempt to recast

266

the dominant representational codes, so that the form of film as well as its content promotes radical alternatives. Form, or means of representation, as much as the content of film, needs to be transformed because the prevailing patterns of thought, perception, and behavior that help sustain capitalism and patriarchy are determined, we would argue, by representations, the dominant forms or modes through which people experience the world. Whether one represents the history of the United States as an epic of realized destiny or as a series of only contiguously related episodes of alternating idealism and brutality makes a difference for how one acts in the world. In addition, socialism would imply a new *form* of life, a new (more democratic and egalitarian) *style* of social organization, which would be inseparable from different modes of representation. If the maintenance of capitalism is dependent on the prevalence of cultural representations that construct a shared social reality, then the development of socialism necessitates different cultural representations, different forms or ways of constructing the world and a sense of one's place in it. If current representations position women as passive objects, blacks as dancers and comics, and poor people as somehow inferior to white male businessmen, then a more egalitarian social arrangement would require different representations.

Form inheres in the very substance of social life. Form not only determines cognition, how one experiences the world; it also determines the shape of social institutions, practices, and values. Morality is a question of ways of being, modes of action, and forms of behavior. And the same can be said of politics, economics, or psychology. The political struggle between Left and Right comes down to a contest over the shape of life, the form it will take. The form of Hollywood film has in recent years come to be characterized as inherently ideological because it tends invariably to reinforce the dominant forms of patriarchal and capitalist life. We differ from the common characterization of this ideological procedure in that we see it not as a matter of cognition, the positioning of spectators as spuriously self-identical, specular subjects who are lured into an imaginary identification that is inherently ideological. Rather, Hollywood forms are in our view ideological because they replicate the figures and narratives that constitute the very substance of those values, practices, and institutions that shape a society of domination.

Spectatorial cognition is merely the end result of a broad process of rhetorical replication whereby those grounding figures of the society (the narrative of individual success, the metaphor of freedom, the synecdochic privileging of efficiency over democracy, the litotic liberal ideal of pluralist neutrality, etc.) are transcoded into specifically cinematic forms—the male quest narrative, the camera positions of individuated identification, the domestic *mise-en-scène*, shot continuity as a realization of a spurious model of psychological motivation, the instantiation of a dichotomous Christian morality through contrapuntal editing, and so on. Rather than disable the question of form, this reconceptualization of ideology gives it even more force as a required concern of a reconstructive politics. But it does displace the specific importance accorded the undermining of narrative realism, of the basic film illusion, by structuralist film theory. Our argument will be that while such work is necessary for a broader project of reshaping the grounding figures of society, it misses the mark by concentrating on the phenomenal consciousness of film viewing. It may be more important to accept the viewing assumptions of narrative realism in order to be better able to change the dominant figures of thought, value, and action that are the substance of society. Instead of only different camera angles, editing techniques, or framing devices which rupture realist narratives, also different character representations, different plot strategies, different moral configurations, different tropes of actions, etc., within the frame of realist narrative. These things are also matters of form, and they go more to the heart of those forms that constitute society as a set of material figures and practices than do the cognitivist forms of the phenomenology of film viewing. We will argue, therefore, that while such modernist formal revisions are essential, they can also get in the way of gaining access to popular audiences in ways that work to reshape the dominant figures and narratives of patriarchal capitalist social life.

1. On the Left Edge of Hollywood

The radical film avant-garde argues that films with leftist content are conservative if they use traditional Hollywood representational forms. Some would push this argument further and argue that only modernist non-Hollywood forms are "progressive." This leaves open the question of what a "progressive text" is.[1] Is a film with conservative content in a modernist form a progressive film? The trouble with this position is that it ignores the role of modernism in cultural history, where it was frequently (as in Eliot and Pound) allied with reactionary politics. Modernist form alone, without a leftist content, is not necessarily progressive. Indeed, as we have noticed in the case of Coppola (who, interestingly, has Brando read Eliot in a scene in *Apocalypse Now*), modernist forms can be welded to quite conservative thematics. A purely formal criterion of progressive politics in film also ignores crucial substantive issues of race and gender. Feminist and non-white progressive texts may operate under a different set of exigencies altogether.

The ideal would seem to be films that are both thematically leftist and formally modernist. But the criterion for judging such matters should be pragmatic, one that measures the progressive character of a text according to how well it accomplishes its task in specific contexts of reception. What counts as progressive varies with time and situation, and what works in one era or context might fail in another. Moreover, the notion of progressive is always differentially or relationally determined. Something is always progressive in relation to something else. Modernist texts tended to be progressive in comparison to the stultifying and ideological bourgeois realism of the late nineteenth and early twentieth centuries (Bennett, Galsworthy, etc.), but as modernism itself became detached from social concerns and became a marketable commodity in the world of art, modernism as such was no longer progressive.

While the idea of the progressive text is variable, it is not entirely indeterminate. Certain uses of certain forms are ideological—camera techniques that suggest natural hierarchies, spectacles that idealize violence as a solution to social problems, voyeuristic objectifications that debase others. The ideal would seem to be forms that provoke critical thought regarding the world, that associate pleasure with egalitarian and empathetic social procedures, that link narrative resolution to ideals of justice purged of militarist and chauvinist themes, etc.—a mix of the best of modernism and classical realism.

Such an ideal is difficult to attain within the Hollywood frame, as we will see in the case of Robert Altman. Most left-liberal filmmakers like Michael Ritchie (*Downhill Racer, The Candidate, Smile*) work within fairly traditional formats. The one consistently experimental filmmaker, John Cassavetes (*Shadows, Faces, Woman under the Influence*), limits his experimentation to *cinema verité* devices and strategies (nonprofessional actors, improvisation, long "real life" sequences of conversations, etc.). Radical formal experimentation is more likely to be used by people whose political and aesthetic interests require a break from the past and from the reigning conventions of representation. Those people generally have to work outside Hollywood. One exception from this is the Chicano film *Zoot Suit* (1981), directed by Luis Valdez and based on his Teatro Campesino play, which combines realist and fantasy modes and uses an unconventional, discontinuous narrative form to tell the story of the trial of three Chicanos and their white friend in the Sleepy Lagoon murders during World War II. The use of a Brechtian narrator (Edward James Olmos) and the frame-rupturing forays into the theater in which the film is being shot distance the audience from the story and force reflection on the events. The contrast between the fast and colorful musical numbers, which often contain utopian visions of various races interacting and dancing together, and the grim realism of the prison scenes marks the distinction between fantasy and reality experienced by many Hispanics. And the "ending" presents a variety of possible conclusions to the story that calls attention to the conventional nature of film, indicates how different endings contain different ideological closures and positions, and depicts life as a narrative that can be constructed in any number of ways.

Arthur Penn has successfully worked on the margins of the prevailing Hollywood conventions, injecting leftist themes into forms that, if they are not modernist, are at least subversive at times of the dominant conventions. His *Mickey One* (1964) represents alienation stylistically through the use of discontinuous narrative and nonnarrative sequences that break the rationality of the logical story line. Jazz music heightens the effect of disjunction. The film, however, was not popular; in effect, it was too formally radical for the audience. Penn fared better with *Bonnie and Clyde* and *Little Big Man*, one of the most popular films of 1970, in which a picaresque episodic structure permitted narrative discontinuity to work in the service of a critique of western myths. Yet in the seventies Penn's films became increasingly traditional in their narrative formats, although the critical thematics of films like *Night*

Moves, *Missouri Breaks*, and *Four Friends* are still allied with a questioning of generic conventions (the detective, the western, the working-class success story).

Most Hollywood liberals and leftists seem to accept Penn's fate, working within the traditional representational formats (image, narrative, and character) while tinkering critically or playfully with the generic and action conventions. Jane Fonda's films, for example, are consistently recognizable as traditional Hollywood realist films on the level of narrative, image, and character construction, yet they usually push against generic and action conventions. Both *Comes a Horseman* (1979) and *The Electric Horseman* (1980), for example, use yet depart from the western conventions. In the first, a woman wins out against a cattle baron (even Vienna couldn't do that without having to cook breakfast for her man), and in the second, the "post-western" conventions are hybridized with the corporate conspiracy genre to produce a sense of generic nonsynchronicity that aids the critical theme. *Fun with Dick and Jane* (1976) turns a middle class melodrama into an absurdist satire of success and economic survival. An unemployed bourgeois couple resorts to bank robbery to maintain their lifestyle.

Clearly, there are significant limits to what can be done with actional and generic conventions. Normal people can be shown doing uncustomary things, and normal generic boundaries can be crossed, but hewing to all-American representational forms requires playing in some way to the attitudes and beliefs about the world that are linked (via the cultural system of representations that includes the Hollywood system) with those forms. Thus, in *Rollover* the plot requires that Arabs be represented in a somewhat populist xenophobic manner appropriate to the Iran hostage era of intolerance. Nevertheless, Fonda's films usually portray strong women, though the left liberal slant that informs the work usually skews these portrayals toward optimistic celebrations of the possibility of individual efficacy in changing society.

The filmmaker who most successfully links social criticism with alternate representational strategies during this period is Robert Altman. The trouble with Altman is that he was so successful that he managed to work his way out of Hollywood altogether. Thus, although he may prove how possible it is to do radical work within the Hollywood representational system, his case may also prove how impossible it is to remain within that system if you become too radical. Altman's work is distinguished by the fact that he operates both on the plane of generic and action conventions and on the plane of image, narrative, and character formatting. His early seventies films (*M*A*S*H*, 1970, *Brewster McCloud*, 1970, and *McCabe and Mrs. Miller*, 1971) subvert the traditional war and western generic conventions and use exorbitant action ploys to satirize conservative values. *M*A*S*H* positions the audience against militarism and authoritarianism by injecting farce into the traditional war format. *Brewster* is based in an absurdist action device—a young man learning to fly—and it concludes with a title sequence that underscores the illusoriness of the Hollywood cinema—the actors appear as clowns engaging in buffoonish acts.

And *McCabe* resorts to historical realism to undermine the traditional western conventions. The West is depicted as mean and direct, and the traditional action codes for the western hero (honor, romance, etc.) are left lying in the dirt.

In *Nashville* (1975), scripted by Joan Tewkesbury, Altman intensifies his social criticism at the level of image, narrative, and character construction. The film follows the lives of numerous characters—a BBC reporter, a political campaign worker, a folk group, a housewife, an aspiring country singer, a successful country singer—in a fairly random manner during a weekend in Nashville. All the different narrative strands come together in the end at an outdoor political rally, highlighted by the appearance of a famous country singer, who in the final segment is shot by a neurotic young man. In this and in his next several films, he breaks more radically with Hollywood practices that produce an ideological vision of the world by inviting identification with privileged characters, or through narrations that connote a sense of world order, or through camera strategies that promote a false sense of dramatic intimacy. The narrative of *Nashville* is discontinuous; the characters are multiple (24 in all), with no privileged hero or even privileged object of sympathetic identification, since all are flawed, venal, or manipulative; and the images are constructed in such a way as to distance the audience from the habitual sorts of engagement with the spectacle. On the whole, the multiplicity of points of view and the narrative discontinuities require more attention and thought from the audience than is usual in Hollywood film, and indeed, a theme of the film is that Americans are passive victims of political and culture industry manipulation, so much so that they can sing "You may say that I ain't free, but it don't worry me" when someone has just been shot.

The film is concerned with the distance between image and reality, both on the broader cultural level and in personal relationships, and for this reason its reflexive signaling of its own departure from Hollywood illusionism (by, for example, having Elliot Gould and Julie Christie play themselves) is significant. Thus, what Altman was after was a certain materialism, showing what Hollywood never shows—the sleazy underside of the American Dream of success that is concealed by the stage of cultural spectacle. For this reason it is important that much of the action takes place on or around stages. Private as much as public life is a performance, often deceptive, and what matters is show, spectacle, and platitude, rather than honesty or fidelity. Even the presidential candidate never appears in person; he is only a set of slogans broadcast over a loudspeaker (although his one early slogan sets the theme of the film: "We're all deeply involved in politics whether we know it or not.")

Throughout the film the discourses of religion, family, and political democracy are shown to be out of sync with reality, and Altman's editing juxtapositions unfold the contradictions between illusionary ideals and real social practices. Songs about love and family are contrasted with acts of crude manipulation and exploitation in relationships. In one scene the hypocrisy of religious righteousness is underscored by a sequence of shots at different churches depicting characters who have been shown behaving immorally in

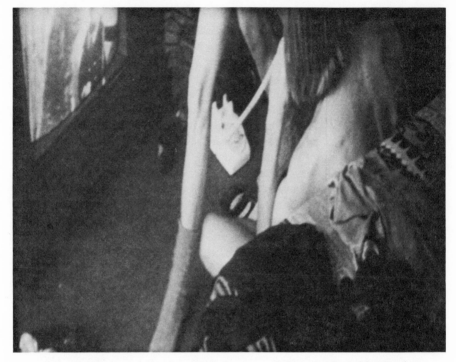

Nashville. The impersonality of predatory, casual sex in the mid-seventies.

other contexts feigning piety and demonstrating the class and race differentials that underlie a supposedly Christian society. In the bicentennial world of *Nashville* patriotic sentiments conceal intolerance, public moralistic stances conceal corruption, and the semblance of romance conceals opportunistic exploitation. It is, with other films and film strands we have noted that culminate around 1977, the cinematic highpoint of mid-seventies cynicism.

The film contains few close-ups and few shot-reverse shots that privilege individual points of view and elicit identification with characters. Its style is distinguished by the use of medium and long shots, even for extremely intimate scenes that usually require a different, more personal camera rhetoric. The camera work instantiates a sense of alienation, since no one seems very close to anyone else. This is particularly evident in one scene in which a woman who has just slept with a man gets dressed while he calls another woman he wants to sleep with. His back is to the camera, while all we see of her is her legs. Similarly, the narrative randomness—that the plot shifts have no determinate logic—seems a correlative for the dominant ethos of this world: infidelity. The film is faithful to no story line nor to any character; both the camera and the narrative treat all with equal coolness, as if they were themselves characters in the world—aloof, indifferent, manipulative.

The film departs from individual-based Hollywood narratives by depicting characters as part of social relations and collectivities. This is the point of the intersection of so many different narrative strands during the film, and at the end. It also suggests everyone's complicity in what goes on in society. Indeed, the strategy brings out the theme of failed responsibility. The complex narrative is the objective correlative of social responsibility; it underscores the networking of metonymic social relations between people and the embeddedness of individual subjects in society.

Nashville is a striking example of a metonymic representational rhetoric which projects a world that is egalitarian, nonhierarchical, negotiable, and oriented toward the continual displacement of all instances of power and authority. The film emphasizes the displacement of meaning, the constant movement away from the absolute stabilization of conservative metaphoric social ideals. The narrative moves without any paradigmatic order through a number of different strands or chains of events, none of which moves toward a teleology of resolution. Instead, a contingent event interrupts the climax and institutes an indeterminacy which classical narratives usually occlude or avoid. No character is granted special metaphoric status as a hero who transcends social context. Altman's world is one without conservative monuments or ideological myths.

Yet if Fonda seems occasionally to pander too much to popular prejudices, Altman's cosmopolitanism seems to feed into an excessively derisive attitude toward American popular culture that risks losing the very audience that probably stands most to benefit from the critiques his film offers. In addition, Altman's left-liberal political vision is limited; it does not target the underlying institutions of American society, but instead concentrates on fairly epiphenomenal problems like hypocrisy and crassness. He fails to see how those surface disturbances emanate from a social system that by its most fundamental laws promotes opportunism and manipulation. In Altman's vision, those things seem instead to be faults of the very victims of that system and those laws. His films thus demarcate a major limitation of the antagonistic attitude toward mainstream culture we ascribed to the sixties sensibility. Altman's films evidence all the wry cynicism of that era, laced with some mid-seventies nihilism. Indeed, the hope of the sixties seems entirely absent from later films like *Quintet*, which depicts a world of mercenary people who cannot be trusted. The films point to the giving up of hope by seventies left-liberals, the sense that no change was possible in a citizenry obsessed with celebrity, self-interest, and the spectacles of popular culture. Altman's subsequent films pursue some of the same representational strategies in carrying out social criticism (*Buffalo Bill, Health, A Wedding*). But except for *Popeye*, all of his later films lost money, and eventually he managed to fall from Hollywood grace, and turned to non-Hollywood video production of theatrical drama (*Come Back to the Five and Dime, Jimmy Dean, Jimmy Dean, Streamers, Secret Honor, Fool in Love*).

The lesson Altman offers is that what lies beyond ideology is neither realism (as traditional Marxists suggest) nor modernism (as other radicals argue) exclusively. What is missing from Altman is not a sense of experimentation with style or with the traditional conventions and representational forms, nor is it a sense of reality or objectivity. It is rather an ability to represent or conceptualize abstractly what the social system as a system is about, while also empathizing more justly with its victims and seeing the rules of the system in all their impersonality. His failures make all the more acute the question of what the most appropriate and most effective forms for a leftist cinema would be.

2. Within the Hollywood Codes: Political Films

The acceptance of narrative realism as a viable terrain for leftist film work foregrounds the issue of figuration within realism. Rhetoric, the question of which figures will be used to represent and construct the world, shifts to the center of the analysis. Rather than the ideological operations of realist narrative, the crucial issue becomes the rhetorical operations for constructing the social world in a certain way.

The representation of the social world is political and that choice of modes of representation instantiates differing political positions toward it. Indeed, every camera position, every scene composition, every editing decision, and every narrative choice involves a representational strategy that embeds various interests and desires. No aspect of film merely reveals or depicts "reality." Rather, films construct a phenomenal world and position the audience to experience and live the world in certain ways. We will consider here how differing political interests construct the social world in different ways through representation.

Left and Right vie for a shared terrain, and although each inflects the issues differently, they both deal with the same problems. Three aspects of that social terrain are the individual, history, and society. The Right makes the individual, conceived as an isolated unit, the basis of its political program. We have examined the ramifications of this in regard to the hero. The Left's program also addresses the individual, but as a relational entity and a responsible part of a collective, not as a lone survivalist warrior battling others in the market jungle. Nevertheless, the statist and enforced collectivist biases of the Left have led Left theorists of ideology (Althusser particularly) to condemn the individual (the "subject") as a political category. This position has been picked up by film criticism as the condemnation of all cinematic devices that reinforce an "ideological" sense of "imaginary" ego identity. We disagree with this position, and argue that in general the Left should not dismiss subjectivity as a primary concern, but that the ideology of individualism should be criticized. In film, this means that films that promote individual viewing pleasure or that adhere to representational continuities that reinforce the ego or that use individual heroes are not necessarily ideological. Indeed, psychological research has found that people are more amenable to therapeutic change when an empathetic atmosphere is created in which their fears, desires, and even their most neurotic fantasies are taken seriously and accepted, rather than being sternly dismissed. The same principle no doubt also applies to film.[2]

Just as the Left and the Right represent and use the category of the individual differently, both politically and cinematically, so also they conceive of and use the concepts of history and society differently. For the Right, history is tradition, an authoritative source of truth and power. Usually it is represented as a time of "simpler" (more conservative) social values and institutions (as in the Indiana Jones films or *Star Wars*). For the Left, history is not an authoritative tradition that sanctions the existence of inequality; it is, rather, a domain of struggle between the interests of inequality and those of inequality in which the outcome is undecided. In Left films like *Little Big Man* and *Buffalo Bill and the Indians*, for example, history as myth or as tradition is shown to be a lie, an exercise of representational power in a political struggle.

Similarly, society is conceived and represented differently by Left and Right. As we have seen in fantasy and hero films, for the Right, society is a potentially totalitarian power that threatens the individualist with curtailment of his property, engulfment of his identity, and diminishment of his sexual power. It is a faceless, deindividualized mass. For the Left, society is a source of cooperation and mutual help, as in films like *9 to 5* or *Blade Runner*. It is a network of multiple, interconnected, expanding relations.

Thus, both history and society, like the individual, are terrains of representational struggle shared by Left and Right. How each is represented on the screen helps determine how it will actually be *formed* or constructed in the world. In this section we will concentrate on Left films that deal with political problems and that all foreground some of the problems raised by trying to deal with such issues as the individual, history, and society within the traditional Hollywood representational codes without succumbing to the conservative ideologies that frequently inhabit them.

Two eighties films, Warren Beatty's *Reds* (1981) and E. L. Doctorow and Sidney Lumet's *Daniel* (1983), exploit the traditional representational codes and push against their limits. *Reds* in part rewrites the traditional Hollywood formulae of historical representation, and uses traditional romanticist and individualist conventions for progressive ends, although it could also be accused at times of a fairly traditional male exercise of self-aggrandizement that requires an adulatory woman as well as masses of people as confirming others. The film depicts the lives of John Reed (Beatty) and Louise Bryant (Diane Keaton), two early twentieth-century journalists and radicals who witnessed the Russian Revolution. Their love affair is the primary focus, although the film also represents Reed's attempts to form a Communist Party in the United States.[3]

Reds' most innovative feature is the use of "witnesses" who interrupt the narrative with comments about Reed and Bryant, both pro and con, as well as recollections of the era. The reflexive device works to establish the credibility of the historical narrative and gives it a documentary aura. And the witnesses take the film down off the screen, so to speak, by underscoring the historical reality of the events depicted. Thus the traditional audience tendency to distance itself from films ("It's only a movie") is undermined.

The strategy also demythologizes history; by making the characters seem everyday and real, it places them closer to the people in the audience. Frequently Hollywood narratives about historical figures do just the opposite. Thus, history itself comes to appear less as a distant tradition, the inevitable working out of a conservative and unchanging fate that is unamenable to reconstruction or intervention. When history is made to seem less mythic and more "real," it seems more like something anyone could step into and change. In consequence, the representational strategies of the film position the individual in a questionably privileged place regarding history, but they also undercut the conservative representation of history as the property of an elite of great men or as a great tradition that is beyond human intervention. They display history as a malleable phenomenon.

Daniel breaks with the traditional sequential mode of historical narration; its dual narrative, shifting back and forth between the present and the past, creates a sense of historical embedding, of the continuity of struggles between the thirties and the eighties. If the establishing of continuities frequently is a characteristic of conservative narratives, which hope to make history appear as an organic development from a ground of authority to current social institutions, this film demonstrates that narrative continuities can also serve radical ends by keeping the memory of injustice alive.

Based on the novel by Doctorow that fictionalized the Rosenberg case, in which two Jewish radicals were executed ostensibly for treason, *Daniel* moves between the story of the parents and that of their two children (Timothy Hutton and Amanda Plummer). The film pushes as much as a Hollywood film probably can against the prevailing representational conventions, and this may in part account for its short life in the theaters (though the story is also decidedly downbeat). It resorts to a highly discontinuous narrative, and the cinematic illusion is broken by nonsequential editing and by direct addresses to the camera by Daniel regarding methods of capital punishment and their function in social oppression. Finally, the film both exploits and departs from a traditional use of sentiment and emotion to elicit audience attachment to characters or ideas. By focusing on the plight of the children, the film gains emotional support for the cause of the parents, yet it doesn't hesitate to represent emotional alienation realistically—the child who withdraws from a condemned mother, the condemned father lecturing manically, incapable of displaying his feelings.

For the Left, there is a stake in representing a continuity between the struggles of the past and those of the present, but there is a greater stake in representing history as being discontinuous, a text yet to be written; it is a representation appropriate to those who have yet to win, just as the rightist representation of history as a closed narrative is appropriate to those who have power to protect.

The struggle of representations between Left and Right over the individual and society is particularly evident in films about the sixties. John Sayles's *Return of the Secaucus Seven* (1980) undermines the Hollywood narrative code of developmental action that reaches some dramatic resolution by using a discontinuous and collective story line; not much happens other than games, conversation, fights, and lovemaking between a group of ex-activists. And the film maintains a sense of collectivity and resists the ideology of individual heroism. As a result, it also raises a political problem characteristic of the difference between leftists and conservatives. The sense of narrative discontinuity is so strong that the ex-activists seem to have little direction in their lives. Conservatives, because they espouse a violent defense of power possessed, using ideals of authority, discipline, and aggressivity, usually come off looking firmer, more continuous. To an audience of dispossessed, powerless people, of course, that representation is likely to be more attractive, and this is a symptom of what we have called the tautology of power.

If *Secaucus* presents the sixties as a lost golden era that survives by fragile collective threads, Lawrence Kasdan's *The Big Chill* (1983) is a yuppie anthem celebrating the burial of sixties radicalism and the passage to a more "mature," self-interested, upwardly mobile outlook on life, in which a group of ex-sixties friends gather to mourn the suicide of Alex, the one among them who had not sold out and who had attempted to maintain the sixties lifestyle.

The film has a dynamism that *Secaucus* lacks. Conservative money buys the best actors and editors, of course, and the film also more successfully deploys attractive representational strategies. "I Heard It through the Grapevine" plays while a woman hears news of the death and turns to look at her husband and child. The personalist/sentimentalist figure tugs the audience into a fast identification with the situation. The "group" in *Secaucus* simply does not accomplish the same thing; the characters' lives are all too alien from mainstream mid-American concerns.

Chill's dynamism is particularly evident in the character of Harold (Kevin Kline), the host for the weekend who is the center of the film. He is called "Christ" by accident at first, immediately after being privileged with an establishing shot of him looking over a fallow autumn field, and he lives up to his name—rejuvenating the group with revivalist music when they are in a slump, giving running shoes to all so they can jog their way to yuppie heaven, bringing Alex back to life in the form of Nick by allowing Nick to take Alex's place on his land, giving a woman a child, and in general sowing seeds of emotional and economic enrichment that will guarantee the brown field will blossom in spring. And he also voices some of the most conservative lines of the film. Of blacks, he says "some of them are scum"; of his still-too-liberal friends, "help me with these bleeding hearts." He is a model of conservative economic success, as well as being the only one of the bunch with a successful family. Thus, although it is a "group" movie, *Chill* is subliminally survivalist and individualist. It privileges the active jogging male as leader and provider. He is the only man not to be made to seem foolish in some way, and the film ultimately legitimates his cynical worldview.

Nevertheless, the film can be analyzed diagnostically to gain insight into the processes of successful ideology, in this case, the early eighties socially liberal yet economically conservative yuppie ideology. It is a worldview that privileges Harold, both for doing liberal things like domestic labor (bathing his child and inseminating his wife's best friend at his wife's request) and for doing conservative capital intensive things like trying to induct his friends into illegal, lucrative, opportunistic business deals. The schizophrenic character of that worldview is instantiated in the dominant attitude or pose adopted by the characters—cynicism. That pose consists of seeing the world as it really is without illusions and of having nonetheless to accept its premises in order to survive. One lives one's life within quotes, and something of this emerges as the quotable character of so many of the lines of the film ("Friendship is the bread of life, but money is the honey"). They are delivered from a post-earnest position of cool detachment and enact a salving of guilty conscience through a tarnishing of all idealism. This attitude is historically derivative and is characteristic of the ambiguous position of an entire social group. It combines the socially critical insights of the sixties and early seventies with the recession-induced economic survivalism of the early eighties. It allows young yuppies to go for wealth while retaining a socially liberal conscience that nonetheless disparages radicalism. Nevertheless, like reactionary crime dramas of the early seventies, yuppie films tell something about the reality of American life. After a recession that redistributed wealth upward and increased poverty, the gentry is better off. And increasingly, money is the only means for obtaining just the basics of subsistence (let alone honey). Thus, the yuppies of *The Big Chill* may be less craven than realistic.

To use our rhetorical vocabulary, *Chill* is a metaphoric film, while *Secaucus* evidences representational traits that are more metonymic. *Chill* idealizes Harold, elevates him above the serial relations of the group and grants him special status. He provides the code for properly understanding their lives, and correlatively, the social structure constructed by the film's rhetoric is more one of subordination than coordination, hypotaxis than parataxis. The implicit politics is individualist and elitist, one which sanctifies the singular ownership of wealth and justifies a defense of it along class lines, the sort of thinking that would claim that the poor deserve their lot because the rich so well deserve theirs.

Secaucus, in contrast, does not resolve around a singular center, a consciousness which, like the class to which it belongs, transcends the everyday world through an act of will. The camera assumes multiple points of view on different people, creating a sense of emotional and experiential stitching between them. For this to work, they must all be on the same general social level, and this leveling is evident as well on the plane of meaning construction. No paradigm is offered, no source of truth or motor of resolution. Instead, a syntagmatic or open-ended and progressive mode predominates. The people interact, move through encounters, and at the end, their relationships are pretty much as they were when they entered the frame. No transcendence occurs, no myth of rebirth which reaffirms the founding (capitalist) values of the group, as in *Chill*. At the end, their relations are indeterminate rather than resolved.

The self-idealization of the white capitalist male which operates in *Chill* also takes the form of the denial of materiality. In *Secaucus*, there are numerous references to bodily functions, everyday reproductive concerns. Nothing of this sort contaminates *Chill*, a world in which no one ever defecates and even the radical drives a Porsche. Such purity and idealization bolster the sense of a sacred self in the film, the inability to step outside one's narcissistic frame, another characteristic of individualism defined as a sense of private superiority. *Secaucus*, on the other hand, is pervaded by a strong sense of self-irony, especially toward the sixties. If the yuppies of *Chill* never even discuss such key sixties terms as revolution and war, the ex-radicals of *Secaucus* discuss them in a way which makes clear their continued material commitment to the causes signaled by those terms as well as their self-debunking lack of righteousness regarding them. And of course, the title is itself an ironic reference to a failed attempt to reach an antiwar demonstration in Washington.

The extreme narrative closure of *Chill* says something about the difference between Right and Left representations of history. For a rightist like Kasdan, the history of the sixties is closed; there is no continuity between the past and the present. Sayles's narrative is more open-ended, but that suggests a continuing historical stream that passes through the film and that has not yet ended. Thus, while closure does seem to serve ideological ends in this instance, a sense of historical continuity does not. In other political films like *Under Fire* and *Missing*, closure is used for radical ends, and narrative continuity shifts political valence as well, coming to represent the ideological stories that hold power in place and that must be interrupted if power is to be undermined. The representational tension in these films has to do with the problem of choosing between narratives of individuals and the representation of social movements, historical events, and structural social change that results from groups, not individuals. The Hollywood representational conventions and the reigning narrative regime enforce an individual focus, even when films deal with historical movements. Radical filmmakers who attempt to depart from this model risk losing audiences long habituated to thinking of history in individual terms.

Missing (1982), directed by Costa-Gavras, recounts the story of the disappearance of a young American in Chile after the American-sponsored right-wing coup that overthrew the democratically elected socialist government of Salvador Allende in 1973. The story focuses on the efforts of the father and the son's wife to discover what happened to him. Narrative movement is defined by the transformation of the father, a conservative businessman who is at first skeptical of the wife's story that the United States was involved both in his son's murder and in its cover-up, into a critic both of the coup and of the United States, after he witnesses the brutality of the fascists and uncovers evidence of U.S. involvement.[4]

Missing can be said to use traditionally ideological representational codes to make a counterideological point. But it can also be justly accused of focusing on the personal tragedy of a white North American in a situation in which thousands of Latin Americans were murdered. The personal focus highlights a problem of historical representation in general. The events were the result of an exercise of imperialist power, yet that system of power is impossible to represent in a biographical narrative of this sort. Indeed, it is the prevalence of such narratives and of such ways of understanding life and history that creates the climate that allows structural and historical descriptions of events like those in Chile to be branded "propaganda." If individuals are involved, it's a movie; if classes, it's propaganda. Hollywood narratives tend to frame history as personal events, and while this enlists audience sympathy with broader concerns, it can also reduce those concerns to pathic rather than ethical matters.

Nevertheless, our survey suggests that the film was extraordinarily successful (in a political sense) with audiences: 27% said that it initiated doubts in them regarding U.S. foreign policy. Moreover, 13% said they were shocked and surprised at the events depicted, 23% said they were somewhat surprised, and 55% said that it was "hard to admit we do such things, but we do"; 60% claimed the movie provided them with new information regarding the events in Chile, and 75% said it convinced them that the "American government does wrong things for its own self-interest in foreign countries." On the question of the focus on one American, 80% felt it was "a good way to enlist audience sympathy." Still, as one might expect, the film appealed to a liberal upper-class audience. Only 40% of our sample saw it, and 75% of those earned over $30,000 a year, while the largest percentage of nonviewers earned less than $30,000. And liberals seemed more possessed of information on the events than conservatives or moderates; of the latter, 71% and 67% respectively said it gave them new information, as opposed to 43% of the liberal viewers. Nevertheless, in our interviews with people of various classes and races about the film, the most common words used to describe it were "upsetting," "frightening," "enlightening," and "realistic." A number spoke of being converted by the film to a critical position in regard to American foreign policy, although several people also seemed to indicate that the criticism the film inspired was directed at "the government" in general, rather than at any one specific group's use of the government apparatus to attain its ends. For one, the "realism effect" tended to have a counterideological effect; very few people reported disbelieving what they saw on the screen. In fact, one interviewee remarked that she had not known that the United States "would or had gone that far."

Films in the same leftist vein as *Missing* such as Roger Spottiswoode's *Under Fire* (1983) also demonstrate the possibility of recoding the conventional formulas in ways that transcend some of their ideological limitations. It depicts how foreign journalists in Nicaragua come to sympathize with the Sandinista revolution against the Somoza dictatorship. While a white male hero "saves the day," and the mass-based revolutionary movement is made to seem dependent on one great leader, the film nevertheless uses Hollywood representational forms to gain sympathy for a progressive movement. At one point, audience sympathy is elicited for a young revolutionary who loves North American baseball. This ploy is a familiar motif of war films, but in this case, sentiment is attached to a revolutionary, rather than to the usual

A major issue around which leftist filmmakers rallied in the eighties was the revolutions in Central America. The United States conducted a covert war against Nicaraguan socialists and supported the Right wing in El Salvador against a people's revolution.

patriotic figure when the young man is brutally murdered by an American mercenary.

The crucial (and perhaps unfortunate) importance of identification is clear in a comparison of the public fates of Haskell Wexler's *Latino* (1985) and Oliver Stone's *Salvador* (1986). *Latino* depicts the problematic situation of an American soldier who is Latino, yet who must fight against Central Americans. *Salvador* portrays the worst elements of rightist repression and frankly points to U.S. participation in the atrocities. The importance of using formats which appeal to popular audiences is signaled by the relative success of *Salvador* and the box-office failure of *Latino*. *Salvador* employs a dynamic and comedic representational mode that situates the Right as a narrational nemesis and alternates scenes of violence with fairly traditional scenes of humor or romance. *Latino* is on the whole more didactic, less characterized by concessions to popular conventional representations. But the film is also a lesson in the limits on leftism within Hollywood. Most companies refused to distribute it.

What we are suggesting is that while certain formal devices, such as closure, subjective narration, and personalizing camera work, do serve ideological ends, this does not mean that all closure, all narration, and all personalization are inherently conservative. The Left must begin by reconsidering the values that inform such judgments (the critique of subjectivity, for example, which haunts much leftist thinking). "Personalization" and "subjectivity" can waylay structural understandings of class realities, but they also, as our survey has shown, work to enlist audience sympathies and advance such understandings. While we would argue that certain supposedly ideological representational forms can be recoded and used for counterideological ends, we also suggest that the question of the politics of form should be taken to a different level by emphasizing the way film representation fits into broader rhetorical procedures for constructing the social world. Rhetoric removes the question of politics from the realm of the simple condemnation of subjectivity or realism and brings it closer to the actual processes of political struggle over the construction of the social world in which representation plays a major role. And it makes possible a concept of progressive texts that sees them not simply as departures from identification or realism but as alternative modes for formulating worlds, different constructions of social realities.

3. Beyond Hollywood: The Independent Sector

The Left is on the whole more alive outside of Hollywood than inside. The social movements of the sixties and seventies in conjunction with the invention of new, cheaper filmmaking technologies (Super 8 cameras and video, most notably) gave rise to a thriving radical independent film and video movement. While the independents have made some remarkable political statements on film during this period—from documentaries like *Harlan County, U.S.A.* to fictional pieces like *Born in Flames*—their significance, we would argue, depends as much on whether or not they will succeed in insinuating their perspectives into mainstream cinematic culture as on the continuing development of an alternative culture of representational possibilities.

The independents came of age in the seventies. If one follows the work of filmmakers like Chris Choy (of Third World Newsreel) from *Teach Our Children* (1971), about Attica, to *To Love, Honor, and Obey* (1981), about domestic violence, the development from interventionist direct cinema to a more reflective and complex style that mixes representational strategies (from interviews to documentary) and examines the deep context of a social problem is striking. By the late seventies and early eighties a number of independent films had attained national distribution, including *Harlan County* and *The Atomic Cafe*. As the baby boomers grew up, they created an audience for alternative films. But independent filmmakers themselves were becoming increasingly sophisticated at their craft, to the extent that the mid-eighties witnessed the emergence of a distinct counter-current of semi-mainstream independent filmmakers like John Sayles (*Brother from Another Planet*), Jim Jarmusch (*Stranger than Paradise*), Lizzy Borden (*Working Women*), Spike Lee (*She's Gotta Have It*), Victor Nunez (*Flash of Green*), Eagle Pennell (*Last Night at the Alamo*), and Susan Seidelman (*Desperately Seeking Susan*).

The problem we see facing independents is how to translate superior political vision into a cinematic practice that will attain a sufficient audience to make that vision effective. By definition, avant-garde filmmakers like Yvonne Rainer and James Benning are unconcerned with this problem. In *Journeys from Berlin*, Rainer meditates on the relationship between public and personal politics as she examines the issue of terrorism in the seventies. Her use of discontinuous editing, scene repetition, multiple perspectives, disjunctive juxtapositions, and nonrealist narration is designed to question the sorts of perceptual procedures which accompany mainstream narrative. Benning's *Him and Me* is a series of painterly images that suggest such social themes as industrialization and urban decay; radio voice-overs recall the struggles of the sixties; and ironic subtitles suggest parallels between modern urban life and Vietnam. These and other "deconstructive" films seem unamenable to a popular politics. They are sites of advanced research for the radical intellectual vanguard. Nevertheless, they may well be the testing ground for alternative representational strategies, alternative ways of constructing the social world.

Those independents who are most concerned with political effectiveness are the documentary filmmakers. In such important radical documentaries of this era as *Hearts and Minds, Harlan County, Union Maids, Rosie the Riveter, The Wobblies, Controlling Interest, On Company Business,* and *Seeing Red*, something like a distinct critical documentary aesthetic has made itself evident. While many of these films are fiercely partisan, some adopt a more "objective" style which allows the images to do their own proselytizing. In *On Company Business*, for example, there is no narration or evident point of view, yet the film clearly vindicates the position of the CIA critics through skillful contrast editing. Patrice Lumumba, a radical leader in the Congo before he was overthrown by CIA-supported reactionaries and murdered, is shown in historical footage as a world leader, and this is juxtaposed to images of him being taunted by soldiers after his fall. In another contrast, a rather disreputable-looking CIA man is shown describing how he drove around for days with Lumumba's body in the trunk of his car, not knowing what to do with it. Yet concerned as the documentary filmmakers are with reaching audiences in ways that are convincing, the documentary form itself suffers from an essential drawback. Audiences of working people who generally go to films to be entertained may avoid them, even if the filmmakers are fortunate enough to obtain distribution—a much too rare event save for a few films like *The War at Home* and *Harlan County*. A number of people in our survey sample spoke of avoiding certain films because after a long day or week the last thing they want or need is a serious film. Consequently, many of the documentary films may be inherently limited to informed audiences of professional class people. Documentaries can, however, accomplish certain representational tasks which fictional feature films cannot.[5]

The example of Cine Manifest is instructive in this regard. The group made a documentary, *Prairie Fire*, in 1975 about the Non-Partisan League, a grassroots coalition of northwestern farmers who opposed banking, grain, and rail trusts. They followed up that film with a fictional feature about the same topic, *Northern Lights* (1979). *Lights* merges the personal and the political in a narrative about the radicalization of a farmer who becomes a League organizer. The film was quite successful and was widely distributed through a plan whereby the filmmakers would accompany the film to discuss it with audiences. Nevertheless, *Lights* was criticized for permitting the personal story to overwhelm the historical narrative.[6] The historical context of the events, something more easily rendered in the documentary, is left out. But it could be argued as well that it was precisely the personal focus in the film which was more successful as a lure for audiences than the distant and impersonal style that documentary seems to entail.

A growing number of filmmakers are turning to fictional features, and it is in this movement that the most obvious direct possibilities for using film to help transform American cinematic culture are to be found. Two remarkable and controversial films in this genre are Charles Burnett's *Killer of Sheep* and Lizzie Borden's *Born in Flames*. *Killer* is a highly praised film about a black man who works in a slaughterhouse. The effects of the oppressive conditions of blacks on his family are disastrous; he becomes impotent, and alienation pervades his everyday life. Nevertheless, the film is characterized by a sense of ironic humor, a tolerance that transmutes oppression into a resistant whimsicality. The dominant metaphor of the film is the relation between the slaughtering of sheep and the life to which most blacks are reduced in white America. The film privileges the everyday events of life, the ordinary as opposed to the extraordinary adventures that are standard Hollywood fare. In so doing, it seems to elicit a different order of recognition or identification from the audience, one based on shared memories of experiences rather than on fantasies.

Flames is a daring future fiction about a postrevolutionary social democratic society in which sexual oppression continues to exist. A group of women radicals grow fed up with the situation and stage a revolution. The film is concerned with collective solidarity, and so there is no singular focus of identification. Nevertheless, it succeeds in creating a plausible adventure plot, and its format includes the use of radio announcements to advance the story and to provide the sorts of background information that we noted above as being difficult to represent in fictional films. The film has been criticized for making it seem as if sexual politics should supersede issues of economic justice, but the film is probably more important as a statement against the leftist tendency to shunt sexual politics to the back burner until the supposedly more important issues are resolved.

Striking as each of these films is, especially in their representation of issues usually marginalized in mainstream cinema, neither was what one would call a major commercial success. Not that such success is a criterion of anything. But it is clearly important to develop a viable alternative cinema which would operate within the frame of popular film in order to be politically effective. Such effectiveness involves making some compromises with the Hollywood codes of representation in the hope of reinflecting their use and meaning, but increasingly it also entails having the funds to generate the Hollywood effect, something which is becoming increasingly expensive to produce, especially in science or future fiction films like *Born in Flames*, although *Android* manages to be a relatively inexpensive yet extremely high-quality radical science fiction film.

Several independent filmmakers have attempted to work more within the prevailing Hollywood codes of representation, and easily the most successful of these is John Sayles. His *Brother from Another Planet* (1985) is a science fiction film which uses the metaphor of an escaped black slave from another planet to criticize the exploitation of blacks in America. The mute slave wanders wordlessly through Harlem chased by two white bounty hunters. The ploy forces the audience to observe social conditions from a naive point of view that underscores their brutality. Moreover, the narrative consists of a series of displacements that suggest a network of decentered relations between people. Even the Hollywood-style apotheosis, in which the slave is freed, is due to collective strength, not individualist superiority. Because the primary character is mute, he is experienced through the effects he has on people. This strategy permits the creation of a web of relations between the characters, all of whom come to participate in his characterization.

A rhetorical and deconstructive approach to the problem of political effectivity through film would dictate a more malleable and multiple strategy than now emerges generally from the Left. Discussions of Left uses of film have been handicapped in recent years by a purism regarding form and an absolutism regarding contamination by popular media. Generally more educated and culturally sophisticated, Left film activists tend to favor forms more appropriate to their own taste culture—documentary realism and avant-garde modernism. Concentration on these areas of work has resulted in a tremendously rich variety of work. But such concentration leaves the entire terrain of mainstream narrative cinema untouched. When leftists do venture into the Hollywood mainstream, they do so usually to make fictional versions of historical events like *Missing* or *Reds*. Such work is extremely important, as our audience survey has shown. But effective work also needs to be undertaken in other cinematic arenas like fantasy, melodrama, and even comedy. Socialism won't work if it doesn't feel good, and the Left tends to be altogether too dour in regard to "politically correct" cinema, enjoining pleasure while privileging cinematic techniques that punish audiences. What is gained in self-righteousness is lost in effectivity.

Moreover, there are serious political problems with a model of progressive cinema which, like that prevalent in structuralist film theory, excludes pleasure and defines ideology in terms of self-identity or the ego. It should be remembered that Louis Althusser, who stands behind this approach to film, subscribed to the idea that the Party subsumes the will of the masses. Modernist film theory is equally committed to a philosophical program that denies validity to the self and that consequently points toward a political arrangement which would require self-denial and would marginalize self-development. Another, different Marxist theory would make the subjective potentials of the mass of people, their power of "self-valorization," not the Party, into the basis of socialism. And it would promote a different sense of what a progressive cinema is.

Such a cinema would seek to reconstruct the dominant cultural representations which construct social reality. Rather than conceive of the Hollywood representational system as being inherently ideological, it would assume instead that what matters are the *effects* representations have, how they are used in specific historical contexts, and how they affect specific audiences. The notion of effect would not be limited to psychological reaction or opinion. It would also include the way in which representations posit worlds, construct a sense of social reality by orienting perception and feeling in certain ways, so that a common set of psychological dispositions results in a common phenomenal and institutional world. And as we have suggested, we find that the sort of representational rhetoric associated with the horizontal, leveling, and contextualizing movement of metonymy generates a sense of the world that is in effect more socialist, more equal and collective. Such a cinema would not, however, think of progressive film merely as a set of formal devices or representational practices. It would assume that the meaning and effects of films are always determined and shaped by historical and contextual constraints, by the audiences to whom films are addressed, and by the prevailing social contexts. Such a progressive cinema would be situational and contextual in approach; it would modulate its use of film conventions according to the constraints in existence as well as according to the particular effects or ends that are likely to be generated or gained. It would be a cinema that would, in a certain sense, be noncinematic, in that it would also rely on such things as studies of audiences in order to gauge what representational strategies are likely to be effective. We are clearly assuming that such a cinema would work within the formulae of mainstream cinema, importing to them the advances in representational (and socially constructive) rhetoric developed in the more sophisticated realm of independent filmmaking. It would be a cinema attuned to the desires and the perceptual codes of popular audiences in order to better work with them, reshaping and reinflecting their meanings. Not no narratives, as modernist theorists argue, but more, different narratives, narratives which posit a different world and allow the living of different life stories.

CONCLUSION:
FILM AND POLITICS

In *The Current Crisis in American Politics* Walter Dean Burnham argues that the prevailing ideology of individualism in American political culture prevents a socialist alternative from developing in the United States: "On the ideological plane, there is still no room for a coherent socialist opposition to the liberal individualism that has always dominated American political culture. This 'liberal tradition' stacks the deck against the public sector in its dominant role, and it creates serious problems of legitimating that role in direct proportion as it expands. Accordingly, its intrusiveness and still more its mistakes will be much less tolerated than will those of any part of the private sector . . . . This quasi-permanent bias is an inevitable by-product of hegemony in the cultural-ideological domain."[1] In the absence of such a socialist opposition, American politics can only fluctuate between the neo–laissez-faire ideology of the Republican Right and the welfare state programs of the Democratic liberals.

We have documented the accuracy of these remarks in our study of American film of this era. But we have also documented signs of hopes and desires that suggest antipathy for the predatory values of conservative economic policy and that would, we argue, be responsive to socialist ideals of equal distribution, social security, and democratic governance in a communitarian arrangement.

During the 1980s Americans demonstrated in polls that, although they had elected a right-wing conservative president, they were not in favor of the right-wing agenda, especially in regard to social and military matters. Indeed, on certain crucial conservative issues, the population was decidedly liberal. While a majority had come to oppose preferential treatment or affirmative action in hiring for minorities and women by the late seventies, in 1986, 66% still favored some government intervention to remedy discrimination.[2] The same year, a majority were in favor of busing and abortion, and a large majority (averaging 80% across the classes) favored more rather than less government spending on cities, health, and education. These majorities stood in opposition to what conservatives hoped to accomplish. In a similarly oppositional vein, most Americans (66%) favored cutting defense spending in 1986, while over 60% opposed more cuts in social programs, and a large

By 1987, the era of conservative ascendancy was coming to an end.

number (88%) opposed cuts in social security and medicare. On the whole, conservatives did not succeed in convincing Americans that the federal government should relinquish its paternalist role as a provider of security and welfare and as a regulator of business. For example, in 1984, in the middle of the conservative reign, 74% of the people were in favor of more spending on social programs, a public position directly at odds with what conservatives were arguing at the time. In the mid-eighties, large majorities also favored gun control, the Equal Rights Amendment, the nuclear freeze, and a government sponsored national health program—all issues conservatives opposed. Majorities also opposed the conservative program to reduce pollution controls, to intervene in Central America, and to reduce government aid to the poor so that they could fend for themselves.

It was probably on this last point that the public and the conservatives were most at odds. During this time, strong arguments were mounted by conservative ideologues against liberal social programs. Conservatives claimed that such programs did more harm than good by disarming poor and black people of their individual initiative. Essentially, it came down to accusing liberalism of being incapable of alleviating the worst effects of capitalism, and the conclusion was that capitalism should be left alone to work its wonders. The blindness (or cynicism) of the conclusion was evident. Yet what it did accomplish was to make clear that capitalism could not indeed be made humane by even the best liberalism had to offer. The demolition of liberalism cut simultaneously against capitalism, since the corollary conclusion was that capitalism was too vicious a social system to be dealt with through small-scale liberal acts of remedial or compensatory generosity. The viciousness of the system—and this was the lesson of the post-1978 conservative revolution—was such that even these measures would be overridden by the larger logic of the capitalist economy, one that structurally placed self-interest and greed before considerations of community. If the Right successfully defeated the liberals at this time, it also prepared its own defeat by making clear to many people that liberalism and pure capitalism (like capitalism and democracy) were incompatible.

Indeed, if anything, the conservative revolution gave the public a lesson in the real nature of capitalism. Americans in the early eighties very quickly caught on to the class, race, and sex gender allegiances of the conservatives. Asked whether Reagan cared about serving all people, 67% said yes in 1981, but only 36% did so in 1984. Asked whether he cared more about serving the rich, 24% said yes in 1981, and the figure had grown to 54% by 1984. By 1982, 62% felt that the poor were unfairly treated by Reagan's programs, while only 3% felt the same regarding the wealthy. Blacks and lower income people consistently recorded much higher percentages of disapproval for Reagan's performance in office. In 1982, a recession year when 58% expressed disapproval of how he was handling the economy, 87% of blacks recorded disapproval, as did 64% of those earning less than $15,000. For those earning over $40,000, it was only 40%. The conservatives cured inflation with unemployment and a military buildup, and fittingly, the most important problem on people's minds shifted from inflation in the early eighties to unemployment and international unrest in the mid-eighties. But the simulated war economy could not be realized as an actuality, since public opinion during this period consistently went against the conservative position on war.

If fifty years of social liberalism had gotten Americans used to state guaranteed security, to the extent of frustrating the conservative desire to roll back the New Deal, two decades of antiwar sentiment had also accustomed them to being cautious regarding the more bellicose desires of conservative leaders. While Americans on the whole felt Ronald Reagan had built up the country's defense capacities, a majority (68%) also felt by 1984 that the world was less safe than when Reagan took office, and 66% cut against the grain of the conservative agenda by expressing a desire to live and let live with the communists. Majorities throughout the period expressed opposition to the conservatives' policies in Latin America. In 1983, 68% opposed aid to El Salvador, and in 1985, only 36% favored sending military supplies to the counterrevolutionaries fighting against Nicaragua.

The acute public perceptions of the class character of the conservative revolution and of the notoriously false claims the conservative administration made in order to rally public support for its war agenda took their toll on the public's sense of trust and further eroded public confidence. The index of confidence in the leaders of business fell from an average 32% in the seventies to 26% by 1984, while the same index for military leaders fell from 37% to 30%. Public perception that government was primarily responsible for the problems facing the country rose from 39% in 1978 to 48% in 1982.

The conservatives had managed to make the government the target of public resentment, but increasingly what people resented was the conservative use of government.

The conservatives had initiated a "new class war," and increasingly in the mid-eighties issues were divided along class, race, and gender lines, as the white, male, business-oriented inflection of the conservative agenda became more and more evident. On the issue of further cuts in domestic spending, for example, of the 55% who expressed disapproval in a 1985 poll, more women and blacks disapproved than white males. And of those earning over $50,000 a year, 57% approved further cuts, while of those earning less than $15,000, 61% disapproved. Public belief that the conservatives would reduce government spending and taxes fell by thirteen percentage points between 1982 and 1985. And by 1985, 77% favored more taxes for corporations. The conservative revolution did not succeed in convincing people, and they for the most part saw through the public agenda to the private interests being served by it. Only 31% in 1985 felt that the nation's wealth was fairly distributed, and 60% felt that it should be more evenly distributed. Moreover, even as his personal approval rating climbed from only 38% in the early eighties to a high of 63% later in the decade, Ronald Reagan consistently received low ratings from the public on specific issues. In 1985, only 44% approved of his handling of unemployment, 37% his attempts to reduce the federal budget, and 33% his position on South Africa. He managed to oversee an erosion of the relative parity with the Democrats which the Republicans achieved in the early eighties, so that by 1985, those calling themselves Republican stood at 32%, while the Democrats stood at 37%.

All in all, the conservative agenda did not win over the hearts and minds of the American people. And indeed, by 1986, the conservatives had done such a good job of displaying their race, class, and sex biases that they seemed to be losing their ability to advertise the specific interests of wealthy white conservative males as universal interests—their great accomplishment in the post-1978 period. Their success at promoting a procapitalist agenda seemed to be turning against them, since its working out (curing inflation with unemployment, gutting social welfare programs, bringing a large homeless underclass into being, creating a simulated war economy to heat up business) had such clearly negative effects (an increase in poverty, homelessness, and hunger, a rise in the threat of war, a scarcely concealable overflowing of corporate coffers at the expense of poor people). Nevertheless, the conservative revolution was correct on two counts: that the only way to cure the ills of capitalism is conservatism, that is, the institutionalization of brutality, and that liberalism cannot remedy a social system whose operative   legitimate viciousness. If anything, the conservative revolution proved ism—a radical equalization of wealth of the sort a major desires as well as a leveling of social power—is indeed the alternative.

If a socialist alternative is to be developed in the Un out of the impasse of possibilities we have called the Am

Left, we would argue, must overcome its traditional distrust and distain for popular culture. The Left's dismissal of culture in favor of politics and economics (elections, strikes, party and coalition building, grassroots organizing, etc.) must give way to an understanding of the crucial importance of culture as the seedbed of that support which would allow socialist ideals to be politically acceptable in the United States. We have demonstrated that the politics of the eighties merely confirmed the culture of the seventies, the mobilization of arguments, images, and ideology that answered the popular desire for hope and renewal by turning that desire in a conservative direction. One of the consequences of a society which mixes rule by an economic elite with democratic procedure is that political power must be ratified by the electorate. Culture is the realm in which the psychology of that electorate is formed. Economic power determines the right of access to political institutions, the ability to shape social policy. But political power must also have a cultural base. And this is what we have noticed particularly in the seventies and eighties: the Right successfully developed cultural ideals before it assumed political power. To a certain extent, culture precedes and determines politics. If this has clear implications for understanding conservative ascendancy in the political realm, it also has implications for formulating a socialist alternative to that power.

Popular film articulates fears, desires, and needs that are pre-political in character and that could be channeled in politically progressive directions. Moreover, popular film demonstrates in its repetitive nature, its hyperbolic forms, and its displacement procedures the impossibility of meeting those needs and desires (for self-worth, community, security, freedom, etc.) or of allaying those fears (of aggression, domination, powerlessness, indignity, social disintegration, etc.) in the current institutional context of the United States. This is so because the needs, desires, and fears on display in popular films arise from the very system that is advertised in film as the only way to fulfill those needs, answer those desires, and assuage those fears. As a result, they exceed the solutions proffered, solutions which merely reproduce the original problems that provoked fear and desire in the first place. Thus, there is an antinomy at the heart of ideology, and it indicates that the tautological closure of ideology is also an irreducible opening. The American social system is condemned to repeat its initial imbalances, and the oscillation between conservative individualism and liberal welfarism can do nothing to resolve the problem or to close the opening. It is an opening that the Left can exploit because it suggests that the only way out of the antinomy and the repetition is an altogether different social model. This opening, we suggest, is what leftists must take advantage of if they hope to develop a viable socialist politics in the United States. But they can do so only if they learn to address the needs, fears, and desires that register so clearly in popular film.

While some needs and desires are ideological and are programmed by the society of domination as part of its operation—the need among conserv-ative women for patriarchal men or among such men for proofs of manhood th violence—others reflect aspirations that are not likely to disappear with capitalism or patriarchy. For example, the need for empathy and care that is such a strong theme of many films seems structural and permanent, although it is now channeled into a family model dominated by men. Rather than equate the need with the social model and condemn both, progressives should attempt to develop alternative institutions that supply the same needs without reproducing the inequality which in the patriarchal family is the price of care.

Another need evident in popular film is the need for a social structure of reassurance. Our study has taught us that when such structures collapse or are weakened without any healthy substitute being offered, people tend to seek neurotic compensations which frequently take fascist forms. What the power of these needs suggests is that socialism, if it is to be feasible in the United States, must offer the possibility of such reassurance. And this must take the form not only of guaranteed incomes and rewarding employment, but also of means for meeting psychological needs through cultural representation.

The fears evident in popular films are often ones that would be dispelled by a secure social system, where survival and fulfillment were guaranteed. Other fears we have described are more problematic—the male fear of women so evident in horror movies, for example. The sexual anxieties that provoke male violence arise in part from economic insecurity and can be allayed in an alternative social arrangement. But other fears are endemic to patriarchy and to male socialization. The problem of male hysteria requires an extensive transformation of male attitudes and socialization processes, and our description of how this hysteria saturates more public concerns such as militarism and conservatism suggests that this is not a marginal issue. It must be as central to social reconstruction as income redistribution.

The fear of the loss of individuality is central to American culture. That fear is laden with conservative prejudices, and it also derives in part from male socialization, as we have demonstrated. But the broad prevalence of that fear should provide a lesson to the Left. Simple collectivism or statism is not likely to succeed in a cultural context in which such a fear is as powerful as it is. The Left should take a theoretical and political lesson from that problem. The individual is not an ideological category, though individualism as a social policy may be. One lesson we take from our work is that a society devoted to the common good must also make it possible for all people to be autonomous and self-determining. And, once again, that is not only a problem of political rights, but also one of psychological dispositions and cultural representations. If our examination of the two poles of social rhetoric (metaphor and metonymy) suggest that no autonomy is possible outside of a determining context of social relations, the inverse seems no less true as a formulation for socialism: the condition of genuinely unforced collectivity is individual autonomy. If the Left is to succeed in the American context, the liberal ideal of autonomy must be deconstructed. That is, it must be inhabited, and its potential for exceeding the semantic boundaries now put on it must be exploited. Only by working within the existing ideological structures of a

society can the Left hope to appeal to a broad mass of people. By inhabiting
the fear of a loss of individuality, the Left can turn it toward socialist uses.
A first step in that procedure is to counter the prevailing cultural representations that associate freedom with capitalism; it is imperative that a social
system that permits powerful individuals to dominate and exploit others be
shown to be responsible for the very anxieties and fears that are exploited
by cultural representations which bolster the power of those individuals. It
is only in a society where individual assertion is privileged that individuality
is threatened. This procedure also requires a reconceptualization of such
collective institutions as the state, which must be reformulated and recon-
structed in such a way as to cease being perceived as constraints on individuality and instead to be seen as facilitators of autonomy. This strategy has
negative implications for the naive formalism of the Left regarding collectivity, which has been abstracted out of its material networks into a state
form which is then imposed on a recalcitrant society. Our contention is that
the collective good can only be realized in a situation in which individual
self-development and collective well-being support and guarantee each other.

Not all of the fears expressed in film can be of use to the politics we
advocate. It would be difficult to say how progressives could use monsters
and disasters to their advantage; the revolution is not a Halloween party,
after all. Nevertheless, the very striking fear of uncontrollable forces determining peoples' lives which are projected or metaphorized in the horror and
disaster genres are at least indicators that the social system of capitalism is
not working smoothly. And what our analysis suggests is that it cannot work
smoothly, because it rests on fundamental anxieties regarding survival (idealized as "freedom") that tear the temporary pacifications of the system apart
from inside. Thus, even those fears and aspirations that seem least political
can be read politically, for what they indicate is the presence of desires that
are not being satisfied under the current system of domination. The desire
for self-worth and personal achievement, even in its most ideological cultural
forms, confronts capitalism with an indictment every time it is frustrated and
displaced into metaphoric substitutes. And it must be frustrated broadly if
capitalism's minoritarian monopoly on social wealth is to be maintained.
Moreover, the very necessity for metaphoric substitutes throughout American
film culture indicates that those desires *must* be deflected. The pervasive
presence of those desires suggests that the Left is not operating in a vacuum,
without a mass base. A politically conscious base is not there, but a base of
counterhegemonic desire is, one that can be the source for progressive change.

But if the Left is seriously to take advantage of the possibilities we are
describing, it must come to see that the desires and needs which conservative
cultural representations seem to satisfy are not themselves necessarily conservative. For much too long, the Left, especially the cultural Left, has adopted
a dismissive attitude toward the culture of the very people in whose interest
the Left supposedly works. The Left assigns an inherent, noncontextual meaning to prepolitical desires and needs that are essentially indeterminate and
undecidable, that change content according to the material circumstances

which shape them (either prosperity or recession, for example) and according to the representations which exist in the culture to guide need and desire. Those representations operate like mental representations in the psyche; they organize the psychological dispositions of social agents and create a common sense of social reality. Cultural representations are not merely added onto an already constituted social substance, a body of feeling and thought which those representations reflect as something external to them. That body of feeling and thought could not exist without those representations, just as desire in the mind cannot exist apart from representations that orient it. Consequently, the political meaning of a culture is not given as something which preexists the representations in that culture. Those representations are themselves constitutive of that meaning. Consequently, such meaning is malleable, constructable, indeterminate. It can change according to which material circumstances prevail, which representations hold sway. The needs and desires which the Left condemns in popular culture appear conservative precisely because they are shaped by conservative cultural representations, and they will continue to assume conservative shapes as long as a conservative rhetoric of social construction is not opposed by leftist attempts to develop an effective rhetoric of cultural representation in the American public sphere. For socialism to be possible in the United States in a fully democratic manner, it must first become possible in people's minds. To a certain extent, in order for the actuality of socialism to be realized it must simultaneously be represented as something realizable. This is the nature of desire, both personal and political. All such desire is to a certain extent utopian, in the sense that its actual object is always absent from the representation that signifies it. It is for this reason that one could say that Ronald Reagan was actually elected somewhere around the mid-seventies, when cultural imagery first began to summon him forth. The same must be true of an alternative socialist society. To be desired, it must be represented. And it won't be realized if it isn't an object of desire. We will conclude, then, by suggesting that the Left must construct socialism as a possible object of desire in the realms that most attract popular desires—film, but also television and music. The Left must develop an effective politics of cultural representation at the same time that it builds coalitions and formulates economic programs. The latter will make no difference in the world without the former.

Postface

The year 1986-1987 was a pivotal one in Hollywood film and in American culture. The tide of political and social change began to turn leftward, and the hegemony of conservatism as a political force effectively came to an end. The Iran hostage/Contra aid scandals displayed a dangerously antidemocratic corruption behind the veneer of high-sounding patriotic platitudes that had been one crucial key to the Republican successes of the eighties. As conservatives once again found themselves at odds with a recalcitrantly liberal Constitution, the Reagan administration produced a per capita rate of criminal investigation and indictment higher than that of any previous presidency. The very clear plight of the homeless poor, whose numbers swelled during this period of public meanness, displayed the cruel agenda behind the revolt against the state, and the obvious injustice of the administration's illegal wars in Central America ignited strong public opposition to further militarization.

By 1987, the era of the hero was over, both cinematically and politically. The patriarch had proven to be a duplicitous coward, the entrepreneur a conniving con artist, and the warrior a pusillanimous bully and a bumbling incompetent. The liberal state, that foil which had defined the hero's virtue as a rebel, could no longer be held accountable for taxes and deficits when it was the conservative heroes themselves, the supposed bearers of deliverance from big government, who were draining the country through borrowing for a by now unpopular defense build-up and who were skewing the wealth of the nation in their own direction, doubling the number of billionaires while trebling the poor and underemployed. In 1987, more people desired help from the federal government than ever before, and liberalism, the belief that the state should provide such help, seemed once again on the rise. The Republicans had clearly lost the moral confidence of the nation, and as the Soviet Union entered a period of democratic reform that included calls for peace and disarmament, the conservatives were deprived of the mobilizing force that had helped them to victory around the issue of "standing tall against communism" in the post-1978 era.

Moreover, as hemlines rose in a reminder of the sixties, so also, it seemed, did expectations that the nineties would belong to the postwar baby-boom generation that was about to come of political age, bringing with it a more open, generous, and fair-minded set of values than had been in evidence during the mean-spirited eighties. With a black serving as its moral conscience and more women assuming leadership roles, the Democratic party seemed to gain in progressive stature. The new spirit of the times was as much advertised in the films of that year as anywhere else.

In the summer of 1986, the two top-grossing films (and the first and the fifth for the year as a whole) were *Top Gun*, a rightist celebration of penis-brained militarism in which a narcissistic macho air force pilot triumphs over communist fighters in a pyrotechnic air battle, and *Aliens*, a quasi-feminist horror film in which a powerful woman does battle with monsters and corrupt corporate executives alike and wins. The juxtaposition was striking and probably important, for it would seem to suggest that as the rightist, militarist patriarchal strain in U.S. culture came to full realization—and toppled into a mannerist period of almost ridiculous excess—another period began that momentarily overlapped with the first; *Aliens*, while it contains negative attitudes toward cynical corporate yuppies, also retains some of the militarist trappings of the preceding era. The possibility (and probability) of a more liberal post-Reagan era made itself felt in a number of other films of that year. The immensely popular *Platoon*, by Oliver Stone, while still mired in very questionable Americanist values and perceptual patterns (the "gooks" are a threatening, faceless other; a "good" frontiersman killer is valorized over a bad, redneck one; and male bonding seems the only solution to the world's ills), nonetheless offered a picture of the war as a messy, dirty, dubious undertaking, a portrayal strikingly at odds with the mythologizing films of the conservative era. *Blue Velvet*, by David Lynch, one of the more significant cinematic events of 1986, brought an ironic post-modernist perspective to bear on the Reagan ideal of the good, virtuous, small-town, mid-American life and showed that Andy Hardy world of vapor-headed platitude to be not all that distinct from the underworld of violence and perversion that it kept at bay. That same year, the popular *Crocodile Dundee* (number three in gross), an Australian import, portrayed a genial semi-hero who articulated a good-humored debunking of the standard inflated male ideal of the tough, self-reliant frontier phallocrat. The fourth *Star Trek* film (number four in gross) argued for an ecological perspective distinctly antagonistic to the reigning conservative agenda for the environment. *The Color Purple* (number six in revenues), despite its evident limitations (made by a white male, it looks like it was made by a white male), sympathetically portrayed the lives of the group least favored by Reagan's economic and social agenda—black women. Mazursky's *Down and Out in Beverly Hills* (twelfth in the standings for 1986) lampooned the myth of self-made wealth that sustained the Reagan Revolution. In the same period, *Mad Max: Beyond Thunderdrome* satirized the business-consumer mentality. And Brooks's *Spaceballs*, a satire of *Star Wars*, made evident that the mood of the country had shifted sufficiently to allow the savior-hero ideal to be treated comically.

In 1987 as well, Cannon Films, the major producer of right-wing fare in the early eighties, began to lose money and retrench, while Stallone, on the brink of making a rightist *Rambo III*, decided to postpone the project. Things seemed to be changing, and if Sly wanted to keep up with what the times seemed to be portending he might have thought instead of making an anthem to empathetic liberalism (*Stand By Me*), or of going in drag for a sympathetic portrayal of lesbian love (*Desert Hearts*), or of doing a critical examination of male sexual identity (*Angel Heart*), or of debunking conformist white professionalism in favor of a female flim-flam artist reminiscent of the sixties (*Something Wild*), or of portraying yuppie parochialism (*After Hours*), or of satirizing sci-fi hero worship from a hip, post-mod, antiracist perspective (*Buckaroo Banzai*), or of promoting empathy against the aggressivity of small business life (*Tin Men*), or of diagnosing the sleaze behind the gleam of wealth (*Wall Street*), or of arguing that sports heroes and children should lead a revolt for disarmament (*Amazing Grace and Chuck*), or of leveling a cinematic acetylene torch at America's national myths regarding Vietnam (*Full Metal Jacket*), or of taking down the hero myth and arguing for leftist revolutionaries (*Ishtar*), or of using a power hero figure to criticize nuclear policy and argue for peace (*Superman IV*), or of exploring the difficulties of handicapped life from a liberal perspective (*Children of a Lesser God*), or of comically exploring the complexities of southern sisterhood (*Crimes of the Heart*), or of siding with a popular struggle against economic power (*The Milagro Beanfield War*), or of sympathetically portraying union struggle (*Matewan*).

Sociologists spoke of a coming of age of the generation of the sixties, now old enough to assume power in American public life in the nineties. The baby-boom generation was more educated on the whole and more liberal than its parents, and with its maturation came as well a changeover from the muzak world of seventies melodramas to the more literary world of "serious" films like *Out of Africa* and *A Room With A View* in 1986–87. The popularity of these films suggested that an audience existed for more sophisticated films, and indeed, major actors, once the trend became evident, began searching for more serious roles to play (Stallone notwithstanding). After years of pandering to youth audiences, Hollywood seemed to begin to realize that young people grow up and still go to movies. But more important, perhaps, a more educated and literate audience was also one less likely to embrace the kind of imbecility on stilts that Ronald Reagan represented. The shift in Hollywood therefore also had this other meaning, that of signaling the emergence of a generational group whose core values were likely to be antagonistic to the values and ideals that dominated Hollywood from 1978 to 1986. With them had grown the public belief that government is run by a few big interests for their own gain, from 20% in 1960 to nearly 80% in the early eighties—a significant, indeed telling statistic.

It was most saliently the sixties generation in independent filmmaking that led the way as Hollywood cinematic culture switched directions and headed left, becoming in the process more filmicly sophisticated and more thematically complex. At the cutting edge were films like *River's Edge* and *Blue Velvet*, but included also should be films like *Down by Law*, *Working Girls*, *Raising Arizona*, *Swimming to Cambodia*, *She's Gotta Have It*, *Hollywood Shuffle*, *Sherman's March*, *True Stories*, and *Sid and Nancy*. In *River's Edge*, the "burn-out" generation of young people without future prospects, whose suicide rate accelerated under Reagan's system of economic apartheid, is looked at sympathetically. The style of the film is markedly non-Hollywood; the drab locations and unedifying dialog stake out a psychological terrain of limited possibilities that is in no way elevated to cinematic metaphoricity. The film's point of view is unremittingly materialist, and the camera refuses to swerve away from the banality of life at the bottom of the great American ladder of success. The style of *Blue Velvet* is more cinematically reflexive, drawing on *noir* motifs (nearly black compositions), exorbitant camera work (close-ups of ants), grotesque images (a severed ear), symbolic intercutting (a harsh candle flame blowing in the wind between scenes of violence), rambunctious color coding (strikingly red, white, and blue makeup), and a deadpan irony that situates the audience either as on the naive side of the narrative or as on the cynical, debunking, worldly-wise other side that lies in wait for those innocent or benighted enough to take the images of picket-fenced mid-American bliss seriously. The film, a dissection of the power system of male sexual violence, is most unremitting in its critique of the all-American middle-class value system with its Hallmark card romances, its ideal of small-town provinciality, and its blindness to its own violence. Yet the film can arguably also be read as an extreme example of traditional misogyny, as well as being extremely derogatory toward the working class.

If *Blue Velvet* suggests the beginnings of a new strain of critical, post-modernist cinema, one that destroys the mid-America illusions which allowed the white middle class to save itself at the expense of workers, blacks, women, and poor people during this era, *River's Edge* points forward toward the coming-of-age of a generation of people who were the victims of that class warfare. And if Reagan's success at serving the needs of the rich at the expense of the poor through deficit spending for defense without raising taxes created an enormous debt whose terrible burden will be felt in the limited lives the future generation of young, especially lower-class people will be obliged to lead, his success also created a bill-collector in the form of those young people, one who would probably not be disposed to be forgiving or accepting of a charming wink and a nod as an excuse for villainy and greed. Just as in the cinema of the early and mid-seventies evidence of future probabilities were detectable, so also in the cinema of the late eighties it is possible that portents were to be divined, signs deciphered of future potentials that await realization.

Yet in this same nihilism can also reside rightist possibilities. Enforced undereducation and low-wage job tracking can also engender resentments and desires that can easily be oriented toward redemption through strong leadership. It would therefore be a mistake to ignore the obvious rightist undercurrents in American culture. They too tend to be augmented during periods of economic stress, as we have seen. Often, the easiest solutions to right-wing economic policies are right-wing political practices. Even though the conservative hegemony of the era seemed by 1987 to have run its course, the desires, needs, and fears that made it possible had not. Hero-worship was still a potent factor in the American psyche, and the sense of ego righteousness that accompanies it still had the potential of attaching to nationalist and militarist endeavors, regardless of questions of justice. Though by 1987 the economy was temporarily stable, the structural imbalances that unhinged it in the seventies and early eighties had if anything become more grave. The possibility of a complete economic collapse became more imaginable, the kind of collapse that in history had been the precursor to right-wing putschism or seizure of power. And such putschism seemed all the more possible in a climate of cultural triage that left many by the wayside, underemployed and undereducated, awaiting a salvation that certainly was not about to be delivered by an economic system that depended on their exclusion from the sharing of economic rewards, diminished since the seventies and increasingly divided up amongst a smaller and smaller group of white professionals.

Thus, any assessment of the potentials inherent in American society as seen through Hollywood film must take the dual strands of populism into account—the radical, which contests the power of the wealthy, and the fascist, which imagines salvation through strong individual leaders. Both exist in American culture, and although Hollywood seemed, with the political tides of the times, to turn leftward around 1987, producing more films with radical and critical dimensions, Hollywood had also proven by the late eighties that strong rightist currents existed that could be drawn upon at time of crisis. For the moment, the leftward tendency seemed the stronger; the Right was without a leader and thus without a movement. And conservatism had so exhausted its rhetorical reserves on the public stage that it had become an easy target of critical farce. Films of the late eighties indicated a shift in sensibility, one that, if it did not constitute a return of the sixties, at least suggested that the critical spirit of the sixties had not entirely departed. If to a certain degree the direction signs pointed both ways at once, one thing at least seemed clear as American culture negotiated its way into the nineties: the failure of liberalism and the triumph of conservatism, the two narratives we have traced in this book, had come to an end, and another narrative was about to begin.

Appendix

Our survey was conducted in the Boston, New York, and Chicago areas in May 1986. It entailed 22 in-depth oral interviews with people of varying races, sexes, and classes, and 153 questionnaires. Participants in the oral interviews were solicited from the audiences at movie theaters, as well as from the parents of students at Northeastern University in Boston, a school which is attended primarily by working and middle class students. A number of the participants in the interviews were working-class black women, and about half were corporate office workers of varying levels. We also spoke to several white middle-class housewives and to a few upper class Westchester County residents. It was more difficult to obtain interviews with white working class men, although we fared better in our written survey, which we distributed to classes of white and black students at Northeastern who were assigned to give it to adults. Ten students in one of our classes and ten in a colleague's completed the survey. We also distributed it to office workers, and obtained about fifty responses by distributing it at movie theaters in upper-class areas of Boston. Of the 153 respondents, 50.7% were men, and 49.3% were women; 14% were black, 82% white, and 4% Asian. The political positions of the respondents were distributed in the following way: Reactionary 2%, Conservative 27%, Moderate 35%, Liberal 29%, and Radical 2%. The family backgrounds of the participants varied in the following way: Working and lower middle class 26%, middle class 47%, and upper middle class 27%. The income of the respondents was distributed in the following way: 34% under $30,000 a year, 27% $30,000 to $40,000, 9% $40,000 to $50,000, and 31% over $50,000. Our sample reflected the opinions that recent polls have suggested are the standard opinions for most Americans. That is, they mix liberalism on certain social issues with conservatism on others. For example, 79% favored more punishment for criminals, while 67% opposed reductions in welfare. Similarly, the large majority favored the ERA, but 58% favored the use of force to deal with enemies abroad. For our own interest, we asked two questions which other polls do not ask. When asked if they feel the "American economic system is fair and just," 61% of our sample said no. When asked if they would prefer a society in which wealth was distributed equally, 50% said they would.

The poll was constructed with the help of Pat Golden, a sociologist at Northeastern University who specializes in data research. Although a sample of fifty is assumed to produce "significant" results, our poll can only be taken as a partial indicator, not as a statement about all Americans. A poll that would legitimately lay claim to universality would require a much more selective approach to the construction of the sample. Our aims have been altogether more limited. We simply wanted to get a sense of how a random selection of people were processing movies. The range of answers given to

303

our questions in the interviews probably cover much of the range that would be given by a wider or more scientifically determined sample. A wider or more scientific sample might have given rise to different percentages, but we feel that the general proportions of the percentages would likely remain the same. Nevertheless, it is clear that more work of this sort needs to be done on Hollywood film, and we present our poll as an effort in this direction.

We did this research in full awareness of all the pitfalls entailed in engaging in such work. We do not claim that surveys provide direct access to information concerning the effects of films on audiences or the realities of audience political consciousness. Questions create their own responses to a certain degree, and an audience may not have thought of a film at all in the manner elicited by a question until that question was posed. Moreover, written polls are not ideal ways of eliciting responses, and the role of the unconscious is difficult to factor into our results. Cinematic perception and political consciousness are highly mediated and differentiated; unconscious feelings or effects may be the most important and the least accessible. Free association in interviews can draw out certain material, and we found that people sometimes gave quite distinct responses in the interviews than they did on the poll. Very few people, for example, in the interviews volunteered that they thought the representation of foreigners in *Raiders of the Lost Ark* was stereotypical, but when the option was presented on the written poll, 90% chose it. If open-ended questions in the interviews elicit a greater breadth of response, they also necessarily preclude certain responses that people might not have thought of themselves. No satisfactory method of survey analysis and interpretation has been devised, and more work remains to be done using in-depth interviews particularly. In addition, further research into audience responses would have to rely on more sophisticated surveys than our own.

On the whole, we found that people are quite mixed in their responses to films. They are capable of holding quite divergent political views at once, and of the same film they can make both conservative and liberal statements. We have come away from this work convinced that most people's values are pre-political; that is, they are not conceptualized as either conservative or liberal or whatever. Many people are not even certain what those terms mean. And some label liberal values as right-wing because they entail restraint, while they call other things radical because they are individualist and rebellious.

We also found that different social groups view the same film quite differently. Perhaps the most noticeable of these divergences occurred in black people's perceptions of films which white people did not find problematic. In our interviews with blacks, we found that blacks noticed the presence or absence of representations of the black experience much more so than whites. And, as one might expect, they perceived problems with stereotypes which whites tended to ignore. The same is true of course regarding women's and working-class people's experiences. Women's perceptions on women's issues diverged from men's, and as we have noted, income and class position influences at least certain responses. We include some tables below which give a more concrete sense of what we are describing.

Each option in each table contains three numbers in a vertical column. The uppermost number indicates the actual number of people who chose that option. The next number down indicates the percentage that number represents of all who chose that option. This percentage should be read horizontally across the range of people. The bottom number of the three indicates the percentage the number choosing that option represents of that vertical category.

For example, our first table refers to the question, "Is *Kramer vs. Kramer* a negative depiction of an independent woman?" The first figure under "Male" is 16, which indicates that 16 men felt it was negative. The equivalent number under the adjacent female column is 28. The percentage on the next line indicates that the 16 men represent 36.4% of those (both male and female) who thought the film depicted independent women negatively while the 28 women represent 63.6% of those (again both male and female) choosing this option. The next figure down in the first column is 30.2%, which means that the 16 men represent 30.2% of all the male respondents. The equivalent figure for the 28 women is 45.2%, since 34 women or 54.8% of the female sample felt the film did not constitute a negative depiction. Thus, while more of the women thought it was not negative, women still outnumbered men in characterizing the depiction as negative (28 to 16 or almost 64% of those choosing this response).

Table 1. Do you think *Kramer vs. Kramer* took a negative position toward women who want to be independent?

	Male	Female	Both
Yes	16	28	44
	36.4%	63.6%	38.3%
	30.2%	45.2%	
No	37	34	71
	52.1%	47.9%	61.7%
	69.8%	54.8%	
Column	53	62	115
totals	46.1%	53.9%	100.0%

The next table indicates that a higher percentage of blacks thought *Saturday Night Fever* offered a false hope as opposed to a real possibility.

Table 2. Do you think the film offers a false hope to working class people that they as a whole group can move up the class ladder? Or do you think the movie depicts a real possibility that all working class people can move up?

	Black	White	Asian	Other	All
False hope	12	28	3		43
	27.9%	65.1%	7.0%		41.0%
	70.6%	33.7%	75.0%		

Table 2. Do you think the film offers a false hope to working class people that they as a whole group can move up the class ladder? Or do you think the movie depicts a real possibility that all working class people can move up?

	Black	**White**	**Asian**	**Other**	**All**
Real	5	55	1	1	62
possibility	8.1%	88.7%	1.6%	1.6%	59.0%
	29.4%	66.3%	25.0%	100.0%	
Column	17	83	4	1	105
totals	16.2%	79.0%	3.8%	1.0%	100.0%

And the next indicates that a higher percentage of those making over $30,000 thought it represented a real possibility.

Table 3. Do you think the movie offers a false hope or a real possibility?

Salary	**Less than $30,000**	**More than $30,000**	**Both**
False hope	18	21	39
	46.2%	53.8%	40.6%
	51.4%	34.4%	
Real	17	40	57
possibility	29.8%	70.2%	59.4%
	48.6%	65.6%	
Column	35	61	96
totals	36.5%	63.5%	100.0%

The following table addresses the same question from the perspective of class. Notice that the percentages for "false hope" decline as one climbs the class ladder, while those for "real possibility" rise.

Table 4. Do you think the movie offers a false hope or a real possibility?

Class	**Working**	**Lower middle**	**Middle**	**Upper middle**	**Other**	**All**
False hope	10	5	19	7		41
	24.4%	12.2%	46.3%	17.1%		40.2%
	55.6%	50.0%	43.2%	24.1%		
Real	8	5	25	22	1	61
possibility	13.1%	8.2%	41.0%	36.1%	1.6%	59.8%
	44.4%	50.0%	56.8%	75.9%	100.0%	
Column	18	10	44	29	1	102
totals	17.6%	9.8%	43.1%	28.4%	1.0%	100.0%

And, finally, the same question from the point of view of political preference.

Table 5. Do you think the movie offers a false hope or a real possibility?

	Reactionary	Conservative	Moderate	Liberal	Radical	Other	All
False	1	6	15	17	2		41
hope	2.4%	14.6%	36.9%	41.5%	4.9%		39.8%
	33.3%	23.1%	42.9%	50.0%	100.0%		
Real	2	20	17	17	0	3	62
possibility	3.2%	32.3%	32.3%	27.4%		4.8%	60.2%
	66.7%	76.9%	57.1%	50.0%		100.0%	
Column	3	26	35	34	2	3	105
totals	2.9%	25.2%	34.0%	33.0%	1.9%	2.9%	100.0%

The following table indicates that blacks, more so than whites, thought *Saturday Night Fever* depicted working class life as a dead end.

Table 6. Do you feel the movie deliberately tries to make the working class world look like a dead end?

	Black	White	Asian	Other	All
Yes	10	41	1		52
	19.2%	78.8%	1.9%		47.7%
	62.5%	46.6%	25.0%		
No	6	47	3	1	57
	10.5%	82.5%	5.3%	1.8%	52.3%
	37.5%	53.4%	75.0%	100.0%	
Column	16	88	4	1	109
totals	14.7%	80.7%	3.7%	0.9%	100.0%

Gender is a factor in many instances. This table indicates that women in our survey were more opposed to Dirty Harry's methods.

Table 7. Do you think Dirty Harry represents the right way to solve crime?

	Male	Female	All
Yes	18	6	24
	75.0%	25.0%	21.4%
	26.1%	14.0%	
No	51	37	88
	58.0%	42.0%	78.6%
	73.9%	86.0%	
Column	69	43	112
totals	61.6%	38.4%	100.0%

The following two tables suggest that people from upper middle class backgrounds and people who make over $30,000 a year are more likely to think that a disaster film like *Towering Inferno* is about one bad sector of business than about business in general.

Table 8. Do you think the corrupt construction people (in *Towering Inferno*) represent (a) one bad sector of business but not all business or (b) the way most big business operates?

Class	Working	Lower middle	Middle	Upper middle	Other	All
(a)	9	5	39	23	1	77
	11.7%	6.5%	50.6%	29.9%	1.3%	77.0%
	56.3%	71.4%	78.0%	88.5%	100.0%	
(b)	7	2	11	3		23
	30.4%	8.7%	47.8%	13.0%		23.0%
	43.8%	28.6%	22.0%	11.5%		
Column	16	7	50	26	1	100
totals	16.0%	7.0%	50.0%	26.0%	1.0%	100.0%

Salary	Less than $30,000	More than $30,000	All
(a)	24	49	73
	32.9%	67.1%	76.8%
	68.6%	81.7%	
(b)	11	11	22
	50.0%	50.0%	23.2%
	31.4%	18.3%	
Column	35	60	95
totals	36.8%	63.2%	100.0%

The table below suggests that conservatives more than moderates or liberals are likely to perceive *Star Wars* as supporting the conservative ideal of peace through strength.

Table 9. Do you think the movie is in favor of the conservative idea of "peace through military strength"?

	Reactionary	Conservative	Moderate	Liberal	Radical	Other	All
Yes	1	25	16	16	2	2	62
	1.6%	40.3%	25.8%	25.8%	3.2%	3.2%	54.4%
	50.0%	75.8%	44.4%	45.7%	66.7%	40.0%	
No	1	8	20	19	1	3	52
	1.9%	15.4%	38.5%	36.5%	1.9%	5.8%	45.6%
	50.0%	24.2%	55.6%	54.3%	33.3%	60.0%	
Column	2	33	36	35	3	5	114
totals	1.8%	28.9%	31.6%	30.7%	2.6%	4.4%	100.0%

The next tables concern social issues. Tables 10 and 11 indicate that blacks and people earning less than thirty thousand are more likely to prefer an egalitarian society.

Table 10. Which would you prefer—a society in which the wealth is spread out unevenly with a small rich group at the top and a large middle or low income group at the bottom, or a society in which the wealth is spread out evenly between all?

	First	Second	Row Total
Black	3	14	17
	17.6%	82.4%	14.0%
	5.1%	22.6%	
White	52	46	98
	53.1%	46.9%	81.0%
	88.1%	74.2%	
Asian	4	1	5
	80.0%	20.0%	4.1%
	6.8%	1.6%	
Other		1	1
		100.0%	.8%
		1.6%	
Column Totals	59	62	121
	48.8%	51.2%	100.0%

Table 11. Which would you prefer—a society in which the wealth is spread out unevenly with a small rich group at the top and a large middle or low income group at the bottom, or a society in which the wealth is spread out evenly between all?

	First	Second	Row Total
Salary less	13	24	37
than $30,000	35.1%	64.9%	33.9%
	24.1%	43.6%	
More than	41	31	72
$30,000	56.9%	43.1%	66.1%
	75.9%	56.4%	
Column Totals	54	55	109
	49.5%	50.5%	100.0%

The final two tables concern the question of whether or not the American economic system is fair and just. Notice that working-class and black participants chose "no" more often than white or upper-class respondents.

Table 12. Do you think the American economic system is fair and just?

Family Class Background	Yes	No	Row Total
Working	7	18	25
	28.0%	72.0%	18.2%
	12.7%	22.0%	
Lower Middle	3	8	11
	27.3%	72.7%	8.0%
	5.5%	9.8%	
Middle	26	39	65
	40.0%	60.0%	47.4%
	47.3%	47.6%	
Upper Middle	18	17	35
	51.4%	48.6%	25.5%
	32.7%	20.7%	
Other	1		1
	100.0%		.7%
	1.8%		
Row Totals	55	82	137
	40.1%	59.9%	100.0%

Table 13. Do you think the American economic system is fair and just?

	Black	White	Asian	Other	Row Total
Yes	2	52			54
	3.7%	96.3%			38.6%
	10.0%	45.6%			
No	18	62	5	1	86
	20.9%	72.1%	5.8%	1.2%	61.4%
	90.0%	54.4%	100.0%	100.0%	
Column	20	114	5	1	140
Totals	14.3%	81.4%	3.6%	0.7%	100.0%

Notes

Introduction

1. P. Biskind, *Seeing Is Believing: How Hollywood Movies Taught Us to Stop Worrying and Love the Fifties* (New York: Pantheon, 1983). See also D. M. White and R. Averson, *The Celluloid Weapon: Social Comment in the American Film* (Boston: Beacon, 1972).
2. See T. Louis and J. Pigeon, *Le cinema americain d'aujourd'hui* (Paris: Seghers, 1975), who claim that 1967 is a "revolutionary year." Their point is disputed by Callisto Cosulich, who argues for 1969 as the turning point: *Hollywood Settanta: il nuovo volto del cinema americano* (Florence: Vallecchi, 1978). On dating and terminology: the dates cited for films in the text refer to year of release; sometimes the source is the film itself, though we also rely on film guides (Maltin, Halliwell, etc.), which sometimes provide different dates. We might note also that the year of the box-office gross rating is sometimes different from the year of release, as many films released late in the year appear on the following year's list. For box-office grosses, we have relied on *Variety* as well as the book *Film Facts*. Some of the films we discuss are not strictly speaking "Hollywood films" in the traditional sense. Some were co-produced; others were made in other countries and were given primary release in the United States. Hollywood has indeed become international, and our continued use of the term "Hollywood film" is meant more to refer to a specific type of film production than to a localizable regional product.
3. See J. Mellen, *Big Bad Wolves: Masculinity in the American Film* (New York: Pantheon, 1977).
4. On changes in U.S. capitalism during this period, see the Union for Radical Political Economics volume *Capitalism in Crisis*, ed. D. Mermelstein (New York: Random House, 1975). On the New Right, see A. Crawford, *Thunder on the Right: The "New Right" and the Politics of Resentment* (New York: Pantheon, 1980).
5. Our psychoanalytic model consists of a mixture of traditional Freudianism and more contemporary "object relations" theory. We have employed the latter more than the former because it emphasizes the cultural, social, and "superstructural" determinants of the psyche, things which strike us as more amenable to change than the instincts. Indeed, in some ways, this work deconstructs the metaphysical prioritizing of the instinctual dimension of the unconscious, the so-called primary processes, in Freudian theory. See P. Noy, "A revision of the psychoanalytic theory of the primary process," *International Journal of Psychoanalysis* (1969), no. 50, pp. 155–78. The theory emphasizes the internalization of external objects in the form of mental representations, an idea that derives in part from Freud's work on mourning. See K. Abraham, "A Short Study of the Development of the Libido," *Selected Papers* (London: Hogarth, 1949). It was developed by Klein particularly, but also by Kohut, Kernberg, Winnicott, and others. For general overviews of the approach, see E. Jacobson, *The Self and the Object World* (New York: International University Press, 1964), pp. 3–69; J. D. Sutherland, "Object relations and the conceptual model of psychoanalysis," *British Journal of Medical Psychology* (1963), no. 36, pp. 109–24, and "British Object Relations Theorists," *Journal of the American Psychoanalytic Association* (1980), no. 34, pp. 829–60; and H. Guntrip, *Personality Structure and Human Interaction—The Developing Synthesis of Psychodynamic Theory* (London: Hogarth, 1961). On the internalization of representations of objects and their mediation by cultural codes, see especially R. Schafer, *Aspects of Internalization* (New York: International Universities Press, 1968), and G. Platte and F. Weinstein, *Psychoanalytic Sociology* (Bal-

311

timore: Johns Hopkins University Press, 1972). On the concept of mental representation and its role in psychopathology, see D. Beres and E. Joseph, "The Concept of Mental Representation in Psychoanalysis," *International Journal of Psychoanalysis* (1970), no. 51, pp. 1–9; S. J. Blatt and S. Shichman, "Two Primary Configurations of Psychopathology," *Psychoanalysis and Contemporary Thought* (1983), vol. 6, no. 2, pp. 187–254; Blatt, "Levels of Object Representation in Anaclitic and Introjective Depression," *Psychoanalytic Study of the Child* (1974), no. 29,, pp. 107–57; Blatt, C. Wild, and B. Ritzler, "Disturbances of object representation in schizophrenia," *Psychoanalysis and Contemporary Science* (1975), no. 4, pp. 235–88; S. Fraiberg, "Libidinal Object Constancy and Mental Representation," *Psychoanalytic Study of the Child* (1969), no. 24, pp. 9–47; L. Freedman, "The Barren Prospect of a Representational World," *Psychoanalytic Quarterly* (1980), no. 39, pp. 215–33; A. Loewald, "On Internalization," *International Journal of Psychoanalysis* (1973), no. 54, pp. 9–17; Loewald, "Instinct Theory, Object Relations, and Psychic Structure Formation," *Journal of the American Psychoanalytic Association* (1978), no. 29, pp. 39–106; P. Noy, "Symbolism and Mental Representation," *International Review of Psychoanalysis* (1975), no. 2, pp. 171–87; J. Schimek, "A Critical Reexamination of Freud's Concept of Mental Representation," *International Review of Psychoanalysis* (1975), no. 22, pp. 171–87. For a more sociological elaboration of object relations theory into theory of social relations, see N. Chodorow, *The Reproduction of Mothering* (Berkeley: University of California Press, 1978).

6. We use the terms "metaphor" and "metonymy" to name the two major axes of representation, with metaphor being the vertical or idealizing axis and metonymy being the horizontal or materializing axis. This should not be taken as a condemnation of metaphors. Actual metaphors can themselves be part of a metonymic approach to the representation of the social world. And metonymy can itself be a conservative trope in certain contexts, as Judith Harris argues in regard to law (see "Recognizing Legal Tropes: Metonymy as Manipulative Mode," *American University Law Review*, Vol. 34 [Summer 1985], pp. 1215–29). We use the terms to name general rhetorical strategies, not specific tropes. In our use, metaphor is linked to ideology for several reasons. Metaphor consists of an empirical image (an eagle, say) and an absent, or ideal meaning ("freedom"). Metaphor suggests a static or spatial structure; the hidden or unstated meaning is simultaneous with the vehicle of its communication. It is associated with tradition and authority in that hidden meanings have to be known and in that because invisible they have to be believed. Metaphor as a general rhetorical strategy also implies codes of meaning from which the significance of an image is deduced. Metaphors privilege analogical thought of the sort which favors identities over differential thinking. That is, an image is analogically identified with a meaning. Metaphor is context-free and universalistic; its meanings transcend material ties and are not contingent upon specific circumstances. Metaphor implies an autonomous ego, the determiner of meaning and the deducer of truth. Metaphor is paradigmatic (implying order), hypotactic (implying a subordination of image to meaning), and disjunctive (operating as either/or propositions). A metaphor means one determinate thing specifically. Metaphor is vertical and hierarchical in that it places ideal meaning over material image and privileges the first.

Metonymy, on the other hand, orients thinking horizontally and equally. In metonymy, an image or sign signifies or means something with which it is connected by part to part or part for whole. Eagle rather than mean freedom would mean nest, or forest, or threatened species. Metonymy connects concrete things on an equal plane of reference, without idealizing one over the other. If metaphor lifts thinking out of reality and toward meta-material ideals like "freedom," metonymy has a realist, concrete, and materialist orientation. Because no ideal meanings stand in to stop the flow of material references or connections, the lateral dissemination of meaning in a metonymic rhetorical mode is potentially endless. In contrast to the traditionalist orientation of metaphor, metonymy is future-oriented, dynamic, and indeterminate. Contiguous relations and connections are unpredictable, multiple, not limitable to an order of subordination (of image to ideal meaning) or of semantic equivalence. Rather than identify things analogically, metonymy affirms their difference while acknowledging their connectedness. Metonymy tends to be empirical, differentiated, and particular, rather than universalistic and identitarian; it decodes or runs down semantic paradigms of equivalence which determine meaning in fixed patterns; it is contextual and combinatory, paratactic (or coordinative) and conjunctive (operating as both/and propositions). We associate it with such deconstructive values as indeterminacy and undecidability, and it has clear similarities to what feminists pose as an alternative "woman's" cognitive mode.

Nevertheless, we emphasize that metonymy is itself the name for the breaking down of simplistic distinctions such as that between metaphor and metonymy. If we use the opposition as we do, it is because in an ideological universe the world tends to end up divided in ideological ways. In a postideological world, it may be possible that such distinctions will no longer hold, but it is a feature of ideology as we see it operating in Hollywood film culture to subordinate the metonymic mode to the metaphoric.

7. For an expanded discussion of these methodological and theoretical points, see M. Ryan, *Politics and Culture* (London: Macmillan, 1988). A final word on vocabulary. We occasionally use technical terms like "undecidability" and "imaginary." We assume a familiarity with deconstruction in our audience, but readers unfamiliar with a term like "undecidability" should consult the works of Jacques Derrida or the introductions to his work by Culler, Leitch, Norris, Ryan, and Spivak. The term "imaginary" derives from Lacanian psychoanalysis, although we do not use it in its technical sense. We employ it to describe a shared or culturally instituted ideological consciousness. For a good explanation of this expanded use of the term, see J. Thompson, *Essays on the Theory of Ideology* (Berkeley: University of California Press, 1984). We also use the term "homosocial" to refer to the bonding that is crucial to male power. Although homosociality has erotic components, homosocial does not mean homosexual. See E. Kosofsky Sedgwick, *Between Men* (New York: Columbia University Press, 1984).

1. From Counterculture to Counterrevolution, 1967–1971

1. See A. H. Cantril and C. W. Roll, *Hopes and Fears of the American People* (New York: Universe, 1971); D. Yankelovich, *The New Morality: A Profile of American Youth in the 70s* (New York: McGraw-Hill, 1974); J. Veroff et al., *The Inner American: A Self-Portrait from 1957 to 1976* (New York: Basic Books, 1981).

2. On the reactionary thematics of the film, see M. Shedlin, "Police Oscar: *The French Connection*," *Film Quarterly* (Summer, 1972), pp. 2–9. Debate over whether the film is "fascist" is found in articles by G. Epps and R. Leary in *Film Critic*, Vol. 1, No. 1 (1972), pp. 54–72. Although we do not believe that this and other similar films are "fascist," we agree with Epps that they provide a "breeding ground of the fascist mentality" in their depiction of violence as the best means of eliminating crime as well as in their primitivism, racism, and authoritarianism.

Right-wing thinking in the U.S. tends to be overwhelmingly populist, although populism itself can also take radical forms. Populism appears in U.S. culture as a celebration of the virtue of the common man, resistance to large impersonal institutions, and a privileging of nature, rurality, and simplicity over urban, cosmopolitan modernity. On the dual politics of populism, see K. M. Dolbeare and P. Dolbeare, *American Ideologies: The Competing Political Beliefs of the 70s* (Chicago: Rand McNally, 1976).

2. Crisis Films

1. See S. M. Lipset and W. Schneider, *The Confidence Gap: Business, Labor, and Government in the Public Mind* (New York: Free Press, 1983).

2. On disaster films, see N. Roddick, "Only the Stars Survive: Disaster Movies in the Seventies," *Performance and Politics in Popular Drama*, ed. D. Bradby, L. James, and B. Sharratt (Cambridge: Cambridge University Press, 1980); O. Eyquem, "Sur fond d'apocalypse," *Positif* 179 (March 1976), pp. 39–45; I. Znepolsky, "Films catastrophiques, spectateurs catastrophes," *Ecran* 50 (Sept. 1976), pp. 34–40; and three articles in *Téléciné* 199 (May 1975), pp. 11–14.

3. *Variety* (Jan. 5, 1977) lists among the "All-Time Film Rental Champs": 8, *The Towering Inferno* ($55 million); 14, *Airport* ($45.3 million); 16, *The Poseidon Adventure* ($42.5 million); 20, *Earthquake* ($36.1 million).

4. See *Jump Cut*, no. 1 (May–June 1974), pp. 3–4.

5. R. McCormick, "The Devil Made Me Do It! A Critique of *The Exorcist*," *Cineaste*, vol. 6, no. 3 (1974), p. 21.

6. See P. Biskind, "Jaws," *Jump Cut*, no. 9 (Oct.-Dec. 1975), pp. 13–14, 26; F. Jameson, "Reification and Utopia in Mass Culture," *Social Text* 1 (Winter 1979), pp. 130–48. For a more formal ideological analysis of the film see S. Heath, "*Jaws*, Ideology, and Film Theory," *Film Reader 2*, ed. P. Erens and B. Horrigan (Evanston: Northwestern Film Division Publication, 1977), pp. 166–68.

7. See E. Rapping, "The View from Hollywood: The American Family and the American Dream," *Socialist Review*, no. 67 (Jan.-Feb. 1983), pp. 71–92; J. Hess, *Jump Cut*, no. 7 (May–June 1975), pp. 4–5.

3. Genre Transformations and the Failure of Liberalism

1. See W. Wright, *Six-Guns and Society*.

2. See W. Wright, "The Empire Bites the Dust," *Social Text* (Fall 1982), pp. 120–25. We do not suggest that capitalism, operating as a spurious collective subject, generates myths that reinforce its legitimacy. Rather, myths advocating values and institutions central to capitalism are integral to the cultural discourse of the United States from its origins. See A. Trachtenberg, *The Incorporation of America* (New York: Hill and Wang, 1982), and R. Drinnon, *Facing West: The Metaphysics of Indian-Hating and Empire-Building* (Minneapolis: Minnesota University Press, 1980). This mythic discourse, which assumed different though related forms in previous eras, is worked out in the mid-twentieth century in the film western.

3. Dan Georgakas, however, argues that even in those films that are more sympathetic to Indians there are fundamental distortions of Native American culture and continuing negative Hollywood stereotypes. See "They Have Not Spoken: American Indians in Film," *Film Quarterly* (Spring 1972), pp. 26–32.

4. P. Roffman and J. Purdy, *The Hollywood Social Problem Film* (Bloomington: Indiana University Press, 1981) point out that whereas social problem films comprised 28% of Hollywood's total film output in 1947, during the height of the blacklist period they decline significantly and by 1954 make up only 9.2% of films produced.

5. See, for example, H. Hertzberg and D. D. K. McClelland, "Paranoia. An *idée fixe* whose time has come," *Harper's* (June 1974), pp. 51–60. In a review of *The Parallax View* in *Time* (July 8, 1974, p. 16) R. Schickel talks about the new genre of the "paranoid thriller," and S. Farber in *The New York Times* (Aug. 11, 1974) and P. Kael in *The New Yorker* (Aug. 5, 1974) discuss the paranoid vision of such movies. G. Weed analyzes basic traits of the new "paranoid genre" and contextualizes it within film history in an article, "Toward a Definition of Filmoia," in *The Velvet Light Trap*, no. 13 (1974) pp. 2–6. Film critics continued to see paranoia films as a dominant trend of the 1970s. J. Cawelti, for example, discusses "Fascination with Conspiracy or Paranoia as Norm" in "Trends in Recent American Genre Fiction," *Kansas Quarterly*, vol. 10, no. 4 (Fall 1978), pp. 13–15.

6. See the article by R. T. Jameson, "The Pakula Parallax," and the accompanying interview with Pakula in *Film Comment* (Sept.-Oct. 1976), pp. 8–19, where Pakula states: "I think that paranoia is a terribly misused word, the sort of word that's used

constantly today. . . . I use it to represent an excessive fear of the unknown, the unseen."

7. See Pakula's interview in *Film Comment*, where he states: "I had just made a film, *The Parallax View*, which someone . . . said had destroyed the American hero myth. If that's true, *All the President's Men* resurrects it. One film says the individual will be destroyed, it's Kafkaesque that way, Central European. . . . The Woodward and Bernstein story is the antithesis of that. Film students have asked me how I could do one and then the other, and I say, it's very simple: *Parallax View* represents my fear about what's going on, and *All the President's Men* represents my hope" (p. 16).

4. Class, Race, and the New South

1. T. B. Edsall, *The New Politics of Inequality* (New York: Norton, 1985), p. 213; W. Watts and L. A. Free, eds, *The State of the Nation* (New York: Universe Books, 1975); Watts and Free, *The State of the Nation III* (Lexington: Lexington Books, 1978), pp. 9–14; A. Campbell, *The Sense of Well Being in America: Recent Patterns and Trends* (New York: McGraw-Hill, 1981), pp. 168–73; J. L. Goodman, Jr., *Public Opinion During the Reagan Administration: National Issues, Private Concern* (Washington, D.C.: The Urban Institute, 1983); P. E. Converse et al., *American Social Attitudes Data Resourcebook 1947–1978* (Cambridge: Harvard University Press, 1980).

2. For a good assessment of the working-class film phenomenon of the seventies, see A. Auster and L. Quart, "The Working Class Goes to Hollywood: *FIST* and *Blue Collar*," *Cineaste*, vol. IX, no. 1 (1978), pp. 4–7; and P. Biskind and B. Ehrenreich, "Machismo and Hollywood's Working Class," *Socialist Review* no. 50–51 (Mar.-June, 1980), pp. 109–31.

3. More than working class or New South films, films about blacks have elicited a good amount of critical and scholarly attention. Most books concentrate on film history through the early seventies. See L. Patterson, *Black Film as Genre* (Bloomington: Indiana University Press, 1978); D. J. Leab *From Sambo to Superspade: The Black Experience in Motion Pictures* (Boston: Houghton, 1975); J. Pines, *Blacks in Films: A Survey of Racial Themes and Images in American Film* (London: Macmillan, 1975).

4. On the ideology of the new black bourgeoisie, see M. Marable, *How Capitalism Underdeveloped Black America* (Boston: South End Press, 1982).

5. A. Hacker, *U.S. A Statistical Portrait of the American People* (New York: Pantheon, 1983), p. 123.

6. See P. T. Johnson's excellent historical assessment in *The Crisis*, vol. 93, no. 1 (1986).

7. On the development of the New South, see A. Watkins and D. Perry, *The Rise of Sunbelt Cities* (Beverly Hills: Sage, 1977) and K. Sale, *Power Shift: The Rise of the Southern Rim and Its Challenge to the Eastern Establishment* (New York: Random House, 1975). For a good account of the transformation from Old South films to New South films, see E. Campbell, *The Celluloid South: Hollywood and the Southern Myth* (Knoxville: University of Tennessee Press, 1981).

8. M. Davis, *Prisoners of the American Dream* (New York: Verso, 1986), p. 222.

5. The Politics of Sexuality

1. See *Sexual Stratagems: The World of Women in Film*, ed. P. Erens (New York: Horizon, 1979); E. A. Kaplan, *Women and Film* (New York: Methuen, 1983); A. Kuhn, *Women's Pictures* (London: Routledge & Kegan Paul, 1982); and T. de Lauretis, *Alice Doesn't* (Bloomington: Indiana University Press, 1984).

2. D. Denby, "Men Without Women, Women Without Men," reprinted in *Film 1973–74*, ed. D. Denby and J. Cocks (New York: Bobbs-Merrill, 1978), p. 168.

3. M. McCreadie, "Latter-Day Loreleis: New Screen Heroines," *Cineaste* (1982), vol. XII, no. 2, pp. 16–18.

4. See the excellent discussion of the rhetoric of images in *Kramer* by R. A. Balin, *Jump Cut* (Oct. 1980), pp. 4–5.

5. On the scapegoating of women, see T. O'Brien, "Love and Death in the American Movie," *Journal of Popular Film and Television* (Summer 1980), vol. IX, no. 2, pp. 91–92; and M. Haskell, "Lights. . .Camera. . .Daddy!" *The Nation* (May 28, 1983), pp. 673–75.

6. See O. Eyquem, "Un retour du melodrame," *Positif*, nos. 228–30 (March, April, May 1980), and D. Kehr, "The New Male Melodrama," *American Film* (April 1983), pp. 43–47.

7. See the panel discussion "Out of the Closet and on to the Screen," in *American Film* (Sept. 1982), pp. 57–64, 81.

6. Horror Films

1. See A. Britton, R. Lippe, T. Williams, and R. Wood, *American Nightmare: Essays on the Horror Film* (Toronto: Festivals of Festivals Publication, 1979). *Variety* claimed that in 1980 horror and science fiction films would generate more than one-third of all box-office rentals, and predicted that by 1981 the figures would reach 50%. See "Horror Sci-Fi Pix Earn 37% of Rentals—Big Rise During 10-Year Period" (Jan. 1981). *Cinefantastique* reported in a decade recap that half of the top ten money-making films of all time were horror and science fiction; see 9:3/9:4 (1980), p. 72.

2. At a time when the genre cycle of demonically possessed children films began to accelerate, an article appeared in *Esquire* (March 1974) titled "Do Americans Suddenly Hate Kids?" In *Newsweek*, an article on "The New Child" (March 4, 1974) claimed that "The latest perception is that adults don't even like children" (75), mentioning increased brutality toward children and the growing tendency of couples not to have children.

3. Wood, *American Nightmare*, p. 91.

4. M. Mackey, "The Meat Hook Movie, The Nice Girl, and Butch Cassidy in Drag," *Jump Cut*, no. 14 (1977), p. 12.

5. M. J. Murphy, *The Celluloid Vampire* (Ann Arbor: Pierian, 1979), pp. ix–xi.

6. See G. Brown, "Obsession," *American Film* (Dec. 1983), pp. 29–34, and S. Bathrick, "Ragtime: The Horror of Growing Up Female," *Jump Cut*, no. 14 (1977), pp. 9–12.

7. See *Film Quarterly* (Fall 1981), pp. 44ff., and the De Palma interview in *Film Comment* (Jan. 1983), p. 38. See also " 'Double Trouble'—an interview with Brian De Palma," *Film Comment* (September–October 1984), pp. 13–17.

8. Thompson suggests that "psychos escape so easily in these films that the case for capital punishment is subtly emphasized." See *Overexposures* (New York: Morrow, 1981), p. 184.

9. G. Gerbner and L. Gross, "Living with Television: The Violence Profile," *Journal of Communication* (Spring 1976), pp. 172–97.

7. Vietnam and the New Militarism

1. See G. Adair, *Hollywood and Vietnam: From THE GREEN BERETS to APOCA-LYPSE NOW* (New York: Proteus, 1981); L. Suid, *Guts Glory: Great American War Movies* (Reading: Addison-Wesley, 1978); J. Smith, *Looking Away: Hollywood and Vietnam* (New York: Scribners, 1975); A. Britton, "Sideshows: Hollywood in Vietnam," *Movies* 27–28 (1980–81), pp. 2–23; and "Preparer a une troisieme guerre mondiale: les films americains mènent campagne (1970–1980)," *Cinethique* (1981), pp. 1–36.

2. On returning vet films, see Adair, *Hollywood and Vietnam*; Smith, *Looking Away*; and A. Auster and L. Quart, "Man and Superman: Vietnam and the New American Hero," *Social Policy* (Jan.-Feb. 1981), pp. 61–64, and "The Wounded Vet in Political Film," *Social Policy* (Fall 1982), pp. 25–31.

3. F. Liebowitz, "Recycling American Ideology: The Second Coming of Michael Vronsky," *Telos*, no. 47 (Spring 1981), pp. 204–208.

4. See the provocative reading of *The Deer Hunter* as nihilistic tragic epic in F. Burke, "The Deer Hunter and Jaundiced Angel," *Canadian Journal of Political and Social Theory* (Winter 1980), pp. 123–31. Also, see R. Wood, *Hollywood from Vietnam to Reagan* (New York: Columbia University Press, 1986), pp. 270ff.

5. For a discussion of the relation between films about military life and the new militarism, see *Tabloid*, no. 4 (1981), pp. 3–17.

6. See G. Mosse, *The Crisis of German Ideology: The Intellectual Origins of the Third Reich* (New York: Grosset & Dunlap, 1964), pp. 55, 60, 62, 94, 281.

8. The Return of the Hero

1. See F. F. Piven and R. Cloward, *The New Class War* (New York: Pantheon, 1981).

2. G. Gilder, *Wealth and Poverty* (New York: Basic Books, 1981). Gilder demonstrates the neoconservative abhorrence of rationality and the desire to return to primitive faith and instinct (biology) as a basis for social hierarchy. Society should be governed by a "supply side political" elite of male businessmen.

3. For a good ideological critique of the film, see D. Ruby, "*Star Wars*: Not so Far Away," *Jump Cut*, no. 18, pp. 9–13. Ruby points out that the rebels are in fact restorers of an old order, like the fascist revolutionaries in twentieth-century Europe. The fascist elements in *Star Wars* are criticized in R. Jewett and J. S. Lawrence, " 'Pop Fascism' in 'Star Wars'—or vision of a better world?" *Des Moines Sunday Register* (November 27, 1977). Jewett and Lawrence quote the film's director, George Lucas, in the novelistic version of the movie and compare these passages to ones from European fascist writers to argue convincingly for an ideological parallel: " 'The Jedi have been . . . the most powerful, most respected force in the galaxy . . . the guarantors of peace and justice,' [Lucas writes.] . . . [Jewett and Lawrence continue:] The Fascist thinker Palmieri described such warriors as capable of 'that magic flash of a moment of supreme intuition' which comes 'to the hero and none other.' Just as the European heroes of the 1930s proclaimed, 'We think with our blood,' Skywalker is informed that his father was a Jedi who would never hesitate to embark on an 'idealistic crusade' because his decisions came to him 'instinctively.' " In Lucas's book version of *Star Wars* (New York: Ballantine, 1976), his description of the Imperial Troopers echoes right-wing denunciations of the Soviet Union and the New Deal welfare state: "These fearsome troops enforce the restrictive laws with callous disregard for human rights. Quite often they are tools used to further the personal ambitions of the Imperial governors and bureaucrats." For a sense of the right-wing use of the word "empire" as a metaphor for big government and urban cosmopolitan liberalism, see C. N. Wilson, "Citizens or Subjects," in R. W. Whitaker, ed., *The New Right Papers* (New York: St. Martins, 1982): "[An empire] consists of subjects, interchangeable persons, having no intrinsic value, to be manipulated in the interests of that abstraction, the empire." It is interesting that a number of critics have pointed out that the storm troopers are all the same size and shape, interchangeable, in other words.

4. See R. Wood, "Wood on Cimino," *Cine Action!* no. 6 (August 1986), pp. 57–65.

5. See the article " 'I'm the Boss'," *Film Comment* (July-Aug. 1980), pp. 49–57, where Lucas takes credit for the idea of *Raiders* and asserts his control over the conception and editing of the film.

6. See "Case Histories of Business Management: A Memo from Francis Ford Coppola," *Esquire*, vol. 88, no. 5 (November 1977), pp. 190–96. Coppola reorganized his production unit in an authoritarian manner: "This company will be known as American Zoetrope and . . . it is me and my work. . . . There is only one person in authority and that is me. . . . Don't presume anything. When in doubt, go back to my original directive." His wife even noticed this during the shooting of *Apocalypse*: "More and more there are parallels between the character of Kurtz and Francis." See "Notes," *New York Times Magazine* (August 5, 1979), p. 39. As further examples of Coppola's fascination with authoritarianism, Milius refers to him as the "Bay Area Mussolini," and in 1967 Coppola said that he patterned his life on that of Hitler. Not surprisingly, by 1979 his company would be distributing *Our Hitler*. See *MacLean's* (August 27, 1979). Given his conservatism, it is interesting that he originally intended to include a segment in *Apocalypse* which blamed student rioting for the French defeat in the war. See "Dialog on Film: Martin Sheen," *American Film*, vol. 8, no. 3 (December 1982), pp. 20–28. On Coppola's petit-bourgeois propensities, see S. Braudy, "Francis Ford Coppola: Portrait of the Godfather's Film Father," *Atlantic Monthly*, vol. 238, no. 2 (August 1976), pp. 67–73.

9. Fantasy Films

1. In an interview with *Rolling Stone* (Jan. 26, 1978), Spielberg explicitly notes that he intended to make the ending a quasi-religious experience (p. 23). See the critique of the vacuousness of Spielberg's religiosity in A. Gordon, "Close Encounters. The Gospel According to Steven Spielberg," *Literature/Film Quarterly*, vol. VIII, no. 3 (1980), pp. 156–64.

10. The Politics of Representation

1. See B. Klinger, " 'Cinema/Ideology/Criticism' Revisited: The Progressive Text," *Screen*, vol. 25, no. 1 (Jan.-Feb. 1984), pp. 30–44.
2. See S. Blatt, J. Schimek, and B. Brenneis, "The nature of psychotic experience and its implications for the therapeutic process," in *Psychotherapy of Schizophrenia*, J. Strauss et al., eds. (New York: Plenum, 1980).
3. See "Talkin' Reds" in *Socialist Review*, no. 62 (March-April 1982), pp. 109–24; J. Trinkle in *The Guardian* (Dec. 23, 1981), p. 22; and the dossier assembled by C. Kleinhans and J. Hess, *Jump Cut*, no. 28 (1983), pp. 6–11.
4. On *Missing*, see "The *Missing* Dossier," *Cineaste*, vol. XII, no. 1 (1982), pp. 30–38.
5. On the aesthetics and politics of U.S. documentary, see B. Nichols, *Ideology and the Image* (Bloomington: Indiana University Press, 1981), and "The Art and Politics of the Documentary: A Symposium," *Cineaste*, vol. XI, no. 3 (1981), pp. 12–21. Our discussion has been aided by an article by Chuck Kleinhans and B. Ruby Rich, "The Relations of Avant-Garde and Radical Political Cinema in the U.S.," *Cinemaction* (April 1980) (mimeo). See the special issue of *Jump Cut* (no. 28—1983) on independents. *Framework* devoted three important issues to the U.S. independent movement (nos. 19, 20, and 21—1983). For a full listing of social issue films, see *Reel Change: A Guide to Social Issue Films*, ed. P. Peyton (Film Fund, P.O. Box 909, San Francisco, Calif. 94101).
6. L. Garafola, "Independents at the Crossroads," *Jump Cut*, no. 28 (1983), pp. 35–37.

Conclusion

1. W. D. Burnham, *The Current Crisis of American Politics* (New York: Oxford University Press, 1982), pp. 259–60.

2. We have relied on *Public Opinion* and *The Gallup Survey* for our polling information. Our position is confirmed in T. Ferguson and J. Rogers, "The Myth of America's Turn to the Right," *Atlantic Monthly* (May 1986), pp. 43–53.

Selected Bibliography

This bibliography contains references to the main texts in film criticism and social theory and history that we consulted. Other works that we used are found in the notes.

T. W. Adorno and Max Horkheimer, *Dialectic of Enlightenment* (New York: Seabury, 1972).

Louis Althusser, *Lenin and Philosophy* (London: New Left Books, 1971).

Albert Auster and Leonard Quart, *American Film and Society Since 1945* (New York: Praeger, 1984).

Walter Benjamin, *Illuminations* (New York: Harcourt, Brace & World, 1968).

Walter Benjamin, *The Origin of German Tragic Drama* (London: New Left Books, 1977).

Peter Biskind, *Seeing is Believing: How Hollywood Movies Taught Us to Stop Worrying and Love the Fifties* (New York: Pantheon, 1983).

S. J. Blatt, "Levels of Object Representation in Anaclitic and Introjective Depression," *Psychoanalytic Study of the Child* (1974), no. 29, pp. 107–157.

S. J. Blatt, C. Wild, and B. Ritzler, "Disturbances of object representation in Schizophrenia," *Psychoanalysis and Contemporary Science* (1975), no. 4, pp. 235–288.

Barry Bluestone and Bennett Harrison, *The Deindustrialization of America* (New York: Basic Books, 1982).

David Bordwell, Janet Staiger, and Kristin Thompson, *The Classical Hollywood Cinema* (New York: Columbia University Press, 1985).

Pierre Bourdieu, *Distinction* (Cambridge: Harvard University Press, 1985).

Harvey Brenner, *Mental Illness and the Economy* (Cambridge: Cambridge University Press, 1973).

Andrew Britton, Richard Lippe, Tony Williams, and Robin Wood, *American Nightmare: Essays on the Horror Film* (Toronto: Festivals of Festivals Publication, 1979).

Walter Dean Burnham, *The Current Crisis of American Politics* (New York: Oxford University Press, 1982).

Angus Campbell, *The Sense of Well Being in America: Recent Patterns and Trends* (New York: McGraw-Hill, 1981).

Albert H. Cantril and Charles W. Roll, *Hopes and Fears of the American People* (New York: Universe, 1971).

Peter Carroll, *It Seemed Like Nothing Happened* (New York: Holt, Rinehart and Winston, 1982).

Manuel Castells, *The Economic Crisis and American Society* (Princeton: Princeton University Press, 1980).

David Caute, *The Great Fear: The Anti-Communist Purge Under Truman and Eisenhower* (New York: Simon and Schuster, 1978).

Centre for Contemporary Cultural Studies, *On Ideology* (London: Hutchinson, 1979).

Centre for Contemporary Cultural Studies, *Culture, Media, Language* (London: Hutchinson, 1980).

Nancy Chodorow, *The Reproduction of Mothering* (Berkeley: University of California Press, 1978).

Nancy Chodorow, "Beyond Drive Theory. Object Relations and the Limits of Radical Individualism," *Theory and Society*, Vol. 14 (1985), pp. 271–319.

Harry Cleaver, *Reading Capital Politically* (Austin: University of Texas Press, 1979).

321

Philip E. Converse et al., *American Social Attitudes Data Resourcebook 1947–1978* (Cambridge: Harvard University Press, 1980).

Callisto Cosulich, *Hollywood Settanta: il nuovo volto del cinema americano* (Florence: Vallecchi, 1978).

Alan Crawford, *Thunder on the Right* (New York: Pantheon, 1980).

Thomas Cripps, *Black Film as Genre* (Bloomington: Indiana University Press, 1978).

Philip Davies and Brian Neve, editors, *Cinema, Politics and Society in America* (New York: St. Martin's, 1981).

Mike Davis, *Prisoners of the American Dream* (New York: Verso, 1986).

Teresa de Lauretis, *Alice Doesn't. Feminism, Semiotics, Cinema* (Bloomington: Indiana University Press, 1984).

Barbara Deming, *Running Away from Myself* (New York: Grossman, 1969).

Jacques Derrida, *Of Grammatology* (Baltimore: Johns Hopkins University Press, 1976).

Kenneth M. Dolbeare and Patricia Dolbeare, *American Ideologies: The Competing Political Beliefs of the 70s* (Chicago: Markham, 1971).

Thomas B. Edsall, *The New Politics of Inequality* (New York: Norton, 1984).

Barbara Ehrenreich, *The Hearts of Men* (New York: Doubleday, 1983).

Patricia Erens, editor, *Sexual Stratagems: The World of Women in Film* (New York: Horizon, 1979).

Stuart and Elizabeth Ewen, *Channels of Desire* (New York: McGraw-Hill, 1982).

Sigmund Freud, *Standard Edition of the Complete Psychological Works* (London: Hogarth, 1963).

George Gallup, Jr., editor, *The Gallup Poll: Public Opinion* (Wilmington: Scholarly Resources, 1970–1985).

George Gilder, *Wealth and Poverty* (New York: Basic, 1981).

Gerald R. Gill, *Meanness Mania* (Washington: Howard University Press, 1980).

John L. Goodman, Jr., *Public Opinion During the Reagan Administration: National Issues, Private Concern* (Washington, D.C.: The Urban Institute, 1983).

Andre Gorz, *Farewell to the Working Class* (Boston: South End Press, 1982).

Andre Gorz, *Paths to Paradise* (Boston: South End Press, 1984).

Bertram Gross, *Friendly Fascism* (Boston: South End Press, 1980).

Michael Harrington, *The Twilight of Capitalism* (New York: Simon and Schuster, 1976).

Molly Haskell, *From Reverence to Rape* (Baltimore: Penguin, 1973).

Stephen Heath, *Questions of Cinema* (Bloomington: Indiana University Press, 1981).

Godfrey Hodgson, *America in Our Time* (New York: Random House, 1976).

Fredric Jameson, "Reification and Utopia in Mass Culture," *Social Text* 1 (Winter 1979), pp. 130–148.

I. C. Jarvie, *Toward A Sociology of the Cinema* (London: Routledge & Kegan Paul, 1970).

I. C. Jarvie, *Movies as Social Criticism* (Metuchen: Scarecrow, 1978).

Robert Jewett and John Lawerence, *The American Monomyth* (New York: Doubleday, 1977).

Marty Jezer, *Life in the Dark Ages. A History of the United States from 1945–1960* (Boston: South End Press, 1982).

Richard Johnson, "What is Cultural Studies Anyway?" (Mimeographed Occasional Paper #74, Centre for Contemporary Cultural Studies, Birmingham).

Gareth Jowett, *Film: The Democratic Art* (New York: William Morrow, 1976).

Stuart Kaminsky, *American Film Genres* (Dayton: Pflaum, 1974).

E. Ann Kaplan, editor, *Women in Film Noir* (London: British Film Institute, 1978).

E. Ann Kaplan, *Women and Film* (New York: Methuen, 1983).
Russell Kirk, *The Conservative Mind* (Chicago: Gateway, 1978).
Joel Kovel, *The Age of Desire* (New York: Pantheon, 1981).
Siegfried Kracauer, *From Caligari to Hitler* (Princeton: Princeton University Press, 1974).
Annette Kuhn, *Women's Pictures* (London: Routledge & Kegan Paul, 1982).

Ernesto Laclau and Chantal Mouffee, *Hegemony and Socialist Strategy* (London: New Left Books, 1985).
Seymour M. Lipset and William Schneider, *The Confidence Gap: Business, Labor, and Government in the Public Mind* (New York: Free Press, 1983).
Theodore Louis and Jean Pigeon, *Le cinema americain d'aujourd'hui* (Paris: Seghers, 1975).
Theodore J. Lowi, *The End of Liberalism* (New York: Norton, 1979; second edition).

Pierre Macherey, *A Theory of Literary Production* (London: Routledge & Kegan Paul, 1978).
Manning Marable, *How Capitalism Underdeveloped Black America* (Boston: South End Press, 1982).
Karl Marx and Friedrich Engels, *The Marx-Engels Reader*, edited by Robert C. Tucker (New York: Norton, 1978; second edition).
Joan Mellen, *Women and Their Sexuality in the New Film* (New York: Dell, 1973).
Joan Mellen, *Big Bad Wolves: Masculinity in the American Film* (New York: Pantheon, 1977).
David Mermelstein, *The Economic Crisis Reader* (New York: Vintage, 1975).
Kate Millet, *Sexual Politics* (New York: Avon, 1971).
Juliet Mitchell, *Psychoanalysis and Feminism* (New York: Random House, 1975).
James Monaco, *American Film Now* (New York: New American Library, 1979).
Robin Morgan, editor, *Sisterhood is Powerful* (New York: Random House, 1970).
George Mosse, *The Crisis of German Ideology: The Intellectual Origins of the Third Reich* (New York: Grosset Dunlap, 1964).

Victor Navasky, *Naming Names* (New York: Viking, 1980).
Bill Nichols, editor, *Movies and Methods*, Vols. I and II (Berkeley: University of California Press, 1976 and 1985)
Bill Nichols, *Ideology and the Image: Social Representation in the Cinema and Other Media* (Bloomington: Indiana University Press, 1981).

Michel Pecheux, *Language, Semantics, and Ideology* (New York: Saint Martin's, 1982).
David Perry and Alfred Watkins, *The Rise of the Sunbelt Cities* (Beverly Hills: Sage, 1977).
David Pirie, editor, *The Anatomy of the Movies* (New York: Macmillan, 1981).
Francis F. Piven and Richard Cloward, *The New Class War* (New York: Pantheon, 1981).
Gerald M. Platte and Fred Weinstein, *Psychoanalytic Sociology* (Baltimore: Johns Hopkins University Press, 1973).
Michael Pye and Linda Myles, *The Movie Brats: How the Film Generation Took Over Hollywood* (New York: Holt, Rinehart and Winston, 1979).

Robert Ray, *A Certain Tendency in the Hollywood Cinema, 1930–1980* (Princeton: Princeton University Press, 1985).
Keith Reader, *Cultures on Celluloid* (London: Quartet, 1981).
Peter Roffman and Jim Purdy, *The Hollywood Social Problem Film* (Bloomington: Indiana University Press, 1981).
Majorie Rosen, *Popcorn Venus* (New York: 1973).

Sheila Rowbotham, Lynne Segal, and Hilary Wainwright, *Beyond the Fragments: Feminism and the Making of Socialism* (London: Merlin, 1979).

Vito Russo, *The Celluloid Closet* (New York: Harper and Row, 1981).

Kirkpatrick Sale, *Power Shift: The Rise of the Southern Rim and Its Challenge to the Eastern Establishment* (New York: Random House, 1975).

Thomas Schatz, *Hollywood Genres* (Philadelphia: Temple University Press, 1981).

Thomas Schatz, *Old Hollywood/New Hollywood* (Ann Arbor: UMI Research Press, 1983).

J. Schimek, "A Critical Reexamination of Freud's Concept of Mental Representation," *International Review of Psychoanalysis* (1975), no. 2, pp. 171–187.

Michael Schneider, *Neurosis and Civilization* (New York: Seabury, 1975).

Eva Kosofsky Sedgwick, *Between Men: Male Homosexual Desire in British Fiction* (New York: Columbia University Press, 1985).

Robert Sklar, *Movie-Made America: A Social History of American Film* (New York: Random House, 1975).

Julian Smith, *Looking Away: Hollywood and Vietnam* (New York: Scribners, 1975).

Peter Steinfels, *The Neo-Conservatives* (New York: Simon and Schuster, 1979).

David Talbot and Barbara Zheutlin, *Creative Differences* (Boston: South End Press, 1981).

Richard Terdiman, *Discourse/Counter-Discourse* (New York and Ithaca: Cornell University Press, 1985).

Sara Thomas, editor, *Film/Culture: Explorations of Cinema in its Social Context* (Metuchen: Scarecrow, 1982).

John Thompson, *Studies in the Theory of Ideology* (Cambridge: Polity Press, 1984).

Alan Trachtenberg, *The Incorporation of America* (New York: Hill and Wang, 1982).

Union for Radical Political Economics, *Radical Perspectives on the Economic Crisis of Monopoly Capitalism* (New York: 1975).

Joseph Veroff et al., *The Inner American: A Self-Portrait from 1957 to 1976* (New York: Basic Books, 1981).

William Watts and Lloyd A. Free, editors, *The State of the Nation* (New York: Universe Books, 1973).

William Watts and Lloyd A. Free, editors, *The State of the Nation III* (Lexington: Lexington Books, 1978).

Cornel West, *Prophesy Deliverance: An Afro-American Revolutionary Christianity* (Philadelphia: Westminister Press, 1982).

Robert W. Whitaker, editor, *The New Right Papers* (New York: St. Martins, 1982).

David M. White and Richard Averson, *The Celluloid Weapon: Social Comment in the American Film* (Boston: Beacon Press, 1972).

Paul Willis and Philip Corrigan, "Forms of Experience," *Social Text* (Spring-Summer 1983), pp. 85–103.

Alan Wolfe, *America's Impasse* (Boston: South End Press, 1982).

Martha Wolfenstein and Nathan Leites, *Movies: A Psychological Study* (Glencoe: The Free Press, 1950).

Robin Wood, *Hollywood from Vietnam to Reagan* (New York: Columbia University Press, 1986).

Will Wright, *Six-Guns and Society: A Structural Study of the Western* (Berkeley: University of California Press, 1977).

Daniel Yankelovich, *The New Morality: A Profile of American Youth in the 70s* (New York: McGraw-Hill, 1974).

Index

Michael Ryan is Associate Professor of English and Film Studies at Northeastern University. His publications include *Marxism and Deconstruction* and *Politics and Culture.*

Douglas Kellner is Professor of Philosophy at the University of Texas. He is the author of *Karl Korsch: Revolutionary Theory* and *Herbert Marcuse and the Crisis of Marxism,* and is coeditor of *Passion and Rebellion: The Expressionist Heritage.*